HALLELUJAHS FROM PORTSMOUTH CAMPMEETING
1896-1899

B. L. Fisher Library Camp Meeting Series ; vol. 1.
Series editor: Robert A. Danielson, Ph.D.

HALLELUJAHS FROM PORTSMOUTH CAMPMEETING 1896-1899

EDITED BY

SETH C. REES,
W. D. WOODWARD
AND
BYRON J. REES

First Fruits Press
Wilmore, Kentucky
c2016

Hallelujahs from Portsmouth Campmeeting, 1896-1899.
Edited by Seth C. Rees, W. D. Woodward and Byron J. Rees.

B. L. Fisher Library camp meeting series ; volume 1

First Fruits Press, ©2016
Previously published by Christian Unity Publishing Co.(1896-1898) and Christian Workers Union (1899).

ISBN: 9781621714620 (print), 9781621714637 (digital) 9781621715313 (kindle)

Digital version at http://place.asburyseminary.edu/firstfruitsheritagematerial/127/

First Fruits Press is a digital imprint of the Asbury Theological Seminary, B.L. Fisher Library. Asbury Theological Seminary is the legal owner of the material previously published by the Pentecostal Publishing Co. and reserves the right to release new editions of this material as well as new material produced by Asbury Theological Seminary. Its publications are available for noncommercial and educational uses, such as research, teaching and private study. First Fruits Press has licensed the digital version of this work under the Creative Commons Attribution Noncommercial 3.0 United States License. To view a copy of this license, visit http://creativecommons.org/licenses/by-nc/3.0/us/.

For all other uses, contact:

First Fruits Press
B.L. Fisher Library
Asbury Theological Seminary
204 N. Lexington Ave.
Wilmore, KY 40390
http://place.asburyseminary.edu/firstfruits

Hallelujahs from Portsmouth Campmeeting, 1896-1899/ edited by Seth C. Rees, W. D. Woodward and Byron J. Rees. - Wilmore, Ky. : First Fruits Press, ©2016.

4 volumes in 1 ; illustrations, portraits ; 23 cm. -- (B. L. Fisher Library camp meeting series ; volume 1)

Reprint of the first 4 volumes of the annual, Hallelujahs from Portsmouth. Previously published: 1896-1899.

ISBN: 9781621714620 (paperback)

1. Portsmouth Camp Meeting Association (R.I.). 2. Camp Meetings -- Rhode Island -- Portsmouth. 3. Rhode Island--Church history. I. Title. II. Asbury Theological Seminary. B.L. Fisher Library. Camp meeting series ; volume 1. III. Portsmouth Camp Meeting Association (R.I.) IV. Rees, Seth Cook, 1854-1933. V. Woodward, W. D. VI. Rees, Byron J. (Byron Johnson), 1877-1920.

BV3799.P67 R44 1896-1899

Cover design by Wesley Wilcox & Amelia Hegle

asburyseminary.edu
800.2ASBURY
204 North Lexington Avenue
Wilmore, Kentucky 40390

First Fruits Press
The Academic Open Press of Asbury Theological Seminary
204 N. Lexington Ave., Wilmore, KY 40390
859-858-2236
first.fruits@asburyseminary.edu
asbury.to/firstfruits

BOOK 1

HALLELUJAHS

FROM

PORTSMOUTH

OR

A REPORT

OF

PORTSMOUTH CAMPMEETING

HELD AT

PORTSMOUTH R. I.

JULY 31 TO AUGUST 17 1896

CHRISTIAN UNITY PUBLISHING CO.
Evangelist Building
SPRINGFIELD MASSACHUSETTS

1896

PREFACE.

PORTSMOUTH camp meeting opened July 31, 1896. Souls were saved and sanctified at the first meeting. Great power fell upon the camp, and much was accomplished during the first three days which cannot be recorded in this report, as our reporter W. D. Woodward, did not arrive until Monday August 3rd. May the readers of this report be greatly helped and refreshed.

Yours and His,
SETH C. REES

INTRODUCTION.

ON the island of Rhode Island in the midst of the blue waters of Narragansett Bay are two remarkable watering places. The one is world-famous Newport, at the southern extremity of the island, swept by breezes from the broad Atlantic, picturesque with its beauties of landscape and sea. Here the multi-millionaires of the great metropolis have their summer palaces. Clothed in broadcloth and fine linen, they sweep down Bellevue avenue with their costly equipages; dressed in latest styles they entertain invited guests in their palatial homes; lolling in luxury on downy pillows, they drink deeply of the world's cup of pleasure. They lavish thousands while others struggle for dimes. They adorn their homes with pictures and works of art, while others creep for crusts on the sidewalks of the slums. They laugh and dance and pipe and sing, while others cry and mourn and sorrow in silent suffering. They spend hundreds of dollars in grand illuminations. They sail in superb pleasure yachts in and out of the beautiful bay. They have a good *time*, and—die.

There is another watering place upon the island, about seven miles north of the city of millionaires. Not so many of the inhabitants of the "wide, wide world" are familiar with this second Newport, nor can it boast of so great antiquity as the city of the famous "old mill." But we have an idea that this new heavenly watering place of six summers is far-famed throughout the golden streets, and many will have cause for eternal rejoicing because godly men chose the grove on Quaker hill as the spot upon which to plant a spiritual Newport, a watering-place for weary souls.

While Portsmouth is naturally picturesque and healthful, it is its supernatural characteristics which endear it to the thousands who have plunged into the Fountain of living waters, and come forth with the strength of an eternal refreshing. It is swept by breezes from the hills of heaven. Here come the multi-millionaires of the New Jerusalem with faces aglow with the cosmetics of the skies, and tongues on fire with songs and testimonies of redemption. To be sure they live in tents, as befitting those who are pilgrims and strangers on the earth, seeking a better country, that is, a heavenly. But they have mansions which millions cannot buy. Clothed in the finest of white raiment, without spot or wrinkle, they sweep down Hallelujah avenue in chariots of love; dressed in the latest styles of heaven, the beauty of that holiness ordained for the saints before the foundation of the world, they entertain guests who will accept their invitation at the royal banqueting table of the King of kings; resting betimes at their Master's request on the luxurious pillows of Almighty grace, they "drink with joy absorbing all the love He would disclose." They accept "the riches of His grace," while others struggle in spiritual poverty "because of unbelief." They adorn the halls of memory and imagination with heavenly pictures and works of the Divine Artist, while others choose to creep along Grumbling Alley and feed on crusts of criticism. They have holy laughter, holy dances, holy songs, while their doubting brethren strive and weep over failure, or plunge into despair. They, too, have grand illuminations of the Holy Ghost, yet "without money and without price." They sail in the superb pleasure ship Zion, and are heading for the port of Heaven. They have a *good* time, and —live forever.

It was a pleasure to the writer to accept the invitation of Brother Seth C. Rees, president of Portsmouth Campmeeting Association, to spend several days at this spiritual watering-place, and chronicle some of the sayings and doings of what has proved to be the most remarkable session ever held upon the grounds. Of course we realize the imperfections of this compilation, yet are glad to present what we have secured of the winged words of truth spoken in the Holy Ghost, with the hope that they may prove a blessing to many souls. Thanks are especially due to Revs. G. W. Wilson and S. C. Rees for revision, and to Mr. John Fenton and Miss Mary Macomber for stenographic aid. We trust "Portsmouth Hallelujahs" may find an echo in many hearts.

W. D. WOODWARD.

HALLELUJAHS FROM PORTSMOUTH.

AFTERNOON TESTIMONIES.
Monday, Aug. 3.

SETH C. REES. It is a wonderful thing to be saved, to be saved all the time, to be saved through and through, to be saved and sanctified and filled with the Holy Ghost. I'm glad I'm saved. The way the Holy Ghost has made me behave myself under various tests makes me think I'd go with Him anywhere. Oh its time we got saved from folks. Many people have been sanctified, but oh, they are so dry! God has a satisfying portion. Does He satisfy all the longings of your soul? If He does, you won't need a committee from Heaven to notify you.

DEACON KIES. The Lord has blessed me since I came on these grounds a few hours ago. I have to confess what the Lord has done for me. I want to say that the blood of Christ cleanseth me from all sin.

BRO. WOOD. I am in God and God is in me. I know that He has sanctified me wholly. I don't want anything of the world.

BROTHER. On the 15th day of last September I got soundly converted, and on the 17th day of September I was thoroughly sanctified, and have been kept ever since. It doesn't take sugar to keep me, but the blessed Holy Ghost keeps me sweetly.

BROTHER. I want to praise God that I've nothing to do but to praise Him. Hallelujah!

SISTER. I have not only the blessing but the Blesser. He satisfies every longing of my soul.

AFTERNOON SERMON.

BY G. W. WILSON.

Text, Mark 11: 24. "Therefore I say unto you, what things soever ye desire when ye pray, believe that ye receive them and ye shall have them."

THE act of receiving being a conscious volitional act, you know when you receive. Let us look at a few principles concerning faith. If the world was full of faith, it would be full of love. The reason we do not love God and each other better is because we have not faith in God and each other. The very same power or faculty of faith exercised toward material things is to be exercised toward the immaterial or spiritual, but the objects differ. There are three things peculiar to faith.

1. The intellect must perceive the object to be received. No heart faith can exist without preceding intellectual faith. The heart does not think. An idiot or undeveloped child is graciously saved without intelligent faith. The heathen's consciences are a law unto them. A heathen mother throwing her child into the Ganges often exhibits a far more supreme devotion to her faith than some of us Christians who whine when we are called to give up a child for Africa.

Now holiness does not consist in emotional raptures. There must be an intellectual conception of your need. So until you find a manifestation of carnality after regeneration you cannot intelligently seek for holiness. God's method of getting light into the church is by the presentation of the truth of holiness. God hasn't turned us loose after we are converted to drift. We are to go on, but to a definite point. The truth won't run by the Holy Ghost without any agency. Holiness literature thus helps to understand God's Word. What did God endow us with reason for, if He proposed to ignore it after He had given it to us? Get pride out of the intellect and God can let light shine through. The Holy Ghost will make the best He can out of what intellect you have. A perverted intellect will often prevent the progress of holiness. God proposes we should discern the truth. The Holy Spirit does not teach the same truth differently to different people.

Another act involved in faith is that the will must yield up to the truth as soon as it sees it. God gives you light on your appetites and passions, for example, and you refuse to obey. You are a rebel in God's sight. You say you can't do better. You could if you would. Christ can cast down all evil imaginations. You have will power enough, but it must be subject to God. Have no will but His. You made up your mind you were going to get it in a certain way, but you didn't get it that way. Submit, and let God have His way, and do it in His manner.

Again, another act involved in faith is this, your *heart must love* what it sees. A great many people would like to have holiness, if it did not strip them of every thing else. You must have holiness for no selfish purpose. Simply love God even if

He puts you in a nook all the rest of your days. No cold intellectual faith can bring this heart-love. You must give up all other loves for Christ's love. A divided heart can't keep Jesus. You, young woman, can't keep company with a godless young man and with Jesus Christ at the same time. He is exceedingly jealous of your love. If you are coquetting with anything worldly, God will take away your holiness. When your heart fully goes over to God, it is as easy to believe as it is to breathe. Are you over? Until you get through with this point of utter abandonment, you will not get the genuine thing. Then your faith is perfect.

EVENING SERMON.

BY SETH C. REES.

Text: He shall baptize you with the Holy Ghost and with fire. Matt. 3:11.

Fire has always been regarded with superstitious reverence among heathen nations. It was always a special feature of their rites and ceremonies. Fire has always been used by God as a symbol of His glory. Material fire in its higher forms, as electricity, though known a century ago but comparatively little, to-day is becoming very familiar in daily life. So previously to the dispensation of the Holy Ghost, the fire from Heaven fell at comparatively rare intervals, but to-day He is at the command of even a child. As the sun causes millions of seeds to spring into life, so the Holy Ghost causes dead souls to be quickened into life. God has pledged success along Holy Ghost lines.

Fire is a wonderful purifier. Some things can be cleansed by water outwardly, but only fire can cleanse others. So fire leaping over the battlements of Heaven is what is needed to purify our hearts from every unclean thing. Fire is a powerful energizer. Science has become wise enough to touch a button and harness the powers of nature that God has had locked up for centuries. But we have not learned how to touch the button and draw down the fire of the supernatural.

The Holy Ghost is a cure for laziness. It is time we were soldiers instead of babies. He will make you go. It is impossible for us to have the Holy Ghost and fail. He never fails. The Holy Spirit is indivisible. If He comes into your life, He does not do so in instalments. I never pray for *more* of the Holy Ghost. He comes in Himself, and not a little at a time. We can then afford to be persecuted, to be trampled upon, to be made, like our Master, of no reputation.

Precious altar services followed these inspiring sermons. Souls plunged into the fountain, and came forth with hearts made clean in the precious blood of Jesus.

> "Oh the blood, the precious blood,
> That Jesus shed for me,
> Upon the cross in crimson flood
> Just now by faith I see."

TESTIMONIES.
Tuesday, Aug. 4.

G. W. KIES, Norwich, Conn. Not long ago I had a dream reminding me of the promises of God. You see I am about 14 years old. But I have taken God at His Word, and tarried at the upper room, and though I can't be a preacher I can be a witness. It is my business to serve the Lord and get as many at it as I can. When the Lord sanctified me one cold winter night, I heard wonderful music. I wish I could have put it down. I heard a preacher say recently we would have more visions if we lived nearer to God. We ought to be able to say not only that the Bible is inspired, but that God inspires us. We should not quench any manifestation of the Spirit. Only a little while ago I was led to do what to me was unusual in holding an altar service, but God blessed, saved and sanctified precious souls.

BROTHER. God has saved me and sanctified me wholly. I look back occasionally and it gives me courage to go forward. A few years ago one morning my little three years old girl put her arms around my neck, and said, "Papa, don't get drunk to-day." Nobody had told her. But that very noon I went to the bar-room. I could not help myself. That night I went home drunk. My dear wife put me to bed, and bathed my head the next morning. I'd often promise that for her sake I'd let it alone, but couldn't. I went to Providence. Brother Rees got me into the church and down upon my knees. Then he put his arms around me. This broke me down. I found out, too, that God could entirely sanctify my soul. And God has been keeping me ever since.

SISTER WILLIAMS. I went to Camp-meeting expecting a big blessing so I could go home a booming. But I found instead of booming me up He boomed me way down. I went home with a little bundle, but oh, how He has been opening it up to me!

BROTHER KENNEY. The age of miracles is not past. I, too, have been saved from a drunkard's life. I was well brought up by Methodist parents, but fell in with evil companions and got to drinking. I tried to stop. I'd get periodically converted. Then I was intoxicated periodically. And when I went for it I went for it everlastingly. Brother Reed came over and pitched a tent near my house, and Brother Rees came and preached full salvation. I tried to drown the truth in rum. But on the 15th day of last September God saved me. Two days later I sought for full salvation. I found I had to be just like clay in the potter's hands. I'm a potter by trade. I find the clay don't have anything to say as to what kind of a vessel it shall be made into. And the Lord has been keeping me sweetly these eleven months. Why, He came in and cast out the old man, and then He cast out all the furniture, to put in a new set of furniture, and then the blessed Holy Ghost came in to dwell.

BIBLE READING.

BY REV. JOHN NORBERRY.

If we are not doing something for the cause of God we certainly are not at our best. We need the unction of the Holy Ghost to-day more than anything else. If we are not moving things where we live, there is something wrong. We ought always to be stirring the devils in hell. Your experience don't amount to anything unless some one gets mad. We

have got a finished touch, fixed up sort of holiness
that needs to get sanctified, unless we make things
move. We are all agreed as to the doctrine of
holiness, but we need something that will make things
move at home, in the church, on the camp-ground.
Anything but stagnation. It has got to this point in
this country to-day that nothing is being done in the
way of conversions except by holiness teachers. The
Lord wants a few sample saints with a real patent-
leather shine on the faces. Get the oil shine on your
face.

God gave me a Bible reading in the second
chapter of Joel showing His plan of revival.
In the 15th verse of the 2nd chapter of Joel we are
told to "blow the trumpet in Zion." God begins with
Zion. Then He says, "Sanctify a fast." Holiness
people get dry from indulging in nonsensical talk, and
foolish jesting. We talk too much. We need to have
the lock-jaw awhile. Pray more. Fast from our own
talk, and talk with God. "Call a solemn assembly."
You must begin with solemnity, not with dancing.
Get the elders of the church together, and the young
people and the children. God wants them altogether, and never meant that they should be
separated. Then the prophet says we are to
come from the closet, with the weight of souls
upon us. Then he says we are to "weep between the
porch and the altar," and weep for His heritage, lest
the heathen reproach them, and say, "Where is thy
God?" Then God promises to strengthen His people
with corn and gladden them with the Holy Ghost
champagne, and shine them up with oil. The stale

forty-year old people have lost their dried-up looks, and appear as fresh as a new-born babe. Then the promise is, we shall be satisfied.

You will have greater persecutions than ever before, but God says, "Fear not. Rejoice in the Lord your God." Then you notice God promises the former and the latter rain in the first month. That is, when the church is where God wants it to be, people will get converted and sanctified in the first month. "And my people shall never be ashamed." Then God says that "Afterward I will pour out my Spirit upon all flesh." You notice nothing is said yet to sinners. Not until the last verse is reference made to sinners. Then God says "It shall come to pass, that, whosoever shall call upon the name of the Lord shall be delivered, for in Zion and in Jerusalem shall be deliverance as the Lord hath said." After the church gets in the right place, sinners will come, and then all they will do is to "call" and pop through like popcorn on a hot fire.

Brother Norberry was most wonderfully free in the delivery of this Bible reading. There were shouts in the camp, and a rousing altar service was held with fire falling on every hand. A number of seekers got through to God.

A grand evening song service preceded the preaching. Some of the saints had a holy dance in their heels, while the command, "Oh, clap your hands!" was enjoyed by many as a real privilege. Deacon Morse of Putnam, offered an earnest prayer. Rev. G. W. Wilson, of Moulton, Iowa, was the preacher. His subject was "Crucifixion."

EVENING SERMON.

TEXT. "I am crucified with Christ; nevertheless I live; yet not I, but Christ liveth in me; and the life which I now live in the flesh I live by the faith of the Son of God, who loved me, and gave Himself for me." Gal. 2 : 20.

Holiness people should get thoroughly established. I want to call your attention to the twofold crucifixion in the text. There is a crucifixion which you may know, and have no doubt about it. Human nature is abnormal not by what it does, but because of an element in it which does not belong to it. That element is sin. When this element is out, the spiritual life of man is in perfect harmony with the nature of God, so there is no room for doubt.

You can get to the end of the sin question, so there will be no further doubt about it. When holiness drives out carnality, you will not find any heart response to sin. Outward temptation will only show to you what a good thing you have got. It is your business, with the light of the Holy Ghost, to hunt up and drag out the old man: nor passively wait for the Holy Ghost to do the business. You can't destroy the old man a little at a time any more than you can get the new man *seriatim*.

You will never get after the old man simply to deliver you from the mortification occasioned by his misbehavior. That is but to please pride. But until you see the awfulness of depravity in God's sight, you won't get rid of the old man. You are an active agent together with the Holy Ghost in this matter. Quit talking about getting rid of your pride, and get rid of the old man. Pride will go then. Sin is a life, not a thinking. It is a life you are just as conscious of, as you are conscious afterward of the life of God. The sin-life must be killed. Have a first-class funeral. Too much trifling exists to-day on the subject of regeneration and entire sanctification. The old man must die. Holiness people have to die to holiness people. So many holiness people are living on other holiness people. Some say, I prefer this type of holiness or that type. There are no types. Holiness is godlikeness. You can't dress the old man up in religious clothes and make anything but the old man out of him. Bless you, some holiness people are just as proud of their old poke bonnets and plain gowns, as they were formerly proud of their silk dresses and gold rings.

No other man but the man Christ Jesus has the throne of my heart. Your religiosity and churchianity have got to die. Holiness was before the foundation of the world. Until you are through on the death line, you can't get the baptism of the Holy Ghost. You don't want coddling, you want killing. When you die, and attend your own funeral, and do your own shouting, have your own wake, then you'd better wait a bit and see if he is dead.

Now you are not to be crucified with Christ in any sense that Christ had any carnality to crucify. After the sin is killed, then really comes the crucifixion with Christ. You are now where your normal loves must be crucified. You will love wife and children, all the more, if entirely sanctified. It is a trick of the devil that when one is entirely sanctified he can run off to camp-meetings and turn wife and children over to the

Lord. It takes more grace to stay at home with the chrildren than to be free at camp-meeting. But there is a sense in which every natural affection and impulse must be subject to His will. We must give up lawful enjoyment and hallelujahs and find some Gethsemane in which to bring to birth lost souls.

Jesus left a home of spotless purity and sinless society because He, a pure soul, could not bear to see human souls lost without doing His utmost to save them. Jesus gave Himself for me that He might give His divine nature to me. I must give myself, the new man, back to God. If God wants you to stop making money and go slumming, you had better go slumming. Does your holiness take in slumming, if God wants you? If you shrink from the cross, you are shrinking from the glory. Holiness costs something. It doesn't wear kid gloves but rolls up its sleeves to suffer. Will you die to sin, and will you live to suffer? He will put His Spirit in you and cause you to love to do His will. Thank God for a chance to give Him one little life. Are you through forever? Are you dead to every self-interest and ready to die for the Master's sake? God help us. Our holiness must be genuine,

MORNING SERMON.

BY REV. C. HOWARD DAVIS.

Wednesday, Aug. 5.

Text: Acts 1: 14; 2: 1, 4. "These all continued with one accord in prayer and supplication, with the women, and Mary the mother of Jesus, and with his brethren. And when the day of Pentecost was fully come, they were all with one accord in one place. And they were all filled with the Holy Ghost, and began to speak with other tongues as the Spirit gave them utterance."

It appears in these days that the Holy Ghost is being ignored by people of this age, just as Jesus used to be spit upon by the old Jews. Few give the Holy Ghost His proper place. Many speak of Him as a power or an influence, the same as Christ was thought to be a mere man or prophet. Let me ask, supposing the Holy Ghost were living as a visible person in your home, would any things be different in your life? Now we are always interested in the last words of a dying friend. They are important words. What did our dying Friend, Jesus, speak of in his last words? It was the promise of a Comforter; and the disciples had a good experience before Pentecost. Why, they went to Jerusalem "with great joy." To get the baptism of the Holy Ghost you must have something on hand. Getting under conviction don't mean getting under condemnation. When you have the latter you had better go forward for prayers. But if you have conviction, (bless you, I get under conviction every sermon I hear,) why, you just measure right up to it as soon as you see new light on any point.

"They all continued of one accord." A divided heart can't get the blessing. We need a united heart. Are you agreed on this one thing in your own soul that you will seek until you receive the gift of the Holy Ghost? All denominations can agree on the same thing as the 120 in the upper room did, viz: the baptism of the Holy Spirit. Their peculiar differences of temperament did not prevent them uniting on this. Well the day of Pentecost did fully come, and it is still here. The Bible nowhere says the Holy Ghost has been called back to Heaven.

"They were all filled with the Holy Ghost," not with a "great blessing." They may not possibly have all jumped, but they all began to move, and make other things move. They began to speak. They had spoken before, but now it was with other tongues. Get filled with the Holy Ghost, and people will remember what you say. They spake "as the Spirit gave them utterance." As we walk with Jesus more and more, we learn to know the voice of the Spirit, and He tells us when to speak. The multitude got stirred. Fine preachers and grand quartets won't move the people. Oh, for the baptism of the Holy Ghost on the church of the living God! The multitude were confounded. They didn't understand it. No more do they to-day. They mocked. The mockers are not all dead yet. In those days they called them drunk. To-day they cry "Fanatics!" "Religiously crazy." How Peter stood, whom a little girl had made back down a little while before!

AFTERNOON TALK.

DEACON MORSE spoke on Prov. 29: 18. "Where there is no vision the people perish." God wants every Christian a soul-saver, and wants every regenerated soul entirely sanctified. I started in on this line of holiness by faith, not by growth, some twenty-five years ago, and I am still in the "vision." It is a wonderful revelation, this salvation that changes a man from sin to heavenly-mindedness. Before I was born again through the soul travail of my own mother, my highest ambition was to sail up and down this bay in a ten thousand dollar yacht, and spend money and have a good time. It is a perfect wonder to me how I got changed, and the life I have lived since. Through false teaching I didn't see the privilege of entire sanctification for thirteen years. I was all that time hungering for God. The "vision" continued, and I sought meetings and God's people.

I went once to Martha's Vineyard years ago, and I heard Phebe Palmer pray. I said, "That is what I want." But my pulpit teaching didn't make it clear. One minister said we were sanctified at death, another through the truth by just ransacking the Bible, a third that it was all done at conversion. Oh, praise the Lord, it is the blood that cleanseth! Now it is going through the country and the world, and you can't stop it. Heaven is in favor of it. Put one foot before the other, and claim every foot of land you walk upon. There are beautiful unfoldings of the "vision" which Jesus gives me night after night as I lie awake.

I found this blessing of entire sanctification November 15, 1870, at 5 o'clock in the afternoon. The next day I testified at home in my church vestry, and most half the people went out. But I preached about three hours. Some of those who could not understand it afterward came into the light. Perhaps sixty may have come in in a few years. Jesus saves me to-day fully.

AFTERNOON SERMON.
BY REV. G. W. WILSON.

Text: 1 John 1: 7. "If we walk in the light as he is in the light, we have fellowship one with another."

A good deal has been said upon this ground about stagnant holiness. Technically there is no such thing.

Holiness is the divine life in you at its best up to date. Hence it means progress. Walking does not mean feeling good. It means taking advance ground, greater power with greater usefulness. The *state* of moral purity never changes. The *character* of the morally pure is forever growing grander. So far as the sin question is concerned there is no difference in the outward life of the justified and sanctified, yet there is a greater power in the character of the latter. What holiness people need is to get a move on, if you will allow this mannerism in the cultured East. Too many are living on a remembered holiness. If you have got it, people will know it, even if you don't always testify. Not that you are to withhold your testimony, especially if you are tempted to keep still. Now no amount of walking in the light can make you any purer. There is no comparison,—pure, purer, purest—in holiness. Then you have 40,000 things to learn and unlearn, and there will be lots of outward things to change, but your purity will not change.

For instance, you get entire sanctification and you'll shed a lot of things. Let us take a walk out with Jesus this afternoon. Walking in the light means walking in knowledge. The most teachable folks in the world are holiness people. Holiness keeps you out of ruts. I've seen fifty million glorious and grand and beautiful things since that wonderful Wednesday night when I was entirely sanctified at 19 years of age. It is God's business to furnish light, and yours to walk in it. Don't try to walk in other people's light. Every act of walking in the light implies obedience and faith. It means also laying hold of some new object of faith as God reveals it to you.

The sanctified life means you are prompt at obeying any new light God gives. Obedience and faith along these lines will enlarge your character, that is, your knowledge of God. He will give you a knowledge of Himself which will increase your capacity for Him. Where hearts have things in common a hint will make them understand. Holiness sensitizes your spiritual powers so when God begins to whisper you say at once, "I see it." You are on the stretch to know how you can love him more and more, and serve him better and better, and suffer more and more. If patriotic soldiers can die for their country, can't we die for Christ? Why, if God wanted you in hell as His messenger, you would have more heaven there than up in heaven if He didn't want you up there. Some folks think light means refinement. It may mean scrubbing the kitchen floor. After sanctification we are to increase in righteousness, and grow grander and nobler. Stop glorying in your idiosyncrasies and glory in the cross. If you don't let the great Sculptor chip off your failings, you will lose your holiness.

In a pure heart there is an absolute impossibility of mistaking on spiritual lines. You can be a pre- or a post-millenarian and get to Heaven, but you can't be impure and go to Heaven. When we say we are walking in the light as He is in the light, we see the things we do see as clearly as God sees them, though not to the same degree. If you are quibbling about revealed truth, you are not walking in the light. Lots of preachers are spiritually color-blind, and don't know the difference between higher criticism and the blood of Christ. Oh, if you are pure you will grow as beautiful in a nook, as in the Queen's household. You are to bloom for Me, as God's lily. The soul that is walking in the light and has fellowship with God is a perfect representation of the church of Christ. No other fellowship is necessary for your happiness. When a man is walking in the light, he can do as he pleases. A loving heart can be turned loose anywhere, and will always do right. How many here will begin and walk in every ray of light from this time on?

EVENING SERMON.
BY REV. JOHN, NORBERRY.

SISTER JENNIE STROMBERG sang a solo prior to the sermon.

TEXT: Luke 18: 1. "Men ought always to pray and not to faint."

This subject ought to interest the sinner, the regenerated, and the entirely sanctified alike. How easily some of us faint and give up. If you hold on in prayer, sinners will be converted. He is as willing to answer you and me as He was Abraham, Isaac and Jacob. Don't any of you dear sanctified folks get an idea you can pray less. Rather you ought to pray more. I have been to holiness campmeetings and felt the critical curiosity. It makes a great difference with the power and result of the sermon whether the hearers are critical or prayerful.

First, pray for yourself, if you are not right. If you have got light on full salvation, and won't walk up to it, you are regarding iniquity in your heart and God will not hear you. Jesus prayed all night. The disciples before Pentecost prayed ten days. Cornelius was earnestly praying four days. You can't experiment with God, saying, "Well, I'll try it and see how it pans out." God shows us the value of importunity in this parable of the unjust judge, and in the case of the humble Syro-Phenician woman. When you come to stay, God will see to your case and see that you get the desire of your heart.

A certain man who has been instrumental in saving thousands of souls, went up one evening on a mountain to pray, determined to stay all night. He set himself out for an all night prayer meeting. But God saw he was determined, and he got the blessing of full salvation in less than three minutes. I remember one Saturday afternoon when getting out of my work I went to my room with perfect agony of soul for this blessing. I intended to stay until the work was done. I kept saying, "Yes" to God. The last thing I gave up was being willing to be misunderstood. God came at once.

MORNING TESTIMONIES.
Thursday, Aug. 6.

SISTER BYE, of Indiana, spoke at the 8.30 service. "Consider the high-priest of our profession, Christ Jesus." God has given us the name of the holy people, "holy brethren." It takes us all in, takes all shame out of our heart, and fills us with perfect love. We ought to rejoice that God has not left His people without a name. He is looking down from Heaven this morning to see who belongs to the royal family. You have a blood-bought title. As soon as you are born of the Spirit, you have a hunger for holiness. Several years after I was born of the Spirit I received this title. Are you willing to stand by your colors? To bear this appellation? Jesus has made us His witnesses at home or abroad. When Christ takes us up into these mountains of heavenly vision, how small the world looks! I believe He gives His children understanding hearts. The Lord himself converted me to himself at 18 years of age, in an old-fashioned Methodist revival. I had a wonderful baptism of the Spirit at the time, and God gave me a soul that very night. Living up to the light, and hungering after more I got entirely sanctified. I like to have got swamped by this fair and festival, grab-bag business, but I got into a holiness meeting and got thoroughly sanctified. How He has kept and preserved me! He has taken care of me. Why, I had become so sour, I had then no use for a class-meeting. But now this meeting seems the next thing to Heaven. Oh, He has made me free from the bondage of sin and death.

BROTHER KENNEY. Its rich. We don't have to go to California for gold. They talk about sixteen to one. I've got the sixteen. I used to buy champagne, and fifteen and twenty-five cent cigars. But God took it all out. I even threw up part of my business, threw my bread and butter in the face of the devil. But God has put sugar on top of the butter.

SISTER. I settled one thing yesterday I never did

before. I was ashamed to be called one of the holiness people. But it is settled now forever.

BROTHER NELSON REED. I realize I have the nature of God in my heart this morning. I don't love sham and hypocrisy.

SISTER STEERE. I am a child of God, thoroughly saved and sanctified. And it was all by the Holy Ghost. I had a tremendous consecration at conversion, and had to say "Yes" to every last thing. There was a letting go when I laid myself on the altar for entire sanctification, and oh, how the Spirit came into my heart. Lately I had a peculiar test. It came to me, "Ought I to take up a duty that really belongs to others?" And when I was falsely accused, I felt a little rising. But I know now that God has delivered me.

MORNING SERMON.
BY REV. C. H. DAVIS.

Text: 1 Sam. 17: 16. "Inquire thou whose son the stripling is."

THE real Christian is not out on dress parade, or with a doll-baby for an enemy. He is engaged in real warfare, and must learn how to handle the sword of the Spirit.

King Saul asked the question in the text. The stripling was a sheep-tender, the son of Jesse. Yet "the Spirit of the Lord came upon David." That's the main thing. With this we can plough our way through with victory on our banners. To-day there are enemies as great as the ancient Philistines. I am inclined to think Goliath is a type of our worst enemy, the giant Inbred Sin. Like Goliath, he is well armed, and has great power. Old Depravity says through preachers and presiding elders, "You can't be delivered." Oh, we have got foes as great as Goliath to fight.

Genuine holiness will take the corns off every one of your toes. So many are afraid of sore spots, afraid of getting whipped. The Israelites were greatly dismayed and afraid. For forty days morning and night, this old champion kept them shivering and shaking. Lots of folks to-day shiver because somebody chins them a little. The most monotonous thing in the world is an unsanctified church trying to fight with a round of dull prayer meetings. What a reproach to the church unless they are on the victory side! How sarcastic David's elder brother got! "What have you done with those few sheep?" Oh! we have just as big a battle on to-day.

People will fight you if they don't fight the devil. "I know the pride and naughtiness of thy heart." You'll meet just the same thing when you get home. There is a real fight on, brother and sister. Are you stripped? Are you stripling enough to go home and make a fight? David says tearfully, "Is there not a cause?" David tells Saul his experience in the sheep fold, tells of his victory over the lion and the bear. David told Goliath, "I come to thee in the name of the Lord of hosts." Like Goliath, old Depravity must have his head cut off. Note that David was on the way to the throne, though he had to go through the cave first.

I remember one Sunday morning when I got the

blessing, what a peace came into my soul. I didn't get the baptism of the Spirit until the next Wednesday. Brothers and sisters, if you are small, you can be clean and empty. A most precious altar service followed, in which both young and old went into the cleansing fountain and came out with clear testimonies as to God's purifying power. It was a time of melting, moving and refining. Holy fire consumed baser fires, and then itself kept burning with its own heavenly heat and lustre.

AFTERNOON SERMON.
BY REV. JOHN NORBERRY.

Text: Romans 15: 29. "I am sure that when I come unto you, I shall come in the fulness of the blessing of Christ." R. V.

PAUL was true to his ministry, preaching a full gospel of pardon and cleansing. You remember the great light which fell on him on the road to Damascus. God told him there he was to be a minister of the things he had heard, and a witness of what he should reveal unto him. Before Felix and Agrippa, before saint and sinner, everywhere Paul was true. He did not flinch under great persecution and opposition. Now it is one thing to be a minister and proclaim the gospel message, and another to be a witness of an experience of which we know. The latter is what tells on people.

Don't testify to holiness like a poll parrot, but because you feel it in your very soul. Paul longed to see the Thessalonians that he might press holiness upon them. He also found the Galations were sidetracked and told them the bond woman and her son could be cast out. For the Ephesians he offered that wonderful prayer culminating in wishing "that they might be filled with all the fulness of God." Paul was so earnest about this, that he would get up nights and pray for them, "night and day praying exceedingly." As for the Hebrews, he urged upon them the privilege of going "on unto perfection."

The text shows plainly that Paul was preaching to believers. There is a blessing of fulness. Webster says the word means "a swelling." Oh, how it does give the man who has it a sensation of swelling! Too many feel a lack, and are lean. Paul also says it is distinctively "the blessing." It is a definite blessing so you can put your hand on it, know when you received it. It is a special blessing for God's people, a gift from God,—"the gift of the Holy Ghost." The Bible speaks of *the* Comforter, *the* promise of the Father, *the* gift of the Holy Ghost. It is definitely expressed in such familiar hymns as "Rock of Ages," "Love Divine," etc. It is "the blessing of Christ." He is willing to give this to anybody who will seek it. It is undenominational, not confined even to the National Holiness Association. God ordained before the foundation of the world that man should be holy. Jesus was very definite in praying that his disciples should be sanctified, that His branches should be purged, that He would give life, and life more abundantly, that his believing children should be perfect as the Father in heaven is perfect.

Again, Paul was sure about it. "I am sure when I come, I'll come in the fulness." There is an error going about, that holiness people are to live on naked faith. And they go about looking like skeletons. God wants to make us sure about this thing, to be "fat and flourishing."

Brother Norberry had to go for the train, but the Holy Spirit remained, and He poured out a special blessing upon seekers at the altar.

EVENING SERMON.
BY REV. G. W. WILSON.

SUBJECT. The Great Commandment. Thou shalt love the Lord thy God with all thy heart, and with all thy soul; and with all thy mind."

SOME here may think there is a tendency on the grounds to speak slightingly of the visible church. Remember there was unity and life long before there was organization. Organism cannot produce life. It is always the other way. Huxley admitted that spontaneous generation is impossible. Organism is but an exterior form of the type of life organized. Jesus did not need to go to a school of philosophy to know nature. He had the holy art of knowing nature as it is. Now you can't make people love on a basis of mere organism. You can massacre those who oppose you religiously on that basis, but you can't love without life. Church organizations wear out, but the religion of Jesus Christ is going to live forever. Even infidels love the character of Jesus, though they may deny His doctrines. Jesus is the foundation of life because He is the foundation of love. We can't be loyal to holiness apart from being loyal to the personal Christ, and you can't do this without love. God has given us a glorious, personal Jesus upon whom we may bestow our affection. "The holiness movement" is the heart of God moving toward humanity. Think anybody can stop it? You might as well try to dip the river dry with a spoon.

"Oh, who that loves can love enough?" There is a great difference in holiness people. Some say, "I hain't got your kind." Bless you, there is no difference in kind, but a vast difference in quantity. Get your capacity increased. Love is the only basis broad enough for us all to be united on. There are many manifestations of love, and these make different experiences. For example, if you have healing of the body in answer to prayer, glorify God for it, but remember it is but a passing thing. Paul says if you don't have love with it, it amounts to nothing. If you want glory, get some more love. Your joy is your own, but recollect it is but an emotion. That is not real love. No matter how much joy you may have here under these exhilarating circumstances, it won't be worth the flip of your finger when you get home, unless you have love.

Now love always blesses other folks. The measure of our love we get here will pour itself out in showers all through the year. Love is a desire for an object outside of ourselves. "Set your affections on things above." You must love something, unless by a damning, hellish selfishness you destroy the power of love. Men can never be won to God without a loving heart. We want the fragrance of the Rose of Sharon without having it all cut up with botanic criticism. One love never fails, nor betrays the one who trusts it. "Love never faileth." Until you love for love's sake, you don't know what it is. When a heart is truly captured, it is won to be kept. What are you in the church for? You don't have to love Christ, if you don't want to. But in the constitution of our spiritual nature, He has so made us we can look upon Him with complacency, and pour out our affection upon Him. We are not to look upon Him as a great reservoir from which to draw satisfaction but as One whom we can love more and more to eternity and never exhaust it.

The ground fact of our love is not something we get, but something desirable. We love what we desire, and seek what we love. I used to have a little business life, but I could smell a prayer meeting five miles off. I didn't want to go to the theatre. I went where I loved to go. You can't hermetically seal love. When you love God, you desire Him, and you'll get to Him though earth and hell oppose. Legalism, churchianity and formality may run themselves to death, but they can't catch you. If you love, you will find your lover! Get dead in love with Jesus, and you'll speak of your lover; you'll let it out so folks will know it.

Love always acts from the spirit of righteousness. If you love, you will do right. If you get a pure heart, you will do right without the training. So many are trying to teach people correct habits. Love never suggests intellectual difficulties. Hence God's way of getting men straight intellectually is to get them to have a pure heart. Love can detect intellectual fallacies. It is the keenest thing in the universe. It knows when deception is practised upon it. Love will make us at our best, intellectually and every way. Love transforms you into a being not imputationally lovely, but really lovely. If you really love God, you will hate everything that appears evil, and contrary to H m. A positive proof that you are not regenerated is that you are not dead in earnest for purity. You know the heathen will suffer everything to get purity after their manner of penance. The reason people backslide is because they refuse to get the love that will purify their hearts. Because I love Him, I'm the eternal foe of everything that hinders others from loving Him. When people get to loving, they do favors for each other that no law compels them to. Do you know Jesus loves some people you don't? He can see their lovely qualities. Love is the richest thing in the universe. Brethren, we must love less or love more.

At the close of this remarkable sermon, delivered with the blessed unction of the Holy Ghost, a large portion of the audience spontaneously came forward, and bowed in the straw. A sweet, pervasive spirit from Heaven settled upon the worshipers. Jesus as the One altogether lovely, appeared. Hearts were transformed into His likeness, but it is impossible to put in words the Pentecostal breezes that swept so gently yet powerfully through the camp. Songs of devotion, ejaculations of praise, quiet hallelujahs, prayers of faith, words of counsel, hearts swelling with unutterable emotion, tears of joy, sounds of holy laughter,— all intermingled. Jesus has gone away, said Brother Wilson, bodily, but His Spirit is here. But He wants eyes and ears and hands and feet. The church is

His body. He can so put His Spirit in us, that we will do as He would if He were here.

One precious soul back in the audience was reclaimed. Others were converted or sanctified. Sixty-five souls fell at the altar. It was, indeed, a night of glory. The Holy Spirit had sole lead. Jesus was glorified. The meeting broke up without dismissal.

MORNING SERMON.

BY REV. SETH C. REES.

Friday, Aug. 7.

Text: By faith Moses, when he was come to years, refused to be called the son of Pharaoh's daughter ;
Choosing rather to suffer affliction with the people of God, than to enjoy the pleasures of sin for a season;
Esteeming the reproach of Christ greater riches than the treasures in Egypt; for he had respect unto the recompense of the reward. Heb. 11: 24-26.

GOD made this Book and bound it, bound the two testaments together, so that fire and blood, infidels and higher critics have never been able to unbind them. In the old testament are types and shadows, in the new testament, principles and practices. God has locked the two testaments together so that to tear away the one ruins the other. The miraculous part of the old testament has been brought over by Jesus and His apostles into the new.

Perhaps as much as any other, Moses is a type of Christ, and he also gave to us wonderful types and shadows. Note first that Moses' circumstances were against him. Most of those who shine on the pages of sacred history have been schooled in oppression and persecution. He was born in human slavery, and at a time when the edict of the king had gone forth to destroy all the male children. But God changed that to a means of advancement to the court and culture of Egypt. Why, Jochabed's faith left Moses absolutely in God's hands, and God made the force of evil conspire to train up Moses and pay all the bills. Oh, we have a God greater than all circumstances! God don't come to change your circumstances but to change you. If you are all the Lord's and sin is gotten out of you, God will make your circumstances all combine for your advancement.

Then again Moses had a wonderful education, a broad and liberal culture that would have fitted him for any earthly position. But God had to take him to the back side of the desert after forty year's training in Egyptian schools, in order to educate him. God taught him more in five minutes by the Holy Ghost than Moses could have learned in a year with unanointed brains. God emphasizes heart education.

All God wants is an earthern vessel, empty and clean. We don't discount anything good. But the foot of the cross is a grander school than Harvard or Yale or Simpson's or a thousand and one little schools all over the country. But whatever you have got naturally or acquired by education must be laid in the dust long enough for God to anoint it. The Holy Ghost can make the Bible the living truth to our souls.

Look next at Moses' choice. Every man must choose. It cost him something. It was a real sacrifice.

People are taught to-day that they can join the church by a formal profession without separating themselves from this godless world. Moses was not driven out. He deliberately chose when he had come to years of understanding to give up the pleasures of Egypt. Modern pulpit thought would have said to Moses, "Your being in a palace is very providential. You can by-and-by sit on the throne and release your own people." Moses renounced it all. Why, they told me I'd starve if I renounced my all for Christ! (Brother Wilson. "You look like it!")

Moses went down to his people to suffer with them. Many to-day would like the blessings that come along with holiness people, but don't want their reproach. So many patronize holiness people. Holiness don't need any apologies and patronage. There are parasites who try to get the drippings of holiness.

Notice, too, that Moses not only forsook all these things, but had to have his enduement. He saw the God of fire at the bush, where the old carnal nature hid its face. So you must get your Horeb experience, and get all the snakiness out of you. Some are so uncertain as to whether they are entirely sanctified. Oh, I'm so glad for what Christ has done for me! I have "respect unto the recompense of the reward." How many are divorced from Egypt? How many want to say "yes" to God? How many will never patronize holiness again but will fellowship it?

Another precious altar service followed, and some came through with shoutings because the capstone of grace had been added to their experience.

AFTERNOON TALK.

Brother Kies spoke at 2 p. m. That was a wonderful meeting last night. I have felt like keeping still all day. I am willing to stay here always, if the Lord wants me to, and be separated from dear ones. I have a dear mother in the nineties, and God has let me assure her I should live as long as she. I told her that I told the inmates of the prison that if mother was willing to give good things to her children, surely God was willing to give the Holy Spirit to them that ask Him.

Brother Kies read from the first epistle of John, more especially from the third chapter. I love the ninth verse. I live there. "Whosoever is born of God doth not commit sin, for his seed remaineth in him, and he cannot sin, because he is born of God." This is justification. But we can't stay here without going on. When I was a little seven-year-old boy I went away to pray for conversion. I was thought to be too young. Some later I was converted in a school house, joined the church, later I was entirely sanctified.

Brother Kies' experience is told in a tract entitled "Sanctification," more than a hundred thousand copies of which he has scattered abroad. Some hundreds of copies were for distribution on the grounds.

Before the preaching service Brother Rees presented the subject of stock and 183 shares of Five Dollars each were taken. These aid in paying for the improvements of the past year, including the new tabernacle, one hundred tents, etc.

AFTERNOON SERMON.

BY REV. G. W. WILSON.

Text: "Thou shalt love thy neighbor as thyself." [A continuation of the sermon of the previous evening.]

To live a life of love we must have a desirable object to love. All this is, of course, eternally and abidingly in Jesus. But God never made us for ourselves. We are all bound together associationally by laws of relationship. Nobody is in right relations until he has nothing in his heart contrary to love to his neighbor. God has endowed us with natural human love apart from divine, and we want to be with the object of our love though it be in a hovel, and we covet not the palaces on the way. Love will find its object. We might as well learn it now as at any time that human love dies with this life. In heaven "they neither marry nor are given in marriage." The love God imparts by His spirit life to our natures is far deeper than that of blood kindred. A great many people have a sweet disposition, and mistake a precious human love for divine love. Not a particle of the love of consanguinity will exist in heaven. I can love every one male and female with the divine, pure, heavenly love.

Human love must be crucified. We must put wife, children and all our relations on the altar. No amount of human love will make a mother love her children religiously. Only divine love will do that. No holy man has any right to form heart love with any unholy man. No holy heart can neighbor with an unholy neighbor, and be one with him. Only natural love can intermingle with any other love when one is immoral. A man may have a natural love for his holy wife, though he has none for her Christ.

Modern church socials are based on human love. A false doctrine is honey-combing the church to-day, that every man is our neighbor because God is our Father and all we are brethren. No man is a brother, unless he is born into the kingdom. If you love God you must do it for what He is. But now comes the question, how can you love an unholy object? God, to be sure, loved his enemies, but how can we? It is philosophically impossible. Human nature, at its best, can't love an enemy. That is why I like the religion of Jesus, because it enables me to love every body, even my enemies. The more you give of love, the grander your character. All benefaction bestowed on any object from a mercenary point of view is damning. If you have got divine love, you can't help loving your neighbor.

Another fallacy the devil tries to put before some is: thou shalt love thy neighbor and hate thyself. So he tries to get them to kill themselves by asceticism. Others give for a good cause, and yet won't pay their debts. The great crime of the church to-day is that she is bowing before wealthy men, who rob the poor of their wages. If men loved God with all the heart, there couldn't be cliques and parties, the sharp distinctions of poverty and riches.

How shall I treat my neighbor according to the text? Never do anything contrary to his interest. You will remove from him everything that weakens and hurts him. You will not be to your neighbor what you would not want him to be to you in anything harmful. When you get real, divine love, you will love your neighbor as God loves him. You have no harmful purpose toward any man. Your servant and you, remember, are on a level at the family altar. If you love your neighbors you will want to share your good things with them.

The man who loves God with all his heart pours out his love for Him upon needy and suffering humanity. If you have real love and not an emotion, you will have an indescribable desire to bless somebody. Every act you do for others must be disinterested and unselfish. Do you ever get a blessing from anybody whom you know is doing you a favor selfishly? When you saw that God gave Jesus for you from an unselfish motive, it broke you all to pieces. His love can't help but bestow. God wants hearts to pour great floods of heavenly love into. The best way to send your love is not in a letter, but go and bear it like Jesus did. God might have sent His love by an angel, but He knew He could show it to the poor, wicked world himself best.

A heavy thunder shower sprang up and continued through the latter part of the afternoon, but the ardor of the campers was not dampened.

EVENING SERMON.
BY REV. G. W. WILSON.

TEXT: "Ye shall know the truth and the truth shall make you free." John 8: 32.

THE apostle John understood more of the inner spiritual life than any other apostle. Forty-two times he uses the word "know" or its equivalents. Now the man that knows is worth a dozen of these "don't know" fellows. Lots of folks know a good deal more on certain lines than any of us. That which we know cannot be otherwise than as we know it. There is a vast difference between knowledge and certainty, and between certainty and doubt. Once you know a thing, you know it forever. You can't really lose your experience. That's all you have left. That which we know becomes an abiding reality, as Bacon says.

Now there are some things we *know*, praise the Lord! Some of these depend on antecedent knowledge. No man can know God, but by faith in Jesus Christ. The God of the average church-member is so poor that the sinner don't think He can do anything for him, because He don't do anything for the church member. When you know God, you know that though your dearest loved one should fail, God's promises never fail. What a small God we have! How we whimper! Why, if we only know Him, we can be like a little child in its mother's arms. God is only known through the revelation of Jesus Christ through the Spirit. Then we will know Christ not as a lovely character or a good man, but God manifest in the flesh.

We must look out lest we sub-divide the Deity. God is one God, the Father, Son, and Holy Ghost. The first essential to salvation is a right revelation of God. God wants to found us on truth. Truth is an ever present reality. There is no new truth. We have such a craze for something new, we have personified our craziness into crazy quilts and such like. Get out of harmony with the laws of life and you destroy it. You can't be pure and misuse life. Holiness people want to learn this. When you can't get communication with Heaven, you must know there is at least a spider's web between you and the earth. You can have impure thoughts taken from your spirit, so there will not be a thought but what is prompted by the Holy Spirit.

To Luther was revealed the doctrine of justification by faith; and he got rebuked for rebuking the sins of the church. But God revealed to him that "the just shall live by faith." God flashed a great divine truth into him, and joy came into his soul. The divine ideal is that men should repent from every sin and make every possible restitution before conversion. No man will know his sins are forgiven until he knows he has got to the bottom of his repentance. It is so blessed when the devil brings up your past, that you can say to him, that's all settled. Never mind the date of your conversion. God don't care about time. He fixes you up for eternity.

Don't ever go to seeking holiness unless you know you are thoroughly regenerated. It is also a matter of consciousness that after regeneration the carnal nature stirs itself. Some few modern preachers have broached the doctrine that we are made pure at conversion. Holiness is begun then because the life God puts into you is holy, but *you* are not holy. Hence arises the need of a subtraction of the self-life that God's life may have full sway. It is hard work to keep the old man under. It keeps one on a constant strain. A man out west liked to have worn himself out trying to keep from swearing and getting mad for ten days.

God never intended you should keep justified and keep carnality. Lots of folks think because they have got amiable dispositions that they are sanctified. Your carnal self is what you need most to get rid of. When you want purity enough so you can't live without it, you'll get it. When the Holy Ghost reveals the heart-depravity, you can't do anything but want it cast out. Seeing it as God sees it, you want it taken out. Think you won't know when this loathsome leprosy is taken away and purity takes its place? Why the very absence of defilement is a blessing itself. You can't know this fact and be true to yourself without witnessing to it. "Ye shall *know* the truth." But you can't keep it if you don't testify to it, because you can't be a true man. Of all the dark souls it is those who have gone out of Canaan into Babylonish captivity.

"The truth shall make you free." You know it, don't you? Well, tell your experience like Paul did. Stand by the facts. Freedom comes only by knowing the truth. Pay the price and get holiness, and then stand by the facts. Do you know that your heart is now cleansed from all sin? A large number arose in answer to this pointed question, backed by the searching sermon. A number also bowed at the altar, earnestly seeking for real heart-purity. Let's have a clear title to holiness, urged Brother Wilson. There were a number of clear cases of coming into the light either of pardon or purity.

TESTIMONIES.
Saturday, Aug. 8.

Brother W. H. West, of Boston, led the 8.30 meeting. How can any child of God resist His will? It is a perfect surprise that we should stop and argue with Him a minute. It is His will that we should be like Him. We are to be changed—not whitewashed—into His image. Do you agree with His plan in your own heart? This campmeeting is a good place to get unhitched, if you have got hitched up. God gives us here on this ground evangelists and teachers and pastors for the perfecting of the saints. Oh, yes, God is going to bring up His boys and girls in the right way. He proposes to make them perfected saints. He is not going to mix us up with the fandangoes of this world. Children generally act natural, and we are the sons of God. I like that thought, I I am a child of God, and we shall be like Him. Do you want Jesus to see you at your best? Are you doing any. small, mean things out behind the door, where you think nobody sees you? Do you love the Bible better than the newspaper? How about your social and devotional life?

Dr. Bye. I know when Jesus sanctified my soul, He put His image in my heart. I was all melted down. Sometimes of late years it seems as though the image was worn off. I know what it is to walk and sing and pray and talk in the Spirit. I saw an Englishman out west, who got converted and sanctified, and couldn't read. But God taught him how to read the Bible and he read in the Spirit.

Brother Ennis. I've only been converted four and

one-half years. For twenty-seven years I was a drunkard. But God saved and sanctified me. Oh how different my home-life has been! Jesus helps me work for Him.

SISTER BEAN. I praise the Lord this morning that He helps me walk in the Spirit, that means keep step with God. There is a growth in this thing. Married people learn more and more of each other's dispositions as the years roll by. So we can know Jesus better and better after He has saved us from sin. He helps me in the kitchen. (Brother West, "kitchen grace!") It is easy for me to keep step with Him. I have no trouble.

BROTHER. I am in all over, all in. I used to cut off my testimonies, but now I can say I'm sanctified. Six weeks ago at Staten Island I received the baptism of the Holy Ghost. As Dr. Carradine says, I'm no longer at the bunghole getting molasses drop by drop. I'm inside, drowned. Whichever way I turn it's molasses.

SISTER. I know the work is done. Last night I could'nt sleep, it was so wonderful, what He did for me at the altar last evening. I'm so glad I came here.

BROTHER. If any man needs to praise God, I do. I was converted four months ago. I thought some friends of mine who belonged to the Roman church were committing a sacrilege in attending a mission. I went in there to get the friends out. I was under the influence of liquor. I listened to the sermon, and it seemed to go home. The next night I came again under the influence of liquor. The missionary prayed; I could not sleep, and I did'nt. So I thought if they had a religion to keep me awake, they could pray me asleep. They prayed, and I got saved. The trouble with our Roman brethren is they are taught to pray to Mary and John and all patron saints. I used to be afraid of the priest. They never told me anything about Jesus as a saviour. All they wanted was ten cents. If I got off from confession with a few Ave Marias I thought myself lucky. But I have learned to pray to Jesus, and read the Bible. Why they never let me have a Bible in the Roman church! Wife says, we only have been living about six months.

SISTER. I, too, was brought up to pray to Mary. I thought she was a good woman. But about two and a half years ago, I learned to pray to Jesus, and I read the Bible. Since then my whole family has been converted.

These two testimonies were intensely interesting and proved at once the darkness of Romanism and the brightness of Jesus.

MORNING SERMON.
BY REV. G. W. WILSON.

Text: And herein do I exercise myself, to have always a conscience void of offence toward God, and toward men. Acts 24: 16.

THERE is a theory abroad to-day that if you have Scriptual holiness, nobody would be offended. They say, if we were only like Christ, every body would fall in love with our loveliness. This impeaches the divine love, is opposed to the treatment of Jesus. Men don't see goodness. No great and good man was ever fully appreciated as to his moral worth.

The children do honor to the men their fathers slay. John and Charles Wesley were hounded in their day but to-day they have a slab to their memory in St. Paul's. What we need is a character based on undying principles and facts of experience. We need a root of holiness that goes way down to the living fountains of waters. People have an idea that some people are born to be great, while they were unfortunately circumstanced. So they sing, "Oh, to be nothing, nothing." They can never make any progress, for they are nothing now, and content to remain so.

You must swing out into the pathway of God's purposes. Amanda Smith had no idea what God was going to do with her. She moved out on the line of obeying the high behests of God's will. So Paul in the text tells how he secured his high position by obeying the behests of conscience. Paul did not simply get through his trials and persecutions by the skin of his teeth. He was more than conqueror. Paul said he was dead to sin, that he had been crucified with Christ. Paul was not moved by his feelings from principle and right. No fear of bonds or imprisonments deterred him. He went where God called him. So you will crucify legitimate loves and friendships, when you are dead in love with Christ. He always went according to his clear convictions of God's will. This man came to his end triumphantly. You may so live that you can write your epitaph before you die. Paul had no act of disobedience recorded after his surrender to God. Bishop Taylor testified in General Conference he had walked with God forty-seven years without a break. "I exercised myself," Paul says. Lots of people sit down and passively wait for something to come to pass. How many of you will go home and start a meeting? Stir up the temperance question in the midst of a political battle?

If you haven't a holy heart, the devil will flash scintillations of all sorts into your mind, and make you think they are from God. Many are preaching to-day who were never called. Pentecost is not an enforced but an essential necessity to a minister. Now all truth is divinely revealed; God could do this without a printed Word, but He uses it as a means of revelation. The sin of New England in the audacity of exalting the human reason as capable of understanding God's truth without a divine revelation. I am fire-proof against higher criticism. We had the truth long before it was recorded. As Joseph Cook says, there is an "Old, old Testament and a new, new Testament." *We* are personally testators to the truth. I had the privilege of looking once at the great pictures of Christ in Europe. But after enjoying them all, it came to me that the Infinite Artist had stamped the image of the living Christ on my heart, and that so melted me to tears that folks thought I must have had bad news from home, I cried so.

A "conscience void of offence." Why, folks get their stomachs diseased by overeating and then pray the Lord to heal them so they can disease their stomachs again! Did you ever remember the three courts, outer, inner, and innermost? The outer is the body, and that ought to be kept clean. I believe in Gospel soapsuds. That does away with tobacco and lust and such things, doesn't it? Then the mind needs to get rid of a great many unclean things if you are going to walk with God. The conscience is the innermost place where God wants to dwell peculiarly Himself. No one has any authority to direct you in the economy of God. The church, for example, is an organism, not a life. It has no conscience as an organism. A lifeless church always goes for forms and ceremonies instead of heart life. History warrants the saying that ecclesiasticism has always assumed authority not vested in it, when life has gone out. It comes more to my heart, what is to be the relation of the present holiness movement to the church of the day? Ecclesiasticism trying to crush out holiness to-day. So it did in John Wesley's time. Obey conscience, yours, not other folks.' Be sure it is enlightened, however, by the love of God.

Then notice this way of Paul is the only way to become truly manly. I am entitled to everything that can make me more manly. Obeying conscience will bring this. The text says, "Void of offense toward men." 'You can do a right thing, and many people will take it wrong, and then say *you* offended them. No, it is the truth. Telling the truth is no ground for offense. If you speak it in love, it is not your personality that offends. You offend when you do something wrong to somebody. Please God first. I can't make people believe I'm gentle, but I am. Sometimes I offend in some statement. But Jesus tucks me up close to Himself and whispers, "Never mind, I'm well pleased."

In the afternoon at two, Brother Wood, of North

Attleboro, told his experience as a missionary in India. It was intensely interesting.

AFTERNOON TESTIMONIES.

THE three o'clock meeting was a sort of general meeting. Brother Rees asked those in the audience who were seekers to tell how far they had got, and what they wanted.

SISTER: I feel I have Jesus but not the Holy Spirit.

BROTHER REES: You mean as a christian you have not the baptism with the Holy Ghost?

"Yes."

"Do you purpose to go on in all the light revealed to you?"

"Yes."

"Well you are headed right and later on we will have an altar service."

BROTHER: I was converted four months ago. Had a good experience, and God has kept me from sin. But I want a full Salvation.

BROTHER: Jesus has wonderfully saved me, but I feel I have been a hypocrite in professing entire sanctification, and I'm determined to get it at any cost. These sermons have showed me light.

SISTER: I love Jesus, but am not conscious of the witness of the Spirit.

BROTHER REES: If you are honest, God will notify you.

SISTER: I thought I had given up everything yesterday, but I had an awful night. I am determined to get it, too, at any cost.

SISTER: I am a sinner. I have been trying two months to give myself up to God. I want to be saved.

SISTER: I want entire sanctification through the word and through the Spirit.

BROTHER REES: Do you believe God does such things?

"I don't know."

BROTHER REES: Will you turn your back on your doubts and seek this very thing?

"Yes."

BROTHER: I am not fully satisfied. I have been in this sanctified experience many years. I have somewhat lost the experience.

BROTHER REES: Have you toned down your testimony in your church?

"I have not actively done so."

BROTHER REES: You have lost somewhat. There must have been a break somewhere, a letting down in your testimony or something. You can't live at high tide in entire sanctification without a continual overflow. You have got your eyes off Jesus onto folks. God will drive out all this fog.

SISTER: For a long time I have been a Christian, but lead an up and down life. Two years ago I gave up the fair and entertainment business. I went to a holiness church to watch them, and believe some people do really have the experience. I will seek it just now.

BROTHER REES: That "I will" goes all through the courts of glory.

SISTER: I want entire submission to God's will.

BROTHER REES: Are you in any way complicated with worldliness in the church?

"I have no fellowship whatever with these things. But I have not had confidence to speak against them."

BROTHER REES: You should be more definite upon these lines. You want something which will settle you.

BROTHER WILSON: No fallacy is more weakening than to say you have no will power. It simply means your conviction is not strong enough to stir your will to immediate decision. The whole heavenly arrangement is waiting on your will.

SISTER: I was wonderfully saved at conversion, and had about ten years ago a thorough sanctification. I am true to God and loyal to his church, but I have lost the joy.

BROTHER REES: I beg your pardon, but you are mistaken in being as true as formerly, or the joy would have increased rather than decreased. If you will head to the light and keep going, you will find it. How many in the audience have got through during this meeting? I want to see how you look.

Twenty-five arose with shining faces.

BROTHER REES: That's all. I wanted the folks to see you. Now all you that want something come to this altar.

About a dozen came as seekers. The camp became a great altar. Soon shouts of victory arose. One by one as the seekers emerged into liberty, they stood upon the platform and praised God for deliverance, amid the hallelujahs of the congregation.

A large acquisition to the camp's company was noticable at the evening service, many coming for the Sabbath and later.

EVENING SERMON.

BY REV. G. W. WILSON.

TEXT. Blessed are the pure in heart for they shall see God. Matt. 5: 8.

PURITY implies a simple, unmixed element. Pure water has no sediment or defilement. Pure oil has no other substance in it. The purification of anything implies a subtraction of some impure element. There cannot be a pure heart without the process of subtraction. Of course this heart is not the muscular organ that beats in your bosom. Every man of sense knows we mean by the heart, morally speaking, the affections. Did you ever think that God united himself with our nature, but never with that of angels? God has a heart of love, and has made us so we must love love something or somebody.

A pure heart is to love a right thing in a right way. There must be an eternal removal of your affections from a wrong object. We need not give up worldly business, but must hold right relations with the world. Real heart purity, real righteousness, from a pure moral standpoint, implies you are to use every gift or faculty for the glory of God. If you can only make money you are under the strongest moral obligation to do so, provided you can do so honestly and use it to the glory of God. The old world is right and human nature is right. It is only sinful and perverted human nature that is wrong. Human nature, rightly acting, is the most beautiful thing in the world outside of God. Good sense is needed in business rather than love. Your business does not call for the heart. Yet, many men give their whole heart to business, and none to their home. So they neglect to pray, and rush away from home to business. Your own baby meeting you on the street wouldn't know you.

Matter has no element in it that can respond to love. Idolaters exist today. Some women would make more fuss over a lost diamond ring than over their prodigal sons going down to hell. Where there is no love there is sin. People are puffed up with pride. Their hearts are on things the heathen have cast aside. For example Christian Science, which is considered so lovely, is bold pantheism; which was in India 400 years ago, and thrown overboard by them.

Your affections can never be pure unless they are set upon the things God meant them to be set upon. Hence home life does away with clubrooms and secret societies. When a man puts his lodge room or clubroom or card table before his home or loving wife and darling offspring, he resigns his manhood and manliness. Secret orders sap the manhood of God's Sanctuary and leave a few women to weep between the porch and the altar. You will follow your heart every time. I never saw a church where the official members belonged to secret orders but what the church was neglected for the secret society, every time. Get a clean heart, and your heart will be rightly centered. A pure heart will have a right affection for every proper object. No people have a right to marry, for example, unless both parties love each other. Genuine Bible holiness makes us intensely love our home. If you get a pure heart, your wife will not be a slave of unregulated passion, but a companion of your love.

Heart holiness will bring mutual self sacrifice into

the home. All these misplaced affections must be regulated, must be purged, that God's love can be put in. The antithesis of love—hate, jealousy and murder —will all go out. Get a clean heart and you will have no desire to harm anybody, even though they harm you. The only right any man has is to be right. Yet, folks talk so much about their rights. You will rather try to win to Christ the one that hurts you.

A man with a pure heart will love pure beings or pure things for their own sake. Holiness is as broad as heaven, and that is narrowed down to excusing all unholiness. When you get a pure heart, you will love pure folks, and you'll show to them the etiquette of heaven. I want to praise God for the simplicity and love life upon this camp-ground. Oh, when you get a pure heart you won't back down. God can bank on a pure heart anywhere, anytime. "Blessed are the pure in heart." When you get the baptism with the Holy Ghost, you will have a pure heart. A pure heart has no flinch or compromise in it. Have you got a pure heart?

A large portion of the audience arose. Many came to the altar.

What God don't want you to have, said Brother Wilson, and you insist in having, will be a curse to you. What He wants you to have will be a blessing. His voice of prohibition is the voice of a loving Father who does not want His children to hurt themselves.

One young lady said, "I thank God, He has saved and sanctified me all in one day."

Another sister said, "I've been a church member

ten years, but that don't save me. I have a quick temper. I want entire sanctification."

THE LORD'S DAY.
Sunday, Aug. 9.

EVERY day is the Lord's Day at Portsmouth camp. The song, "Every Day'll be Sunday By-and-by," is changed here to "Every Day is Sunday Now-and-now." So heavenlike has this meeting been that the life of eternity has begun in the fact that persons fail to notice the flight of hours. The dinner or supper bell, or night bell, surprises us, it rings so often. The second Sabbath dawned bright and clear, with cool, refreshing breezes from the blue Narragansett around us, sweeping through the spacious auditorium, and warm, tonic, spiritual gales sweeping down from the blue heavens above us.

THE LOVEFEAST. At 8:30, after singing by the assembly with the Spirit and understanding, Brother Wilson read some verses from I. Corinthians 11: 6-16. Don't try to fix up your testimony so the natural man can understand it. It is foolishness unto them, they cannot understand it.

BROTHER. God has saved me thoroughly. He saved me from both using and selling tobacco. I praise Him this morning.

Three young girls testified to having received entire sanctification, to having learned how "to eat honey."

BROTHER. Hallelujah! I love everybody. His salvation turns out concerts and all such things.

SISTER. I more than praise Him this morning for the victory in my heart.

HALLELUJAHS FROM PORTSMOUTH 57

BROTHER. I am so glad I have got into the fire and the fire has got into me. Six years ago He sanctified me, and they have been six years of victory.

SISTER. They thought I was going insane. But my brain got out of the way, and He made me understand it was my heart He was after.

BROTHER. I'd rather have enough salvation to make people think something is the matter with me, than to be so much like other folks.

SISTER FRIEDA STROMBERG. I praise God for a fresh revelation of the Spirit. He sanctifies me wholly, body, soul and spirit.

BROTHER. I know that I have been justified, regenerated, and was fully sanctified nine months since, and received the baptism of the Holy Ghost about seven weeks ago.

BROTHER WILSON. We are here in the interest of the truth and not good feeling. Don't think you can be entirely sanctified for months without the Holy Ghost. You can't know you get sanctification without the Holy Ghost.

BROTHER. I praise God He sanctified me last night. He filled my soul with peace and I know it.

BROTHER. I got a good birthday present of a know-so salvation.

BROTHER WILSON. I want to ask you, beloved, how it is possible for you not to have the witness of the Spirit to entire sanctification and know when you lose it.

SISTER. I wasn't willing to say "Please" to Jesus until last Wednesday night. Then I submitted, and He saved me.

Brother Woodward. I understand they had a grand illumination at Newport the other night. I think this camp meeting is the grandest illumination I ever attended. I believe after receiving the baptism of the Holy Spirit there are many illuminations and anointings. Many confound these things and say they received the baptism with the Holy Ghost weeks, or months, or years after entire sanctification.

Sister Bosworth. I have stepped over onto the victory side. He has set the joy bells ringing in my soul. One reason I know I'm over is because the enemy is so stirred.

Brother Badger. When I first came upon this camp ground I had a great weight over me. When they talked about entire sanctification it scared me most to death. But down at the end of that altar the other night I told God I would take all He wanted to give me. Oh, hallelujah! This is the first time I ever shouted in my life.

Brother. I am glad for the fullness and sweetness of God's love in my soul. His glory is a living reality to me.

Sister. I praise Him for the sweetness of His own presence in my soul.

Brother. I feel as clear this morning as this bright day.

Brother Wilson. Nobody, who has not the experience of holiness can talk the thing straight. I am overjoyed to see so many people here a unit and so free. We bring a chill on the meeting and dishonor the Holy Ghost to slight the work He has done. Nobody can have inbred sin burned out apart from the Holy Ghost.

He is glorified in our telling what He has done, and only in that way. People want to know what He can do, whether He casts out ill temper, and unholy lusts, and improper desires.

MORNING SERMON.
BY SETH C. REES.

TEXT. Who shall ascend into the hill of the Lord, or who shall dwell in His holy place? He that hath clean hands and a pure heart. Psa. 24: 3-4.

THIS psalm was evidently composed for that eventful occasion when the ark of God was returned to its place on the holy hill at Jerusalem. It had been in the hands of its enemies and cursed them. It had been in the house of Obed-edom and been a blessing to him. Now if it was to be restored to the temple, some man must be qualified to go up into the hill of the Lord and stand in the Holy place.

First notice the Holy place. This represents the place of holiness, the blessing of heart purity wrought in the experience of entire sanctification through the baptism with the Holy Ghost. Holiness is a state; entire sanctification is an experience, the entrance gate to the state; the blessed Holy Ghost brings us through the gate by His own power.

Now it is a place of honor, indeed, to be admitted to the presence of the King. What a glorious honor! It is not a place of embarassment. Oh! we ought to see how great an honor it is. I never pity myself, I always pity the other fellows! It is so glorious to be admitted to the presence of royalty. Some day people will take off their hats to us, though they sneer at us now. Don't think that you are coming to this altar to get a blessing on the sly, which you can keep in solitary confinement. Glory to God, I'm not hard up! Get into this Holy place, and everything else will sink into insignificance, and the kingdom will take on such magnificent proportions you will be continually charmed with the splendors of the court.

Again, this is a place of friendship. We are on continual terms of intimacy with the King. We want and may "stand in the Holy place." Too many are sanctified by spells, go in and out. But you have got to forsake this world to have this holy fellowship with the Lord.

Then it is a place of safety. So many say, I don't want to get up so high, for I'm afraid I'll fall. I don't want to make high professions lest I dishonor the cause. Oh, how anxious the devil is about "the cause." The only safe place is the place of holiness, even though it be a lion's den or a fiery furnace. God makes me invulnerable against the attacks of the batteries of hell. Don't feel scared to seek holiness when it means such absolute safety and such perfect security.

Then again, it is the place of power. Queen Esther was in the place of power in the presence of King Ahasuerus. She touched the sceptre of power and revolutionized the condition of her people. So with Daniel and Joseph. So you can touch the sceptre of almightiness and do as you please; for you will please to please Him. Yet how we bemoan our weakness! Oh! if you ever get in, you are in bondage to nothing nor nobody, not even your own church, which you love.

The reason you have not power is because you are not in the place of power. You are trying to work at arm's length. People fail to recognize the Holy Ghost. That is why many think they must have a third experience. [Brother Wilson. That third blessing idea is really restoration to the blessing of entire sanctification.]

Once more. It is a place of plenty. You'll eat your bread without scarceness, have grapes and honey to give away, and then have more left than when you began. You are not lean and hungry, and going round questioning folks as to this thing and that. Glory to God! I want no other thing. Plenty of joy and peace and feeling. There is an awful lack of old-fashioned religious feeling. Faith is all right, but it brings definite results.

Secondly. Look at the conditions of entering the Holy place. First, we must have clean hands. Are you governing your home and your business and dress according to the Holy Ghost? Do you give a pure daughter to a godless young man because he has advantages of wealth or position? I thoroughly believe in old maids. Better stay forever unmarried than yoke up with unbelievers. It is an awful thing to fail to make right what is wrong. Have you paid your grocery bill? "Well, I've got to live." No, you haven't.

Again, the heart must be pure, as clean as Adam had in the Garden of Eden. This is easy, because it is God's side. Anger, envy, jealousy, unholy passions, covetousness, and all these things will go out, and all will be sweetness and heaven. Who wants it? Oh, praise the Lord! Many came and sought an entrance in the Holy place, and were not long knocking at the doors of mercy ere they were thrown wide open, and they came through rejoicing with shining faces. Among the seekers were some young men and boys, who came through on the victory side.

AFTERNOON TESTIMONIES.

W. H. WEST led the 2 o'clock meeting. It was a rousing praise, prayer and testimony service. Success or failure, which? There is only one true line of eternal success, and that is with God. Lots of folks think many people have great success, but they have got to drop it at the grave. I read a little story about the children of the White House the other day which illustrates about the proper emphasis to be placed on worldly honors. The nurse and two children of the White House were out in the park, when up came a policeman with his little girl. The other two children began to make friends with her. Presently little Ruth remarked, "My father is President." "Well," said the other little girl, "my father is a policeman." Little Ruth looked up to the blue suit and shining brass buttons and, attracted by the glitter, said finally, "I wish my father was a policeman, too." Oh, how empty this worldly wealth and fame and show and tinsel! Some people exist and some live, but others *reign*.

BROTHER WOOD. I want to stand as a witness to the fact that there is cleansing in the precious blood. I came to myself at eighteen and thought what my future would be if I should live and die in sin. A few years after I found Jesus was able to give me a second dip and cleanse out anger and impatience and all sin.

BROTHER. I'm glad to-day I'm the child of a King. I was a lost sinner. I wasted twenty-seven years in the gambling den, with my family starving.

YOUNG SISTER. I am glad that we school-girls can be saved and sanctified.

SISTER. I praise God I have entire sanctification and the witness to it. I came here feeling I weighed about two hundred. Now I feel as if I weighed a pound.

AFTERNOON SERMON.
A Perfect Man.
BY REV. G. W. WILSON.

TEXT. And he gave some, apostles; and some, prophets; and some, evangelists; and some, pastors and teachers;

For the perfecting of the saints, for the work of the ministry, for the edifying of the body of Christ:

Till we all come in the unity of the faith, and of the knowledge of the Son of God, unto a perfect man, unto the measure of the stature of the fulness of Christ:

That we henceforth be no more children, tossed to and fro, and carried about with every wind of doctrine, by the sleight of men, and cunning craftiness, whereby they lie in wait to deceive;

But speaking the truth in love, may grow up into him in all things, which is the head, even Christ:

From whom the whole body fitly joined together and compacted by that which every joint supplieth, according to the effectual working in the measure of every part, maketh increase of the body unto the edifying of itself in love. Eph. 4: 11-16.

"Well," some will say, "if he has got such a long text, how long will the sermon be?" I am going, however, to take three words out of that long text, and make them the central thought of the hour: "A Perfect Man."

When we introduce the subject of perfection, we always arouse mental antagonism. No man can think, in its proper sense, of that which he cannot subjectively realize. It is a very common thing to hear men say, "You talk about perfection, but you are just as perfect as I am, and that is all." The trouble with the mass in this tabernacle now is, you do not believe in nor do you think of any possibility of any perfection in this life, and the whole foundation for that form of thinking is in the fact that you are everywhere radically defective yourself. Preachers that preach that kind of material from the pulpit are men who are at every part of them radically defective. When the doctrine calls for one form of perfection, if the preacher has a perfect heart he will find something in common that quickly responds to the doctrine. If he has not a perfect heart he will find moral antagonisms against the doctrine. We need not be surprised if a preacher opposes holiness, for that is the best he can do if he is at all carnal. It is just as natural for a carnal preacher to oppose holiness, as it is for a bull to run at you when you shake a red rag. There is nothing the matter with the rag, but the fact is a bull never liked one, and you had better be on the other side of the fence when he comes around.

All this opposition to holiness grows out of the nature of the opposer, and nothing in the doctrine itself. In everything else, we believe in and like to see perfection. Everyone would like to have a perfect piano in his home, not one that has a lot of chords out of harmony, but one in which each part is harmonized with the whole. Most men would like to have a perfect wife. Young men always look for that. Most men would like to have perfect machines. One of the advertising methods of to-day is to try and convince people that the thing they are selling is perfect.

Now we have perfect flowers. There may be blights and defects, but these blights and defects have been discovered by the existence of perfect flowers. If every flower had a blight and every flower had a defect, you have no scientific process by which you can discover a defect in any of them.

The perfect man Christ Jesus is God's standard of true perfection, and because he is here and on hand as God's standard of true perfection we will have to stand our measurement by Him. He is here to tell us just exactly where we are. Now, when God made man He made him like Jesus. The original human nature in the Garden of Eden was just like Christ's human nature as He walked among men. Exactly! Jesus Christ in His human nature possessed nothing that Adam did not possess in the Garden of Eden. Nothing!

Because of the discovery of that fact the Eastern Unitarians have a very beautiful human Christ, but for want of spiritual eyesight they have looked at the perfect man and tried to copy and imitate him, but they have not seen that in the perfect man dwelt all the fulness of the God head bodily, and so in their system of religion from beginning to end they have not got any Spirit of God working in God's spiritual perfection; but they have development and evolution, and culture and education, and refinement. They have not got down to gospel lines, and recognized that the Holy Ghost is established in the church to reach men, and to sanctify and to perfect them, and to bring them to the stature of the fulness of Jesus Christ. When they do they will find out that the Holy Ghost can put a man in one hour spiritually where a million years of culture and education, and evolution and refinement, can never put him. He is able to lift us into perfection spiritually by a process of His own in perfect harmony with spiritual laws. He lifts us, however far down in our intellectual faculties we may be, and needing a great amount of trimming and training. Don't I love to see a sanctified soul in the raw? I like to see that pure and clean, and bright and happy, pleasing to God, and up to the divine standard and yet having a great many crudities and weaknesses and infirmities, and things they have got to learn, and be taught and disciplined in.

And then some one takes up these crudities and weaknesses, and says, "There is your perfection!" Well, that does not prove that there is no such thing as a perfect man. It simply shows that in producing a perfect man God works inwardly first, and the whole system of religious thought I have spoken against works externally. God works first on the inner spirit life, and then having perfected the inner spirit life, he works through it by mental laws and physical laws, and natural processes and by inspirations of His Spirit, and the education of experience to straighten out the man's life in a great many things which need to be adjusted after He has made him pure. There are many things in connection with wholly sanctified lives in regard to their education and their associations, and their relations to thought which need straightening, and yet the inner man may be spotless, holy and pure and perfectly acceptable to God. We must not forget the fact that holiness does not give us sense, but it takes what we have and makes the most of it, and multiplies it for all there is in it.

Now there is another thing. You know when a man is fighting holiness he will pick out some hypocrite as a sample to judge professors by and will say the whole profession is false. If I should go into one of your orchards and you should say, "Now I want you to tell me what you think of my apple trees," and I should go up to one tree with great, rosy-cheeked, yellow apples, looking very inviting, and especially if I was not very much acquainted with fruit, I should say, "That rosy-cheeked, big thing, that is certainly the finest fruit in the orchard." Then I turn about and see a dwarfed, little tree with small fruit and nothing very inviting in either size or colors, and I say, "I would not have that, that must be very unpleasant." You smile, and as you walk along you ask, "Well, but did you taste this fruit? If you want to know which is the finest fruit you must taste it and not judge by the appearance." I said, "I forgot; sure enough. I was just going to ask you to send us five barrels of these big, rosy-cheeked apples, but I guess I'll taste them." I walk up to the tree and take one of them and put it to my mouth, and it makes my mouth so wry I can hardly straighten it up again. There is no juice in it, and I say to my friend, "Don't send me any of these apples." Then I take one of the little golden russets and they are full of juice, and as my teeth close upon it I say, "Yes, that is the kind; send me five barrels of that kind right away. You may keep all the dry, pithy ones you have, but here is the kind for me." When you run across a truly sanctified heart and close your teeth in it you will find so much juice you will fall in love with it. When you stick your teeth into an unsanctified heart you will find they will stick their teeth into you. But the real, genuine holy heart will bear testing.

I will just enunciate the principle and leave it. Perfection of action or external conduct is an absolute impossibility in this life for this reason, that the instrument you have to do the act with is imperfect, no matter what may be your spiritual nature that lies back of it. So when you look for perfection of conduct among saints you are just going to get left. Now I am not going to excuse any of you folks along this line. I have been so kind to you before I feel like being very plain now.

No act in and of itself has any moral character attached to it, and you cannot judge the moral character of any individual simply by the act that that individual may perform. Let me illustrate. Suppose I am a preacher, I do not believe in Sunday drives, and all that sort of thing. Suppose I am preaching down here and as I am through, some one comes driving down here and says, "I know you are very exhausted, but my grandmother has heard of you and she is very ill, and she will not live till morning and sends a request for you to come and see her." I jump into the carriage and he takes the whip and whips up the horses, and away we go. Now some jockey has a fast horse out on the road and we come upon him and are anxious to pass him, and just as we turn out he whips up his horse and away we go abreast for a rod or two. Well, some one sees me there and says, "Why, I saw your holiness preacher out trotting his horses on Sunday, and if that is your holiness I don't want to hear anything about it." There was no difference in the appearance of the act. The jockey, however, was bound to bring out his horse ahead and feed his pride, while I was hurrying to get to the deathbed of a saint to say a word for my Master that would make purer and sweeter her last moments. One was riding his horse to hell, while I was wearing the livery of earth to help a saint on to heaven. I had got another motive, another spirit of the thing. I want to say right here that holiness people want to quit judging each other until they know that something is the matter with each other. You never will get in love with people you are everlastingly snapping at. Yes, sir, holiness people do it, but holy people don't.

No act in itself has any moral quality, but no individual can put any moral quality into an act without that moral quality being discerned by a pure heart. People can be mad and as mad as can be, and by virtue of well trained habits behave themselves perfectly *outwardly*, and yet they are just brimful of old-fashioned devil mad, and other folks will appear to be mad outwardly, while inwardly they are just as sweet as can be.

Another thing I want to call your attention to. Holiness people do not stop very much to get all their pulpit mannerisms and all their church mannerisms moulded into the lines of worldly conformity to style and conduct. You do not know it, perhaps, but I would have been exceedingly eloquent to-day if I had just tried to be. But I have no time to be eloquent. I am going to let that out when I get to heaven. Just now I am so busy with the truth that I have not time to polish up the sentences. But when a man has nothing else to give to the people he must have some style or polish or else they get nothing. Oh! if my father had willed me a large estate I would not care a flip of my fingers whether the eloquent pleading lawyer of the firm came to read the will or the law attorney who understood all the law of it who had a stammering tongue. What this world wants to-day is a type of ministry that though they may have stammering tongues will tell poor, poverty stricken humanity of their glorious inheritance in Jesus Christ. I would rather hear of my inheritance in Jesus Christ from a stammering tongue than have an eloquent brother try to prove to me that I am rich in my poverty. We have grace for eloquence and the truth is what we want.

"But," you say, "some of these holiness folks do some very queer things." Well, if you get the blessing of holiness you will do some very queer things too.

People say to me, "I was just enjoying hearing you preach and you were just beginning to reach me when someone took a skip and it ruined my aesthetical feelings and I lost all the blessing. Some of us, it is true can't have a good time unless we skip, but suppose you take the truth whether someone skips or not. Take the truth anyhow.

I am not particular about the messenger; the message is what I want. A boy runs in here from the Western Union Telegraph Co., and comes to me and says, "Mr. Wilson, the agent over here has received a telegram that he thinks you will want to see right away." I take a good square look at the boy. He is dirty and I see his clothing is ragged. I do not find any marks of culture and refinement about him, and I say, "You get out of here and tell the agent to send some other boy over here with a clean coat and face." The boy looks at me and says, "But don't you want the message?" "No, not until I get it delivered by a better looking boy than you." He looks at me again and says, "I wish you would take it." "Will you get out of here at once," I say, "and tell your agent to send messages to me only when he has a nice clean boy with hair combed and fingernails trimmed and his clothing whole and nicely brushed to carry them." He goes, and I finish the sermon somehow and by and by walk down to the depot. The agent is there and he says, "Mr. Wilson, I received a message over the wire for you this afternoon, and I felt as though you ought to see it at once, and so I sent that boy up with it. Would you like to have it now?" "Yes, but never send a dirty boy with a message to me anyhow." I open the envelope which has been in the office for three hours and read, "Your wife is dying: come first train," and then I ask, "What time is the next train? I must go at once." The agent tells me the last train for this night is gone.

I take the next train in the morning but am too late, my wife is dead, and I say, "Oh, fool! that I did not take the message no matter who the messenger was." It is the message I want and not the messenger.

It is the truth we want and not the style in which it is given. Take the message whoever the messenger is. Blundering, stammering, what ever he may be, take the message, for that is God's own eternal word.

There is something in the doctrine of holiness that meets the wants of your heart. Take the doctrine and the truth home to your heart and get the blessing and you will love the messenger that bore it. You do not like the unpolished conduct of this one and the violation of etiquette by that one, and so on. I want to tell you something for your comfort. Before the Lord can bring you to your senses and give you the blessing He will make you cut up like everything. How He does love to shake up those fine polished folks that have such perfect control of themselves and their feelings that they can never commit an act of impropriety!

But after all we are the folks that do behave ourselves. We are the folks that have the true etiquette. I want to say that nobody on earth ever behaved themselves till they were brimful of love. Lots of people don't know the difference between starch and fire. I think when the people get my dead body and have dressed me for the last service, I shall look real nice; but I think that my dear wife would rather have me walking around in my shirt sleeves shouting at the top of my voice so long as I was alive. And some of you folks that are so polished and finished that you

HALLELUJAHS FROM PORTSMOUTH

cannot do anything that you think is improper in your religious services, you are so ignorant of real spirituality that when you become spiritual you become bigger fools in the beginning than we are now.

We do not behave nearly as bad as we used to. We have got the machinery adjusted to our new spiritual life so that we can stand it without so much commotion.

And some of you now would like to have the blessing of holiness or perfect love if you were not afraid you would have to go back on all you have said against it. And the last thing that some of you will have to give up before you are ever sanctified wholly is to be willing to go into your old, dead, formal, cold, lifeless church and shout out until every beam and rafter sounds out a loud hallelujah and sends you off again. And some of you who do not think you are anywhere unless you have a big tantrum on, when the Lord sanctifies you wholly He will make you just as quiet as if you were dead. You will be so very quiet, with a great big heaven in your soul without much emotion, and you will say, "I have not got the witness that other people have, but I believe I have got the blessing."

Beloved, don't pay a particle of attention to what people think about your outward manifestation of the inner life, but let the life flow as best it can through your poor defective, perverted human nature and give God the glory and please Him. I think that anybody that understands the blessing of holiness will stand you. If you were all to stand up now on your feet and shout at the top of your voices, I think I could stand you. There are some boats on this river that are built for storms. They are not so nice looking as some, but, oh my! how they stand the waves! When the Lord built me for storms He made me so I could stand a calm, but I was built for storms.

What is perfection as taught in God's word? When we talk about a thing being perfect we simply mean that the thing which we denominate perfect is answering perfectly the thing for which it was instituted. A perfect sewing machine will sew cloth, but it won't thresh wheat. When you say you have a thing that is perfect you simply mean that it answers perfectly the end for which it was instituted.

Now there are only two senses in which we can be perfect in this life. First, our wills can be perfectly conformed to the will of God. No individual has perfection that has not a willingness to say "Yes" to all the known will of God in his case. No individual has perfection that is not willing to suffer all the will of God. No individual has got perfection that is not willing to do all the will of God, and no individual has got spiritual perfection that is not willing to wait on God's will before he makes a pathway of his own. No individual has any business doing anything that he has not orders to do.

We are not proprietors; we are servants. The church of God would be wonderfully blessed to-day if every uncalled preacher would vacate the pulpit and let the people come in throngs to hear the truth from those who have it. We can choose to do the perfect will of God. I thank God that if I want to, there is nothing in the universe can prevent me from having a holy heart and doing the perfect will of God. In that sense I am the arbiter of my own destiny.

But we want not only a perfect will, but we want a perfect affectional nature. No man is perfect spiritually or morally that has any affinity for an impurity. A brother said to me yesterday, "I got wonderfully blessed at a certain place, and since that time I have been able to keep my old nature under control, but lately it got away with me again. I am very sorry, and I want to be renewed so as to keep that old nature under again." Exactly! That brother came forward last night and went down to the bottom of this sin question and is here to-night and can testify to the fact that the difficulty is ended and the carnal affection is removed. Every man has something in his heart-life or love-life that he has an affinity for, that is evil, till God has cleansed him from all sin. Every one has it; and you are not perfect in love until all the old element of impurity is taken out of your nature and you perfectly love God. And this has no reference whatever to *capacity*, but simply to the *quality* of your affection. It is pure, and it may increase and abound more and more.

There is another thing. No heart is perfect until it is perfectly obedient to every ray of light that God may give it. What is the ground work of your sanctification? Entire consecration properly taught. It must be taught in order to receive the blessing. Entire consecration! What does that mean? It does not mean that when you consecrate yourself now you are doing all the will of God that you can do, but it means that you give your will up and always take the will of God. Because of this, God cleanses you from all sin, but an absolutely essential requirement of your retaining purity and keeping the blessing of perfection or perfect love is that every added ray of light that God gives you from any source shall be walked in at all cost. Too many are on the ragged edge of this blessing and have an in-and-out and up-and-down experience, and all that sort of thing. Get away from that. Say you will do the will of God because you love it, even if it takes you back of your yesterday and shows you a new plan for to-morrow and changes all the program. You will dare to walk with God.

The Lord gave me the blessing of a perfect heart at the age of nineteen, twenty-four years ago, nearly a quarter of a century ago. I had nothing but an indescribable desire to do His will and I did it every day up to my light, and it did not require one hundredth part as much to do His will then as it does now. I put myself where the light shined. I see new things physiologically, I see new things in mental philosophy, I see new things in relation to my fellowmen, and I want to say that there is not one with a perfect heart, but if you will live twenty-four hours in the white light of God, something in your talk, something in your methods of doing things, something in your way or plan of life, God will give you additional light upon which you must obey. If you will not, you will become a sort of holiness fossil and will kill any camp meeting on earth if they will let you. If we are to be perfect in love we must be perfect in life and God will show us many things we ought to change if we would keep a pure heart before Him.

Now let me finish the sentence in another form. There is no responsibility for any past mistake or failure until light comes, but just as the light comes you must walk in that light and put away that evil thing, as you will put yourself in the path of doubt and disobedience and will lose your purity. Now when you get that light don't come forward and say you have not got holiness, you have simply got fresh light. If you have got a holy heart when God shows you anything in your speech or conduct or manner of life or anything else you have not seen before, you will be so anxious that your outward life will be a proper representation of what your heart feels that you will correct it in a flash. A perfect heart does not go growling around when fresh light comes, but is looking for fresh light. When added light comes you will learn to welcome it just as an earnest workman would welcome the rising of the morning sun.

I want to speak of another thing. One great mistake that people make is that when you get perfection you ought not to be subject to tests; and yet you cannot develop a life of holiness without tests equal to your added measure of spiritual power. It was enough for Abraham on his first test of faith to leave his country and his kindred, and go into a new land, but he did not get the blessing of perfection then. It was not until he had gone back and forth and went down to Egypt and had other tests that God said to him, "Abraham, walk thou before me and be thou perfect;" and in his ninety-ninth year he got perfection. As far as an Old Testament Saint could get it he got the blessing. But God said, "Abraham!" "What now

Lord?" "Take now thy son, thine only son Isaac, and offer him unto me on a mount that I shall show thee." The greater tests with the greater experience. Abraham would not trust his unsanctified wife, Sarah, with the facts in the case. He arranged to take the boy along and the wood and the fire, and when the supreme moment came God interposed and Himself provided a ram for the sacrifice and he received this commendation: "Now know I that thou fearest God."

Every sanctified heart that is perfect in love is also perfect in confidence in God. There is not a test that He can make that you will not respond to and say, "Where He leads me I will follow. I will trust Him for the outcome."

You can make no progress in the spiritual life until the measure of your test is equal to the measure of your resistance. This is a rule you can bank on. When the measure of test is exactly equal to the measure of your power of resistance you are absolutely free to go either forward or backward and with every choice to go forward you get added strength and power and grace and unction, so that your character is the product of your choice, and not simply the accident of your life. I stand here at this hour with a great consciousness down deep in my heart that He knows and I know that He knows that whatever test He puts on this poor soul I will dare to follow wherever He leads. Have you got it? If not, get to the bottom of everything here and let God have a chance to fix you all up. Amen.

SUNDAY EVENING.

SISTER JENNIE STROMBERG sang a solo, "I'll Go Every Step of the Way." The congregation caught up the chorus, and made the tabernacle ring therewith. After singing and announcements, Brother Rees turned the meeting over to Rev. G. W. Wilson.

BROTHER WILSON. There are some things you can be done with forever. They are finalities. There is some discussion as to the origin or utter disposal of evil. The best fact is we can get rid of it as a cause, and be done with it forever. Every man who wants to can have a divine assurance of pardon by the Holy Spirit's divinely attesting to God's pardon. It is a divinely wrought assurance that God has forgiven us and will not go back on it at the judgment. This is the judicial side of salvation. Nothing in the nature of things requires a man to sin any more. God never pardons a sinner who does not pledge that he will never sin any more. To keep you from sin God regenerates you, hence, "whosoever is born of God doth not commit sin." No man is born from above who has not surrendered the principle of disobedience. If he sins after regeneration, he must first surrender the principle of obedience. Now there is no necessity for such surrender. Only one being in the universe can make me a sinner and that is myself.

You can't be born from above twice. You may be quickened and spiritualized, so if you fall into sin, you must not expect to have the same feelings you had at regeneration over again. You can get restored only by coming back to the point of obedience where you began to disobey. A great mass of backslidden church members began to backslide by refusing to walk up to the light of holiness. The antagonism to holiness comes from your having to accept the truth of God where you dropped it. Then you must get restored, and go forward. If you won't promise in your heart of hearts to go forward to holiness, you won't get restored. The thing you have an antipathy for is just an expression of your depravity, and that's the very thing by which God must kill out your depravity.

Many have to swallow way down the words, "entire sanctification." The trouble is you must surrender your will and nature upon the point God reveals is wrong. You know when you are sorry enough for your sin to be at an end of it. Then you can trust God. You will feel different in returning from backsliding than at conversion. Then you can seek the blessing of heart purity. You must have every form of rebellion given up ere you can seek holiness. You should come to the fountain of cleansing to keep saved. Consecrate once for all, your friends and loved ones and, hardest of all, yourself. Now, if you retain your holiness, you will never have anything to consecrate over. Yet some of you say: "I consecrate every month." You might as well have your marriage ceremony said over every thirty days. Everything is to be the Lord's forever, body, soul and spirit. Until you know the consecration is complete, you will never get holiness.

There is not a soul in this tabernacle who will give up his sins, but God will save him. Are you willing to accede to God's terms? When you get to the point that you are going to be saved, God will save you.

Make your honest confession, and determine you will obey God fully. You see the necessity of bringing on the issue. Who will come?

Again the shouts of the converted, reclaimed and sanctified, were heard after prayer.

MORNING SERMON.
Monday, Aug. 10.

At the usual hour for preaching Brother Wilson talked about three things: First—What is involved in committing sin? Before an individual can commit sin there is a clear conviction in the mind of that individual of the moral character of the choices. Adam did not sin for me and I did not sin in Adam. God couldn't make me guilty for a sin I never did. When you do not consciously and deliberately make a wrong choice, you cannot be guilty. Choice involves freedom *from* as well as *to*. It is impossible to sin without choice. Nor can you make a choice without knowing the moral character of your choice. So you can't sin without knowing it. You first consciously surrender the principle of obedience. Whenever a sinful heart sins, there is depravity back of it. Adam's subjective nature must first have been depraved before he could do a depraved act, i. e., his nature must have yielded to evil intent before he performed the act.

The first stage of salvation, regeneration, saves from unholy choices. A regenerated will, however, can keep down all sinful acts. I cannot feel pride without being proud, but I can feel pride and not act proud. If I feel anger, there must be anger somewhere in me.

Regeneration saves you from acting proud or angry when you feel pride or anger. You will manifest rather the opposite. As long as you retain the life of regeneration, sin does not have dominion over you.

Now entire sanctification leaves you under temptation without anything within to respond. When through the senses temptations arise, nothing within responds. Sin is always the perversion of natural things. Appetites and passions are proper and have their normal uses. Indignation is proper. There is a sort of namby-pamby putty holiness which is undisturbed if everything goes wrong. That is sentimentality. Real holiness rebukes sin wherever it is found. Some folks have no opposition, but a holy heart has a natural antipathy for evil, when before you had a natural affinity for it. The idea you can have holiness and no conflicts and persecution is wrong.

Second—Infirmities lie neither in the will nor affections, but in the body or mind. Neither the will nor the heart are infirm. A weak body may prevent your carrying out the desires of a loving heart. A great many people have such physical infirmities that they press upon the mind peculiar temptations. The Holy Ghost quickens our mortal bodies and tones them up by His own indwelling.

Jesus Christ does heal human diseases, and by two processes—natural and supernatural. He can do it instantaneously or by natural processes, but the individual must forever put away that which causes diseases. I believe many more would be healed if they would put their bodies in line with God's will. Don't consider yourself a poor, unfortunate creature if you have physical infirmities which could be avoided by obedience to health laws. If you don't obey them you are a sinner. Many people get the blessing of entire sanctification and lose it through the unnatural gratification of carnal appetites. The awful crime of lust has its foundation in the wrong idea that appetites must be gratified abnormally. That which yesterday was a mistake becomes to-day by added light a sin whereby you bring guilt upon your conscience. There is a great difference between thoughts of evil and evil thoughts. A pure heart may think of evil yet have no evil thought. Jesus had thoughts of evil. But if you have a pure heart you will at once reject the temptation. The sanctified heart has no sympathy with the sins, but great sympathy with the sinner. Hence our pure women are doing slum work. There is a vast difference between having your mind filled with the awful sinfulness of sin, and your heart full only of love for the sinner.

Now a mistake you make to-day you need not make to-morrow. You may make a big blunder with a pure, moral intent.

You may be falsely impressed with the first appearance of any rough man, for example, but you find on further acquaintance he has more grace than yourself. He suffered for a time from your under-estimation. Here is another polished fellow who shows all he is at first, and you overestimate him. You do him an injustice by inflating him with pride. All your actions are shaded by these things, and you can't help yourself. I like sanctified naturalness. You have a right to inquire about people. Jesus found more in John than others by virtue of what John was. If you are wholly sanctified, you won't feel bad because people don't properly estimate your real value.

Intellectual deficiencies exist in many holy people. Some folks think the Holy Ghost will give new attributes and capacities. A western woman of wealth sent a daughter east to be educated in music. The preceptress after a term delicately hinted to the mother her daughter lacked musical capacity. The mother indignantly sent back word, "I want you to understand I am a woman of means. Give my daughter a capacity and send me the bill."

Some holiness people try to teach, when they ought only to witness. A meek and quiet spirit won't wear flashing adornments and attire. You won't want to. Slouchiness often accuses tastiness of pride. We naturally love the beautiful. Some folks need tidying up as much as others need stripping off outward adornments. Another infirmity is dullness, or physical lethargy. There are times when a good night's rest is better than an all night of prayer. If the devil can't get us to indulge in excess of pleasure, he will try to kill us by over zeal. Good people can get saved and go through to God's kingdom, though they cannot so mend the sins of the past life as to stand clear before society. Some men cannot be trusted with money. Salvation does not repair the marrings of past sins.

Third—Again, people can be holy and have a good deal of unsanctified theology. You must lovingly bear with the false educational bias of folks. Holiness may be especially in Methodist theology, but it is most especially Bible doctrine. Allow great latitude on everything but sin. The stronger you are the more infirmities you can bear in other folks. Isn't Jesus good to bear with us? He never tells of our marks, but just loves us in spite of all our detects and infirmities. They are all under the blood. Why not be loving?

Let me give you an illustration to show you how love looks at the heart and not at the blunders. I had a precious little girl who died when only five and a half years old. One day sitting beside her mamma she asked her for something to sew. Her mother gave her a little piece of cloth, pinned down a hem, and provided baby with thread and needle. She began to take stitches, some an inch long, others a half or a sixteenth. After a while she held it up to mamma and said, "Ain't that dood?" Do you think her mother said harshly, "Why, that's awful! Just look here, some stitches are a quarter of an inch long, some a half, some a sixteenth." Ah, no! With mother love welling up she said, "Yes, that is excellent." So I somehow think our Heavenly Father will take our great blundering stitches and not measuring their awkwardness will say in that day, "She hath done what she could." He looks at the motive of our hearts.

AFTERNOON TESTIMONIES.

Rev. T. H. Crocker led the afternoon meeting at 2, reading Eph. 5: 18. We should be filled with the Spirit. A man this morning was acting just as if he were drunk because his Pentecost had come. If you don't want it, you won't get it. When liquor gets hold of a man it runs him, gets him into trouble. So does the Holy Spirit, but God will be sure to bring you out.

SISTER. One thing there is no danger of getting an excess of, the Holy Spirit.

About ten young people gave exceedingly happy and earnest testimonies to the efficacy of the cleansing blood. Their faces had what Bro. Norberry calls an "oil shine." Yet some folks think salvation is so sad for the young. Ask the boys and girls of Portsmouth camp meeting. Their countenances will tell ere they speak their glad testimonies. Full salvation loosens the tongue. Brother Rees called upon an Episcopalian lady to pray, and she offered her first public prayer as naturally as though she were talking to her dearest friend. She was. She had found the blessing of entire sanctification after a severe struggle a few days before. Jesus had become altogether lovely.

AFTERNOON SERMON.
BY SISTER S. C. REES.

TEXT. If ye then, being evil, know how to give good gifts unto your children, how much more shall your heavenly Father give the Holy Spirit to them that ask Him? Luke 11: 13.

IT is a great comfort to me to know that the blessed Holy Spirit is a gift, a blessing. Every parent desires to see his good qualities and abilities reproduced in his children. How much more does our Heavenly Father desire to see the character of His son reproduced in us. I say, let me go through the fire, if need be, to acquire His character. Jesus was a gift to this sin-cursed world, but the Holy Ghost is God's gift to

His children. Just as the disciples recognized the Messiah in Christ, so we can recognize the Holy Spirit when He comes to us. God gives us the Spirit so we can be in sympathy with Him in His purposes of salvation. If we are to sit on the throne with Christ, we must have the kingly spirit. Have you ever had a friend come to you for spiritual bread, and like the man in the parable, had nothing to set before him? Too many people are occupied with getting fixed up themselves, running around for people to pray for them and have no time to attend to dying souls.

The lesson of importunity is also taught here. Some people who honestly pray say, I am anxious to get an answer, but I don't get any answer. God says, "Everyone that asketh receiveth." The difficulty can't be with God. It is in your own heart. God wants to destroy all our enemies. When you will stop finding fault with God and holiness people and your circumstances, and lay hold by faith, God will hear you and you will be satisfied when you hear from Him. When we are in earnest we will hear from God. The Holy Ghost is faithful to press home the truth.

We want to be not only seekers, but finders. When you light your candle and get your broom you will find it. You will raise a dust. The minister and some of the church members will get their eyes full, but never mind. And then when she had found the silver, she had a little cottage meeting and told her friends and neighbors that she was not a seeker but a finder. Some one has said that God justifies us that He might sanctify us, and sanctifies us that He may keep us justified.

A very blessed service followed at the altar, and among the seekers were several who became finders.

EVENING SERMON.

REV. A. B. SIMPSON, of New York, stopped over an hour on his way home from Old Orchard. Said he, The clocks of heaven do not go by minute hands. I can tell you all I know in less than forty-five minutes. We have had a glorious fifteen days' meeting at Old Orchard. We have had salvation and sanctification and the coming of the Lord and the evangelization of the world. The last week the latter feature was especially emphasized. People got out of themselves in thinking of the world. Yesterday by the close of the meeting we had over $100,000 pledged. One sister gave a dollar and went without her dinner. It set others to giving. One business man sent a pledge of $25,000. Then some gave hundreds and fifties, etc. For two hours the people shouted and wept and gave, until the newspaper men were fairly awed. Over 7,000 people were present.

In Acts 1: 8 it reads, "Ye shall receive the power of the Holy Ghost coming upon you, and ye shall be witnesses unto me," etc. This verse is the keynote ot my work. The great want of the sinner is Jesus. The great want of the Christian is the Holy Ghost, to give us power to be and do whatever God wants us to do. It is power to be holy, power over sin and the world, power over your surroundings. It is not power for service apart from a holy life, but the Holy Ghost comes in in all His cleansing and sanctifying power,

power not only to cleanse from all sin, but to make all the life filled with Jesus. Separated from sin, dedicated to God, filled with God, this is sanctification. Then it will shine forth. There will be a subtle strength in our character which will make people think Jesus has been near. It is the causing power that makes you right. One good old man says he used to be unable to be good if he tried, now he says he can't do bad if he tries.

It is power to minister help to others, to make people feel they are wrong and fly to Jesus. The very demeanor speaks for God. You act in the very authority of God. Parents and Sunday-school teachers, you need this. The Son of God never preached until baptized with the Holy Ghost. What business has a preacher to stand between the living and the dead without the same power? I am so sorry that I did it for ten years. But I didn't know any better. When I saw I could have Jesus, I jumped at the chance. I remember the darkness of the darkest hour of my life when at Saratoga Springs with broken health and discouraging prospects I gave all into Christ's hands. Since then every curse of that hour has been changed into blessing.

Then the Holy Spirit enables us to be witnesses "to the uttermost parts of the earth." Until our sympathies reach out to all men, and are as large as the heart of God, we fail to realize the deepest depths of sanctification. Through false prejudices, want of faith, and a limitation of not receiving, we don't accept as we should all these glorious blessings. We must open our hand and then close it. Believe it is

done and it is done. You must take God at His Word.
Many of us miss the baptism of the Spirit because we
want it to consume it upon ourselves. We want it to
be happy with, or to have our loved ones saved, or a
grand revival for our church. The secret of blessing
is to be a blessing.

Dr. Simpson had to go at once, after this refreshing talk, in order to take the train.

BROTHER WILSON. I'd have Him speak to me tonight or I would not leave this spot. Jesus never spoke to the spiritual ears of anybody without their knowing His voice. Seekers kept coming to the altar after the departure of Brother Simpson, teachers seeking the Holy Spirit, that their classes might be converted, preachers for power, leaders of young people's meetings, precious saints for the Spirit's anointing, souls for sanctification or pardon. Without any word of invitation, save as given by the Spirit, one by one they came to the altar or fell prone in the straw.

"You can trust love," said Brother Wilson, "the universe over. What, then, have you to fear?"

For more than an hour this precious service went on. Blessed songs of prayer and consecration rose upon the air. Some wept aloud. Others quietly drank in the Holy Ghost until their faces shone. A holy hush was upon the audience. The on-lookers in the rear of the tabernacle were awed at the scene.

BROTHER WILSON. The Lord don't make hard places easy, but He goes with us through them. He didn't say to the Hebrew children He would send an angel to put out the fires, but said, "I'll be there myself." That's enough. When I get to Heaven, I'm going to ask Daniel how he felt in the lion's den. It is far more blessed to have God with us than not to have the trials.

The meeting closed with victorious songs and testimonies. It was a precious hour of "sinking out of self into Christ."

MORNING MEETINGS.
Tuesday, Aug. 11.

THIS was an exceedingly hot day, but real salvation does not spoil in summer nor freeze in winter. The usual 6 and 8:30 meetings were held. Brother Rees was the preacher at ten o'clock. Without a text he gave general remarks.

There were the very same objections raised to the children of Israel's going out of Egypt as to-day are made against the godless sinners leaving the Christless world. There was the same objection to the children of Israel going across Jordan, as to-day is made against the Christian finding the Canaan of perfect love.

Pharaoh suggested that they leave their wives and little ones, their flocks and herds, that they should only go a little way. But Moses said everything must go entirely out of the country. All people here are located either in Egypt or the wilderness or in Canaan. Some folks say there are only two classes, the saved and unsaved. But the Bible says there are three classes, the saved, the partially saved, and the fully saved. Those in the wilderness are partially saved; they have manna from heaven, to be sure, but it is a light diet like milk. God wants us not to be dwarfs and babies, but strong men in Jesus. There are too many babies in the church, fourteen, fifteen or seventeen years old, who, like a certain fourteen years old girl I saw a while ago, have to have their hair combed, and be tended and handled very carefully. Let us go in and possess the land.

[Here a young man came right forward to the altar saying, "I want to go in."]

When I was seeking entire sanctification, the night before I found it, was the darkest night of my life. I had my cheeks buried in the carpet, and God showed me what I was to give up. I kept saying, 'Yes,' to God. And when I finally said 'Yes' to giving up my church prejudices, I felt such a peace! Then I went to bed and slept like a baby, and after about three hours' sleep I waked up and about eight o'clock, without my worrying about any witness, the Holy Ghost fell upon me. Oh! I knew it. Glory!

Several seekers began to come to the altar at this point, and the sermon ceased.

BROTHER WILSON. Praying for results is wrong, unless you accept the gift of a pure heart. Then you will have power. As long as there is any unbelief, your heart is impure.

AFTERNOON TALK.

BROTHER LOUIS MITCHELL, who is the efficient helper at the piano, led the two o'clock meeting. He said he had been a poor tied-up Episcopalian, who had in the past stood very tremblingly to speak for Jesus, but after finding full salvation he was not afraid to testify before a bench of bishops that the blood of Jesus Christ cleansed him from all sin.

DR. BYE. It is a kind of ponderosity that will hold a person level. It is the best ballast I know of.

AGAIN the band of young people gave glad testimonies to the cleansing blood. It was a blessed hour.

AFTERNOON SERMON.
BY REV. G. W. WILSON.

TEXT. Having therefore these promises, dearly beloved, let us cleanse ourselves from all filthiness of the flesh and spirit, perfecting holiness in the fear of God. II Cor. 7: 1.

THE preceding verses have a command and promise. If our average church-members were as the closing verses of chapter six describe, we would not have so hard a time preaching holiness. Yet for all that, Paul beseeches these "sons and daughters of the Lord Almighty" to "cleanse themselves," etc. A filthiness here of flesh and spirit are not so much external acts of uncleanness as internal manifestations of uncleanness. After conversion we feel propensities to evil. The struggle with these keeps the individual so busy conquering himself, he has no time to help others. Victory over self precedes helpfulness to others. So the church has to go through various manoeuvres to get folks saved, and then don't always succeed. If you are everlastingly patching and mending yourself, you can't help others. One thing I like about this camp is its watchword, "go dead forever and ever." If any of you folks report for repairs next summer at any meeting where I am, you'll hear music.

Lust, avarice, dishonesty, etc. lurks in the soul. We are not responsible for the inbred sin. The stingy man abhors the lustful, the lustful man despises the covetous man, but both are equally depraved. Our very depravity deprives us of a proper moral conception of moral turpitude. That's why many preachers won't preach holiness. There is some propensity to evil even in the regenerate, though it may be kept under. Not many professing Christians who have regeneration stand the strife very long, without giving up the struggle, and falling into sin. Those who say, "*I can't overcome*," ought to see just the necessity of the cleansing we preach. That is an indubitable witness to the necessity of cleansing. Backsliders say, "I've tried and tried, and now I am not going to try again until I can hold out." They need purity.

Now many fail to recognize the difference between temptation and sin. You can't be tempted unless you desire something. A mere desire is not wrong in itself. Natural appetites and passions can suggest unholy desires but the natural desires themselves are not sinful, unless they become a heart desire or longing to unlawfully gratify natural desires. Jesus proved that purified human nature can go victoriously through a world on fire with hell, and be unsullied. You don't need to get away from unfavorable circumstances. You need a pure heart which will take you through as spotless as an angel. You can't do work in a sinful world without arousing the mind with forbidding and forbidden things. We want something not only that will overcome temptation, but have nothing in common with it. There must be correct outside habits to correspond to inside purity. Heart holiness cannot be retained unless the outward life conform to the inward.

purity. People without purity will flinch from doing what is unpopular. Some people fear being called peculiar.

Our social nature don't need modern church entertainments and sociables. They feed lust. If modern church sociables are Christian, then Jesus was a burlesque on sociability. If holiness is perfected you can go through any temptation that may come upon you, and come out with the consciousness that no defilement has touched you. No temptation the enemy can suggest will settle down even as a light dew or fog. A man may be overcome in his spirit nature, when it is impossible for him to commit a sin act. By continually entertaining unclean thoughts you are as defiled as though you were committing unclean acts. Until you get a holiness that will accord with God's laws in every line, you have got crankism.

No unclean thought will come from a pure heart. "Thinketh no evil." You are a match for society. To ponder over sin is to have uncleanness of mind. Christ can cast down evil imaginations. Bad men cannot make tools of good men. You have no sympathy with unclean thoughts nor thinkers. Sister Hamline had a good way of getting rid of gossiping pests. When one came in she'd say at once, "Don't say anything more, let's go down and see about it." They always had an excuse for not going.

When you are cleansed from filthiness of the spirit, purity of spirit comes in. Then appetites and passions and imaginations are white-vested' elders, waiting at the altar of God's purposes to do His will and to offer holy sacrifice. You are delivered from *unholy* thoughts and appetites, and passions and imaginations, not the things themselves. When you have a pure heart love is a passion in your soul for right objects. It is a fire in your bones. If you have a pure heart you won't have to have especial baptisms of power for service. You will get out of the faucet what is in the fountain. If you have a pure heart, turn on any time you please and your little cup will run over. Purity entitles you to everything God has and is, and you'll not flinch in the asking.

Notice, you are to "cleanse yourselves." Some fellow says, "I'm going to put my tobacco on the altar." You filthy thing! Bury it in a hole too deep for a hog to get at! Cleanse your bodies! Use soapsuds! You can make your mind mind you, if you want to. The supernatural never comes in till you have done your best. A young woman came up very affectedly to Benjamin Pomeroy one time and asked, "Mr. Pomeroy, do you think it will hurt me to read novels?" Mr. Pomeroy looked at her a moment from head to foot and replied, "No, I don't think it would. But it would hurt a Christian."

Whatsoever is right you will love on sight. How many have it or want it? As usual, a glorious altar service followed, several finders among them.

Wednesday, Aug. 12.

PREVIOUS to the morning sermon, Sister Florence Vaillancourt, of the Fall River Deaconness' Home, sang a beautiful consecration hymn.

The preacher was Rev. Byron Rees, son of the beloved president, Rev. Seth C. Rees.

Through the courtesy of Brother John Fenton, a young man who is preparing for work in Africa, we are able to present a stenographic report of this precious sermon.

THE REST OF FAITH.

SERMON BY REV. BYRON REES.

TEXT. Let us therefore fear, lest, a promise being left us of entering into His rest, any of you should seem to come short of it. Heb. 4: 1.

THIS passage has for its keynote and central thought the idea of rest. Prominent I think in the teachings of Jesus is the subject of rest. One time we find him saying, "Come unto me all ye that labor and I will give you rest. Take my yoke upon you and learn of me and ye shall find rest unto your souls." I leave it to learned exegetes to determine whether or not the rest mentioned there are two distinct works of grace in the heart. Personally I think that Jesus spoke of a second rest.

This book from which I have chosen my text has indubitable evidence in it to show that Paul was the writer. There has been much discussion and a great deal has been said and written on the question, but I think from the tone of some of the verses, and many of the lines of argument the way in which he piles up his proof is characteristic of St. Paul, and so it is St. Paul who has written this, inspired by the Holy Spirit.

We first must recognize the fact that he is writing to church members, to men who have been born of God, to people who are no longer of the world, but have been converted. You will find a proof of this in the preceding chapter, the third chapter, in the first verse of which he calls them holy brethren, partakers of the heavenly calling. Paul had more gumption than to call sinners holy brethren. Nowhere do we find Paul coating sin with sugar and calling people sweet names to get their money. He always denominated them by their right names. He always spoke of them by their moral excellency and never in the least allowed himself to shut his eyes to their sins or their character of heart, and if he calls them holy brethren, then they were not sinners, they were not men who had not been converted. They were members of the true church of God and saints of the Lord.

And then again, the very type which Paul uses in this chapter proves conclusively that these men were Christians. If you will read the whole of that chapter you will find that he has been using the history of the Hebrew nation as a symbol of the history of every believer, and one of his great arguments for going on into the second rest is based on the fact that the Israelites, after crossing the Red Sea, had a second crossing in passing into Canaan. You find he says in the seventh, eighth and ninth verses, "Therefore, as the Holy Ghost saith, to-day if ye will hear His voice, harden not your hearts as in the provocation, in the day of temptation in the wilderness, when your fathers tempted me, proved me, and saw my works forty years," showing that the type which he uses, the history of the Israelites, is brought to bear on the Hebrews to whom he is writing as saved men. He says of this Hebrew people, having crossed the Red Sea and been delivered from Egyptian bondage, I will warn you against following their example of tempting me in the wilderness and provoking me by failing to pass into the land of promise, which is the blessing of entire sanctification.

Again he says, "Take heed, brethren, lest there should be in you an evil heart of unbelief in departing from the living God." If there is anything in words, this certainly implies that they had been with God. You cannot depart from a place, thing, or person without first being with that place, thing, or person. The fact that he warns them against departing from God shows they were already with Him, and people with God, who live in His presence, who walk with Him, are not sinners, but Christians.

Now in the second place, let me call your attention to the fact that this rest is not heaven. That is the fallacy that many of us have held to all our lives. That is the idea that has crept into many of our hymns. We sing of crossing Jordan as though it was death. Indeed it is a death, but not the death which occurs when a man goes to heaven. It is a death of the old man, of the carnal man. It is not the death of the physical man, for why should there be giants in heaven? Why should there be walled cities to overcome in heaven, or temptation to be afraid or draw back in heaven? The type breaks down in even the simplest places, for if carried out at all it is not true if we make Canaan heaven.

It cannot be heaven, because the refusal to go into it is because of unbelief, and lack of faith. Now the entrance into heaven is not based on faith. It is based upon the decomposition of the physical body.

Salvation is based upon faith; but entrance into heaven is not. We never find Paul exhorting people to believe themselves into heaven. We do find him exhorting people to believe God and enter into the land of perfect rest.

Again, it cannot be heaven, because Paul says he is there. "We, which have believed, do enter into rest." This epistle was not written by Paul from heaven. He was still on earth, and if Paul is in the land of perfect rest it must be a present experience. It must be an experience that is to occur in our lives here and now. This second rest is for us now. A. B. Earle, years ago as a Baptist evangelist, preached the second rest, and hundreds got the blessing under him. And although some of us have been taught wrongly and our ideas have been moulded, and painted, and colored by our education in regard to this point we will have to concede that everywhere in this book, Canaan is a type of the baptism of the Holy Ghost. This land of Canaan in its physical geography was the promise to Abraham and his seed. Just as truly as the people who had the promise that came to Abraham entered into the land of Canaan, just so you and I receive our inheritance in the baptism of the Holy Ghost.

I notice in this third chapter Paul gives us a number of very plain and practical results that occur if we do not enter into the land of rest. You will find first, he says hardness of heart will come through the deceitfulness of sin. Enter to-day, lest any of you be hardened through the deceitfulness of sin. I find that men and women who hear the preaching of the second blessing, have the opportunity to enter in and fail, as they refuse to obey the will of the Lord have hardness of heart thrust upon them. The failure to enter into all God's will is the missing keystone to many a fallen Christian arch. The failure to obey God has been the occasion of the downfall of many a blessed Christian character.

Then, he says, that not only will hardness of heart come, but the privilege to enter in will cease. "So I sware in my wrath, they shall not enter into my rest." That is, based upon their previous action and upon their refusal to obey me, I in turn say they shall not enter into my rest. There comes a time when your privilege ends and God puts up a divine barrier which you cannot pass over. There comes a time with us when God, having seen that our hearts are hardened through unbelief and the deceitfulness of sin, refuses this experience to us because hardness of heart can never get this blessing. It requires a tender, a meek, a lowly, a teachable heart. Jesus says, "Come unto me, for I am meek and lowly in heart," and none but a meek heart, none but a lowly, and humble, and teachable heart will ever get into this experience.

And then he says, that these men should fall in the wilderness. He does not dignify them by the name of corpses, he calls them carcasses. Not only will your heart be hardened, not only will you be forbidden to enter in, but spiritual death, ignominious spiritual death, will occur as a result of your refusing to enter in. I can point to districts where the land is white with the bones of men who have refused to cross Jordan. The spiritual death, the lethargy, the indifference and the coldness that we find in all too many churches is due to the fact that God's will has been refused and holiness has been rejected. The moment a man puts his hand upon this work he falls dead. The moment you oppose the work of God you begin to draw yourself away from the blood and pull yourself away from the cross and to suicide yourself by your own hands. If a man does it ignorantly, God will close His eyes for a time, but if with open Bible, and open light, and quickenings of the Spirit any man puts himself against God's holiness and God's holiness movement he will bring spiritual death, and his carcass will fall in the wilderness.

Why is it that some of you people here to-day are so indifferent in regard to this question? You simply think that the question of sanctification has nothing to do with your case simply because you are not living on the experience of entire justification. You should not say anything about sanctification. I talked with a man yesterday about this blessing, and he said, "Well, I cannot see it has anything to do with me. I do not see I am required by any divine command to enter into this blessing. I think I am doing about as well as I know. I am a church member, living a good life and giving my money." "But," I said, "brother, do you know that God, by His Spirit, is keeping your heart from sin?"

"Oh, no! I do not believe a man can be free from sin in this life."

"No, but God saith that he that sinneth is of the devil, he that is born of God doth not commit sin." And the reason that we cannot see this thing that has been preached to us for some twelve days on this camp ground is because of some great blot of sin that blocks our eyes, and the reason we have no interest in this matter is because we are holding on to some secret uncleanness, or some bit of pride, or some bit of wilfulness, or worldliness, because he that is born of God is eager for the will of God.

Then I notice that this rest has to be entered into just as you entered into this tabernacle this morning when you came to service. Just as you enter a state or a house, we enter into this experience. I was glad there was an entering process and not a growing process. Lots of people are trying to grow into this experience, but they will never get there. Lots of people are bigger when justified than ever after. They had more of the love of Jesus, and more real humility of heart, and more tender affection for God's word and prayer, and saving sinners than they have had since. I find that these men who grow on the growth theory are growing smaller instead of larger, they are shrinking up instead of expanding and being built up. Instead of their theory working their way, it works the devil's way. It works them down to a mere shrivelled-up, dry experience, where none of the love of God ever comes into their heart.

This is entered into. It does not come by works, by our making an effort, by our making ourselves acceptable to God, by doing a great deal of church and charitable work, and work among the poor, and teaching Sunday school classes, and doing all these good, honest things. Splendid they are, but we never get the experience that way. We will never get the blessing except by faith and entering into it. God sells not His blessings for so much work. He will not sell the blood of Christ and the sanctifying Spirit for your paltry services. You will never get it that way, but when I said, "O, Lord! I am thine forever, come weal or woe, come sorrow or joy, dear Lord, I am thine forever, and I take this blessing by faith and enter into it now," I felt I was sanctified wholly. This is the reason we are testifying to this blessing on this camp ground, because we are now enjoying something we did not make, because we discovered a land that God had prepared for us. We did not create it by our own will power or strength, not by long service and faithful prayer, but because Christ by the divine spirit, by the immortal blood, has done the work, and we cannot but speak of the thing God has done. You people who are discussing and jollying and wondering whether you will be able to testify to this blessing when you get home, ought to be ashamed of yourselves, and ought to be filled with a purpose and a gladness for the privilege of telling men that Jesus Christ made you holy. It is no merit to yourself, it is no goodness of your own, it is no righteousness which you have done, but because of the divine good, the unmerited favor of the Lord you have this blessing this morning. You go home and deny your Lord and close your mouth in regard to this blessed experience, and God will close your heart. You will take the dry rot and blow away.

I notice this rest is a divine rest. Paul says it is His rest. It is not a rest that is manufactured by building a home and settling down in the place where you have located. St. Augustine once said, "Our souls were made for thee, and they are restless till they rest in thee." You may try to fill this great void in your heart with material things. You may have acres of land and blocks of houses and millions of money and yet the hole will be just as large. You may try to satiate your hunger for rest by pleasure, but you will never get satisfied until God Himself comes and fills the vacuum. I read somewhere that one time a great vacuum opened up in the Forum, and the people tried to fill it up and could not fill it. After a while a young man, a brave young Latin, fully armed and on horseback, rode to the brink and leaped in, and the lips of the chasm closed, and there was no more fear of that opening there. And so with this great chasm in our hearts. When we consecrate ourselves to God and say, "Lord, I want this filled, filled with thyself," He will fill the chasm with Himself, and we will have a whole heart, a heart complete.

Oh, brother! you need this rest. Away down miles below the surface of the sea the ocean is never disturbed. There is a calmness that Euroclydon or tempest, or the beat of the screw cannot mar. So there are heart depths of the soul that cannot be disturbed by all the outside tempest and all the opposition that may be hurled against us. Christ Himself has come in with His rest and has made our hearts still forever.

Some of you people are going away from this camp at rest, and some are going away discontented, more so than you ever have been before. You have refused to seek this blessing, and the Spirit of God will leave you and soon you will have no more conviction on the question of holiness. I tell you, brother, God's will is for our holiness, and the only sensible way for you and me to do is to seek earnestly until we find His will in our individual experience. I thank God for this rest, for the experience, that Christ brings his rest into my heart. There is no uncleanness that can spoil our enjoyment and mar our service, nothing to mar the heaven that God put in our hearts here and now. Amen.

AFTERNOON MEETINGS.

THE two o'clock meeting was addressed by Miss Etta Milton, of Winchester, Mass. She said, "God has been bringing to my heart these past few days His promises of peace. If there was any one on the ground who needed this peace, it was I. I have been learning so much here this year of the cleansing power of Christ. I realize God's goodness in giving me sympathy for others, a true realization of friendship. I believe God. I am clean, with nothing between my soul and God. The blood of Jesus Christ, His son, cleanseth me this very minute from all sin." Before Brother Wilson preached, Sister Vaillancourt sang another beautiful solo. As Brother Fenton took his sermon in shorthand, we are able to present it entire.

"PERFECT IN ONE."
SERMON BY REV. G. W. WILSON.

TEXT. And the glory which Thou gavest me I have given them; that they may be one, even as we are one: I in them, and Thou in me, that they may be made perfect in one; and that the world may know that Thou has sent me; and hast loved them, as Thou hast loved me. John 17: 22-23.

IT would be very difficult to understand the Savior's utterances without recognizing the fact that sometimes

He is speaking from the standpoint of His human nature and others from that of the divine. All statements of Christ that imply or declare inferiority to God are the expressions of His naturally developed human nature. He frequently blended the two, and almost with the same breath emphasized the fact of His human nature and then that He was also divine.

There are two errors that are current in regard to Jesus. The first is that He was only a perfect human being. He was a perfect human being. That is admitted by even His enemies. Unitarianism idealizes that with emphasis all through the east here, that His humanity was a perfect humanity. But a perfect humanity of itself, empty of divinity, could never accomplish the end for which humanity was created and could never occupy the proper place in the divine economy. So the human nature of Jesus had to have its baptism with the Holy Ghost. No writer in Scripture ever speaks of Jesus being baptized with the Holy Ghost and fire, because the fire symbol essentially is left out in His case. He did not need any purification, but He did need in His human nature, perfect as it was, the filling of the Holy Ghost. And so the human nature of Christ was not ready for its high office of being the minister of God to bless and save the world and declare the truth until it was first baptized with the Holy Ghost, the symbol of which was at His baptism, the dove coming down out of heaven. Under that baptism He was so unbrokenly yielded to God that He could say in the language of the first sentence of the text, that He was as God with His human nature, and God was in Him in His human nature in a sense in which He never referred to His divinity, that is to the fact that He was God manifest in the flesh. He was always exceedingly careful, and so are the Pauline epistles, to exalt the human nature to the highest possible privilege in the kingdom of God. I am utterly done with the idea that angels and archangels, and cherubs and seraphs, and those beings who have never sinned in the other world are superior to us. I know we do not show up very well on the outside just now, but when we get through with the thing, and when this mortal shall put on immortality, when we shall be raised and have a body like unto His glorious body, and when we shall see Him as He is, and not be comparatively like Him, but be like Him forever, we will occupy with Him the highest place in the universe of God. Glory to God!

There is more possibility in the very nature of things in human nature than anything in the universe of God; else God would not have eternally allied the divinity with it. And when God made man it was not half so much as we hear frequently that He failed on angels, as that He always intended to make a being just like man as the climaxing act of His creative power, beyond which with all His infinite ability He dared not and could not go, else He makes a God. There is nothing in the universe possible above a man but a God, Hallelujah! Isn't that grand? God cannot make anything more than a man. There is nothing that He is capable of creating that is higher than human nature, and He has taken human nature into such relation with Himself that they are now indissolubly joined and human nature is God's visible expression or method through which the divine is forever to flow. You will never see God in heaven or anywhere else, but through human nature.

I am rather fearful here, but we will get through all right if you will keep praying and don't go to sleep. I want to hold along for a little while because there is a fallacy abroad among those who are trinitarians and so-called orthodox that human nature don't amount to much of anything, and the counteracting but other fallacy (for you have to have fallacies to meet fallacies), is the idea that human nature is everything, and that human nature in itself possesses all possibilities and that all it needs is the sunlight, and the rain, and the showers, and the fructifying influences of good environment to develop into a very beautiful type. We got that from New England, and they got it from perdition, and as it came from New England they must be closer to perdition than we are, to hand it up to us. That is so.

The two fallacies are facing us—the one teaching asceticism and monasticism and nunneryism and all that conduct that does violence to human nature, and the other making a god of self, dethroning Jesus from the throne of the universe, and utterly ignoring the process of the divine work in the human nature, and it is just as logical and legitimate in this country to find in your literature utter indifference to the subjective work of regeneration and sanctification, according to their systems of thought, because of their attitude towards humanity, as it is in an unenlightened and darkened country to find idolatry and all these other things— the simple products of their thoughts.

Now the middle ground that this text very clearly teaches, as I understand it, is that Christ first came to earth to reveal to us the lost humanity. No human being ever had a correct conception of what humanity really is and what true humanity ought to be since the fall in Eden. With the incarnation of Christ there came a revelation of true human nature—a revelation from God, a direct revelation by a divinely purposed plan of what human nature really is. Jesus Christ is the only perfect human being since the fall. Spiritually we may have His perfection; otherwise not, and He reveals this fact in His life, death, sufferings, and all the rest of it that human nature has no law against it. Hallelujah! We have got our place in the established order of things to abide forever, and the whole redemptive scheme is just putting us back into harmony with the laws of our being, and all this dying sanctification business and all that other thing is just stuff we have borrowed from the Romish Church and ought never to have been transferred at all. Just what Jesus was in His human nature is just what we will be when redemption's work is complete, and then all the processes of redemption will end in our case, because our perfect nature, brought into harmony with the original law under which we were created, will serve all the ends for which we were created. We will need no prayer, we will need no mediator, we will need no blood of atonement, we will need no pardon, we will need no power. We won't need any of these things that now belong to the redemptive scheme to make our life work efficient and sufficient. Bless the Lord! The whole redemptive scheme will become a thing of the past. Incorrigible, wicked souls that love unrighteousness rather than righteousness will be imprisoned in the blackness of darkness forever, but all who love the Lord Jesus and His appearing, and who are His, He will gather to Himself from the four quarters of the earth, and they shall come in to go out no more, and the whole question will be settled, for we shall see Him as He is and will be like Him forever, and up to the standard of perfection of human nature that Christ possessed. We are to be filled with God, and as human nature in its perfection is capable of endless progression, we will be ever approximating in our thought, and in our life, and in our activities to the divine, absolute perfection, but as we will never reach it, we will have all eternity on hand to be busy and have a good time and enjoy ourselves and serve Him and love Him and live for Him forever. I am out on that line and expect that glorious end on the other side by and by. Praise the Lord!

Well, that is good as far as it goes. Now the only perfection we teach in this life is a perfection of spirit, spirit nature, because it is under different laws than those which govern our mental and physical life, and consequently can be treated by a different plan and by a different method without doing violence to God's economy or His kingdom. We teach that the spirit nature may be perfected, as work can be performed instantaneously upon our spirit natures, transforming them into the moral image of God that could not be done by any mental process or without violating mental laws or physical laws. And so Jesus never perfectly cured anybody when He was in this world so that he could not die any more. He took a few cases off to glory to show us what would have happened if we had not sinned, for I am very well satisfied that Bishop Foster's theory of the earth being covered so thick we would stand sixteen deep on each other if sin had not entered the world and took off the race is a beautiful speculation for a Boston Bishop, but has no ground for fact in it, for after God had done His work He could have translated man off to glory and wiped death out of the whole business. Blessed be God! He wants to give us room for activity here, and there are so few at the work there is plenty of room.

Now Jesus Christ Himself is the real resurrection, is the perfect man going through the whole process from generation up to glorification. He has passed through all the process and given us an object lesson of what humanity will pass through in getting the work completed and consummated where God shall dwell with him in a sense he cannot now here. So Christ is our object lesson and the ground of our faith and when He who is our life shall appear then shall we also appear with Him in glory.

So I have nothing to say against human nature, but I am a stern foe to anything that interferes with it, to anything that enters in to interfere with its organism from end to end. Do you know, beloved, we preach lots of things on this platform that people do not understand, even the preachers who have not gumption enough, whatever else they may have from the schools, or sense enough to see that we are simply defending the laws of our own constitution. For instance, there are constitutional laws in our spiritual life that demand and require certain things, and every true man goes Godward constitutionally. That is, God does not require us to do anything that violates constitutional law in our being. The plan of salvation is to perfect us, and not to smash us all to pieces and ruin us and blight us, and when any body of thinkers or body of men, or organized company of men, or social customs or human laws or mental or moral philosophies conflict with an established constitutional law of human nature you are absolutely free under divine authority to tread that thing under your foot and enjoy the liberty of the law of your own being. Jesus Christ in both His ministry and conduct and life and everything else was simply nature acting naturally. But you know there was a whole lot of customs and traditions and established laws, and they are everlastingly trying to get Christ down into the mould of Judaism, ceremonial laws and commandments and traditions of men, but Jesus did not bring his perfect human nature into line with their perverted human nature.

I thank God that Jesus has come to make us free and whom the Son makes free is free indeed, and if there is one thing that Jesus has taught us by His own teaching and His own life and example and His own nature, it is that we have a perfect light and have a perfect right to follow the law of our own being and be natural according to its light, and along that line we will find righteousness. Glory be to God!

This fact remains, however. However perfect

human nature may become and however complete it is in all its parts, it does not answer the end for which it is made, simple by being perfect in itself. I like to see a nice set on the table when I go to dinner. I like to see a beautiful instrument, I like to see a beautiful form, I like to see a beautiful picture and a thousand other things, but I would not care to sit down at the table and spend all my time admiring the artist's work on the cup if I was thirsty. I would like to have something put into the cup, however beautiful it was, so that my thirst should be satisfied. Now there is an old statement in the Psalms that thousands of people have overlooked and yet it is a wonderful truth. It says this: "Know ye not that God hath set apart him that is godly for Himself?" Glory be to God! And when God calls you to holiness it is not that you may enjoy a certain measure of happiness, but that you may have the moral fitness for Him to come in and occupy you Himself. Glory be to God!

And so in begetting Himself He could not be imperfect in His own begetting. I want to say to-day there is no ground in intelligent thinking for the doctrine of generation by the Spirit as set forth in the third chapter of John if Jesus had not come into the world by the very process that the apostles' creed has taught us from our childhood He came. "Conceived of the Holy Ghost, born of the Virgin Mary." Some people get very aesthetic if you mention the fact that a pure young woman virgin was with child. They will hold up their hands and look crossways at each other as if their high sense of propriety had been shamefully violated. If they were not vulgar they would take that as revelation. The Lord write that on our hearts. I repeat it: If they were not vulgar they would take that as revelation instead of unbecoming a refined pulpit and an educated congregation, and I say if you take out of the thought of humanity, the fact of that begetting of Jesus Christ, you have taken the broad platform for the faith of a believer in being generated by the Holy Ghost and made a child into God's family and you have your wishy washy, get-there-any-way-you-please church; your sinning and getting people to turn over a new leaf and trying to build up character without the work of the Holy Ghost. We folks have been fooled with it. It is a great temptation to an unsanctified heart to shine out as one of these popular evangelists that can crowd thousands of people inside of three weeks into the church of God and have a great reading in the papers, "Five hundred converted in one night." The Holy Ghost was not within a thousand feet of the whole business. How we do like the flaring of trumpets!

Humanity must be divinely begotten to become receptacles for the Holy Ghost. That is the fact, and if you can prove what you may have been taught or is being taught, that humanity is capable of being brought to a point of perfection by any process you can think of, I will stand back of your acquirement and compel you to admit that when you have made it perfect by your processes it must have a divine life in it to meet the law of its being and find harmony in the operations of its inner spirit nature.

It is a good thing to be fire proof against

unitarianism. And against modern chaff and sweet-Jesusism, and all that kind of thing and be down on the solid rock of an inner consciousness that in some inexplicable sense, but as a glorious reality, Christ is in me. "I in them," that is, Christ's human nature, by the reconstructive processes of the Holy Ghost, given to us. He that begot Him can generate us from above and beget us in righteousness and true holiness and take us into the family. Hallelujah! How God loves His own babies!

But you cannot get God to own anything He has not fathered. There is in the church to-day, just as there is outside, a wonderful lot of something that nobody seems to want to father. I tell you when the Spirit answers to the blood and tells me I am born of God, if the mother that brought me physically into this world should leave me to die, God would send angels to care for me and lift me on the bosom of His love and feed me with His own life. Hallelujah! Oh, it is grand when you are born into the family! It is a big thing to be one of the babies. Of course you are a little bit cross-grained and cry a little, yet you are one of the babies. The reason we have such a mass of professing converts on our hands that die in the birth is because they have not been rightly begotten and have no vitality in them to live through being born.

I repeat it: By whatever process you can, you may perfect human nature and yet human nature cannot act normally until God enters into it as its inspiration and life and power. So if unitarianism does get through by its process of refinement and education and culture, the Lord will have to come in at last and set the machinery going and set things right. But we will take another course. We are intent on getting the imperishable thing, the everlasting thing, the spirit nature regenerated and sanctified and perfected, and we will let others take the slow process. If I could not be smart and good I would rather be good and ignorant than smart and vicious. What is the matter with the church of to-day? What is the matter with the pulpit of to-day? We have a whole lot of young men sent to the university under the idea that their future standing in the pulpit depends upon their record in the class-room. A young student said not long ago, "It is impossible (and he was an average student) for me to be thoroughly prepared with my lessons for the class-room and have enough time left to go into the consideration of my own soul." What emphasis to-day is laid in nearly all of our educational institutions upon passing a high grade in your class whatever your moral character may be!

I understand that here in New England a first-class athlete or somebody away up in the base-ball nine is more likely to be called to your first-class pulpits than a member of a praying band. What is the outcome of all this? The cultivation of their mind is made of more importance than the sanctification of their nature, and the whole educational system of the country is based on that principle. Teachers in the schools are sending notes to you if your children don't attend regularly, and we pay the salary of these infidel teachers that think more of the tick of the clock than of the salvation of a soul. The Lord help us! Didn't Jesus make a fuss in the established order of things when He was down here! How does this man know so much, not having learned His letters? It was because He had the inner qualification for knowing things, while we have a lot of pulpit fossils to-day who come before the people with some of their notes tied up with baby ribbon, and some borrowed eloquence and perfume, and a few anthems mixed in, and think it so very becoming, "worshiping the Lord in the beauty of holiness." Their brains are undeveloped and they have no heart material. One of this kind was once invited to preach in the church of a good old fashioned preacher. He fell in love with the daughter of the old man and that softened him worse than ever. But he was a graduate of a college and a preacher and so the old man asked him to preach. His fiancee, anxious to watch the proceedings with great interest, sat up opposite him in the gallery. He took the text from the Song of Solomon. "Thou art fair, my love, thou art fair," at the same time pointing his hand toward the gallery where the object of his love sat and worshiped. He preached on that line for a while, and sat down remarking to the old man that he did not have the inspiration he would have had, had there been a better congregation. The old man, justly mortified with the whole performance, put in another clause in his closing prayer: "Oh, Lord, bless this young man and make his heart as soft as his head."

This is the way that I feel when I hear some of these fellows preach. Exactly. Oh, how they are dabbling with inspiration! There is nothing inspired, there is nothing true, there is nothing real, there is nothing abiding. Eternity is a guess, eternal life is a possibility, and so on and so on, until they have sown the seeds of infidelity with the baptized name of Christianity to raise a generation that will blot the moral atmosphere everywhere they touch. I believe God is going to keep holiness on hand in the country for the sake of having something to show off the difference. Bless the Lord! Something that has the divine in it. And there are some few of us who don't propose that the cause of holiness will go into the grave just yet.

I want to say further that every sanctified heart that has really God in them in the sense in which Jesus expressed it in this prayer is a unit with God on everything. Hallelujah! Do you know that when we get the Christly humanity we have all the attributes in finiteness that God possesses in infiniteness, and they are so related to each other that there is nothing He has that we do not get as much of it as we can hold, and without any pumping either. They got that idea in science sometime ago, and thought they had made a brilliant success. A man down here east somewhere took a notion that he could inoculate an old man with a young boy's blood, and could make the old man young again, comparatively so. So he got a real healthy boy and an old man and laid them down side by side on the table, made the incisions and began pumping. The old man's eye began to clear, and to look better, and he thought he could stand a little more, when he began to froth at his mouth and breathed his last. The process was all right, but they gave him a little too much.

Well, the Lord has his own process of making an

old man young. He just believes in the process of making a new baby all at once, and puts all the life into it that it can stand. This is what He gives us when He regenerates us and sanctifies us, and no other can stand the pressure of divinity but it. This is why He says there is no use trying to take the old bottle and put the new wine in, because the old bottle goes to smash.

I want to state another fact. Every man that has God in him, appreciates every other man by the measure of God that is in him, not according to his intellect or his education, or his gifts and ability. Gifts are just like the color of your eye, like the shape of your nose and hand. Some people have the gift of song, some people have not, but a person that has the gift of song, however sweet the voice, will love an individual that has the gift of the Holy Ghost, just as much as if they had the gift of song. Those who have Christ in them are in unity, in their spirit, the one toward the other. Sometime ago I was at a campmeeting where Bishop Taylor was. Dear old man! There stood a lady looking at him, a crowd around him. She had to take a train in a few minutes. I saw her anxious face and wondered what she wanted, till the supreme moment came when she must go, and at last she touched him on the shoulder as though she was almost committing a crime that was unpardonable. He turned at once, and she says, "Bishop Taylor, I have come three hundred miles to-day to hear you preach and have the pleasure of shaking hands with you, and I must go. I want to know if I can have the privilege of shaking hands with you." The dear old Bishop smiled in his own way. "Well, yes," said he, "any negro has that chance any day in the year." Hallelujah! When you have the Spirit of God in you, your spiritual nature will gravitate towards the poor, spiritual church member rather than the worldly, godless church member. There is no color line in the Spirit of God. Of course I am free here, where the Bunker Hill monument is, but this holds good down south as it does here. I would rather to-day have a thoroughly black skinned father and mother and have God say of them that they were a good man and woman, walking with God and filled with the Holy Ghost, than have a white father and mother and have it said of them that they were lacking in moral character. I don't suppose I will have any wealth to leave to my children, not very likely. But I want to have my children say of me that "though my father did not leave me any wealth he was a good man, full of faith and the Holy Ghost." And I will promise you now that if I make that record they will feel far richer than if I left them untold wealth.

My Father can give to you more worlds on worlds when He gets you ready to receive it. All things are yours, for ye are Christ's and Christ is God's. That is our inheritance. God is our inheritance and our portion forever and ever, therefore we will not be moved though the mountains be cast into the middle of the sea. Where you have a sanctified nature the infinite and eternal Spirit will come in and establish an unbroken union, so that nothing this side of the throne can enter between you and Him and interfere with your fellowship. It was on the ground of that, that the apostle Paul said, "None of these things move me, and nothing can separate me from the love of God."

Now the object of this relation is that you may glorify God by showing Him forth. I want to state it clearly. God purposes to show His own glory through humanity, and as the one human nature that fittingly represents it has gone to represent it to the saints on the other side, what the consummation of redemptive work shall be so that they shall have the full pledge of the beautiful outcome of all of God's promises before their eyes, He has deigned to take you and to take me and make us the medium through which His glory is to be revealed. Glory be to God! What manner of men ought we to be! What kind of a conversation, what kind of a walk ought we to have in this world? I repeat it. God cannot be seen in His true nature and character by his works outwardly. He must be seen in His great miracles spiritually and inwardly. This is an unanswerable argument to all the atheism of the universe.

I want to call your attention now to another fact, and that is that there is nothing greater possible for any of us than for God to dwell in our hearts. It is the greatest possible glory that can ever come to you in this world or in the next, and that is why we have such a heaven here below. We are having more of heaven on this ground than thousands of people think they will get if they go to the place called heaven. We are not going to Mount Zion, we have come to Mount Zion. You will get more genuine heaven in your souls in five minutes after you get sanctified than a million years of your fancied heaven that you think you will go to by and by. I use to sing when I was a boy, "I want to be an angel and with the angels stand," but since the Lord has shown me what human nature is capable of when His Spirit comes to dwell in it, I don't want to sing, "I want to be an angel."

Now one practical form of thought and I close. God in you universally precedes conviction on the part of sinners. God was in Christ reconciling the world unto Himself, and the Spirit of God in you will be the means of bringing men and women to the feet of Christ. Then shall the heathen know that I am God when I am sanctified in you before their eyes.

I want to ask you, How is it with you? Has the Spirit of God sanctified you wholly? Is God dwelling in you, the source of your life, the source of your strength, the fullness of Him that filleth all in all? Have you got it?

EVENING SERMON.

BY REV. G. W. WILSON.

Text. For the kingdom of God is not meat and drink, but righteousness, and peace, and joy in the Holy Ghost. Rom. 14: 17.

THIS universe is full of kingdoms. These have their limitations and laws. Some are transient, some everlasting, but all under law. God himself, even, is subject to the law of His own being, by a spirit of absolute righteousness. Hence His love does not overcome His rectitude and sweep everybody into heaven, regardless of their character. The kingdom in the text is spiritual, immaterial, invisible. These to many are non-realities.

A thoroughly educated man, a husband, a father, a church member—a man may be all these and yet ignorant of the spiritual kingdom. Going out by and by into the eternal world will not make sinners see spiritual truth after death. An individual without a spiritual nature will never discern spiritual things, either here or hereafter. Some have so placed themselves beyond the reach of the influences of the Holy Spirit, they never will be saved. I believe others are just as certainly fixed for heaven. They will always choose the good.

Now one of the curses of the age is that men want to focalize spiritual truth into forms, to make it appeal to the senses. All forms of religious worship are nothing apart from worshiping God in Spirit and in truth. "The kingdom of God is not meat and drink," does not consist of ordinances. What are cantatas and charades and broom drills and clam bakes and fairs and festivals, but saying to the people, this is the way we worship and get people interested in the church. But a holiness campmeeting does away with the whole string of these things, and is not bound by forms. The truth of God is not ritualism and apostolic succession. All we have to do is to handle the truth wisely; no apostle could do more than that.

Righteousness is the first element of this kingdom. That's not action, that's being. It is a moral quality. It means internal rectitude, spiritual perpendicularity. Many are *trying* to be good. Why, if you *are* good, you will do right. Get out beyond meats and drinks and forms and ceremonies. Do you know there is a church within the church? Why, good old-fashioned repentance would put many a church-member into a fright. Righteousness is a quality rather than a quantity. Babies are innocent, but not pure. There is a great difference between innocence and righteousness. Revelation teaches both an imputed and imparted righteousness. No man can be righteous who has not the power to choose right. There is no necessity or compulsion for a man to be right. If you choose anything besides, it is your fault. I am afraid to do anything else than to do right. No child is responsible until he can choose between right and wrong. Some folks think they can spank out old Adam. Depravity plays itself out in the child without the child's knowing why it is naughty. Until they deliberately reject the atonement, the atonement covers them. Jesus don't hold anybody responsible for what they don't choose.

No man can be really righteousness merely by choice, they must love right. These folks say, "I know I'm wrong, but I'm going to do my duty." The spirit of righteousness is a love for righteousness. If people had that, they would vote as they pray. The church members in this country hold the balance of power. Therefore the church members are responsible for the rum traffic. But the church won't pay the price of being right. When you are right you will passionately love the right. Just in proportion to your intensity for righteousness will be your intensity of antipathy toward wrong. This is your chance to do something for God. A man who loves righteousness is a king.

Count the cost. Build a good foundation for holiness. You get inward righteousness, and you will dance when nobody fiddles. You will not be popular here, but will be in heaven. They crucified Jesus because He was righteous.

Righteousness distills its own peace. A righteous man don't have to run around after peace. It may cost you a good deal to stop and get plumb with the Holy Ghost, but it will cost you far more not to stop and get plumb. How many here are all right? How many want to be?

A service of consecration and blessing followed.

"BEFORE AND AFTER."
Thursday Morning, Aug. 13.
SERMON BY REV. WALTER RUSSELL, PRESBYTERIAN EVANGELIST, OF CANADA.

I WOULD like if you would turn to the closing verses of the eighteenth chapter of the Acts of the Apostle, and read from the 24th to the 28th verses, and also to the 3d verse of the nineteenth chapter.

This message I am going to give you to-day I call the "Before and After." This is the thought. You know in all quack advertising literature to-day you find a picture of a poor, emaciated fellow on one side, and there is a bottle, and on the other side a big, handsome fellow, and called "Before and After."

That is what I am going to do to-day. I am going to look at one of the most wonderful characters in history, before and after he received the Holy Ghost. It is the key to all the most wonderful discoveries of the day.

"A certain Jew named Apollos, born at Alexandria."

That is equivalent to saying he was educated. In Alexandria, in the time of Apollos, we find everything we find here to-day. The museum there is the richest and largest in the world to-day and is visited by thousands of scientists and students. If Apollos were living to-day he would pose among the mighty of the land. But, friends, you may be educated until you are a walking cyclopedia, you may understand things until people call you brainy, but still be a perfect stranger to this truth of the Holy Ghost.

The Bible says he was an educated man, but more than that, he was eloquent. This man could draw. If you had him here you would have to take the roof off as well as the sides. There are two things about the gospel; it draws and it drives. It drives very often more than it draws. Every time Christ opened His mouth He drew and He drove. The gospel is a draw cart, but the trouble is men won't stay put. Beloved, let us have God in this thing and men will stay put till the sun goes out. Apollos drew, but he had not the Holy Ghost.

He was exceedingly mighty in the Scriptures. The Greek says he was "exceedingly mighty." I suppose there are people here from all denominations. Well, if Apollos had been around here some time ago, there would have had to be three bishops in the Methodist Conference instead of two, or else Chaplain McCabe would not have gone in. The Presbyterians would have tried to bribe this mighty Apollos to become a moderator of the General Assembly of the Pan Counsel. But do you know you might know the Scriptures by heart and go to the devil.

But that is not all. He was earnest. He was fervent in spirit. The English word is boiling, boiling in spirit. People tell me they are cold. Why, the Lord would spew you out of His mouth if you are luke warm; but if you are cold, where can you be? Oh, for the boiling! He was fervent in spirit, and the book says he taught diligently the things of the Lord. He was evangelical. He worked and toiled, but he did not have the Holy Ghost. He was an earnest Christian worker, living up to the light He had. The reason I believe Apollos was converted is that when he heard of something better he did not kick.

Then again he had the baptism of John. John's baptism is unto righteousness, but the baptism of the Holy Ghost is with fire. Beloved, I am more than ever impressed with the necessity of the fire. Let us seek it, and let us not be satisfied until the fire comes and we are burned clear through and filled with the power of God.

AFTERNOON SERMON.

BY REV. G. W. WILSON.

TEXT: For the law of the Spirit of life in Christ Jesus hath made me free from the law of sin and death.

That the righteousness of the law might be fulfilled in us, who walk not after the flesh, but after the Spirit. Rom. 8:2,4.

THERE are two laws expressed in the first verse, which laws are radical opposites. There can be no sin where there is life; there can be no life where there is sin. Your regenerated nature is like the sensitive plant. If sin touches your righteous life, that life dies. A plant may be carefully trained for a year, but a five minutes' frost will destroy it. It is not our business to make laws, but to discover them and bring ourselves into harmony with them. If you violate law you will suffer penalty, whether it be in our physical, mental, or spiritual nature. You violate law, and you can't avoid evil results. It is better to save a boy from beginning to drink, than an old toper from his cups. One of the fearful things about a lost soul is that it has lost a desire for God. Spiritual death springs from violation of spiritual law.

An abominable doctrine of modern times is that a professing Christian can keep sinning and yet go to Heaven. Righteousness is the law through which love operates. God made us to be lovers, not haters. Fill a man with love, and you can turn him loose anywhere, and he won't harm anybody. The more you love, the more you will feel hatred for the opposite. "Love worketh no ill to his neighbor." We catch the purpose of love by the manner of its manifestation.

The opposite of love is "sin and death." Life would be everywhere if it were not for sin. Everybody under the atonement is just as free to choose right as he is wrong. Hence childhood is naturally believing. The fundamental faith of the race is in the heart of a little child. Every nature has a measure of the divine life implanted in it. There is not a hint in the Bible that a child needs spiritual life in the incipient state. By virtue of the atonement, every child is in the kingdom, but each one needs sanctifying. Each one, too, has a different type of depravity, according to their heredity.

A child feels first a desire for purity. Quit beating

back the lambs. Every child is entitled to divine favor. But every child knows its need of being better. Many children have spells at eleven o'clock because you had one a little while before. A child does not know anything about being wrong, it feels bad.

The sacrifice of Jesus has entitled every child unconditionally to a complete salvation under the grace of God. When you are spiritually born as a baby into the family, you are heirs to all there is in the will, all things. Your inheritance depends upon your being born, not upon your being sanctified. You are an heir of all things. But when you come to a point of light, and God shows you what you are entitled to, if you reject that light you go into disobedience and death. You are not responsible until you have light. Your soul is in peril, if you don't obey God-given light. We love folks for their loveliness whether they agree or differ with us. Even the holiness movement is in danger of becoming divided because of certain preferences for method, certain beliefs of the head, if we forget the one unity of love. It is a burning shame that theories, or organizations, or anything should disunite the church of God because of lack of love. The law reveals to us what right is, but it can't make us right. Many have sanctification all in the head, but lack perfect love. Others after hungering and thirsting after something find the blessing without knowing its name. They go after it heart-first. So many are on the law-line, "I am going to do better." Bless you, you can't *do* better until you *are* better.

Every religion has the idea we ought to be holy,

and has a plan by which we shall be holy somewhere, sometime. Did you ever hear people say, "I have tried, and tried, and tried, but I can't keep my temper? But I expect it is because of my make-up. My father had it before me, and my mother, and I suppose I'll be troubled with it until I die." Until you die! Why not forever? There's your idea of a death purgatory. See? Jesus has provided a sufficient remedy. Now, you are not responsible for having an ill-temper, or an avaricious or lustful nature, but you are responsible for not accepting God's remedy for these things. The law binds us to the right, but has no deliverance. You can't be pure until Jesus comes and takes away the old loves out of the heart, and fills it with the richness and sweetness of the new loves. Let Him search you thoroughly, and then give you freedom from all that defiles. The spirit of love gives you the moral nature which keeps the law. The law of love is more exacting in its requirements than the law of Sinai. It is not doggedly keeping the letter of the law, but a baptism of love that enables you not only to love your neighbors but your enemies, a law that not only enables you not to do the unlawful things, but also not to do the inexpedient things. You can cheerfully sacrifice what may be lawful for yourself, that you may have the opportunity of helping others.

At the song-service preceding the sermon the camp broke loose in a sea of hallelujahs, as the song, "When the Roll is Called Up Yonder" was being sung. The speaker was Rev. Walter Russell, of Canada.

MORNING SERVICE.
Friday, Aug. 14.

At 8:30 Rev. G. W. Wilson read the twenty-third Psalm. Every shepherd wants to give his sheep the best food. No hungry sheep *lies down* in green pastures. That must mean brimful and still in the pasture up to the eyes in supplies. If you are in a barren pasture, gnawing at roots, you will be spiritually lean. Our Shepherd gives us tender green grass, not dry, chopped feed. He wants to make your soul fat. The Lord knows it pays to feed His people well.

"He restoreth my soul." As there is physical waste, so there is spiritual. Here we learn how to replenish the waste of soul. This is by feeding upon the Word, by walking and talking with God. You can't live on good feelings, but upon good, old-fashioned, grandmother slices of the Bread of Life. We need digestive and assimilating processes to get restored tissue. We must chew the cud, to meditate. All you have got of God's Word is what you have assimilated. That makes your blood tingle. "He leadeth me"—zigzag, up and down, in by and forbidden paths, on the mountain top to-day and in the valley to-morrow? Nay, nay! "He leadeth me in paths of *righteousness*." I have got an eternal love for righteousness. I had rather go on foot and be right, than ride in a carriage and be crooked. Righteousness stiffens the backbone. When you are all right, you don't need any props. So many people need to have holiness campmeetings, etc., to fix them up. You can get so fixed that nothing moves you.

"Yea, though I walk through the valley of the

shadow of death." That's as near as a saint gets to dying, it's translation. "I will fear no evil," etc. I lose all my enjoyment, says one, in the midst of holiness fighters. Well, God has a table prepared for you in the presence of your enemies. You keep eating grapes and pomegranates, and honey and bread, made from the finest of the wheat. Sanctified folks haven't any more sense when the table is set than to come and eat. I am not going to stop eating, because I hear the wolves howl. Some folks are so lean and poor waiting to get to heaven for their supplies, they won't have any appetite for them there. Notice, God has a running-over cup. Don't jostle your cup, don't try to be blessed. Some are so afraid of a running-over cup! they are so nice!

"Goodness and mercy *shall* follow me all the days of my life." Promise of dwelling in the house forever, not of backsliding and regaining the blessing. We don't want a "victory-side" sanctification at camp-meeting, and no victory when we get home. Lord help us to get a sanctification that will give us victory at home. Say constantly, "Jesus saves me now."

WHAT IS A CHRISTIAN?

AFTERNOON SERMON BY REV. WALTER RUSSELL.

TEXT: The disciples were called Christians first in Antioch. Acts 11: 26.

THE world wants truth to-day, not tissue-paper charity. Do you know the dignity and destiny of the Christian? We need the fire of God to consume the fiery passions of men. All doubts and difficulties were settled at the cross and tomb of Christ.

1. A christian is a sinner co-quickened with Jesus. Dead in sin and to sin are the two extremes of Christian life. You will either have to be born once and die twice, or be born twice and die once. If you don't kneel at the throne of grace, you will kneel with blistered knees on the fiery pavements of hell. Oh, this salvation is no picnic business!

2. There is a death and resurrection in Christ. We are new creatures, who can look up. You might as well tell a hog to climb a tree and sing like a canary, as to tell a sinner creeping on all fours in sin to look up. We must be *new* creatures. I am suspicious of people who are covered with Florida water; I fear they haven't got their laundry. Only the enemy in Christ's time seemed to believe what Jesus said of his resurrection. You never get very aspiring notions with your head in a sepulchre. If you see your shadow you will have a hard time.

A worldly Christian is a misnomer. A carnal nature is scriptural. We are "risen with Christ," not terrestrials but celestials. We sit "in heavenly places." They call us visionary, but after all it's the unseen that's real. Jesus left the throne of God and took upon Himself humanity, that we might take upon us divinity. The Holy Ghost is to be incarnated in us. Thus He sends out His workers, His yoke-fellows, from high-places to low-places. Jesus is still the carpenter, and knows how to make yokes which fit so beautifully when the skillful Holy Ghost puts them on. A fellow yoked to Christ can be hitched on to anything, and —so much the worse for the anything. I am investing in the joint-stock company of the skies. That company is going to declare dividends of kingdoms. Come and see me when I get one.

3. A co-worker with Jesus is a co-witness. We are pictorial Bibles from the circulating library of the skies. Your life will tell. Did you know the Lord wants preserves? He wants to put you up, pound for pound. "Preserved blameless." Now a witness must know what he talks about. No other man is a scriptural witness but one who has "been there."

4. Then you become a co-sufferer with Christ. If you are like Christ, you will suffer like Him. You won't have invitations to popular assemblies, but dying folks will call you to their bedside. The purer the being is, the less it will take to seem an awful sin. I am glad I am going the upper way. I am not going down.

5. Then we shall co-reign with Him. Somewhere, sometime He is going to let me reign with Him on earth. I expect to wear a crown and wave a palm and hold a sceptre.

PORTSMOUTH CAMPGROUND
AND
HOW TO GET THERE.

IT may interest the readers of this book who have not been to this charming camp, to have a little fuller description of the accommodations of the place, and ways of transportation thither. Brother Rees combines both actual facts and faith facts in his annual announcements concerning the camp, viz:

"Portsmouth camp ground is situated near Quaker Hill, on Rhode Island, about two miles from Portsmouth Station on the N. Y., N. H. & H. R. R. (Old Colony System), and is seven miles from Newport and ten from Fall River.

Portsmouth Camp is a beautiful, clean, maple grove, with many excellent advantages, the island of Rhode Island being a delightful summer resort, with bracing sea air and picturesque scenery. But best of all, the blessed Holy Ghost is to be present in great power. Sinners will be converted, believers will be sanctified, backsliders will be restored. Pentecost will be repeated, fire will fall, apostolic success will return, a cloud of glory will rest upon the camp. 'And these signs shall follow them that believe.' Mark 16: 17.''

Portsmouth campmeeting is not an organization for money-making. It's dividends are to be paid in heaven. If any money is left after paying the running expenses of the meeting, it is devoted to improvement of the grounds, and the cheapening of board and lodging expenses, so that persons of moderate circumstances can enjoy it's privilege at a minimum of cost.

During the past year a new tabernacle has been built which will accommodate 1,300 people. New tents have also been put in the past season, so that there are now over 100 family tents, there are also seven or eight large society tents which can also accommodate transient visitors, if necessary. A fine wooden building has been erected for the free lodging of ministers and their wives. Another frame building stands beside it, containing also twenty furnished rooms, which are let with or without bedding. We subjoin the usual annual announcement concerning these matters. One contemplated improvement is the putting in of an electric plant for lighting the grounds. Other improvements will be made as needed.

LODGING.

THERE are Society Tents where lodging on single beds may be had at 25 cents per night. Family wall tents 10x12 with flies and board floors, each tent containing one double bedstead, straw mattress, straw pillows, pail, cup and wash-basin, chair and broom, for $4 for the first ten days, or $6 for the entire time provided they are engaged by July 15th, otherwise they will be more. In all cases bring your own bedding, towels, etc., not mentioned in tent furnishings. Do not neglect this. Furnished rooms may be had in houses by those who prefer not to live in tents. The tents are owned by us, they are all new, made of 8oz duck and each tent has a fly of the same material. Free lodging for all ministers and their wives in regular standing with any evangelical church.

BOARD.

GOOD table board $4.50 per week, 75 cents per day, breakfast and supper 25 cents each, single dinner 35 cents. Provisions may be had on the grounds for those who wish to board themselves. All persons must procure their provisions and meal tickets for the Sabbath, on Saturday, as nothing will be sold on the Lord's day.

CONVEYANCE.

ROUND trip tickets from Boston $2.40, from Fall River 40 cents, from Newport 35 cents. Stage will leave Portsmouth on arrival of trains at 7.24 and 9.02 a. m., and 3.02 and 6.37 p. m. All persons coming by way of Providence will leave the city at 2.30 p. m. (on Saturdays only at 3.30) on boat "Queen City." Round trip tickets 40 cents. The "Awashonks" leaving Providence at 9 a. m. will carry passengers to and from the camp Saturdays only. The boat landing is about one mile from the camp. Passengers taken to or from the camp ground for 15 cents each, and trunks 15 cents each, from Portsmouth station 20 cents each and trunks 20 cents each. No Sunday trains. Let everybody come up to this feast of the Lord. A tabernacle has been built which will accommodate 1,300 people, and the grounds greatly enlarged and improved. Applications for tents and boarding should be sent in as early as possible.

All communications should be addressed to SETH C. REES, Portsmouth, R. I.

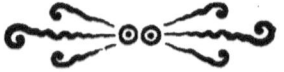

JUST OUT

Do you want to see the absurdity of modern methods of supporting the Gospel?

GET......

"The City of Mundum at the South Pole."

An Allegory on Church Entertainments,

BY REV. W. D. WOODWARD.

Ten Cents Each, Postpaid.   One Dollar Per Dozen.

"A beautiful tract with cover."

"A genuinely original treatment of the subject."

"Bright, argumentative, poetical, attractive, and will convince. We wish it a wide reading."

"A faithful picture of the character and folly of worldliness in the church presented in an attractive and forceful way."

DR. DANIEL STEELE writes: "Its purpose is excellent. It shows the folly of unscriptural methods for the support of the Gospel, which becomes badly contaminated thereby."

"Rev. W. D. Woodward, in his recently issued pamphlet on church entertainments, makes a witty and forcible point in one sentence: 'Rev. A. Muddle on Progressive Indefiniteness.' The whole pamphlet is worth reading."—*Christian Standard.*

Order of....

The Christian Witness Co.,
Boston, Mass.

Or of W. D. WOODWARD, Westport Point, Mass.

BOOK 2

HALLELUJAHS

FROM

Portsmouth

OR

A REPORT

OF

Portsmouth Campmeeting

HELD AT

PORTSMOUTH R. I.

JULY 23 TO AUGUST 8, 1897

CHRISTIAN UNITY PUBLISHING CO.
Evangelist Building
SPRINGFIELD MASSACHUSETTS
1897

PREFACE.

GOD smiles upon the Holiness Campmeeting. As the Holiness movement has increased in scope and power, the number of these annual gatherings has steadily grown until now the land is studded with Mount Zions, up to which God's people troop by hundreds and thousands. Holiness has rescued the campmeeting and made it a force for piety and godliness. As spirituality waned in the churches the old-time "campmeeting" instead of being a soul-saving institution as formerly, became either a species of picnic, an educational convention or a perfunctory "District meeting," remarkable only for platform sky-rocketing and the utter absence of conversions.

But the Spirit saw in the campmeeting a vehicle for spreading Holiness, and under His care it has become one of the most potent battering-rams of all the pieces of God's artillery. This effectiveness is due to a number of causes; chief among them is the fact that from the pulpit of a Holiness camp men are encouraged and expected to speak as moved by the Holy Ghost. Here there is liberty. No backslidden Presiding Elder has a right to enter this domain and browbeat a minister into desertion of his own convictions of truth. Holiness people fear none but God. They of all men can afford to and do invite the light. They have no skeletons to put in appearance at inopportune moments. Truth they will have at any cost.

The utterances therefore of the preachers at a camp like Portsmouth are invaluable. They are unique. They are straightforward. They are Scriptural. We have sought in "Hallelujahs from Portsmouth, No 2." to give at least an echo of the sermons preached during the encampment of 1897. It must, however, be remembered that a report of this character must of necessity be more or less unfair to the man reported. Because of this fact we hesitated for some time before attempting this work. Dr. Carradine's sermons, for example, as given here are but poor representations of those he really preached. It is impossible to do him justice in so brief an account as this must be. Two considerations out-weigh this objection to the publication of a condensed report. First, those who were so fortunate as to be able to attend the meeting will have their memories of the grand feast freshened by the perusal of even so meagre a record as this. The reading over of the bill of fare ought to bring up a recollection of the taste of the viands. Second, hundreds will read this book who were unable to be at Portsmouth; we feel justified therefore in reproducing for their benefit as much of the glorious seventeen days as possible.

The writing of this report has been a labor of love. If inaccuracy and blunders are found, as doubtless they will be, we can only dull the point of criticism a little by saying that much of the work was done in great physical weariness, and that the matter was prepared for press while the writer was going from state to state in campmeeting work. May our Lord use this little book to the refreshment and encouragement of His children!

BYRON J. REES,

Westport, Mass., August, 1897.

INTRODUCTION.

THE State of Rhode Island is not an Island, but takes its name from one bearing that name. This island is washed on the west by Narragansett Bay, and on the east by the Sakonet river, a stream two miles wide. It is something over fifteen miles long and four broad. On it are the towns of Portsmouth and Middletown, and the famous city of Newport, one of the capitals of the State, and the sea-side resort of the wealthy and fashionable of our land. Newport is at the southern end of the island, and Portsmouth is located eight miles north, toward the upper end.

It was late in the afternoon when I got off the Boston train at Portsmouth station. Then followed a hack ride of two miles, through fields and meadows fenced in with stone walls and bordered with golden rod, to the camp ground. As we were driven into the dense, dark, beautiful grove, we will never forget the pleasing effect made upon the eye by the deep shadows of the woods, the many twinkling lights of lanterns swung to the trees, and the long rows of white tents that loomed up spectrally on every hand.

INTRODUCTION.

The founder of the camp ground is the Rev. S. C. Rees, whom I recently commended in *The Methodist* as an evangelist to my friends through the South and West. Some eight or ten years ago, he was pastor of a church in Portsmouth. Near his house was this large and beautiful grove. He felt it ought to be used for God's glory in the way of a camp ground. One evening near sunset he pushed his way through the tangled underbrush and explored its depths. The beauty and perfect fitness of the place, at once struck him, and kneeling down in the shadows among the trees, he began praying about it to God, and promising to get it for Him, when the Holy Ghost suddenly fell upon his soul, and he commenced shouting so long and loud that his wife heard him, thought some accident had occurred, and sent a messenger swiftly to his help. The camp meeting was really born that evening. There have been six regular encampments since that year, and each successive one has been better and more powerful than its predecessor.

According to Bro. Rees, the meeting this year has kept up this remarkable record, and is the best that has ever yet been held on the grounds. It lasted seventeen days, and there was a steady and increasing interest to the end. When we remember that there were five services a day, this fact of unflagging attention and enjoyment becomes all the more remarkable.

This time we did not do the counting, but others did, and their figures show from two to three hundred souls converted, reclaimed and sanctified.

In all my travels I have never seen a "freer" camp meeting congregation. Gospel liberty abounded in pulpit and pew, and the responsiveness of the audience was simply delightful.

On several occasions the holy joy so filled the people that they could not be kept in their seats, but sprang to their feet, with shouts, cries and hallelujahs, while a tempest of glad song fairly shook the Tabernacle. On two nights there was a "march around" the big building, several hundred people being in double line, while as many white handkerchiefs waved like banners in the air, and as many voices swelled forth in the inspiring hymn: "Tis a Glorious Church." On one night it seemed to me that we would surely have a religious dance, and on that very night of uncontainable joy upon the part of the sanctified, fully forty to fifty souls swept into the light. The joy broke out in the preparatory services before the sermon was preached. That sermon was never preached. A perfect gale of glory blew from heaven, and for over an hour there was nothing but shouts, cries, laughter, hand-clapping, and rapturous singing. It did not die down at the end of an hour, but the preacher in the midst of it all, called for penitents and seekers, and there was a rush to the altar.

The singing was led by Rev. John Norberry, whose rich, unctuous voice went with power to hundreds of hearts. He also preached a number of times and worked indefatigably at the altar. After being with him for ten days, I unhesitatingly pronounce him the prince of altar workers. I have never seen his equal, much less his superior, in that important branch of work.

The instruments of music were a piano and a tambourine. I had no idea they could be made to agree so well. The manipulator of the tambourine was a colored man in the full enjoyment of sanctification. How he did bend over that jingling instrument, and how he made it speak forth some of the joys that overflowed his soul. Now and then in the midst of a full swell of the music and flood tide of congregational enthusiasm, his voice could be heard above all, crying out, "Yes, Lord"—"Glory to Jesus"—"Oh Yes"—"Hallelujah to the Lamb," etc.

Prof. L. F. Mitchell, of Providence, R. I., was at the piano. He is an accomplished musician, and gets high prices for his instruction in the city, but here for seventeen days he played three times daily, hours at a time, without charge. It is needless to say he is a sanctified man. It is wonderful how he put the holy fire of his heart into the splendid instrument before him. Even to-day after the camp meeting has closed, I can hear his rich base chords as they pulsated and even boomed their way through, and even above, the flood of harmony poured forth from the platform, crowded with excellent singers. One day on calling on the great multitude to cry out "hallelujah," by a happy inspiration, Prof. Mitchell struck a number of base chords at the moment of the general shout. The effect was thrilling. I told him afterwards I had heard of accompaniments to hymns and songs, but he had made one for shouts.

The next time this happy combination of sounds was tried, the colored brother added a long tremulo movement of his tambourine. I was convinced as I listened to the shout, heavy rolling base notes of piano and long drawn jingle of the tambourine, that David was right, and that everything can, and should praise the Lord.

The camp ground is located in the midst of historic localities. It is at the foot of Quaker Hill where one of the Revolutionary battles was fought. Over a thousand Hessians fell that day besides Americans, and blood flowed like water down the hill.

On top of the hill is an old Quaker church that was built over two hundred years ago. The roofing and weather boarding has been changed but the frame is just the same. The British used it in the war of the Revolution for barracks, as well as arsenal. Recently in cleaning out the cellar a number of cannon balls were found, buried in the earth and debris of many years. Two of these balls now sit on a mantel-piece in the church.

In this building George Fox preached two hundred and fifty years ago, when he came on a visit to this country in its colonial and early settlement history. He preached entire sanctification on this hill one hundred years before John Wesley ever agitated the subject.

Bro. Rees, who has studied up the Quaker history of those early days, tells of a convention held by the "Friends" on this very hill in the early times. He said that it was to be a six days' church business meeting. But the Holy Ghost so fell on them the first day that the opening minutes could not be read. On the second day the marvellous scene was repeated. On the third day it was the same. Business was simply impossible. Praise, adoration, worship, shouts became the one order of the day. They at last struck business on the fourth day, and were so filled with the Spirit that they finished in two sessions, what they expected would take a week. On the sixth morning they attempted to break up and part for their different works, but there was another downpour of the Holy Ghost, and they were three days in tearing away from each other and the place which seemed so close to heaven. They were two days in transacting church business, and six days in pure, happy, rapturous soul worship of God. May be the Spirit was giving the preachers and churches in the land a picture lesson of what ought to be done in Conferences, Synods and Assemblies, and what He wants to be done.

What a stupendous blow would be given to sin and hell, and what mighty revivals would sweep the entire country if our Conferences would be held after the manner of that famous convention of the "Friends" on Quaker Hill in Rhode Island.

This is not all that is connected with this interesting body of people. Only a few miles from this spot, and on this island, is the grave of Mary Dyer, the Quakeress preacher. She was forbidden to preach in Massachusetts, but with the holy fire of sanctification burning in her, she trespassed the commands of men in obedience to an inward Divine call. So she committed the awful sin of crossing ecclesiastical boundaries in order to preach full salvation to men and women. For doing this she was hung on Boston common. She now sleeps near Newport, awaiting the coming of the Son of God, who will right the wrongs of His people, and bring justice as well as reward to those who for His sake have been slaughtered and killed all the day long.

I took a number of strolls to the top of Quaker Hill, hard by the old church. Whether I went in the morning or at the hour of sunset, the view from the summit of the hill was always lovely. A landscape of twenty to thirty miles in breadth, filled with natural beauty and historic associations, was what held my fascinated eye and drew me repeatedly from the crowded camp meeting grove to the lonelier elevated spot above. Narragansett Bay, island gemmed, sail-flecked, and with smoke trails of passing steamers, stretches away westward and north-westward. A glimpse of the ocean far away to the south with a few sails upon it, is dimly seen. On the east is the Sakonet river, more like a bay than a river, with hilly slopes for its distant shore on which gleams home-like residences, some villages, and still farther the smoky skirt of the great manufacturing city, Fall River, in Massachusetts.

Northeast can be seen Tiverton Heights, from which place some American soldiers rowed one night during the Revolutionary war, got around the British war vessels anchored on the west of this island, and captured the English Commander, General Prescott, who was staying in a dwelling on the shore.

Due north, and four miles away across an arm of the Bay, is Mt. Hope. This looks down upon the swamp in which the celebrated Indian King Phillip was killed. The mountain and swamp are both in full sight from Quaker Hill. The forest is just the same as of yore, the ground being poor soil, the timber has not been cut down. The whole sad history of Phillip rushed over me, as I stood looking at the place from afar. I had read the volume of his life by Abbott, when a boy. How he had lost a thousand of his warriors in a battle, only ten or twelve miles from this very spot. Besides this his wife and only son had been captured, and so broken in spirit, with a few of his followers he drew near to Mt. Hope, in the neighborhood of which he had lived in happier days. Some one, doubtless an Indian, informed the whites, and they tracked him down. I recall the pen picture of the silent, melancholy Indian chief sitting on a fallen tree in the swamp, with his arms folded, his head bent down upon his breast, while his feathery plume drooped in front of his face. In this broken-hearted attitude he was surprised, soon captured, killed and his body cut into thirteen pieces.

One fact that adds much to the sympathy felt for this Indian King, is stated by early writers of that time, that Phillip was opposed to the war in which his great tribe was destroyed, and like his father Samoset, was at heart a friend to the whites.

So as I remarked in last week's letter to *The Pentecostal Herald*, it is coming to pass that every bit of landscape is getting associated with some sorrowful or tragic scene of the past.

The reader can now understand why my steps would

turn so frequently to the summit of Quaker Hill, where Plenty frolicked in the valleys around me, Commerce glistened on the Bay and sea, History waved its hand from the horizon, Beauty smiled everywhere, and God's benediction and presence came down upon all. —*Rev. B. Carradine in The Methodist.*

ORDER OF PREACHERS DURING THE CAMP.

Friday, July 23d.	7.30 P. M., Pheobe L. Hall.
Saturday, July 24th.	10.30 A. M., Wm. H. Hoople.
Saturday, July 24th.	3.00 P. M., F. M. Messenger.
Saturday, July 24th.	7.30 P. M., Wm. H. Hoople.
Sunday, July 25th.	10.30 A. M., S. C. Rees.
Sunday, July 25th.	3.00 P. M., W. H. Hoople.
Sunday, July 25th.	7.30 P. M., Phoebe L. Hall.
Monday, July 26th.	10.30 A. M., F. M. Messenger.
Monday, July 26th.	3.00 P. M., B. J. Rees.
Monday, July 26th.	7.30 P. M., W. H. Hoople.
Tuesday, July 27th.	10.30 A. M., John Norberry.
Tuesday, July 27th.	2.30 P. M., Phoebe L. Hall.
Tuesday, July 27th.	7.30 P. M., W. H. Hoople.
Wednesday, July 28.	10.30 A. M., B. J. Rees.
Wednesday, July 28.	2.30 P. M., S. C. Rees.
Wednesday, July 28.	7.30 P. M., John Norberry.
Thursday, July 29th.	10.30 A. M., —— —— ——
Thursday, July 29th.	2.30 P. M., John Norberry.
Thursday, July 29th.	7.30 P. M., Phoebe L. Hall.
Friday, July 30th.	10.30 A. M., H. A. Rees.
Friday, July 30th.	2.30 P. M., B. Carradine.
Friday, July 30th.	7.30 P. M., John Norberry.
Saturday, July 31st.	10.30 A. M., E. M. Levy.
Saturday, July 31st.	2.30 P. M., B. Carradine.
Saturday, July 31st.	7.30 P. M., Phoebe L. Hall.

ORDER OF PREACHERS.

Sunday, Aug. 1st.	10.30 A. M., B. Carradine.
Sunday, Aug. 1st.	2.30 P. M., John Norberry.
Sunday, Aug. 1st.	7.30 P. M., B. Carradine.
Monday, Aug. 2d.	10.30 A. M., B. J. Rees.
Monday, Aug. 2d.	2.30 P. M., B. Carradine.
Monday, Aug. 2d.	7.30 P. M., John Norberry.
Tuesday, Aug. 3d.	10.30 A. M., B. Carradine.
Tuesday, Aug. 3d.	2.30 P. M., H. A. Rees.
Tuesday, Aug. 3d.	7.30 P. M., B. Carradine.
Wednesday, Aug. 4.	10.30 A. M., S. C. Rees.
Wednesday, Aug. 4.	2.30 P. M., B. Carradine.
Wednesday, Aug. 4.	7.30 P. M., —— —— ——
Thursday, Aug. 5th.	10.30 A. M., B. Carradine.
Thursday, Aug. 5th.	2.30 P. M., John Norberry.
Thursday, Aug. 5th.	7.30 P. M., B. Carradine.
Friday, Aug. 6th.	10.30 A. M., B. Carradine.
Friday, Aug. 6th.	2.30 P. M., —— —— ——
Friday, Aug. 6th.	7.30 P. M., B. Carradine.
Saturday, Aug. 7th.	10.30 A. M., B. J. Rees.
Saturday, Aug. 7th.	2.30 P. M., B. Carradine.
Saturday, Aug. 7th.	7.30 P. M., Phoebe L. Hall.
Sunday, Aug. 8th.	10.30 A. M., B. Carradine.
Sunday, Aug. 8th.	2.30 P. M., John Norberry.
Sunday, Aug. 8th.	7.30 P. M., B. Carradine.

Portsmouth Camp Ground.

FRIDAY, JULY 23, 1897.

The day on which Portsmouth Camp Meeting opens has come at last. The grove, never more beautiful than to-day, is alive with campers hurrying hither and thither, anxious to be settled in their tents before the opening service. The clouds which frowned so inauspiciously in the early morning have disappeared and the bright sunlight filters through the trees and strikes the ground in yellow splotches. From the verandah of "Rest Cottage" the eye can cover nearly the whole encampment. To the northeast is the tabernacle, westward is the dining hall, and everywhere through the dark columns of the tree-trunks glimmers the white duck of one hundred and eighteen tents. Here and there a cottage is seen, but the mass of the people live under canvas.

FRIDAY, JULY 23, 2.30 P. M.

Promptly at the stroke of the bell the campers, hymn-book and Bible in hand, gather from all directions to the Tabernacle. We are surprised at the number who come. We scarcely thought so many had arrived. Providence people have not put in appearance yet—they will come by the evening boat,—but Nantucket, Block Island and Wickford are well represented. Among the preachers we notice Rev. Phoebe L. Hall, a Friends' minister of Washington, D. C., Rev. Thomas C. Crocker, Olneyville, R. I., Rev. Mr. Crandall of Wickford and the President of the Association, Seth C. Rees.

The meeting opened with the hymn, "All hail the power of Jesus' Name." Seth C. Rees then read a Scripture lesson from Isaiah, the 58th chapter, accompanying it with comments. "I was never more fully convinced of the immense possibilities of grace than I am at this hour. I am someway assured that the miraculous, supernatural power of God belongs to us if we will but humble ourselves and meet the conditions necessary for its bestowment. My faith looks up! God will scatter all his enemies! Let us stretch our tent and strengthen our stakes. Let this service result in our taking new spiritual ground."

At the close of his remarks Bro. Rees said, "Let us go to our knees." Nearly all in the audience knelt and a season of unctuous, self-abasing prayer followed. Singing "I'll step out on his promise."

Brother: The moment I stepped through the gate, God blessed my soul. Hallelujah! I am believing for great things in this encampment.

Singing: "Fill me now."

Nelson R. Reed of Fall River: Never was I more sure than to-day that He fills me now. I am looking, however, for advancement. I am here with the full determination that I shall know more of the heights and depths than ever before. I want to be of the most possible use to God.

Singing, "On the victory side."

Sister Phoebe Hall: My faith does not shrink. God will give us great triumph in this campmeeting. Thank God, I am on the victory side. I always expect to be.

Sister Lucy Phetteplace of Wakefield: Satan seemed to especially hate the thought of my going to Portsmouth campmeeting, but through the grace of our God I am here. Praise His Name!

Louis Mitchell: Friends told me I ought to wait until to-morrow before coming to this place, but I am here and praising God.

Sister: I am come for rest, physical, mental and spiritual. I lack the victory which I desire. Pray for me.

Seth C. Rees: Keep headed to the light and victory will be sure.

Singing: "Walking in the Light."

Rev. T. C. Crocker: I am kept in peace. God is running me. I have given all to Him.

Serena Chrestenson, missionary to Alaska: Since I was here last year God has kept me. I have looked forward to this meeting for weeks. I am here, not simply for myself, but for others. Sinners will surely be saved in this campmeeting.

Sister Hinckley: When I sang last year that chorus, "I'll go every step of the way," I had no idea it would lead me to the grave of my daughter, but God has sustained me.

Thus with testimonies filled with faith and victory the first service of the Seventh Portsmouth Camp Meeting closed.

In the interim between the afternoon service and the evening hour there were many new arrivals. Wagons piled high with trunks and bags labored up and down the shady roads seeking the tents where they might drop their load. Superintendent Chase was here and there and everywhere, directing his assistants and answering the questions of the new-comers. Rev. Wm. H. Hoople of Brooklyn came by the evening train. Rev. D. W. Dean of Centredale greets us cheerily under the beeches, and over on the verandah of his beautiful new cottage we see F. M. Messenger and family. Providence people have come by steamer, and the faces which we see at Emmanuel are so frequent that it seems as if the spiritual portion of the city had come to us bodily.

HALLELUJAHS FROM PORTSMOUTH. 23

FRIDAY, JULY 23, 7.30 P. M.

We do thank the Lord for our Tabernacle! As we look at it now, with its broad, generous stretch of space, its brilliant lights, its solid platform, and its rows upon rows of chairs, we say to ourselves "there never was a better building for the purpose to which it is put." Bro. Hoople is leading the singing to-night, and with Louis Mitchell at the piano and the Spirit-touched voices in the pews, how the hymns ascend to God! Portsmouth does not feel herself a stranger to Bro. Hoople. His stalwart figure, his stentorian voice, his bass "Amens," his frank, open manner—are they not all known to us? Yea, and loved by all the Portsmouth saints. As we watch him standing on the platform and throwing his whole manly soul into the singing and think of what God has wrought through him, and that though scarcely twenty-eight, he is practically the father of a movement which we have all learned to love because of its fire and power and spirituality, we say "Thanks be to God for men like William Howard Hoople." After a number of hymns were sung, F. M. Messenger of No. Grosvenordale led us to God in prayer. The President gave out the order of services and introduced Rev. Phoebe L. Hall as the preacher for the evening.

My subject this evening will be found in three words: "Mighty to save" (Isaiah 63:1.). I used to think of a lovely little Christ saving me from lovely little sins and carrying me to a lovely little abode with Himself. Later, I realized that sin was infinite, that Hell was infinite and that Christ must needs be "Mighty to save" if he was to save me from sin. God is able. I submit that if he was of sufficient might to create us, then surely he is able to correct and righten us. On this platform, in this audience before me, all over this broad land of ours, are people who can testify to God's ability to save to the uttermost.

God is infinite in wisdom. Satan from the very first has been warring against the human race, but God in his infinite wisdom prepared a plan of salvation by which the enemy might be defeated completely. A brother on the platform said that we have something worth making a noise about. Surely a salvation so great as this of which I speak is sufficient cause for great demonstration. In Calvary's sacrifice we see God's wisdom. Standing in the beginning and looking down the long course of the years, God saw what scheme of salvation would suffice and that scheme has for its central point the death of Christ. Every knee shall bow and acknowledge that Jesus is Lord. All of us owe our salvation to this, the wisdom of God manifest in the atonement. My salvation from being a prim, stiff Quaker who never smiled, and your salvation, whatever you may have been saved from, all come from the hallowed cross.

God is "mighty to save" in that He is infinite in love. It was hard for me to believe that. I could see how he might love everyone else but *me*. Can it be *love* with which he comes to *me*? Hallelujah! It is. Reared in a denomination whose ministers said little concerning the new birth, a genuine conversion taught me as by a scriptural revelation the real nature of regeneration. My habits became new, my associates, my thoughts, my life, all these were new. Shortly after it became known to me that God had a second work of grace for me, my need was shown to me by the Spirit, and at last with my consent He came in with his fire and burned out all the dross. For my body, for my temporal needs, for everything, God is more than sufficient. In closing, let me say that Christ's salvation is mighty in that those who possess it go on to victory, heedless of frowns, heedless of disapprobation, resolute and true because they are filled with God.

Singing: "Oh, now I see the cleansing wave!"

Brother S. C. Rees: We will close the meeting on our knees. Let us pray.

SATURDAY, JULY 24, 10 A. M.

The ten o'clock service opened with the singing of several songs. Our number has grown considerably since yesterday. Newport, Fair Haven and Westport are all well represented among the arrivals, while many are in from the immediate locality. Sister Phoebe L. Hall led in prayer. Wm. H. Hoople then arose and took his text for preaching. Matt. 5: 8. "Blessed are the pure in heart for they shall see God."

Formerly little attention was given to God and salvation. To-day while it is fashionable to take a certain amount of interest in religion, perhaps sufficient to belong to a church, very few care for real salvation. One bane of the church to-day is that we are unduly emphasizing head culture to the neglect of *heart* training and experience. The questions put to the candidates for the ministry by the church to-day indicate interest in his "educational advantages," in his "culture," in his intellectual training rather than in the training of the heart. But God says, "Blessed are the pure in *heart*." We are making it hard for the heart by our over-stocking the head.

In the twinkling of an eye God can educate a man in divine things so as to prepare him for spiritual work. "Heart" means the affectional nature, and our affections play an imporant part in our lives. Bad affections ruin the work of a good head, but good affections will frequently supplement marvellously the work of a poor head. Intellectual lack need not hinder you in spiritual and holy advancement. Even if your brain power is small, if you will surrender to the Lord he will make you independently rich in spiritual things. Hallelujah!

I. "Heart." I am not speaking now of the physical organ. I refer to "the seat of the affections." God is interested in the condition of our hearts. Naturally the heart is "prone to wander," leading us to the shades of hell. This evil heart is towing this continent to infidelity and scepticism. But the new heart pulls us toward heaven and righteousness. Therefore God is pleading for our hearts. If He can get them, He knows He can establish us safely. Resolutions, tears and sighs won't take away the blackness. Nothing but the fire of the Holy Ghost will do it.

II. "Purity." Bengal says that something more than ceremonial purity is meant here. Imputation will not do. What Christ does for and in us alone avails. Adam Clarke says that this text is directed against Pharisaical purity. Purity implies fire, for only fire will produce it. Many people move through this world accomplishing nothing, but the Lord Jesus wants to baptize us with effective fire. Matthew Henry says "True religion consists in heart purity." We agree with him here. Purity means unmixedness.

God can so work in us that we will be all the same kind, and that kind the right kind. All the soul's desire will be for God. Every evangelical church says in its creed or statement of belief, that the soul must be pure before it enters heaven. Many say that sanctification is at death, but not a passage in all the Bible even implies it, but the number of texts which say we are to be sanctified *now* are innumerable.

III. We "see God" when we are sanctified. Can we have a pure heart now? If not then all the beatitudes are meaningless. "Poor in spirit" is not a characteristic meriting commendation or blessedness in either of the next worlds. There will be no good in "mourning." Thirsting for righteousness will be of no avail beyond death. So heart purity is for the *present*. My brother, let God kill the stinging, biting, crawling, twisting thing called inbred sin. He will do it. He will do it now!

The following altar service like the sermon was rugged and strong. Brother Hoople's sermons are plain, and "meaty," Anglo-Saxon discourses. His growth in the ministry is truly phenomenal. We hear no preaching which is more lucid or more convincing than that of Brother Hoople.

SATURDAY, JULY 24, 3 P. M.

After an unusually happy song service Rev. F. N. Messenger, of North Grosvenordale, was introduced as the afternoon preacher.

"If you will bear with me I will read some rather lengthy selections from the 14th, 15th, and 16th chapters of II Chronicles." Brother Messenger then read passages treating of the life of Asa. These scriptures bear two indubitable marks of inspiration. I have no more sympathy with the Higher Criticism of the schools than with the lower criticism of the streets. I believe the Bible to be God's revealed will.

King Asa was in the experience of heart perfection. This the Word states. I find a proof of Divine inspiration in the fact that the man of God administered a stinging rebuke to the King. All through the ages God has laid his hand upon men and sent them here and there doing his bidding and obeying his commands.

King Asa got into a tight place. The army of the opposer was twice as great and vastly better equipped. The situation was a critical one. But Asa fell back on God. "Oh! Lord, it is nothing with thee to help." It doesn't matter about our circumstances nor environment nor power nor wisdom; for if in His name we go "against the enemy we will triumph. So the Lord smote the Ethiopian." God always helps the man who depends upon him. After this great victory Asa needed instruction. Sanctified people often need instruction. The Spirit fell on Azariah and sent him to the court of the King. This was the message: The Lord is with you while you are with him, but if you forsake him he will forsake you. There are many ways of forsaking God. If the tippler backslides and again goes to his cup all know it; but in the higher experience of holiness, we may lose it without it being so generally known.

There came another time of testing. A second army came against Asa. It seems strange that Asa should now take a suicidal course. In the face of the former victory he effects a league with the King of Syria. A Christian is supposed to stand for God in the world. He is God's ambassador. What a misrepresentation of God then when Asa seeks aid of the uncircumcised heathen. And the children of God wofully misrepresent him when they go to the lodge or to any secret order against Romanism. Striking hands with the sceptic, the Unitarian and the world. Even among holiness people we find now and then a man entangled in these evil institutions. This is what is meant by profaning the name of God. Putting it down in the dust, lowering it, degrading it before the unsanctified eyes of the world; this is profaning the name of Christ. It is no wonder that sinners have no reverence for Christianity when they see such poor examples of the Lord's grace. Holiness brethren, we can't be too careful in keeping ourselves unspotted from the world. How can we impress people with a second rest if we are not restful?

Asa was wroth with the seer. This was a mark of his being backslidden. When men do not relish the message of a man of God they are backslidden. Asa was diseased in his feet. Clarke says he had the gout. Gout as you know is caused by the violation of natural laws. Spiritual gout is caused by the violation of spiritual laws. The feet stand for the will. If we violate the laws of God our wills become less capable of putting forth right volitions. Inability to submit to God ensues. "Thou hast done foolishly." Ah! the sadness of having this sentence pronounced by God himself upon our career. May the Lord help us to act honestly and do that which our hearts and the Spirit tell us is right. Amen.

Owing to the necessity of our being away on the Sabbath we are not able to give reports of all the services at this stage of the camp. We learn, however, that Wm. H. Hoople preached Saturday night, S. C. Rees Sunday morning, Wm. H. Hoople Sunday afternoon and Phoebe L. Hall Sunday night. The cloud of glory which had come upon the people already continued to rest upon the camp and the results were blessed and manifold.

MONDAY, JULY 26, 10.30 A. M.

Rev. F. M. Messenger, whose messages have been so blessed to the people this year, again preached. His addresses glow and burn with personal piety. In appearance Bro. Messenger is a business man, and in repose would pass for an ordinary bank-cashier; but in the pulpit he is a flame of holy fire and is instinct with the power of the Holy Ghost. We rejoice that Bro. Messenger ever came amongst us. As usual the altar service followed the sermon and Jesus was present to save and cleanse.

MONDAY, 2.30 P. M.

In the afternoon service Byron J. Rees preached from the text, "Unto him that loved us and washed us from our sins in his own blood."

In the paean of praise both the church militant and the church triumphant may join. All the saints of all ages, the martyrs of all persecutions, the holy army from all climes, the children of God of every color, one and all their voices mingle in this note of gladness and thanksgiving, "Unto him," unto Christ, about whose white brow should cluster the laurel of all our gratitude and praise.

No doubt we furnish merriment for holiness-fighters by our frequent instances of strained scripture. Take for example the two words, "Sin" and "Sins." Without controversy the word "sin" in the singular number refers very often to "the carnal mind," the body of sin, "the old man." The plural number likewise is used constantly as a synonym for transgression, but this mode of interpretation has been abused. In the text before us the word "sins" is of far vaster scope than mere "actual transgression." It covers all sin, whether actual or original.

Love was the moving cause of the sacrifice of Christ. It was this that drew him from the skies and led him to throw away his life for rascals. A parent in seeking to rescue his son from drowning loses his own life and we say that he loved him; but the pain was only momentary. In Christ we see agony and shame and disgrace and suffering, not only infinite in bulk but long-continued. Gethsemane is scarcely over when the trial succeeds upon whose heels swiftly follows Calvary. And yet to add hopelessness to extremity the ones for whom he died were yet sinners, rebels of the vilest character. Surely he "loved us."

It was the blood that made the atonement efficacious. Without the shedding of blood there is no remission of sins. Literally that red stream drawn from the tortured body of Jesus Christ is the ground of our salvation. It is the font to which old Zechariah pointed in the old days. I have noticed that those testimonies and sermons and meetings which emphasize and honor the blood call out the snarl of Hell and uncover the fangs of the hounds of the Pit. Satan *hates* the blood. It has lost none of its efficacy in all these centuries. Sweet and clean and fresh and potent as on the day of its spilling, it still cleanses the soul submitted to its action.

The very word "washed" implies filthiness. As we look at men's deeds we are frozen at their blackness, but they are but indices to states of heart far worse. The heart is the opulent *source* of unclean deeds. He who knows his own heart even slightly, dares not trust himself in certain networks of circumstances. The turpid maelstrom is too stout for the will. The stream is too swift for any of our stemming. The tide is running out with a swiftness inconceivable, the wind is dead against us, the main sheet is in tatters, while the oars are gone by the board. The force of the stream of vileness overcomes us. The blood of Jesus Christ is the panacea, and nothing else will cleanse us. Penance, be it ever so severe and protracted, will not avail. St Simeon Stylites may rot upon his pillar, but only the blood can help him. Resolution is futile without it is braced and pilastered with the power of God. Endeavor will end in endeavor and accomplishment will be far beyond our grasp if the blood is not sought.

Allow me to notice in passing that washing is not imputation, neither can it be thus fairly construed. The very words are contradictions. These are they which have washed their robes and made them white; not wrapt themselves in the skirt of Christ's robe. The whiteness is imparted by the application of the blood.

The magnitude of sin's gravity is seen in the nature of what it took to remedy it. Sin is more than merely "missing the mark." It is not merely a failing, a lack, a negative quantity. It is a veritable, positive, forceful *Ungehener* with a scaly hide impenetrable to all attack but that of the sword of the Spirit. The blood of Christ can cleanse the heart and make it holy.

A number were blessedly sanctified in the altar service and two or three were graciously reclaimed.

MONDAY, JULY, 26, 7.30 P. M.

Wm. H. Hoople opened his Bible to Heb. 12:14. "Follow peace with all men, and holiness, without which no man shall see the Lord." The question of sanctification is one that has puzzled many, many people. Strange to say, the wise and learned are puzzled by it more than the simple. Someway God will not let us burst this wall through with our heads, but wear it through with our hearts. We can afford to receive God's light on this important question. The text very plainly says that we must get "the sanctification" if we are to get into heaven. God insists upon our being sanctified.

The churches say we must be sanctified. All evangelical churches confess that there is something lacking in the human heart that needs cleansing. The Catholic Church proposes the Purgatorial fires as remedial of indwelling sin. But they count on the wrong fire—hell fire will not damage sin. Only the fire of the Holy Ghost can destroy sin and unless it strikes us before death it will never strike us. The trouble with the most of churches is that they mistake the time of being made holy. They put it at "the hour and article of death." There is a death, but it is not physical. May God help someone to die to-night.

"The sanctification." The Apostle uses this definite article "the" to distinguish the sanctification spoken of from all other kinds of sanctification This is vaster and more profound than all other kinds. There is a sanctification which consists in setting oneself apart for special work. The Mosaic accounts tell us of the sanctification of whole congregations, in which they separated themselves from dead bodies and unclean beasts and other things pronounced unhallowed by the law of God. Ordination to the ministry is a sort of sanctification. The dedication of a child to God is a species of sanctification. Moreover, there is sanctification at conversion. This, it is true, is not entire but it is sanctification for all that. But these sanctifications are but partial. They are not *the* sanctification. Conversion is a complete work, but it is not *the* sanctification. The work of purity is begun in conversion, but it is only completed in entire sanctification. It is one thing to be alive and quite another to be clean. When we are converted we love God and God's gospel; but when we get wholly sanctified we love with all the heart. When we are regenerated we trust God with many things, but the sanctified soul trusts him all the time. When you are saved, when first born of God, you are helped and strengthened by the Bible, but when entirely sanctified it is the foundation of everything. The new convert feels anxiety for souls on the dark road to Hell. When we are sanctified we have only one business and that the salvation of souls. I say to my charge, "I'll have a revival until I die. July and January are equally good." Even in vacation time you'll talk salvation.

Conversion imparts to the soul strength and dignity. The justified heart can endure much, but the sanctified can "endure all things." In a justified experience we have joy at times, but there are bare spots where the sleigh runs hard. But when sanctified how the honey drips! There is such a mighty upheaval in conversion that we enjoy holy people though we do not care to be seen with them before everyone, but sanctified we are delighted to be marked men and women, ostracised, if necessary, for the sake of Jesus.

Brother, there is no such battering-ram against the sinner's bulwark as a consistent holy life. Men are convinced when they see the Christlike graces blooming in our hearts and lives. Hallelujah!

The discovery of sin in the heart is a painful revelation to the soul which is truly converted. How you fear your own heart! It is not simply the manifestation of sin that disturbs you, but oh, how you mourn over the inclination you feel in your soul toward sin! But there is a place of felt safety. Blessed be God! Sin in the heart is first cousin to the devil and is ever hollowing for him to come and lend a hand, as it twists and crawls and schemes. Oh! there is deliverance. We have a hell-discomfiting, sin-destroying, devil-driving salvation. Come my brother, and find this blessed remedy.

Many did come and soon the air was filled with the joyous shouts of those who had found the remedy.

TUESDAY, 10.30 A. M.

Among the ministers on the platform this morning we notice Rev. Mr. Hartwig, Swedish minister of Newport, Rev. Mr. Ridgway of Fall River, Rev. Mr, Simonson of Oklahoma and Rev. Olin W. Rose of Iowa.

Rev. John Norberry is the preacher this morning. This is the third meeting this summer in which we have been associated with our dear brother John. There is a peculiar, tender unction which inevitably comes to us under his ministry that is like a zephyr from the skies. In the old days they burned God's men at the stake, now the Lord's preachers burn themselves up in work for Christ. Like Jesus, "He who saves others himself cannot save," but we pray God that the delicate constitution of our dear Bro. Norberry may stand the strain for many years to come. The message this morning was in the form of a Bible reading.

"For Zion's sake I will not hold my peace." Isaiah was a radical preacher of holiness. When a man or a woman gets the experience that Isaiah did in the sixth chapter of his prophecy they will be anxious about Zion. You "want to reach sinners." Amen! Get sanctified and get Zion cleansed and the heathen will get reached. Isaiah says he "will not rest until righteousness goes forth as brightness and salvation as a lamp that burneth. When the brightness goes forth, the rum-seller, the sabbath-breaker, the incontinent, will be convinced. The devil's folks plaster their saloon floors with silver dollars to attract the masses, while our big gray stone piles of churches are enough to give people the chills. But when the "brightness" comes the masses will flock to us. Why, some unconverted men, while they will not give up and get saved yet refuse to attend any other kind of meeting but a holiness meeting. "The Gentiles shall see." They must see purity and Christlikeness in the church. The trouble to-day is that they can't *see anything* worth having in the church, but when the bride of Christ gets sanctified "All kings will see the glory." They will see the lustre, the shine, the glow.

"They will call you the holy people." Oh! that is our name. We do not consider it a reproach, no indeed! Hallelujah! "No more termed forsaken." Presiding elders may forsake, and preachers and official boards, but God will not. Blessed be his name! Instead of the poorhouse God will give us a white house. "Crown of glory." A decoration for God himself. He will show us to the angels. He will "present us faultless to the father." "The sons of the stranger shall not drink of the wine for the which thou hast labored." Oh! sir, some of us have been going around and having revivals and giving our life and strength to the salvation of souls, only to see fighters of holiness fatten their salaries and oppose God with the substance God gave. No one to conserve the work, the false shepherds have made themselves drunken on the Lord's heritage. But we have a promise here that it shall not always be so. Bless the dear Lord. "Cast up, cast up, the highway; gather out the stones." The church must take away the stones of prejudice and inconsistency, that the sinners may come trooping to God. Let us do it now. Let all who want to be sanctified come forward.

Quite a number were blessedly sanctified at the close of this glorious talk. The fire in the camp is increasing and conviction settling upon the unsaved and unsanctified.

TUESDAY EVENING, 7.30 P. M.

In the afternoon Sister Phoebe L. Hall preached a most gracious sermon on the text, "If God be for us who can be against us?" Sister Hall is new to the New England holiness people, but the welcome she has received amongst us has been both general and cordial. In her sermon to-day, she referred to her work in the South, where thousands of dollars were needed annually, and God supplied every need. As we listened to her burning words we thanked God that she belongs to a church which believes in "women's ministry."

New faces greet us this evening. Ex-presiding Elder Hill, Rev. Mr. Jewelson of Baltimore, Md., and Chauncy A. Lockwood, one of the younger holiness pastors, are on the platform. Sister Hattie Livingstone of Colorado is also with us, but in poor health. May the dear Lord strengthen and heal her. This is Bro. Hoople's last service with us, as he insists upon it that he must press on to Clintondale, N. Y. So after Bro. Jewelson had led in prayer our dear Bro. Hoople rose and preached from Luke 3: 16, 17. "He shall baptize you with the Holy Ghost and with fire." Thank God for the promises! Our hopes would languish and die were it not for them. They say there are 32,000 of these, and every one of us may have all of them fulfilled.

Some people can not seem to get the promises to work, but it is because they themselves are wrong. God is all right, and when we meet the conditions the things promised will be deluged upon us. The promise which I have read in your hearing to-night is, strange to say, a very popular one. I have seen the presiding elder nod, and the members of the official board smile, and the preacher grin, and the young people beam, and the President of the Ladies' Aid Society swing into line and say, "yes," when this text was read in their hearing. Not a tear shed, not a sigh, no one gets into the blessing. Why? Why, because they have no right understanding of the text. Oh! there'll have to be a desperate heart fight if you get this blessing. In one of our meetings a woman came tripping down the aisle and knelt daintily on the velvet cushion, and laid her little gloves on the altar rail, and the little feathers waggled on the top of her little head, and she said, "Now let it come." We said to her, "Sister, will you give all you've got to obtain this blessing!" "Oh! I didn't suppose it cost anything!" and she tripped her little person out of the door and down the steps and up to her little room, but God talked to her, and soon after she tumbled in and got the blessing. Hallelujah!

Ah! it means something to get this blessing. Quit your dabbling around the full salvation pool and plunge in all over. Some folks look upon this blessing as a sort of finishing touch—a sort of a "tack-on" a "bay window," a kitchen "lean-to" that will enhance their beauty and add to their attractiveness. "Oh! I'm all right. I have only a little temper, a little pride." That is the self-life talking. Before you get the blessing you'll shrink up until you can hardly see yourself. When you strike rock bottom the bottom of heaven will drop out and saturate you with glory. You will lose caste on earth, but your stock will go up in the exchange of the skies. You think you will have no opportunities for service if you get sanctified. You will have so much to do you will wish you had five bodies to serve God in.

Yes, this blessing is a finishing touch. It is a finishing touch to carnality. It is a finishing touch to some of your friends. They will gravitate out of your life. Give your little plans and little thoughts up to God and go the lone way with Jesus. Amen.

The usual call was made and several hungry souls obtained this blessed baptism—the baptism with the Holy Ghost.

WEDNESDAY, 10.30 A. M.

After John Norberry had prayed, Byron J. Rees read Ephesians 1:15-23.

This magnificent prayer is read by thousands who fail utterly to get its meaning. It has a spiritual swing and balance and cadence to it, which, if we are not on our guard will waltz us clear through to the finish with no comprehension of what the inspired apostle is saying. Let me give you the skeleton of this prayer. "I pray that the Father may give unto you the spirit of wisdom and revelation, that ye may know Jesus and the hope of Christ's calling and what is the magnitude of his inheritance in the saints and what is the greatness of his power toward us." This it seems to me is the kernel of this great petition. The clause, "The eyes of your understanding being enlightened" simply calls attention to one of the concomitants of the gift of the Spirit to the soul. Verses from the 19th to the end of the 23d merely explain the nature of the power which we who believe are to know when the Holy Ghost comes.

In the first place the Christians at Ephesus are *real* Christians. They are not mere professors, neither are they backsliders. Paul says that he does "not cease to give thanks for them." He has likewise heard of their "faith in Christ and of their love to the saints," Moreover, in the salutation he calls them "saints," a term he never uses except to children of God.

The Spirit referred to is, of course, the Holy Spirit, and Paul calls him the Spirit of wisdom and revelation. Conversion is a revelation. Sanctification is a revelation, but wisdom enables us to utilize the revelation to the best advantage in the work of God. Information is excellent, but wisdom alone will know how to make the most of it. Many a rich experience is lying unused because the owner fails to recognize in the Holy Ghost the blessed source of wisdom as well as revelation.

The Apostle parenthetically describes one of the accompaniments of the coming of the Holy Ghost, the eyes of the soul are opened or illuminated. We see this typified in the healing of the blind man by our Lord. After the first touch men were indistinct, gigantic, monstrous, but with the second application of the Divine hand he saw clearly. We can't *see* sanctification as it is, until we get the experience. We may see something we hunger for and pant after and wish we had, but our ideas of this sunny experience are crude and more or less false until "the eyes of our understanding are opened" by the blessing itself. We either set it too high or place it too low. It is either angelic or uncanny, when the truth is, it is neither.

The Holy Ghost is a gift. "That God may *give* unto you the Spirit." I am so glad it is a present and cannot be bought. Our struggles and tears and groans and night prayers and day fastings only bring us to a place after all where we receive a gift. They do not purchase it, do not count an iota so far as paying for it is concerned.

O, how vast is this gift! Four years ago at Old Douglas God gave me this gift; and I am astounded every day of my life at the inexhaustible character of it. When I least expect it I touch as if by accident some hidden spring, and a new receptacle is discovered. I unwrap bundles by the score, but the supply shows no sign of failing.

One object for which the Spirit comes is that we may know Jesus. Christ to the sanctified is far more precious and delightful than to the merely regenerate. We get to see his inner heart life when we are pure. To the disciples even he was for three years an enigma.

A Messiah, yes, but so odd, so strange. Pentecost reveals to us the real Christ. The word "knowledge" does not mean "knowledge about." It means "spiritual communion." It means "close communion." It means, Spiritual intimacy. In the office, on the street, in the exchange, among our books, there is ever by us a fragrant Being whom time does not change nor events fluctuate. What boots it if people grow chilly toward us? Supposing that reverses of the most painful kind do come? That fair Talisman is within, and we can smile right in the frowning visage of Hell.

The second knowledge is that of "the hope of his calling," God has called us unto holiness and the Baptism with the Holy Ghost causes us to know experimentally what the calling is. Men may doubt and pass resolutions and browbeat and gnash their teeth, but if we meet the conditions we will know purity. And a personal knowledge is the final, triumphant answer to all cavil; you can't down testimony. The blood of Jesus and holy, fire-touched testimony will throw the devil every time.

And when this blessing comes we will have a new appreciation of Christ's riches in the saints. We don't appreciate God's people. They are the salt of the earth. If they had not lived in the world it would have turned putrid and rotten and fell to pieces long ago. Hid under convention and etiquette and under-estimation and suspicious-looking circumstance, what stores of fidelity and cleanness and rightness and self-denial and Christlikeness there really are in God's children. The sanctified man sees this more than other people. He puts the best possible construction on everything. He attributes the spirit of love to many a deed which afterward proved a blunder. Rather than be suspicious he blindfolds his eyes to the pictures of dishonesty and unfairness which Satan throws upon the faces and lives of his brethren and seeks to make him believe are real. He will not lose faith until he is driven to it.

The last knowledge which the Apostle here emphasizes is that of "the exceeding greatness of God's power to usward who believe." He says that the power of Pentecost is the same kind of power that raised Christ and enthroned him beside the Father. This is the power we are to have. Whirlwinds, holocausts, tempests, earthquakes, death-beds, funeral tolling cannot disturb us if we get this power. It makes us masters. It causes us to rise above the paralysis of sin's clutch. It makes us rejoice in hours of blackness. It gives us perfect and eternal victory over "the world, the flesh and the devil." Amen.

Five or six souls found this blessed experience in the altar service. Thank God for the work of the Holy Ghost among the people.

WEDNESDAY, 2.30 P. M.

Every service marks new additions to our audiences. From all over New England they are coming. Every train brings reinforcements. Portsmouth was never before so large at this stage of the meeting as it is now. This hour was given up to testimony to-day. Brother Norberry is in charge, and in his delightful manner is interspersing the glad witnessing with equally glad songs. We cannot give much of the great volume of praise which ascended in a few minutes, but we will cull here and there.

Brother: I thank God that he has clearly sanctified me since I came upon the campground.

Mrs. Ballentine of North Attleboro: I wish to register. This is my first visit to this camp. I know by experience that the Holy Ghost can cleanse the heart and come in to abide.

Evangelist Hattie Livingstone of Colorado: I am so glad of the privilege of living in God. No longer does the world attract or annoy.

Harlan Ballentine: I praise the Lord for the consciousness that all is right between me and God.

Sister Shrader of Washington: "Ye shall receive power to witness." I want to witness to this blessed experience. God has sanctified me wholly.

Sister: I praise God I have a "know so" in my heart.

Sister Lilly Lewis of Westport: I am glad the Lord abides in my soul. He has come and sanctified me.

Sister Edith Trafford: I praise the Lord that I am saved, sanctified and satisfied.

Brother Norberry: "Let us close this meeting with the Yorkshire Doxology." This was sung with a will and was followed with a season of silent prayer.

3. P. M.

Rev. Seth C. Rees, President of the Association, preached from Hebrews 5: 14.

We have inspired authority for saying that the five physical senses are types of five spiritual senses, the gateways of the soul. In the spiritual babe these senses are present but undeveloped; in the "old babes," dwarfs, they are vitiated; but in the "man," they are exercised to know things with supernatural certainty. Men are willing to talk of perfection in anything else but salvation. We speak of perfect gentlemen, perfect ladies, perfect machines, a perfect flower, a perfect day, but when a word is said concerning perfection of heart, men lift their hands in holy horror.

I. Spiritual illumination is one result of the Baptism with the Holy Ghost. While other people see clouds, opposition and difficulty and dungeons and stakes, we see the glittering walls and burnished towers. The stoning Pharisees saw nothing unusual, but the dying Stephen looked straight up to heaven and saw Jesus standing. "You can't see sanctification," but that doesn't prove there is nothing in it. The Spirit-touched eye can see what other people cannot see. The fact that you cannot see the Premillenial Coming of our Lord does not by any means prove that it is not in the Word of God. You say you "don't see Divine Healing." Well I do, and so satisfactory is the view to me that all the sneers and jeers and taunts of doubters have not yet been able to beat me out of it. Hallelujah!

II. The Baptism with the Spirit gives us good spiritual hearing. Most of people are so dull of hearing that they do not recognize the voice of God when it comes. They think that "it thundered" or possibly "an angel spoke." If you are unsanctified, the chances are that you hear lots of things that are never said. You think the preacher said things he never dreamed of uttering. You are ever accusing others of things that were never said.

III. Sense of smell. When the Holy Ghost sanctifies you wholly you will not only scent the heavenly perfumes which sweep down from the skies, but you will smell brimstone and escape it. Talk about "moral accidents" and "sin taking us by surprise!" There is no need of smirching ourselves with soot before we know what it is. No, sir! The Spirit will make us like Jesus, keen of scent.

IV. Taste. Someone has said that "holiness was a matter of taste anyhow," and they said more truth than they supposed. God has so made the ox that he will pick the sweet grass here and ignore the poisonous weed there, and choose the luscious plant yonder, and surely God can give us discernment enough to avoid swallowing unwholesome sermons and venomous doctrine. Egyptians take to garlic, onions and leeks; wilderness people like manna and quails; but Canaan-dwellers enjoy "old corn."

V. Feeling is tabooed in many quarters, but "the kingdom of God is righteousness, peace and joy in the Holy Ghost" two-thirds feeling after all. Genuine faith will bring the evidence that the work is done in the heart.

People who do not get the experience of entire sanctification are unstable, children tossed about with every wind of doctrine. These people who are so easily disturbed by heterodoxy have not had their Pentecost. Be careful now. If you *claim* to be sanctified and some preacher, with scathing, skinning truth disturbs you, the place for you is at the altar. Come on! Come on!! And they *did* come and Heaven kissed Rhode Island in a marvelously deep and spiritual altar service.

WEDNESDAY, 7.30 P. M.

Bro. John Norberry preached from Hebrews 2: 1.

We cannot insert all the good things said by these men of God, and to-night for lack of space we will give only a few notes from the best.

We will be held responsible in the day of judgment for not only the things which we have heard, but also for what, in a land of churches and Bibles, we might have heard if we would.

Some folks are waiting for some irresistible force to pick them up and carry them to the altar, but you can't depend on feeling and you may go to hell without ever having the feeling you are anticipating. The Bible is so full of holiness that it has boiled over, and some of it has stuck on the cover (*Holy* Bible).

This was a sermon of great power, and many were clearly saved, among them nine or ten children. Praise the Lord.

THURSDAY, 10.30 A. M.

The heavy storm of the night is abating this morning. Inquiry shows that of the one hundred and eighteen, nearly every one was proof against the copious rain which fell in the darkness. Rain does not dampen the ardor of Portsmouth campers. We were not able to report this morning's service, but we learned that the

Lord very graciously poured out his Spirit and many souls sought releif from sin, either actual or original, in the "gifts of the Holy Ghost."

THURSDAY, 2.30 P. M.

This service was in charge of Bro. Norberry. After the instructive and spiritual sermon, the altar was filled with seeking souls. Hardened sinners melted and came to God. Souls were reclaimed and many sanctified. Thanks be to God.

THURSDAY, 7.30 P. M.

According to Bro. Norberry's afternoon suggestion the Christian children, especially those who have been saved, reclaimed or sanctified during this campmeeting, sit upon the platform. What a sight they are with their bright happy faces! And their child voices touched as by the finger of God float out on the evening air and fill the camp with their sweetness. Marvellous is the presence and power of God in this encampment. We have been going to holiness campmeetings for years but we have never been in a meeting like this. Surely God is in the place. Chronic cases are being cured, gospel-hardened sinners are being saved, the carnal-minded are being sanctified. Hallelujah! Remarkable cases are too numerous for individual attention. The fire has caught among the youth of the congregation. Frank Messenger, Bro. F. M. Messenger's son, has been blessedly sanctified. The hymns to-night seem to be bearing to the stars melodious praise to Christ for what he is doing in our midst. Even as in the old days in Galilee, he is stopping here and there, healing our sick. To him is the glory.

There, walking up the side isle, comes Dr. Carradine. How the faces gladden as the people catch sight of this man whom they have learned to love, both by his presence and his books. He is but little changed since we saw him a little over a year ago—a little grayer perhaps, the result of long conventions, and laborious campmeetings, arduous battles with little respite. Upon the platform we note Rev. Delia Rees of New York, now connected with "The King's Messenger."

Sister Phoebe Hall preached from the text, "Be not drunk with wine wherein is excess, but be filled with the Spirit."

This world is drunk. Alcohol is not the only intoxicant. Politics, pleasure, money, fashion, any or all of these may just as effectually intoxicate as liquor. As we saw all Washington recently staggering under the influence of political excitement, frenzied by the enthusiasm for an earthly candidate we said to ourselves, Why cannot we be just as enthusiastic for *our* candidate to whom we owe so much? Let us throw up our hats for Him! Let us elect him with an overwhelming majority!

Bro. Norberry took charge of the service at this stage leading off in exhortation and opening the altar for the coming of the seekers. Many came and God poured out His Spirit.

FRIDAY, 8.30 A. M.

The clouds are entirely dissipated and the blue Rhode Island sky is as serene as if no storm had ever marred its brightness. It is a delight to be in this clean hard-wood grove on a morning like this. The trembling leaves, the cool earth figured with light and shadow, the rows of white tents, the singing congregations, the ringing "Hallelujahs," all enhance the beauty of the spot. We are especially impressed with the character of the conversation upon the grounds. As we pass the little groups scattered here and there, the words which come to our ears are words of intense piety. Preachers are discussed but little. Sermons are received with love and attention and rarely subjected to that unhallowed criticism which so often wrecks the spirit of a meeting of this character. Bro.

Morse is upon the camp ground and cheers our hearts with his praises to God.

Sister Hattie Livingston, of Colorado, was in charge of the 8.30 a. m. meeting. She spoke for a little time upon "the gifts," and then turned the meeting over to testimony.

10.30 A. M.

After Deacon George Morse had led in prayer Rev. Huldah A. Rees preached from Num. 32:5.

"Bring us not over Jordan."

These are words of distrust and disbelief. God for many years had been telling Israel about "the land." He had described its harvests, its vineyards, its olive-yards. That they might dwell in Canaan he had subdued the enemy. Now at the very point of going over Reuben and Gad refused.

Jordan means "death," not physical, but the death of the "old man." We cannot receive the Holy Ghost unless we are willing to die. This campmeeting stands for a definite death to sin, selfishness, the "old man."

The reason for the action of these two tribes was that they were grazers and the country across Jordan was a grass country. Beloved, if you are not sanctified, the hitch is on your side—not on God's. If you seek him with all the heart, you will surely find him.

Let me call your attention to certain results which attend upon failure to go over Jordan. (1) The heart of the people is discouraged. (2) The ark of God, symbol of communion, passes from you. You cannot retain the communion with God which your soul needs unless you get sanctified. Many a minister should look here for the cause of his failure. (3) It leaves you without a place of prayer for your families. This sad fact ought to stir our parent hearts. The departure of the ark of God accounts for the fictitious literature in our libraries, the immodest pictures on our walls.

Beloved, we will have to walk in the light. We are not pressing Divine Healing on this camp ground, although we are accused of doing so, but we are pressing you to walk in the light. We cannot help but praise God that when facing eternity only a short time ago he said to us, "Thou shalt not die, but live, and declare the works of God."

This reference by Sister Rees to her recent marvellous healing brought tears to the eyes of the people as they thanked God for his power and willingness to heal the body.

(iv) Farther on in the history of Reuben we find that he did not go out against the enemy. He "abode among the sheep-folds." Deborah rebuked the lack of interest manifested by this tribe. These people were backslidden. The love of cattle had filled them. The thing you choose instead of holiness will become the passion of your life and will stifle the cry of dying souls in your ears.

(v) Reuben was taken into captivity. The devil got them. There is no safety but in utter surrender to God. Launch out this morning.

In the prayer service which followed, the fire fell and God bared his arm to cleanse and save.

FRIDAY, 2.30 P. M.

Dr. Carradine preached his first sermon at Portsmouth at this hour. The doctor selected for his text Job 1:8. We shall not attempt a full report of Dr. Carradine's sermons, for they are, as all know who have heard him, unreportable. We shall give, however, such parts of his messages as are especially choice, or, at least, seem so to us.

"Hast thou considered my servant Job, that there is none like him in the earth, a perfect and an upright man?"

There's that word "perfect," again. Oh, how that word used to meet me in my study! Paul said, "Let us go on unto perfection," and I wanted to go on to be Bishop.

We see perfection in nature and even in man's inventions and why can't God make a perfect heart?

Yes, but you say, "It is impossible, because God is dealing with spirit-nature which, though created by him, has been given the power to defy him." But suppose by entire consecration that spirit nature submits itself to God: then God can mould the consecrated soul to his will.

We are not talking of angelic perfection. We are never to be angels. I don't want to be an angel. I'd rather have skin than feathers any day. If you "want to be an angel and with the angels stand," you want to stand one step lower down than I do, for God plans for redeemed humanity a position *above* angels.

Neither are we referring to a perfection of the body. Paul says he has "not yet attained" to that. We have weariness and pain here. In the resurrection body the death principle will not be present; but while yet in this body we may have perfect hearts.

In the altar service several souls received the blessing for which they sought.

FRIDAY, 7.30 P. M.

As we glance over the platform this evening we are glad to see Dr. Edgar M. Levy of Philadelphia, Rev. I. T. Johnson of Douglas, Mass., Rev. Mr. Penny of Barbadoes, W. I., Rev. Mr. Gosline of Adamsville, Rev. Mr. Graham of Westport Head, and Evangelist Ingersoll of Stamford.

Rev. John Norberry preached from Luke 13: 5. "Except ye repent ye shall all likewise perish."

The word on this important theme of repentance was pungent and powerful. As Dr. Levy prayed in the opening prayer, the Spirit was poured out in conviction and the altar was speedily filled with sobbing penitents. We have not space to tell how the clouds of condemnation cleared and the sunlight of grace poured down, nor how quickly the blood showed itself effectual in cleansing the believer's heart, nor how marvellous was the work of the Spirit in quieting and subduing the sinners, but God is keeping account of all in his great book and some day the angels will read to us blessed annals of this mighty campaign. Hallelujah!

SATURDAY, 8.30 A. M.

The meeting began this morning with the enthusiastic singing of some of the blessed hymns which have been the battle-crys in many a spiritual triumph. Sister Shrader sang, "I feel the fire burning" with great liberty and power. In the season of waiting upon God which followed a great many prayers were offered. Brother Rees, who was leading the meeting, then asked that the strangers and those of God's children who had not had opportunity to speak, should take a little time. Brother Penny, who has been laboring for some years in the West Indies and South America, was introduced. He spoke at some length of his work for God in Martinique. He baptized the first convert ever baptized in the Orinoco River. He contrasted the self denial of the converts in foreign lands with that of professed Christians in America. "We find that when we have real revivals the devil is stirred. We find that the same Satan hates God and his work in other countries as in this. Real piety rouses antagonism. The popular church with its popular preacher does not stand for the real old-fashioned gospel. 'The gospel of the Kingdom must be preached to all nations for a witness.' Will you go if *he says so*?" (Brother Rees and others, "Amen.") The people seemed to heartily endorse Brother Penny's talk. Surely there should be an increase of the missionary interest amongst us.

Bro. Rees: Beloved, the true Baptism with the Holy Ghost inspires the heart with a love for God's work in foreign lands. And, thank God, we are proving it in this campmeeting. Last year Sister Minnie (Lindberg) went to East Africa from this camp ground.

Singing 203.

'Tis a glorious liberty
Oh! the wondrous story,
I was bound but now I'm free
Glory! Glory! Glory!

10.30 A. M.

Sister Huldah A. Rees led in prayer. In her prayer she made especial mention of Dr. Levy. And as she prayed we thought of how much it ought and does fill our hearts with gladness that this holy man of God is at Portsmouth. Dr. Levy has stood for holiness for twenty-six years. In appearance the doctor is of average height, robust build, smooth faced, white-haired, —a singularly clean looking man, a true exponent of holiness both by life and precept.

Dr. Levy: I want to be very simple this morning. I want, if I can, to be of comfort and help to some of God's children. I will begin by telling you a dream which I had some time ago. I do not as a rule place much importance upon dreams. They are many times due to irregularities of the physical system, but if we can get any good out of a dream, let us use it. I dreamed I was in heaven. Angels waited upon us as we sat at a great table. I asked who a certain venerable, gray-bearded man was whom I saw. An angel replied that he was Abraham.

"And who is that woman whose beauty I never saw equalled on earth?"

"That is Mary, the mother of Jesus."

"And who is that upon Jesus breast?"

"That is John, but there is room for you there as well."

"Why," I said, "this is glorious. And when shall this come to an end?"

"This will last forever and ever and ever!" (Cries of "Praise the Lord!")

Christ is going to have the majority. The infants who die are saved and they are half the world's population. Surely more will be saved than lost.

Dr. Hamilton, that golden-mouthed orator of England, who recently passed to heaven has said that for many years one nation furnished the great mass of the saved, but now the middle wall of partition has been broken down and men of all peoples and tongues and from all parts of earth swell the number of the redeemed.

And from all centuries the saints come trooping up to glory. I believe we will see Adam and Enoch and David and the Magdalene. They were sinful once. They were black and vile, but now in the blood of Jesus they have cleansed, they have washed their robes.

This company will *sit down*. Some of you see but little time for sitting down, you are so busy in your shops or in your homes. But there will be at that day an eternal unbroken Sabbath of rest. Not the rest of indolence, but a rest unmarred and undisturbed.

There will be a feast to sit down to. There will be a feast for the intellect. There will be a feast for all our faculties. "Then shall I see and hear and know,

All that I have wished below," says old Watts in one of his hymns. We will see our loved ones and the shadow of separation will never trouble us. Now, even in our marriage ceremonies, we must bear with the fatal clause, "Until death shall separate us," but then there will be no end to our happiness.

This feast denotes familiarity and friendship. Friends only are invited to feasts. Enemies are not asked to feast together. And we shall know each other. What would be the sense in Christ saying that we should sit down with Abraham, Isaac and Jacob if we are not to know them? We will hear Adam tell of Eden. And we will listen to Methuselah tell his experience of a thousand years and no one will say, "Brother Methuselah, be short. Don't take too much time." Oh, to see Daniel and listen to his tale of the lions! But best of all we will see Jesus. How we will listen to the voice that once fell on human ears in Galilee! How we will drink in the light of his eyes!

One question. Will you be there? ("Yes." "Hallelujah." "By the grace of God, I will.") The only matter that ought to concern you now is the fitness for entering. Get clean, get pure, rush forward and let the blood cleanse you. Amen.

Brother Norberry now took charge of the altar service.

SATURDAY 3 P. M.

Although the storm which has been gathering, black and terrible, in the southwest, has doubtless frightened away a considerable number, yet a large and happy audience is waiting for Brother Carradine to preach. Storms do not disturb Portsmouth people—not at all. Judged by the shining faces and hearty shouts of holy triumph, one would not think there was storm within a thousand miles. Brother Norberry led in prayer. Just before Dr. Carradine arose, the offering was taken. Portsmouth abhors begging for money and it is never necessary. As Brother Rees says, "The Lord loveth a *hilarious* giver" and the people invariably give liberally for the support of the gospel.

Singing: "I have found it."

Dr. Carradine: Isaiah 35: 8, 10.

A very marvelous experience. I used to think it was a description of heaven, but as you see they are on the way to heaven. It is a wonderful experience that God gives us in which we have no sorrow or sighing. A little child that used to say to its mother, "Mamma, what makes you sigh so?" changed its question when the mother was sanctified and said, "Mamma, what makes you laugh so?"

Isaiah, the St. John of the Old Testament, knew about the blessing and he describes it in these verses. We do not minify the grace of regeneration. They don't come to hear us who say we minify regeneration. No, sir, it is a "highway." Isaiah said so. It is a marvellous work which will wash away the sins of a life time. Regeneration does that. But I have a message. God has sent me out to speak of a neglected doctrine, and yet I do not belittle justification.

When a men repents we all know it. A man who repents quits sin. Repentance is so great that though it isn't salvation yet the angels rejoice. It is a great step. Faith is a big step. You ask a man at the altar to believe and you'll see it is a big step. It is so big that God always blesses a man who believes. A man who repents and believes is on a high-way.

But Isaiah is talking about a *way*. There is the highway of regeneration and the way of holiness. "It" refers to the "way." What! two roads to heaven? Yes, one inside the other. A man in N. Y. rode about through the city quite a while on the surface cars, but suddenly he heard a rush and a roar overhead, and he looked up and found he could go up about forty feet and drop a nickel in a box, and ride more swiftly, with better air, a broader outlook, and be nearer the skies. I used to ride on the car of justification, but I heard a rush and a roar and, lo! it was a holiness meeting. Now the outlook is broader, the air is purer, and I am nearer heaven. I am on the elevated.

The news of this "way," is out. It has escaped the

confines of ecclesiastical councils. The report is being scattered. The demand for holiness and holiness literature, and holiness preachers is increasing. I have a quiet sense of victory concerning this movement. Isaiah says some comforting things about it. Isaiah says it is in the highway. He also shows that it is hidden. You can't see it at a great distance. The man on the highway will see the way if his attention is called to it. Why, it is hidden in the text. I read this text fourteen years before I found it said *"and a way."* And then it is a hidden *experience* in a sense. Preachers admit that they are the best people, these sanctified folks, but "a little off." Two preachers whispering in the pulpit. "I call on them to pray every time but they are not quite all there."

The more precious a thing is the more God hides it. God don't hide brick-bats and cobble-stones. He hides gems and diamonds. Conviction is patent to all. Anyone can understand it; but holiness, what a mystery it is to the masses!

Now, I notice that God hides this blessing from the very people that you hide things from. You hide your heart secrets from careless people. And God hides this great grace from careless people and careless talkers. When a man says, "What do you think of this here sanctification?" he isn't in a thousand miles of holiness. When a preacher goes to the altar and kneels on one knee, or when a woman sets back and fans and wiggles her ear-bobs, he or she is not in a long way of the blessing.

You don't tell your secrets to the unbelieving. And you don't gain anything by doubting God. Sanctification is the secret of the Lord, and God's got to tell it to us for no one else can, and if you doubt God you lock him up. The man that believes, knows most about God. God can't keep secrets from men who trust him and believe in him.

And I notice that God hides this from the wise and prudent; Jesus himself said so. A revelation must be revealed. You can't find out God by searching. We say to these wise people, "You will have to throw away your scientific opposition and begin to pray and believe."

You and I can have a blessing that these big men and these college presidents and these bishops haven't been able to get with all their knowledge. God wants to cut off all our heads to the collar buttons. They say that "faithful exegesis" (which so often means "exit-Jesus") "doesn't teach this blessing." But if we humble ourselves and seek we will find it.

The men of Sodom couldn't find the door of Lot's house because they didn't seek in the right spirit, and the big heads now-a-days are bungling and blundering and saying, "There aint no door here." "Why, yes there is! and I am looking over the transom at you now."

Yes, and it is hidden from the prudent. The preacher who claims to be following a man who had no reputation, and taking care of his reputation will never get the blessing on that line. Moses identified himself with the Hebrew crowd and ignored what he might have had.

And God says a fool can have it. A man with a cracked-brain, or a man with a teaspoonful of brains, he can have it. And I have seen a man with a quart ful of brains make fun of the man with the teaspoonful, while the former was miserable and the latter gloriously happy. That man that speaks in one language and breathes in another, and sneezes in a third, he can't have the blessing if he doesn't go down and be humble.

People have an idea that periodic washing is the best thing possible. Bless your heart! Your eye-ball is kept clean all the time, and can't God keep the heart clean all the time?

No lions there. Doesn't say that there *are* no lions, but no lions *there*. You may feel their breath, but you won't feel their teeth or their claws.

It is a joyful way, and the joy is everlasting. For seven years I have had a bird twittering in my breast. I have several children. When some days they are still for a bit, I am not frightened. I have some spiritual children. There names are Hallelujah, Bless the Lord, Praise the Lord, Hosanna, and Glory. And if I find I havn't heard from my spiritual children for some time, I call up the staircase, "Hallelujah!" and here they come, the whole troop; and, Oh, what capers! When we think of what God has done for us, we ought to wake up all the children.

This blessing is "obtained." I tried for years to "attain," but it is *obtained*. We can't attain. God gives it to us. You say you want it. Well, there are only two steps, consecration and faith. Come and meet the conditions, and the one that wants it worst, you get here first. And the hungry seekers filed out of the pews and down the aisles to the altar. Bro. Carradine with infinite skill and tact, usually talks with each seeker, getting him to pray and trust in the Lord. To-day a large number came into the light with that ease and rapidity which inevitably marks the presence of great spiritual power.

SATURDAY, JULY 31, 7.30 P. M.

The usual influx of people on Saturday evening has enlarged the audience very perceptibly. Bro. Rees has the young converts sitting upon the platform. And what a choir there is of them! Thank God for a holiness campmeeting where sinners are converted by the score.

What a vast number of places are represented here to-night. Glancing over the sea of faces we see people from New York, Philadelphia, Brooklyn, Providence, Washington, Baltimore, Boston, New Bedford, Fair Haven, Stamford, Wakefield. The places are almost innumerable. Surely the salt of earth is gathered to swell the white robed, conquering, fire-baptized throng at Portsmouth campmeeting.

One thing characteristic of Portsmouth is the vast number of its visitors who have never attended a camp meeting before. They are for the most part comparatively recently sanctified. Many Douglas people, many Rock people, and other holiness workers are of course here, but the mass of the campers never go elsewhere than Portsmouth.

While we have been writing, the spiritual tide has steadily risen and now what a sight! Is a similar one ever seen in a meeting other than a *holiness* meeting? Who can describe the holy enthusiasm, the spiritual rapture, the "Solar light" playing on the upturned faces, the waving handkerchiefs, the uplifted hands! Surely the Pentecostal Spirit has fallen upon us. Praise the Lord!

The collection is being taken now. "We do not sing while we take the offering" said Bro. Rees. "We consider this an act of worship and therefore do not confuse it with anything else."

Rev. Phoebe L. Hall: We were so inspired and helped by the word of the Lord through Dr. Carradine this afternoon that surely we are all in love with the elevated "way of holiness." But Isaiah teaches us the same truth by another figure. "For there the glorious Lord shall be unto us a place of broad rivers." It is hard for me to get by the word "glorious;" it is so rich, so replete with beauty and blessedness! This text brings to my mind an adventure of my childhood which my brother and myself passed through. We were trying to cross a lake in Michigan. The boat was leaky and I was detailed to bail while my brother with a cumbersome rail tried to row the craft. That, it seems to me was a "galley with oars." But God says in my text that "thereon shall go no galley with oars." "Nor any gallant ship." Jonah was in a gallant ship. The disciples on the Sea of Galilee. Paul on the Mediterranean, these were in "gallant ships," but the experience of the text is something far higher than this. John saw this experience. He saw the sea of glass. He saw upon it the holy company with the palms and the golden harps. These harps I imagine correspond to the "Hallelujah children" which Dr. Carradine told us about this afternoon.

At one time I visited the State Prison in the city of Richmond, Va. I saw sights there which broke my heart, and I said then, "I will give my whole being for the salvation of souls." As I saw the sin and misery which the prisoners were in, I saw the resemblance to the human family's condition under bondage to evil. As we plead with souls we find that "Satan hath bound" them, that the fetters of depravity are upon their limbs. This world is a seething caldron of broken hearts, bruised souls and disappointed hopes, and I pray God for a sympathetic spirit to cry out for souls and work for them and, if need be, to die for them.

After I had been saved for some time, I found certain things in my heart which troubled me. I was often astounded at a dearth of joy, at my coldness in prayer, my timidity in testimony. The "old man" was present. This was the "old man" which Paul said we must "put off." I find many people who want to set me right. They are sure I am deluded. But, Praise the Lord, it is possible for the Lord Jesus to kill the "old man" by the baptism with the Holy Ghost. I was on a train at one time when we suddenly halted. I looked out and saw the conductor putting an intoxicated man off the train. I said to myself, "God has stopped my train and taken off all disturbing elements."

It is not God's thought that the finishing touch to our purity shall be accomplished in heaven. God's time is "now." Write it down, John, and say to the church that "it is granted to her now to be arrayed in white linen." Glory be to God! Our robes are on. We are betrothed to the Bridegroom, and we are waiting for the wedding. You may have these white garments to-night.

Some time ago a man came to me to ask that I join with him in prayer that he might get access to the President for a few minutes. He told me in the course of the conversation that he knew a man who had traveled five times from Cleveland, Ohio, to Washington, for a five minutes' conversation with Mr. McKinley and even then had been denied. But our Christ is not so. If we have any desire to speak to him he is accessible to every one. Will you come to him now? Amen.

Brother Norberry, singing:

> "And when I was willing with all things to part
> He gave me my bounty, his love in my heart.
> For the Lion of Judah can break every chain,
> And give us the victory again and again."

Brother Norberry had the audience repeat the chorus a number of times. Then the converts on the platform, standing and with uplifted hands, sang, "I believe Jesus saves and his blood washes whiter than snow." And while they sang the seekers came to the altar. The revival spirit is manifest. The sanctified stand about the altar and with the tears streaming down their faces sing their faith in Jesus' blood, while the hungry hearts come streaming down the aisle to the front, where Jesus saves and cleanses.

SUNDAY, AUG. 1, 6 A. M.

This early morning service is in charge of Rev. I. T. Johnson of Douglas, Mass. The spirit of prayer is upon the people and the air is charged with faith for a wonderful day in the Lord. The people are out in force this morning. It is by far the largest sunrise meeting since the camp opened. Bro. Johnson read a portion of Scripture and in his happy style delighted the audience with a short exposition. The meeting closed with shouts of victory.

SUNDAY, AUG. 1, 8.30 A. M.

This praise and testimony meeting is filled with a tide of joy. The hallowed songs float out upon the still Sabbath air like tunes from heaven. The Tabernacle by a providential arrangement of ledge is high enough to cause the sound of holy hymns and sanctified preaching to go out for miles around. Elder Mix of Newport, a blessedly saved colored preacher, led in prayer. Thank God that he makes no distinction as to race or color in the bestowment of his great grace.

Singing "Lo! he comes, Lo! Jesus comes."

"Yes, thank God," said Bro. Rees, "he has come in my heart and he is coming again to this earth even as he went away."

One thing is noticeable at Portsmouth. The professed holiness people do not squirm and frown and fidget when the Second Coming of our Lord is mentioned. That narrow, pusillanimous counterfeit of holiness which has nothing to do but turn away from fighting sin, and slur Divine Healing and the *parousia* of Jesus, has no place at Portsmouth.

The meeting was turned into a love feast, Bro. Rees insisting that many should speak, especially those who had recently been saved or sanctified.

Sister: When I came upon the camp ground I was unsanctified. I have been a Christian for many years, but God has now cleansed my heart from all sin. Praise His Name!

Bro. Crandall: I thank God for the definite work of God in my heart. He has saved me fully and sanctified me entirely.

Sister S. F. Paul. I haven't words to express myself this morning. God is saving and keeping me.

Bro. Lamond: God has given me perfect love and filled me with the Holy Ghost.

Bro. De Moranville, of New Bedford: The dear Lord has given me this great blessing. I feel like singing

"Oh! glory to God, the Savior has come,
He has come in my heart and made it his home."

Sister (recently sanctified): I can say in the strength of my Savior's promise, "The blood of Jesus Christ his son cleanseth me from all sin."

Sister Hallett of Nantucket: I have seen Jesus and he hath spoken unto me.

Rev. M. D. Jewelson, Baltimore, Md.: I sought to be sanctified for six years in my way and did not succeed; but when I said, I will seek in God's way, I got the blessing.

Frank Messenger. I praise God he has saved and sanctified me.

Young Boy: I can stand on my feet and say that God has saved and sanctified me too.

Sister: God has satisfied my heart; he has given me full salvation.

Presiding Elder Hill: Refining fire goes through my heart and sanctifies the whole.

Aged Brother: When I came on the camp ground I was unsaved. I got mad. I was going home, but I couldn't get away, and now God has gloriously saved me. Thank God for Portsmouth camp meeting.

Bro. Annis of Brockton: I have been through fires of affliction, but this blessing stands me in good stead. He keeps me sweet in everything.

Mrs. I. T. Johnson: My whole being praises the Lord this morning. I have an experience that I cannot express, but it is blessedly real.

Sister Amanda Chase: I do praise the Lord for what he has done and is doing for me.

HALLELUJAHS FROM PORTSMOUTH. 79

Y. M. C. A. worker: Entirely sanctified by the blood of our Lord Jesus Christ.

Bro. Mix: I praise God for the blessed truth I have heard since I came to this meeting.

Mrs. F. M. Messenger: My soul cries, "Glory to God!" I came here weak in body, but he has strengthened me both physically and spiritually. Bless the Lord!

Miss Julia Ellis: I feel the assurance that I am dead to sin. God has killed the "old man." I do praise the Lord for this.

Sister: Glory to God! You must bear with me if I am a little noisy. God has done so much for me that I can't keep quiet. Jesus has saved my husband and filled our home with salvation.

Bro. Wordell of Smith's Mills: I want to praise God for the work of God in me. I have it in my heart. Bless God!

Bro. Bercander of Providence: I praise God. He has cleansed me from all sin.

Bro. Wallace: I am under the blood. Jesus keeps me.

Brother: I was a drunkard seventeen years, but God has saved me.

Sister Cunningham: That's my boy! I prayed for him for many years, and, glory to God, he has answered my prayers.

Singing: "Then I'll trust him, fully trust him."

SUNDAY, 10.30 A. M.

After a few moments of silent prayer Bro. Rees voiced the desires of the people in an unctuous vocal petition. By this time one of our large Sunday morning congregations had assembled. Rows upon rows of people with a holy look upon their faces, very evidently born in heaven, sat and sung the praises of Jehovah. Brother Rees in his announcements made the statement that at least fifty souls have been either saved or reclaimed during the first week of this camp Praise be unto God!

Dr. Carradine preached another of his heaven-sanctioned sermons this morning: I came upon the platform with four texts struggling in my heart, but the Lord wants me to speak on this one and I always obey him: Acts 1: 8. So far as I can see everyone is after power. In the society realm, in the political ring, in the Christian circle, we all know when a man gets power. Regeneration is not power; it is life, but not power. Churches make the mistake in thinking that the disciples were unconverted before Pentecost, but Jesus said that they were "not of the world," they cast out devils, their "names were written in heaven." They were saved, but they were to tarry until the power came, and when it came they did more in a day than they had accomplished in years before.

There are two ways of saving this world, God's

way and the churches' way. The short way and the long way. God's way is to wait at Jerusalem until the power comes. The churches' way is "Go for sinners, go for sinners!" But the seemingly long way is the short way after all. If you get this power you will do more in a minute than you did before in a year.

I suppose the disciples were jeered at for seeking this power. People are now. But the result proved the wisdom of their course. We are ridiculed for holding meetings like this. "Look at them up there. Mutual admiration society. Telling each other how good they are. If you want more religion come down and work with us and go for sinners." "Yes, but we are not ready for sinners. We are saved but can't save anyone else."

When you get this blessing people will know it. Oh! there is a big difference between the sound of hitting two bones together in a pulpit and hitting two tenderloins. When tenderloins go together the gravy flies! Samson could shake himself, but could shake no one else. The congregation knows it when the preacher is unsanctified. This blessing is for the laity as well as the preachers. Peter told the people so on the day of Pentecost. Even the daughters will prophesy, Joel said so. Which is the better, for ten jaded preachers to strike a town Monday morning, or ten congregations to hit the city with an irresistible force?

This blessing is not something that will make you popular. Jesus was not popular until hundreds of years after he was dead. The church that will kick a holiness man out of a church, would kick Christ out if he were here. If you get this blessing you'll miss many a tea-drinking they used to give us preachers, but you'll have a private luncheon inside. I appeal to this crowd, this holiness crowd, if we aren't having a better time than the folks who are laughing at us.

You will be interviewed when you get this blessing; you will be antagonized. If you say you are sanctified, they will say, "It reflects on the brethren." The Presiding-Elder will write to you; the Bishop will say he "is praying for you that your eyes may be opened."

They say that we are going to split the church. Its because they are afraid for us to see something wrong.

"Let her split," says Sam Jones, "I always did want to see what's inside." Why! these people who dish oysters and serve strawberries and claim to be such profound church people, never read the standards of our church—they think we are talking about Fairbank's Standard Scales.

They say you are "going to the lunatic asylum." Well, aren't you glad you got the blessing before you go? "Your prospects will be ruined." What right have I, a follower of Jesus, to expect anything but a hard time? I have no right to *have* any prospects but those of reproach and persecution and death itself.

They will commiserate and yet envy you. They wish they had your experience, but not your theory. They see something that they want, but are repulsed by the forbidding conditions of its obtainment. We haven't got the nabobs, but we've got the ark. I know we're a rough looking crowd, but we've got the ark. They will envy us at death. I mean to die exhorting from my pillow, with seekers for pardon on one side, for purity on the other, and backsliders coming home to God at the footboard. They will envy you when you are crowned.

This blessing brings self-control. Look at the impulsive, sharp-tongued Peter. See how fearful he was. Frightened because a woman got mad at him!. But when he got this blessing, he was so brave that though he supposed he was to die the next day, he slept so soundly that an angel had to hit him three times to wake him up.

If you get this evil thing in your heart out of you, you will find it easy to control your body. Not that the lawful appetites are destroyed, but sanctified and kept under rightful authority. It becomes a luxury to live for God.

Witnessing is connected with sanctification. A sanctified man has dynamic power to throw his experience into mid air where folks can see it. You don't have to beg Vesuvius to tell her experience. Bless you, a man with a volcano in him doesn't consider testimony "taking up a cross."

This grace will enable us to stand. Many a preacher is in bondage to the Colonel and the Major and the Doctor. If they are not in favor of a thing he lets it drop. But if he gets this blessing he will *stand*. It will enable him to stand under all circumstances. I have seen a hundred men turn white at the roar of one man. Look at Peter. He was preaching and the Sanhedrim roared at him and the next day he got up and said, "As I was saying yesterday morning." There is a blessing that will deliver us from all fear. Hallelujah! You and I can't afford to trade off this blessing for the fear of a man who will die and the worms will eat.

This blessing enables us to win and woo and save souls. What are we good for anyway if we cannot save souls? No kind of substitute will go in the Judgment if we don't get folks *saved*. But Lord, we have the highest spire in town. We have the biggest organ and the finest choir. "Yes," says Jesus, "but where are the souls?" Oh! the souls, they are lost.

This blessing will make you suffer well. It will help us die well. Oh! this is God's grace for us this morning. Who will take it now?

Amen.

During the precious altar service which followed, Bro. Carradine sang his new hymn, "The Wanderer." Never has he sung this hymn but someone has been saved during the singing of it. Both words and music are Dr. Carradine's.

SUNDAY, 1.15 P. M.

The throngs which move about the grounds suddenly disappear within the tents as the bell strikes for closet prayer. Silence creeps over the entire area of the camp ground. Hundreds of people are in close communion with God. The air seems heavy with the subtle nameless perfume of prayer. Thank God for this institution of closet prayer! Now and then the silence is broken with a glad, "Hallelujah!" or a joyful, "Bless the Lord!" Never does that old thread-bare phrase so common with some Christians, "Perceptibly and feelingly near," seem so true of God as during one of the silent prayer services at 1.15 p. m.

SUNDAY, 1.30 P. M.

The people seem unwearied though this is the fourth meeting to-day; for they are here and singing with energy. They are here in crowds and look as if fresh enough for twenty-four hours more of meetings without a respite.

Bro. Jewelson led us in prayer.

Bro. Rees: This meeting is the same meeting as that of this morning. Let us go on with the testimonies.

Mahlon Chase of Swansea: I praise God for the privilege of witnessing for Jesus. He saves and sanctifies me.

Mrs. Lily Lewis: I want to thank God for what he has done for me. He has saved and sanctified me.

Bro. Brooks, of Fall River: I can say I am a child of God.

Thomas Lewis: I have not been on the way so long as most of you, but I find it joyful and blessed. Praise the Lord!

Herbert Skinner: I praise God for salvation. He does great things for me.

Bro. Gardiner: The Holy Ghost is giving me my education. Glory be to God!

Isaac Fish: That sermon put me under conviction. I am determined to go out farther than ever before.

Sister Phetteplace: God has a sample-room at Portsmouth. There are sample saints here, and I am rejoiced to mingle with them.

Bro. Chapman: I am glad this afternoon that God has made me more than conqueror.

Sister Chapman: I am saved, sanctified and kept this afternoon.

Lemuel Chase: Since the first campmeeting held here, God has kept me sanctified.

Bro. Kenney: Two years ago I was converted in a tent. God has been keeping me ever since.

Singing "Is not this the land of Beulah?"

Mrs. Clara Trafford, of Westport: I thank God for victory all along the way.

Singing "I'll go every step of the way."

Sister : I thank God for sanctification.

Lela Lewis: The Lord has saved and sanctified me wholly.

Brother : The Lord has given me a very good thing —it is a clean heart.

Singing "There is joy in my soul."

SUNDAY, 3 P. M.

Rev. John Norberry, Matthew 5: 20.

The Bible reveals to us two kinds of righteousness: that of works and that of faith. One is our righteousness, and the other is God's. The righteousness of the Pharisees is better than the righteousness of the moralist. One thanks God for its being, the other thanks itself. The Pharisees were careful as to with whom they associated. They would not mix up with sinners. In that, they were better than the modern church-member, who instead of going to prayer meeting goes to the store and sits about the stove and spits tobacco-juice, and either tells or listens to smutty stories; and when he goes to church, he can't pray and wonders why. Why! You miserable hypocrite, you sinner, of course you can't pray. You "don't believe in holiness." How could you believe in holiness? A Pharisee wouldn't do that, and except your righteousness exceed that of the Pharisee, you will be lost.

I notice that the Pharisee observed the Sabbath; and some of you church-members do not do that. These Pharisees wouldn't talk business on Sunday. And you! Service is scarcely over before you get out on the stoop and talk potatoes, and horses, and calves, and cattle. My dear man, you are a hypocrite! Oh! You forgot the coffee or the rice, and so you have to go to the store and get it on Sunday. A Pharisee wouldn't do that. And God says that our righteousness must exceed that of the Pharisees if we are to be saved.

If you get converted my brother, you will talk just as loud in meeting as you scold your children at home. The Pharisees held out-door meetings. They stood at the corners and prayed. And you, hypocrites, won't do that. If you carry a Bible, you hide it under your shawl. Bless you, you mean sneak, you wouldn't have some folks know you were at this campmeeting for the world. The Pharisees gave much alms. But you haven't given a cent of money to spread holiness in the last ten years. And God says that our righteousness must exceed the righteousness of the Pharisees. The Pharisees gave tithes. You don't do that, and your righteousness falls short of that of the Pharisees.

Many a man who supposes he is all right will be lost. In the day of wrath, some will plead that they were "superintendents of Sunday schools" or "preacher" or "workers," but Christ will say "I never knew you." "I never knew you." God help us!

The word was sharp and effective and many, many stood up as candidates for conversion or reclamation or sanctification. The careless were held as if spellbound. There was no levity, though the crowd was great. The altar service was blessed and fruitful in lightening dark lives and dark hearts. Blessed be the Lord!

Bro. Norberry rightly divides the word of truth. He prays much over his messages and there is always a Divine appropriateness in what he says. His tender messages feed and strengthen and encourage the saints, while his portraiture of law and guilt strikes the sinner with terror.

SUNDAY, 6.30 P. M.

The praise service opened this evening with a burst of glory. The hymn, "'Tis a glorious church without spot or wrinkle," never fails to stir a holy heart to the depths and to-night it seems to have a special fitness in the mouths of God's people. The sort of Christians who assemble in this holy mount for spiritual convocation recognize a fire-touched song when they hear it, and if the writer is in the Holy Ghost the hymn invariably meets with the heartiest appreciation.

What a sea of faces. Available room is occupied and the tiers of faces reach from the platform far, far out beyond the edge of the auditorium. Here is the young convert, joyous in the blessed novelty of salvation. There is a patriarchal looking saint, against whose brow has beat the surges of seventy years, but there is nothing but hope and joy and calmness there. A sanctified sailor is singing over by the pillar; a railroad engineer, with a face shining like the headlight of his locomotive, is waving his hand yonder near the center aisle; a young collegian is shouting not far from him; a fisherman is sitting with the tears streaming down his face a little distance from the piano, while a happy colored brother is beating his tambourine with a will. And yet the order is perfect and there is no discord. Like the day of Pentecost, these days are marked by spiritual intoxication yet spiritual unity. "That they all may be one."

SUNDAY, 7.30 P. M.

Dr. Levy led in prayer.

Dr. Carradine preaches again to-night. Reader, have you ever met this man of God? In appearance he is of rather slight build, a little haggard in the face, grey moustached, keen eyed and gray haired. In repose on the platform, he is a Southern gentleman, rather listless, hands in pockets, legs crossed. Preaching, he is a flame of fire, a hurricane of power, a cyclone of energy and force. God is with him. Foremost in popularity among the holiness brethren, he is humble as a child and approachable as a new convert. He strikes one as a man who would gladly burn to ashes on the altar of service for his Master.

Text, Prov. 29:1. When a verse like that is read a man with any sense at all ought to ask several questions. First, "Is that God's word?" Yes. It is. "Is that a correct translation?" Yes, sir, it has never been disputed. And the third question is, "Have I been often reproved?" If you have, you ought to get your grave clothes ready, for as sure as the truth you will suddenly be cut off.

God's laws always have a penalty. State laws have a penalty, and God's much more. The crime increases in gravity in proportion to the dignity of the one sinned against. Someone has got to die if God's law is broken, and Jesus came down and died on account of that law. In the atonement we see God's mercy, but there is a time when mercy becomes weakness, and justice must come to the front. God has a government to defend.

This is such a dreadful thing that is to come, that we ought to give heed as to who it is that is to suffer it. "Often reproved." That takes in a big lot.

You may depend on it, hell will be a ghastly place, a place of wailing and sighing, and biting of tongues. There is no silence there, and there is no love there, and men will hate each other there who loved each other on earth. And yet no man can say that he was not reproved before he got there.

God is so anxious to save us. He makes it hard for us to go to hell. He has even put a voice inside us which for a better name we call, "Conscience." It is this that makes a man feel miserable when he commits sin, and like heaven when he does right.

God's made his ministers and built his churches to reprove men. God reproves us through nature. The very cloud says, "I go wherever the breath of God blows me; and you, a man, made in the image of God, rebel against him!" The very waves of the sea condemn you. The Holy Ghost takes the sound of a bell, the cry of a bird, the stars, the Bible, and reproves men with them.

The Holy Ghost is sent to this world to reprove the

world. He loves us and is so faithful that he lightens every man that is born. He is ever rebuking, ever convicting. "Yes, but I pay my honest debts." How about your dishonest debts? The Holy Spirit convicts of righteousness, condemns your own righteousness, which is as "filthy rags." He reproves by convicting of judgment. What makes you afraid to die? Nothing in the world but the conviction of the Spirit, which makes you sure of the judgment of God.

"Harden the heart." What does that mean? It means that you fail to discharge any given duty. It means that you, a free moral agent, are rebelling against what you know you ought to do. God entreats a free being. He cannot force it. It is free. He can't damn him if he isn't free; he can't put him in heaven if he isn't free; but he is free, and God deals with him as with a sovereign. I tell you, it is no little thing to knock off God's touch. I say that it is an awful thing to slight the impression of the Holy Ghost.

Do you know what agencies God uses to save the world? I didn't see it for years. It is "by the foolishness of preaching;" not foolish preaching, but "by the foolishness of preaching," that God has chosen to "save them that believe." What if you are congratulating yourself that the preaching of the gospel don't move you? It is as if you hugged death to your bosom and kissed the green, frothy lip of destruction. You are laughing at the only thing that can possibly help you. You are shaking off the only rope that can lift you to heaven. You are throwing away the only remedy.

Oh! brother, you are kindling your own hell-fire. You are selling an eternal heaven for a little gratification of the body. People do not like to hear of this, because they love something dirty, something vile.

And then people don't want to hear of this because the revelation of the heart's condition is painful. A man in a dungeon who is in the dark together with vampires a-hanging by their heels, and hissing snakes, and reptiles, and venomous serpents, and who cannot bear the light which is necessary to his deliverance, is a fool.

God gives every man a chance until he sees how he is going to act. We are all under God's protection until God sees there is no hope. Philip Doddridge saw that in his dream. The arm of the angel protected his head from the sharp rock. But there comes a time when God takes away his arm and the least little accident sends a sinner to hell!

This calamity is *sudden*. Without an opportunity to repent, without a chance to cry for salvation, swept off to the Pit! I am preaching some man's funeral sermon to-night.

"This is without remedy." I do not know a sadder phrase than this. It has become such to us by association with the doctor's expression when there is no hope and death is sure: "Without remedy." There will be such misery on your death-bed that you cannot think of your soul's salvation. What if you are delirious? No remedy! No remedy!

More than this, your parents and the doctor will see to it that you go to hell, young people. This is how they will do it. They won't let the preacher tell you you are dying. Oh! you who are putting it off to your death, you are gone. It is without remedy forever. What makes me leave home and comfort and books? Because I know that once in hell you'll never get out.

We have heard Dr. Carradine preach this sermon several times before, but never with such unction nor such effect. Men who had stood out against God melted and sought eagerly for mercy. Truly it was an awful time, and yet a gracious. Thanks be unto God for the gift of his Son to rescue us from the hand of the devil. Many of us will never forget this hour, for we saw many of our prayers answered and some for whom we had cried to God for months gave up and were saved.

MONDAY, 10.30 A. M.

Though a large number were compelled to leave this morning, yet the congregation was large. B. J. Rees preached from Rom. 12: 1.

We see in this passage the Apostle Paul in his tenderest vein. The language used is that of entreaty: "I beseech you." The relation between the great Paul and the church of Corinth is one of great affection. He is addressing "brethren," not sinners or idolaters nor aliens from the commonwealth, but "brethren," fellow Christians. As a basis for his plea he cites the mercies of God.

Oh, the mercies of God! How they ought to incite us to entire consecration! It is due to God's mercy that we were placed in a land of Bibles and churches and civilization. It was God's mercy that convicted us and led us to repentance, and saved us. Seeing we are under such obligation to God, Paul argues that we ought to present our bodies unto him. Notice the tense of the verb, "present," instantaneous act once for all.

The word "bodies" in this connection refers to the whole man, with special emphasis upon the physical part of him. The body is the vehicle of the soul, the *only* vehicle at present, therefore the necessity of its being clean and holy. Asceticism is not in the Bible, neither is intemperance, but God would purge and rectify the physical nature and make it the temple of the Holy Ghost.

This is to be a living sacrifice, not a dead one. God don't want you to give him your body when you feel the fingers of Death gripping your throat. He wants a vital, living sacrifice which he can use in a world filled with potent forces.

In order for this sacrifice to be "acceptable" it must be "holy." We must cleanse it. We are to "put away, that God may take away," as Bro. Haney used to say. We must take sides with God against all sin and filthiness. So long as we are favorable to any kind of sin, so long we block the gate for the entrance of the blessing. Undying hostility to every form of sin will bring us into favor with a holy God.

We notice that this dedication is made to God. Strange to say, it is not to the church nor to "the work," but to God himself. I am so glad we can give ourselves to God and be accepted. He will make us his property and forever run and control us.

The latter part of verse 2 says that by doing this, viz., consecrating ourselves fully to the Lord, we prove or experience the will of God. "This is the will of God, even your sanctification." This is the road to purity. This is the path to entire holiness. When we get to the end of ourselves, when we have given to

God all there is to give, we can then trust God to sanctify us and he never fails.

The word "rational" should be translated "spiritual." The service of a sanctified man is distinctively spiritual. He is moved by currents that come from beyond the stars. He lives in a world of a far different character than that in which men usually live. New principles, new ambitions, new desires, actuate and thrill him.

The usual altar calls were made and a number quickly responded and knelt in the straw. The ever-faithful Spirit did his work, evidenced by the glowing faces of the soon-delivered seekers.

MONDAY, 2.30 P. M.

The work of the Holy Ghost is seen all over the grounds to-day. Several cases of deliverance during prayer service in the family tents are reported. Salvation is deluging the whole encampment. Men who entered the gates with utter unconcern have been, and are being, wonderfully saved. Glory be to God!

Bro. Rees offered prayer.

Singing, "I have found it."

Dr. Carradine: Matt. 13:4.

One of these men was a tramp, the other a rich man. This cannot mean two men getting salvation in two ways. It cannot mean that, for "there is no difference." No, the wayfarer is the poor sinner getting salvation. The sinner is a kind of tramp walking around, careless, indifferent. Did you ever see a sinner in church, head bobbing around, as if to say, "This (pointing to the head) is empty and ready for rent?" The sinner is arrested suddenly. He is walking across a field and stubs his toe on the top of a box and finds the treasure;—nothing premeditated about the event whatever.

But Jesus says, "Again, the kingdom of heaven is like unto a merchantman." A contrast to the tramp, this man trades in pearls and is looking for bigger pearls. He stands for the regenerated man. The regenerated man is no tramp. He knows he's rich, and you can't get him sanctified by telling him he hasn't got anything. He knows he is rich, for he hears the pearls rattlin' around. This man wanted more pearls. And every regenerated man wants more of the graces of the Spirit. And if a man doesn't want *the* pearl he isn't regenerated. You would think by the way some people act, that Jesus said "the kingdom of heaven is like a mule, which, when he heard of a pearl of great price, laid back his ears and stuck his fore feet in the mud and said, 'I won't move a step.'" But he didn't say that.

The "all" of the merchantman and the "all" of

the wayfarer are very different. They both gave all, but how much greater the "all" of the merchantman than the "all" of the wayfarer. "One thing thou lackest," said Jesus to the young man. He didn't say that he lied when he professed to have kept all the commandments, but he said, "One thing thou lackest." This man was regenerated. The unregenerate need a thousand things, but the truly converted needs one thing, viz., the pearl of great price. "Go sell *all* that thou hast." There is that word *all* again. Sell out. Reputation? Yes, *all*.

Must I part with all these nice things? God will make it up to you. In the first place this *one* pearl simplifies things tremendously. You cannot quote the ten commandments. Few can. So God has simplified them and said, "*Love* is the fulfilling of the law." And when you get this love, you will keep the law. I used to have in the back of my Bible twenty things I wasn't going to do and twenty things I *was* going to do, but I was always getting them mixed. But all I have to do now is to keep perfect in love. If you have only the treasure the wayfarer found, you are always counting it, but you can't count a pearl, its *one*.

I notice the stability of the pearl. If you have money you are always spending it, but you can keep the pearl, cherish it, save it.

The pearl stands for purity. "To him that overcometh I will give the white stone" and "white stone" is the same word as the one here translated "pearl."

Another advantage is that the pearl is the gate of heaven. So if you have this pearl you have the gate of heaven, "for every several gate was of one pearl." Rev. xxi: 21.

The pearl is more easily carried than the box. How that wayfarer tugged and perspired to get it across the country! But the pearl is easy to keep. The man with the box is like this: (dragging the pulpit across the platform with evident difficulty) but the man with the pearl! Bless the Lord, what an easy time he has!

Why, there are two ways of taking hold of hands. In regeneration we catch God by the fingers, but in sanctification God catches us by the wrist.

Well, this is a hidden blessing. Other people can't see its value; but when they laugh we put our hands on the pearl and press it to our hearts. Dr. Peck, when a young man, used to lean against the mantel and say to his mother, whom he loved very dearly, "Mother, what makes you think you have the second blessing? why, no faithful exegesis will show that it is taught in the Bible." But the mother would look up over her spectacles with her face shining, and say, "Yes, George, but your old mother has got it."

Another thing. When we have this "white stone,"

we may ask what we will and He'll do it. I know a man that isn't appreciated in this country. Say what you will, beloved, but why don't you raise $50,000 or $75,000 for missions. You see the human in him. Your mind is on the oxcart, and you ignore the "ark." We have only skirted the possibilities of faith and God's power yet. When will we learn to ask largely?

Next the pearl is of great value. You can't scare a man with this pearl. Supposing the caterpillars do eat up the crop? What if the ships of the Mediterranean do burn up? You can't scare a man with this blessing.

Do you want it? God calls you his temple and his building. This blessing brings Christ into the heart to stay. First, you empty the house. All the bedsprings in the back yard, and all the halves of old brooms and the sardine cans—everything must go. And God comes in and re-scours and recleans and then fills the house with himself.

MONDAY EVENING 6.30.

While the people were singing "Joy in my Soul" this evening, some one raised a handkerchief and waved it in the air. The example was followed by nearly the whole audience. Suddenly Dr. Carradine leaped upon the platform with handkerchief in hand

and shouted, "Everyone march down the middle aisle and back the side one." What a sight it was! White linen in air, glad expressions on the faces, a long chorus of marching, triumphant, blood-washed saints; it seemed like a whiff of the marches of victory in which we will engage beyond the sea. Symbolic it was of that great throng who are "arrayed in white linen," and who press from the various parts of the globe up to the throne of God.

MONDAY 7.30 P. M.

Rev. John Norberry, Acts 19, part of second verse. "Have ye received the Holy Ghost since ye believed?"

This is a very important question. It is one that ought to interest every believer. This question was asked of the Christians at Ephesus by the apostle. I do not know how many were converted in the previous revival, but when the apostle came there were twelve, and that is a large company. I would to God that every church in the land had twelve converts left of the converts of last winter's revival. These men did not know about the Holy Ghost. The people of to-day know but little of the Holy Spirit. They are wofully ignorant of this profound question.

If you are a believer you are eager for this truth. "Have ye received the Holy Ghost since ye believed?"

Apollos was born at Alexandria. A Jew, eloquent, mighty in the scriptures, he spake and taught diligently the word of the Lord. He was fervent in spirit. He was walking in all the light he had. And there was something very sweet about this man and that was that he was willing to be taught. Priscilla and Aquila expounded to him the way of God more perfectly. And I think he got the blessing right there, for when he went over into Achaia, he "helped believers much."

Bro. Norberry here broke off and gave his experience with blessed effect upon the people. Waxing earnest in exhortation, the preacher urged believers to settle the matter of their being made holy at once, and a large number stepped forward to the altar. The worker's crowded around and another mighty altar service was held. In spite of all objections, there is no simpler nor more effective method of getting seekers "through" than the rational and judicious use of the altar. It brings wants and supplies into proximity. It is a check to superficial religiosity. It is a place of spiritual instruction. Personally, we confess to a sort of "home feeling" when in the altar. It is there the fire falls. It is there the blood flows. Hallelujah!

TUESDAY 10.30 A. M.

Bro. W. H. West, of Boston, has just entered the Tabernacle and is upon the platform. Sisters Reed and Williams, well known to all New England holiness people, are also here. Rev. Frank E. Talbee of Bristol, and Rev. Mr. Kilpatrick of Newport are likewise present.

Rev. Beverley Carradine: Text, Gal. 2: 20.

That is an extraordinary experience. There is not a regenerated man on this earth who can put his hand on his heart and say, "That is my experience." I used to want to preach from this text before I was sanctified, and God wouldn't let me. I couldn't unstand it. There were five apparent contradictions in it. But now I understand it—it is as clear as day. Regeneration is a birth and therefore not a crucifixion. A man must be born before he is killed. This is a divine work, but growth is a human work, and therefore crucifixion is not growth. Wesley said that sanctification was both gradual and instantaneous. What did he mean? He meant that man's part is gradual but God's part instantaneous. I was seeking and moving toward God a long time, but suddenly I reached the magic place where the fire was falling and jumped up and said, "I am sanctified."

Sanctification is a crucifixion, and one element of crucifixion is *loss*. When a man goes out to be crucified, he leaves everything else but the beam of wood on his shoulder. Oh, this repulsive cross! But it yields well, and as from the carcass of the dead lion, from it comes the sweetness, and we, Samson-like, go along the road eating honey.

There is pain in crucifixion. Christ never said who should and who should not drive nails. What nails they drive! "Say, wife ain't you sprouting wings?" "Sanctified eh!" But these nails help us to die.

I notice that loneliness is a third feature of crucifixion. Jesus Christ went alone. Favor, friends, reputation, good things, lawful things, all must be left. Oh, the loneliness! We are social beings, but here is an experience, to get which you have got to be as lonely as the sparrow on the house-top. The Holy Ghost digs a chasm between you and your friends. Not a "holier than thou" chasm, but a real chasm. The water-tank department of salvation is not the essential part. You may cry and cry and not get the blessing. You must accept the loneliness. You must be crucified. You can't bridge the chasm. You must give up trying to keep in touch with the other crowd.

Shame is characteristic of crucifixion. Where is the reproach of the cross to-day? Is it in saying you are a child of God? No. Is it in being a church member? No, sir! Is it in being a preacher? Bless your heart. See him get off the train. Beaver hat, twenty-two buttons, gold-headed cane. That isn't reproach. Christ was an object of contempt. There he is, pale, haggard, with the dried, black blood and spittle clinging to him. Oh, if you want to know the reproach you get sanctified.

Crucifixion means death. A dying man don't care what is being said about him. He don't care how he looks. See his eyes roll, mouth open, hair disheveled. What does he care what you say now? A man who is dying gives away all he has got. I gave up my lecture-ship. Preaching is a vocation, not a profession. Jesus wouldn't smile on me after my lecture, though the people did, and now, though large congregations greet me with the anxious look, the apprehensive look, the resisting look, Jesus puts his arms around me and comforts me. What healthy sanctifications we would have if we would but go this route!

Paul says, "I *am* crucified." The old man is dead. It is a luxury to feel that he is dead—that he isn't even wriggling a toe nor arching an eyebrow. And, bless God, not only are you dead to the world, but the world is crucified to you.

Dead folks are not sensitive. If you mash the toe of a corpse he don't say "Ouch!" If you are dead you won't talk back when things are said against you. My precious brethren, don't talk back. You haven't got to have a reputation anyhow to succeed. Let them talk. Go to bed and rest and get ready for to-morrow's work.

"Dead yet alive." The very moment Christ's body died his soul was never more alive or more about his Father's business. He was never more alive than when folks said he was dead. And you are never more alive than when you are sanctified. The sanctified life is a mystery to the man who hasn't got it. Get it and you will understand it. You can't understand a holiness preacher without you get holy. I used to think "Hallelujah" and "Bless the Lord" were automatic, parrot-like expressions. I thought it was habit, but I found it was a nightingale sitting on a rose-bush in a moonlight night, singing itself to death.

This experience will make you a bundle of activity and yet give you rest at the same time. It puts an end to spiritual weariness. This is a kept life. You go to bed kept and wake up kept. Praise the Lord.

Sanctification is Christ keeping house in the heart. For this Paul "travailed in birth again." "Christ" must be "formed within." And then it is a life of faith. That's the way we get it, by faith. "The altar sanctifies the gift." You are the gift, Christ is the altar. And as you obtain the blessing so you retain it—by faith. Not by ecstacy nor feeling nor emtion, but by faith. You'll never have more feeling, but you won't go by feeling. You'll never have more blessings, but you won't go by blessings. You'll go by faith.

These notes which we have taken doubtless sound disjointed and disconnected to those who did not hear the sermon. Those who were present know how symmetrical and finished the discourse really was. And the power which attended it! Of that we can of course reproduce here not an inkling. But the crowded altar bore evidence to the mightiness of the word.

TUESDAY, 3.00 P. M.

At the opening of the meeting Miss Jennie A. Stromberg and Frank E. Talbee sang that blessed hymn which Dr. Carradine brought to us, "Blessed Quietness." Thank God for spiritual songs. After the duet Miss Stromberg led in prayer.

Rev. Hulda A. Rees was the preacher of the hour. She chose for her text those marvellous words, "Because as he is, so are we in this world." This text is, I know, a tremendous, one but, for that matter, the Bible is full of such texts. The more I pry into God's book the more I am struck with its *extreme* character. Neutrality it knows not. Its teachings are as radical as words can express. We are accused of talking about "extreme holiness." The Bible is full of it, and this is only one of the many texts that show it.

I want you to notice especially the last phrase, "in this world." The Apostle is here referring to an experience for this world. He does not say that in the future, in heaven, we are to be like Jesus or are expected to be like him, but he clearly indicates that at the present time, amid present conditions, we are to be like Christ. Now certainly no one will maintain that this text is true of the ordinary church-member. We are taunted every day with the dissimilarity existing between Christ and his professed church. It is the standing joke in the grocery-store. The man on the dry-goods box sees the incongruity, and laughs at it. No, this is a picture of advanced spirituality. No one need be told that there are various degrees of godliness and piety to be seen among the Christians of to-day. Dr. Steele has very happily struck on a classification of mankind on the basis of love and fear. First there are "people who are without fear and without love." These are unfeeling sinners. They have no reverence for God and no apprehension of penalty. Second, there is the class who are "with fear and without love." These are awakened sinners. Third, "with fear and with love." This describes the justified Christian While he feels himself to be a child of God yet there is mingled with this attitude to God a shade of fear. "He that feareth is not made perfect in love." The fourth and last class includes those who are "without fear and with love," that is to say, perfect love has cast out fear. These are those who are sanctified wholly. A man in the last class does not find it at all irksome to love the Lord with all the heart, mind, might and strength.

There is a great gulf necessarily between the true child of God and the worldling. Christ said of the disciples that they "were not of the world." This gulf has not been bridged since the day of Christ's sacerdotal prayer. It means as much to be a real child of God now as it ever did. It means self-denial. It means a spirit of self-sacrifice. It means separation. The world has but little use for us when we get to be Christlike. And the strange part of it is that we are not willing to recognize the breach which in the very nature of things must ever exist between God's man and the world. To be like Jesus means to receive the same rebuffs and the same hatred of which he was the disdained object. We may depend upon it, the world will not patronize or flatter us if we get right. Christ testified against evil both in the world and in the synagogue. And the servant who is not above his Lord, who testifies against evil, will receive the same vituperation which the Son of God was subjected to. My Christian brother, if God does not lead you out of the church, and probably he will not, you must stand and faithfully testify against the evils which you see in the church.

But let not the gloom of severity overcloud the silver sheen of gladness. If we are true to God, we may depend upon it that Christ will reward us with joy. I haven't a particle of sympathy with the notion that Jesus never smiled, for the Bible itself says that God "anointed him with the oil of gladness above his fellows."

And we are to be like him in service. Many a minister will get no reward because he was un-Christlike in the spirit of his service. In that day Christ will say "How came you into the ministry?" "I wanted to sway men," I fancy I hear one man reply. "Did you do it?" asks the shining Judge. "I did." "Stand aside. Thou hast had thy reward." Many and various will be the answers given to Christ's questions. Some will give as their reasons for entering the ministry their preference for an indolent life, and the thought that they could make the ministry such a life. Others were forced into it by the wishes of fond mothers. Some went into the sacred calling because they were of a studious turn and the ministry afforded time for gratifying their love of books. But there will be some preachers on that day who will come up from the battlefields of earth with the scars of war upon their limbs and the dust of conflict on their faces; they will come up peeled and scourged and lashed, but to the question of their God they will answer, "Lord, thou knowest why we preached. Thou knowest the struggle. Thou knowest the nights of prayer. Why should'st thou ask this question. Thou wert there all the time."

Notice the character of Christ's joy and sorrow. They had not their source in anything trivial. His joy was in bringing souls to a knowledge of the truth. His sorrow was for lost men and stubborn hearts. The disciples of Christ to be as he is, must have their joy and their sorrow depend upon the same things that his joy and sorrow depended upon.

Christ was heard by the Father. "I know that thou hearest me always." God hears the prayer of every true child of God. He would leave off making a star to hear the cry of his weakest saint. To think that we have the ear of God, access to the throne of the King!

My brother, sister, would you like to be like your Lord? You may be this very afternoon. If you will meet me at the altar, and will surrender yourself to God without reservation, and let him kill the "old man," he will make you "as He is."

A glorious altar service followed the preaching of this mighty sermon, and many a soul got through to God and victory. "What hath God wrought?" is the language of our heart as we see so many sanctified wholly in these altar services. Hallelujah!

TUESDAY, 7 P. M.

There is a feeling in the air that the camp is drawing to a close. Our number is swelling at every service. The prayers offered for the unsanctified and unsaved are direct and importunate in view of the shortness of the time. The fire of God is burning in the camp. Solemnity profound and effective rests like a blanket upon the unsaved. This evening the people have gathered more promptly than usual, though there are always many on hand when the bell taps. Sister Rose Williams sang this evening "Get Somewhere in Jesus To-day" with the perceptible touch of the Spirit upon it. Her clear, sweet voice floated far out into the leafy grove with touching beauty. God has his singers in this day and, filled with the Spirit, they mightily magnify his name. Dr. Carradine preaches to-night.

Dr. Carradine: I am always fond of preaching hallelujah sermons, but I shall not preach one to-night. I know of no life from which you can draw more spiritual lessons than from that of Samson. One thing about him is that he is hard to locate. Paul says he was a man of faith, but we find him in Judges a man of passion. Sometimes in his life he seems all right, but at other times strangely in the rear. Like some folks now he was sometimes on one side and sometimes the other. One thing about Samson, both sides counted him. His name seems to be on both books. I don't want any doubt about my soul. I don't want devils and angels fighting over my soul when I come to die. I don't want to be like the girl who belonged to the church but who dropped dead in a theatre and there was a desperate fight over her soul. The angels said "she is a church member." "Yes," said the devil, "but she died on my territory" and he whisked her off to hell!

Another thing about men like Samson and Solomon is that you can't tell where they go when they die. They have put God to an open shame and to the last you can't tell where they go. I tell you, my brother, backsliding is an awful thing. When a man is for God for twenty years and then like a hog wallows in the mire or like a dog turns to his vomit, goes back again, that man's death will be peculiar, uncertain. I want to die so that all the children will know where I have gone.

Look at Samson going around in dangerous places. Fooling with danger; getting into trouble but coming back again, and doing the same thing again. Don't you see the "prone to wander" element. Haven't you watched a mouse fascinated by the bait in the trap. He just fooled around and was caught. What are you playing around dangerous places for? Take to your heels and fly from danger.

When Samson lapsed I notice that his power was gone. He could still shake himself, but he couldn't shake anyone else. Don't you see, my backslidden brother, that your grip is gone; that your exhortations and prayers and conversation have lost their point and power?

I notice that he wist not that his power was gone. The dissipation was so gradual, like the sunlight in the West, that he was not alarmed, but the angle of divergence, be it ever so acute, will ultimately separate God and the soul.

Christ was lost *in the temple* by his father and mother. Right in the midst of much activity they got confused by the activity and lost the Lord. Do you know that I find that the hardest folks to move on the question of holiness are these great church workers. Did you know that one-third of the preachers are going to be damned? One third of the stars of heaven, which are the ministers according to John in Revelation, were pulled out of the sky by the devil. So intent are many upon their work that they lose the Christ.

I notice that Samson got the knowledge of his fall from those that pulled him down. Young Christian, ever since you have been converted some people have been trying to pull you down, and when they get you down they will laugh and sneer at you.

Why does God let these folks below you sting this way? Because you have cut yourself loose from all lawful communication with God and he makes you know things through your enemies.

Watch Samson make fun for the Philistines. Cutting capers for the sinners. Look at these preachers telling stories and cracking jokes to keep their places. Lost his power and now he keeps his place by cutting capers for sinners. Oh, how they laugh at fallen preachers and lapsed Christians!

And the pitiful thing about it is that the Samsons are blind and can't see how pitiful is their condition. Brother there was a time when you were a better man.

This is the devil's plan. First, get you away from God and then paralyze your faith that he will take you back.

This was a "boring" sermon. The altar service was deep and searching and some who had been seeking for some time "came through shouting." Praise the Lord for this day.

WEDNESDAY, 8.30 A. M.

Bro. W. H. West, Superintendent of the Kneeland Street Mission, Boston, led this service. After several blessed hymns Bro. West said, "Now we want to have a little season of communion with God. Let us shut out everything else but God." A gracious time of earnest supplication followed. Bro. West then spoke a few minutes with his usual liberty and power. The meeting closed with many testimonies.

WEDNESDAY, 10.30 A. M.

Singing, "I'm over in Canaan now."

Prayer, Phoebe L. Hall.

Rev. Seth C. Rees, Colossians 1:26, Even the mystery which hath been hid . . . but is now made manifest to his saints.

There is no more illustrious man in the Bible than the author of this epistle. His labors were incomparable, his writings unparalleled, and his experience unexcelled. He passes through all the vista of Christian experience. He sees the magnitude of the gospel.

There are two things in our text. First a secret revealed, and second, the secret appropriated or applied. There is a secret in everything, even in the material world. The great electrician of this century has only been discovering the secrets of God. Newton and Bell and Morse and Edison are only finding out secrets. They have created nothing. Human ethics have revealed some important facts; Plato, Buddha, Socrates and Confucius discovered some of our needs as a human race but they created nothing. But by revelation God has shown "to his saints" the great mystery of "Christ within you the hope of glory." In the seventh chapter of Romans we have a picture of a regenerated man seeking for liberty from the "old man" (Dr. Carradine: "Amen").

Holiness is a revelation. My greatest concern is that God may sweep through this camp and reveal Christ in human hearts. For by revelation God makes the soul sure of what it has. If you have got the blessing you will know it, and if you don't know it you haven't got it. Talk about "temperament" and "constitutional make-up!" If you get this blessing you will be sure of it, and though I may question or people may doubt or even Gabriel be dubious, yet you will have such a revelation from the Holy Ghost that you will not have a quiver in your assurance.

This secret was Paul's power for his physical being. The Spirit quickening his mortal flesh kept him going through beatings, and nights of labor, and days of preaching and shipwrecks, and all the malice and hatred of hell.

This is the secret of power. Not gestures, not fine speeches, not ability either natural or acquired. Paul could do all things *through Christ*. We preachers need to learn this. Only by utter dependence upon God can we work spiritual miracles.

Joy is another characteristic of this secret. Nehemiah rebuked Israel for weeping on a holy day. Holiness brings joy. Oh, the secret of joy! Paul stoned and left for dead arises and confronts the disciples and the next day goes to Derbe. His joy could not be killed. "Thanks be unto God which always causeth us to triumph." Look at the miners singing as they go down in the bowels of the earth. Watch the soldier cheered by the sound of music. Notice the sailors helped by their tunes and the fireman encouraged to a deed of bravery by the cheers of the crowd and see what an important element joy is in the Christian warfare.

Oh brother, this a secret. You can't get it by rubbing up against other folks, for it won't rub off. You can't get it by keeping good company. You have got to die out. The self-life must be killed and then the secret is revealed.

George Fox had this secret. He preached it on this very hill (Quaker Hill). Mary Dyer who is buried on this Island had it. You and I may have it. Will you take it this morning?

Bro. Rees' sermon was received with great enthusiasm. Conviction was deep and nearly a score stood up as wanting the secret of the Lord revealed to them.

WEDNESDAY, 3 P. M.

Brother Rees spoke at some length in regard to holiness literature. Dr. Carradine's books, "The Old Man," "Twenty Objections," and "The Better Way," were especially recommended. Prayer by Brother Haden.

Dr. Carradine: I find myself drawn to the lesson taught in the scene at the wedding at Cana of Galilee. There were two fluids, water and wine, and there are two experiences. The disciples lived on a water experience up to Pentecost, but there they found a nobler and profounder grace. There it was that the people thought they were drunk. Peter admitted it but states that it was not the same kind of liquor that they supposed since they had not had time to go down-town. A drunk man will charge at anything from a cyclone down to a wind-mill and when the disciples got drunk they charged the whole creation.

I love to see people get royally drunk on this wine. I notice that they are the people God is using. For I notice that this wine experience is attractive. The multitudes flocked about the disciples after they got this blessing. I have seen in going from town to town that a drunk man always draws a crowd. There is a fascination in seeing a man who is moving in another realm than ourselves. The heaven-devised plan is that if you lack a crowd get drunk and you haven't got seats enough to hold them. The church-bell was the result of the recognized need of something to call the people to the house of God. And then the fine church was tried and then the choir, but all have failed.

But some think that this is the nineteenth century

and the plain gospel will not do. So the truth is emasculated, eviscerated, attenuated, until it is so small that the Holy Ghost can't fall on it. The Holy Ghost don't fall on nothing. He falls on a spherical, rounded-out gospel.

When we get in condition to help them, God will bombard us with sinners to be saved. I notice that the wine experience is a convicting experience. I want an experience that will make men beat their breasts and cry out "What shall I do to be saved?"

Jesus said, "feed my sheep," not "whip my sheep," not "rap my sheep," not "amuse my lambs," but "*feed* my sheep," "*feed* my lambs." And when the sheep are hearty and fat the goats will come up and butt at the door and say, "Will someone please be so kind as to saw off my horns and teach me how to bleat." Bless your heart, you can't conquer people with syllogisms. You take up the major premise and they'll answer with the "colonel premise."

I find the wine experience is the saving experience. I tell you you can't have people converted in a church where the minister is an icicle six feet long, and snow is on the pew, and frost on the choir and the sexton something in the polar region undiscovered. You can't pop corn in a cold skillet. You cannot pop converts in a cold church.

This blessing is a compensating blessing You

won't want something else. You are satisfied when you get this wine. This wine will stimulate you when you come to die. You'll die drunk. Hallelujah!

How to get it. First get water—regeneration. Fill up the firkin to the brim—consecration. Dip out. Dip out what? What did you come after? Wine. Well there it is. "Bear to the governor." Confess it before you taste it yourself. Here is God's order. Believe! Confess! Saved! Tell the governor, tell the presiding elder, tell the Bishop. Don't hide it. Don't do that.

The result of all this was that many believed on him. More than this Jesus was glorified. The physician that does the cure gets the glory.

WEDNESDAY, 7.00 P. M.

This evening witnessed the fall of gladness from the skies upon the people. The great congregation encircled the large tabernacle with a holy march. It was an example of what Dr. Carradine had preached in the afternoon. Oh, the faces, "white with holiness!" Oh, the pure spirits in the congregation! And with these souls, holy, harmless, undefiled, and best of all, with the stainless, lily-white Christ, we are to dwell forever. Hallelujah! for the holy intoxication.

So great was the conviction that no sermon was practicable. Bro. Rees then opened the altar and scores crowded forward. The great company of seekers unanimously broke out in vocal prayer. Bro. Rees exhorted the congregation with great power, and the hungry souls kept coming to the Lord. Those who had once had the blessing of holiness, but like Samson, had lost the power and blessing, were especially urged to seek the Lord anew, and many did so. Thanks be to God!

THURSDAY, 10.30 A. M.

Dr. Carradine. Matt. 5: 8.

The churches believe in purity. It would not be a decent church that didn't. The disagreement is as to the time and manner of the purification. The Catholic Church believes in Purgatory, but the objection to this is that the Bible don't back it up and that spoils it for me. And then the folly of saying that material flames can purge a spiritual thing? Another class of churches look to death as a purifier. But that is spoiled by the same objection, viz: The Bible does not teach it. Death is not our Savior. Jesus is the purifier. I am jealous for Christ. Death is not our friend. We have two enemies, sin and death. But the last enemy that should be destroyed is death; so sin is killed before death. Another idea is reformation. This is the world's idea. But this is really whitewashing. Christ's work is washing white. Then there is the Zinzendorfian theory, that is, that when we get converted we get a pure heart. Wm. Bramwell said that this would be the "devil's big gun," and such it is. And this is his big gun, for by it he makes men believe that there is no second work of purity, and of course with no faith in it, they can't get it. How did Zinzendorf ever come to believe this anyhow? Well, he had a quiet Christian childhood, and when under conviction gave all to God and got sanctified, and thought he was being converted. If this doctrine is true, there must be analogies in nature. It must be taught in the Bible and the experience of God's children must correspond. Now nothing in nature is born clean. The Bible distinctly says that there is a filthiness remains. And experience doesn't show it. Controversy may say it is true, but its ablest exponents do not stand up and testify to it with two or three hundred men of God looking at them.

It is said that growth sanctifies. Where is the man who got it that way? I have seen his camp fires like those of Evangeline's lover, but I never found him. If I had been traveling for forty years trying to get to this camp ground and hadn't reached it I would decide that I had the wrong train. The Word says,

"Grow *in* grace," not grow *into* grace. A tree cannot grow from one field into another. It must be transplanted, and then it can grow in the new field.

Oh, yes, but "first the blade then the ear then the full corn in the ear." Ah! but if that means how to get sanctified you have proved too much; for it must in that case teach that regeneration is a growth. We are talking of purity, not maturity. Common sense will help us along here. When your handkerchief is dirty, what do you do? It is suffering from additions now. What you want is a dose of subtraction. You cannot clean it by adding clean cloth. Hot water and soap will do what growth cannot do.

Another theory is that righteousness is imputed. But as Bishop Mallalieu said, "When Christ comes he will take his white robes and leave you," if you are unsanctified. There is a legal sense in which righteousness is imputed, but sanctification is *imparted*. Imputed holiness is like a snow in a barnyard, and what if there should be a thaw? The Baptism of Fire teaches us that the residuum of sin is to be destroyed. This shows the third blessing idea is nonsensical.

Yes, says someone, but I don't believe God has to do his work over again. All right, but sanctification is *another* work. They are not the same work. It took six distinct touches to make the world. It took two creations to make mankind; first man, then woman. You sisters ought not to fight the second blessing. You are the second blessing.

Why, the disciples gathered in the upper room to receive a second blessing. The way they whooped and shouted and kicked up generally, shows it was novel to them. It was brand new. They had been converted; they "had cast out devils;" "their names were written in heaven;" but they tarried for a new blessing.

You can see the second work in the two touches of Christ upon the eyes of the blind man. In regeneration, bishops and presiding elders seemed as big as trees, but the second touch makes them six feet high and eighteen inches broad.

When we get sanctified we see God. Regenerated people only see God partially, but sanctified, we see him as Moses saw him; gracious, forgiving, loving. Sanctified people don't give folks up. They hold on in prayer and faith until the answer comes.

You'll see God in your heart. You'll see Christ in the faces of God's sanctified people. These holy people have a way of smiling. I used to think it was a self-satisfied smirk, but I have found it is born in heaven. You will see God in the Bible. You see him in trouble.

And then I can't see how anyone who is right with God can become inflamed against the doctrine of

Christ's near coming. A man's accounts must be wrong, or else he's smoking cigars, if he don't want to see Jesus.

As usual a crowded altar rounded up this glorious service. Christ is here, and all through this camp He is stretching out his hands, and the power drops from his fingers upon the people.

THURSDAY, AUG. 5, 3.00 P. M.

Although the rain had fallen steadily nearly all day, the congregation was of good size. Deacon Kies of Norwich, Ct., and Henry Parkhurst of the well-known Pitts St. Mission, Boston, are with us. After the season of song, Rev. Mr. Simonson led in prayer.

Singing No. 222.

Rev. John Norberry, II Tim. 1: 10.

"For God hath not given us the Spirit of fear, but of power and of love and of a sound mind." If there is anything which the Christian church is cursed with, it is the spirit of fear. Go where you will, you will find the same plague upon the people. Preacher and congregation, the bane effects them all; many a meeting is ruined, many a plan of God thwarted, by fear on the part of God's professed people. Lord, help us to get rid of it this afternoon.

Many campmeetings come to failure, many protracted meetings are without effect, because of fear. It is fear of the consequences of a holy plain-spoken ministry which breeds this attack upon the evangelist. Multitudes go home from campmeeting converted, and backslide because of fear. Preachers often fear to preach Jesus as he is, and keep still. Fear does not come from God. If you have fear, it is from the lower regions. God has something that will take all the fear out of us. Fear of going to the poorhouse, fear of this, fear of that, God will take it all out.

"I am naturally of a timid disposition," but God does not want you fearing. Timothy seems to have been a young man of timid disposition. I was a coward until God sanctified me, and now I am not afraid of the devil himself. When you go home you will be tempted to "let down" in your testimony. If you are not careful you will radically change when you get to your own church. There have been preachers sanctified, not a few in the past thirty years, but where are they to-day? They have lowered their testimony and are not heard from any more.

When we go home we will either move men for piety or for evil. The same sun that hardens the clay melts the wax; the same rain that makes the live limb grow, rots the dead one. Power is a characteristic of the baptism with the Spirit. The sanctified man is a force in the world.

"Spirit of love." We must remember than an important element in the sanctified life is love. Don't get raspy. Don't be harsh. Let the spirit of love possess you. The blessing of entire sanctification is, it seems to me, well portrayed in the 13th chapter of I Corinthians. If you get provoked when ill-treated, you haven't the blessing. If you are told by the preacher to sit down, sit down. Don't be bull-dogged, but courteous and polite; but do not cease to avail yourself of every proper occasion to testify to God's power and willingness to sanctify.

Although Bro. Norberry's sermon was chiefly on the line of instruction to those who are already sanctified, yet many who had not yet entered into the perfect land of rest sought and found the experience of holiness.

THURSDAY, 7.30 P. M.

Rev. B. Carradine, 1 Thess. 4: 3.

"For this is the will of God, even your sanctification." You may be sure it is not the will of the devil that you should be sanctified. How he does dread a sanctified man! He knows that he is to be put in hell by a fire-baptized church. It is not the will of the world that we should be sanctified, for it is disturbed by a sanctified man. Neither is it the will of a formal church that we should be sanctified. But it *is the will of God* that we should be sanctified.

Yes, says the sharp-eyed critic, but look at the expression which follow: "Abstain from fornication." I answer that there are discriminating commentators who hold this to be spiritual fornication. And then these men are not fornicators anyway. In the first chapter Paul says they are "ensamples." If they were committing fornication they ought to quit it. But Paul says to abstain, therefore they were not fornicators.

Haven't we got anything else to do but fight holiness, any kind of holiness? I am so glad I never did. Even when I didn't understand anything about it, I never either spoke or wrote against it.

Whatever God says is his will we must do or else go into shadow. If we refuse to do anything which is God's will we will go into darkness. If we love God and yet are not sanctified I don't see how we can ever be quiet and at rest again after we have found out God's will concerning our sanctification.

I would that you who say you are God's children could see the tear-drops of the Son of God on this verse.

"If this is God's will, why don't you get it?" and the answers are as thick as blackbirds in the spring. One says, "I don't understand." Well, don't you know you can get it without understanding it?" You say "you can't see into it." You are not in a position to see into it. I have noticed that though a man cannot see into sanctification from a height of six feet, yet he can see into it from a height of three feet six inches (kneeling).

The reason some people are not sanctified is that they do not want holiness. They do not relish an entire consecration. They want to hold back something. Every sinner is after one certain sin varying in character with the man. And every professedly regenerated man who doesn't get sanctified has something he holds higher than sanctification.

One man says that his little religion makes him miserable and what will more religion do? That is not the way to argue. If justification gives you some peace, what will sanctification give?

Oh, the reasons, the real reasons for not getting sanctified! I can't see what is in the heart. But when you see a man who says he is God's friend, fighting God's blessing, I know there is something wrong in his heart.

Some people who would not commit a crime like to think about it. They enjoy a momentary revery which they know is not right, and they know sanctification will put an end to all that.

Fear keeps many a man from this blessing. Many who believe in the doctrine are afraid to identify themselves with it.

Well, if this is God's will it will come to pass. When Herod made the appointments of the Jerusalem Annual Conference and sent the preachers flying, God had his way. And when men fight the holiness movement, they only help the cause.

O, the sanctification of this world is coming! Why, we are going to have it on the bells of the horses: "Holiness to the Lord": And if it is to be on the horses certainly it is upon the fellow that drives the horses. Ezekiel saw this movement. His vision of waters was nothing on earth but a vision of the holiness movement.

I can't get scared about the outcome of the movement to save my neck. Here is a man who thinks he will stop the movement. God says, "Son, you are in the way;" but he will not move and God knocks him out of the way. If you are fighting this doctrine, you had better get your grave clothes ready. The presumption of some holiness fighters is ludicrous. It is like a craw-fish who says, "I will build a clay dam and stop Niagara," or a knat who stretches out his left wing and says, "Now I'll throw an eclipse on the earth."

Consecration is not sanctification. Consecration is man's work, but God sanctifies. Consecration brings me up to a table and sanctification *puts something on the table*. Sanctification is not regeneration, although they say it is. They say we preach on sanctification and then get a few people converted. Suppose we do; isn't that a good work? But sanctification is not regeneration.

Sanctification is not a recovery from backsliding. If we are getting people reclaimed we are doing a good work. Our bishops and the editors of our papers say the church is burdened with backsliders. If we get two hundred people sanctified and it turns out they are only reclaimed, people ought to endorse us for we are doing as much as can be done. It is not recovery from backsliding, and to say it is, is enough to make John Fletcher turn over in his grave; for he lived a pious life up to the very time he was sanctified. I was no backslider when I was sanctified. Early in my religious life I made it a rule never to put my head upon my pillow until I was at peace with God, and I kept to it even up to the time I was sanctified.

Sanctification is not growth in grace. Sanctification is not a delusion. If we are deluded we are awfully happy for deluded people. We are having a good time with our delusion, do you notice? For several years I have had this "blessing of delusion." I find that this is its character. I find a constant joy. I have a constant conciousness of Christ in the heart. I find a spirit of prayer. And if this is the effect of this "blessing of delusion," may the good Lord delude us all. Bless you, if this delusion will revive our dead churches and quicken the religious life then we want it.

But this is not a delusion. It is a sacred work wrought in the soul subsequent to regeneration. The fact that the regenerated man yearns for a clean heart argues its possibility. The prayers of God's people show it is a possibility. On their knees they say, "Lord, sanctify thy people," "remove the last and least remains of sin."

Praying they are all right, but practically they are infidels. Look at the company praying for Peter. They did not believe it was Peter when he came to the door.

The testimonies of God's people prove this blessing obtainable. Madame Guyon, a Catholic, F. R. Hɩvergal, John Fletcher had it. Geo. Fox, Bishop McKendree and Bishop Asbury had this blessing.

It is the restful experience. Paul said so. It is a purifying blessing for Peter said so.

It is the experience of establishment.

It is the experience of fullness.

It is the overcoming blessing. We can ride the waves of trouble and annoyances and feel as fresh at sundown as at sunrise.

It is the rejoicing blessing.

It is the everlasting blessing.

FRIDAY, 8.30 A. M.

Bro. William H. West is in charge. After Scripture reading the meeting was thrown open for testimonies.

Sister: How can I ever thank God for what he has done for me! Why shouldn't I make some noise when the Lord has done so much? My husband came upon the camp ground a rebel but now he is a child of God. Hallelujah!

Sister: I just want to say that the other night I found liberty at the altar. The devil tempted me not to seek this blessing but I said "I will," and Jesus filled my heart·

Brother: God blessedly saves me and keeps my heart cleansed from all sin.

Singing, "Glory to God, Hallelujah!"

10.30 A. M.

Often some saved and sanctified man or woman in the audience is called upon to lead in prayer. Liberty in prayer among the laity is one of the marks of the falling of fire upon the church. Vocal prayer is not confined to the ministry when holiness has the right of way. This morning Sister Johnson of Providence voiced the petition of the people. Thank God for fire-touched "elect ladies" who know the way to the throne.

Dr. Carradine. I have come upon the platform not knowing which one of three texts to take. I believe I will try this one. Deut. 13: 6.

I believe that God is raising up a class of people who know how to *divide* the word. It has been conglomerated. Whenever the doctrines of the Bible have been lost, God has raised up someone to divide the word and bring the neglected doctrine back to light.

A regenerated man cannot say that his heart is circumcised. I did not see that for many years. But God is anointing men's eyes and causing them to go through this book dividing up the truth as a boat splits the wave with its prow.

Christ's own figures show this to be a second work of grace. Jesus defines regeneration as a birth, but this work is a circumcision. When we are regenerated something is added to us, but in circumcision something is taken away. The Lord give us sense. Circumcision is a removal, an excision, a taking away. When we get this blessing we know something is gone. You needn't argue with a man who has had a tooth drawn that the tooth is gone. If he doubts it for a moment he can run his tongue into the socket and feel it is no more.

God thought we would have sense. He supposed we would have gumption enough to see that a child must be born before it is circumcised.

I look at this text again and find that this experience is not to give us love. And this shows that sinners are not addressed. He is not going to circumcise our hearts to make us love him. The man who led me into this experience recognized that I had love. He did not discount my Christian experience. You cannot cudgel folks into this blessing. There is a good deal of the mule left in the regenerated heart. You cannot drive a balky mule, but you can lead him all over the plantation with a stalk of fodder. This is the object of circumcision that we may love the Lord our God with *all the heart.*

I am so glad I belong to a church that believes in perfect love. In her wisdom she asks every candidate for the ministry four questions:

"Have you faith in Christ?" Yes we said with a vim.

"Are you going on to perfection?" There was a slight tremor in the breast of the candidate. "Let us go on *to* perfection" says Paul. I didn't grow from Madison, Me. to this camp. If I had you couldn't have entertained me. You would have had to coil me around these hills and valleys and feed me from a step ladder.

"Do you expect to be made perfect in this life?" Now you ought to see the brethren swallowing walnuts We have a man in the M. E. Church South who says he answered this question with a mental reservation. Just like the Jesuits, he said he believed but in his heart he said he did not.

"Are you groaning after it." I read this question a few days before the examination. I began to groan at once so as to tell the bishop I was groaning. And I kept it up some time after I entered the ministry but I got lonely. The bishop was not groaning. The presiding elder was not groaning, so I quit after a while.

If you don't believe in the blessing and are an honest man, state your doubt at this point, and give the church a chance to protect herself from your entrance into the conference. If anything makes my heart sick it is to see a Methodist minister walking around with Methodist dollars in his pocket, and getting fat on Methodist bread and butter, and using the strength to fight Methodist doctrines with.

This work is attributed to God. "The Lord thy God will circumcise thy heart." That settles it; it is not by growth. It was a divine work. The priest stood for our Lord and the priest circumcised the child. It may take eight days to get the child ready, but when it is ready, circumcision takes place in an instant. The result of this is that the soul will live. Jesus says "I have come that ye might have life and that ye might have it more abundantly." God takes out the foreign matter and lets in the abundance of life and vitality.

Oh, these tired workers! Come and get the heart circumcised and have life abundant. The unbroken presence of Jesus Christ is the life of the soul just as the presence of the soul is the life of the body.

You want it. Well, you can get it. "In the day ye seek *me*." When a woman is hunting for her scissors, every one knows it; when a man is seeking a wife, the whole town knows it. I have seen a dog asleep dreaming he was after a rabbit and kicking his foot in his dream but any one knows he isn't hunting rabbits. But when you *seek* you'll find.

If any man will do his will he *shall know* of the doctrine. Obedience brings the blessing. Right here the devil tries to help you consecrate. He tries to drive people frantic with preposterous exactions. He seeks to push folks into fanaticism. "My sheep know my voice" says Jesus. Listen to him and "try the spirits."

I don't often say anything on the dress question. The Lord is jealous and wants to tell us himself how to dress. And yet sometimes the Lord leads us to speak on this. Obedience must be perfect even in the minute points if God is to give us a perfect blessing.

Faith is the next step. "How can ye believe which receive honor one of another?" If you are trying to keep in touch with the nabobs and popes whom you know haven't the juice of the spiritual life, you cannot get the blessing.

Confession. Your faith must have oxygen. Like the seed in the clod, your faith must get the air. The absurdity of being frightened out of confession by some ecclesiastical dignitaries. Fear of being put out of the Swine-a-gogue (synagogue), fear of being put out of the Sinnygogue (synagogue). You must confess in spite of the whole thing. "Believe in your heart and confess with your mouth" and the blessing will fall like the oil upon the head of Aaron down over his beard, down to the edge of the garment. Hallelujah!

Many who came upon the grounds last night were put under immediate conviction by this glorious sermon and the altar service found them forward for prayers. Bro. Norberry, that prince of altar workers, is prominent in these services. With great spiritual tact and skill he has led scores into the blessing of heart-purity on this camp ground.

FRIDAY, AUGUST 3.00 P. M.

The testimonies of this afternoon were especially spiritual. Out of the great throng who have been either saved or reclaimed or sanctified in this meeting many gave by testimony evidence of the Divine work in the heart. It was a time of general witnessing to God's grace and power.

Joseph E. Macomber: This is a day of sorrow for

me. Though my eldest daughter is being buried in a distant state yet God sustains and comforts me.

Sister: I came to this camp with bands upon me, but the fire of the Holy Ghost has burned them all off.

Hulda A. Rees: It has seemed to me in the past that if I had been in Judea or Samaria when Jesus was there that I could have been healed. But he is the same to-day. He has shown himself the same within the past three weeks. When I stood face to face with eternity he spoke to me. When I felt all things on earth slipping away from me, he revealed himself. He has healed me perfectly, for which I do now devoutly thank and praise him.

Great numbers testified, and after awhile without a sermon an altar service was held, which was one of the most gracious of the whole encampment and resulted in the sanctification of a number of souls.

FRIDAY 7.30 P. M.

Just before preaching, Jennie A. Stromberg and H. E. King sang a duet.

Dr. Carradine: Ps. 129: 23, 24. "I feel drawn to-night to talk from these two verses. This is one of the numerous prayers of the Bible. It is a prayer that no man who proposes to keep up sinning will pray. It is the prayer of one who wants to be right. It is a prayer of a child of God. It was uttered long years after David had been forgiven for his lapse.

In this prayer is a confession that we do not know ourselves. The sinner does not know himself. A breath fluttering in the nostrils is all that keeps him from plunging into the pit. If it were not for a little organ which God keeps going in his breast, he would drop into hell. I wonder sometimes that I ever dared to go to sleep unsaved, for sleep is so like death.

The regenerated man does not know himself any more than the sinner does. A sin may exist in the heart, unrecognized. Take the sin of covetousness. Did you ever see a Christian who admitted that covetousness were in his heart. I have read in Drummond's book on Africa of a snake that can so shift his colors of crimson and gold that he looks like a bunch of flowers or a cluster of autumn leaves and just as you put out your hand you hear a sort of rattle and jump back just in time to save your life. And sin is so simulative that it can make itself look like virtue. You have heard people say that they "always speak their mind." They call it candour, but God calls it slander. Covetousness can make itself look like prudence.

God lets us see our own hearts before we get them sanctified. He takes us down the winding stair into the cellar to see the vampires hanging by their heels and the fungus growths and the cumulations of filth in the corners and the cobwebs on the walls.

You can tell when a man has gone through his own heart with God holding the candle. When there are no more floors deeper down there is a "cellarian" sound which shows that there is nothing below.

I believe that over in that city yonder are men who will not allow the bookkeeper to draw off a trial balance for they know that it would show that they were ruined. We had a man in St. Louis who, when he saw something was the matter with his nose would not go to the doctor, for fear he would find out it was a cancer; and that was what it was and it rotted off his head. Inbred sin will rot the soul, and if it is not investigated and extracted, it will consume the whole spiritual nature.

This petition rests not only upon our ignorance of ourselves, but upon the fact that God knows us. I don't know how you feel, but it makes me feel glad to think God knows all about me. The heathen king forgot his dream, but God knew and told Daniel, so it must be God knows our dreams. The prayer is that God will search the heart. One way he searches us is with his Book. There never was a sleuth-hound that run down a man in the jungles more surely than this Book. There is no Book like it in the universe. It discovers the thought and intents of our souls. God wrote on the wall of Belshazzar's feasting-hall one text and the king turned to mortal whiteness and his knees smote together and he sent for Daniel. O how the preachers are in demand in times of danger! The fact that I have a sword in my hand arms me with courage to prosecute my work. Go where I will, I am sure of the victory because I have God's sword.

There is a peculiar power in God's Word. Did you ever notice that when the Word of God is quoted exactly, it has greater force than when put in a man's own words?

When I was converted I gave up tobacco. You are seeking sanctification and trying to find out if God's word says anything about tobacco. Yes, it says that any animal which "cheweth the cud and parteth not the hoof is unclean!"

God searches us by his providences. You are going to know what you are before you are in your coffin. Various situations, nets of circumstance, will cause what is in us to appear. Peter says, "I will follow Thee," but a set of succeeding circumstances revealed that his heart had infidelity in it. You will know that you need this thing before you die.

And then he searches us by his Spirit. Usually this is with the Word but often it is independent of it. He "lighteth every man that cometh into the world." Sometimes it comes gradually like the day and sometimes it comes like a flash of lightning. In every man there are four men. There is the man that your friends know, the man your enemies know, the man you know, and the man that God knows, and he is least of any of them. And you want to ask God to show you the fourth man.

The third petition is "Try me, O God," and refers to the trial of fire. "Put the fire in my heart," says David, "and burn me out."

The fourth petition is "lead me in the way everlasting." They say that we profess a blessing which makes us independent of God. That's the way they talk about us. No, sir! Like the boatman's song,

> "O Lord, my boat is so small
> And thy sea is so broad,"

we sing,

> "O Lord, I am so small
> And life is so great, guide us in the way everlasting."

We will walk on and scare up the centuries as a man scares up blackbirds walking through a wheat field. And when the universe grows old and gray and the moss hangs to the stars and blows in the wind we will walk on in the way everlasting.

SATURDAY, 10.30 A. M.

B. J. Rees preached from Luke 3: 16, 17.

"I indeed baptize you with water, but one mightier than I cometh, the latchet of whose shoes I am not worthy to unloose; he shall baptize you with the Holy Ghost and fire."

Without controversy surely a second work of grace is taught here. Notice with care the antithetic arrangement of thought and words: "I indeed," "but one cometh." While I am performing a certain rite indicative of the remission of sins, there is coming a Divine Baptizer who shall perform a holier and more important work than this.

John's preaching bears unmistakable evidences of being strictly evangelical. He was a *gospel* preacher, for in the 4th verse of the preceding chapter he tells his hearers to "prepare the way of the Lord and to make his paths straight." In the second place he was a gospel preacher because he refused the patronage of superficial religionists. The favor of the influential Pharisee was not a thing which this stout soul desired. Moreover, John Baptist insisted upon real repentance, a repentance which by its fruits would demonstrate its existence. The figure of "an axe at the root of the tree" shows that his conception of the work of the gospel was that it was inward and thorough. Yes, indeed, John was a preacher of genuine regeneration, a sterling apostle of justification.

While John's disciples were converted, the preacher gave them no ground for remaining at rest in that experience, but kept them on the tip-toe of expectation of a second work, the baptism with the Spirit. Justification is blessed, but entire sanctification is more blessed. Water is good, but fire is better.

Christ is mightier in the manifestation of his power to cleanse from indwelling sin than in forgiving sins. No one less than God can forgive; but the strength of God comes out more evidently in the removing of depravity, in the crucifixion of the "old man," in the reversal of the currents of the soul, than in pardon.

The mightiness of Jesus in this work shows itself in the might which he imparts to the man or woman sanctified. Nothing less than an impartation of Divine power will enable a man to battle his way joyously through the wilderness of this world; but sanctification does precisely that.

SATURDAY, 2.30 P. M.

Dr. Carradine preached to a large congregation. Text, Lev. 9: 3, 4.

This doesn't look like a very promising subject, but there is more in it than you would think. The offering most familiar to all is the sin offering. The lamb of this offering was without blemish and was a type which was fulfilled in our Lord. The lamb was killed at the full of the moon and so was Jesus. Bitter herbs were eaten with the lamb, and we, when we partake of

Christ, taste the bitter herbs of repentance and faith.

It is worse than useless, it is hopeless, for us to come to God if we have sinned, without our hand is upon the head of the lamb. And men have been always seeking to find some substitute. God cannot accept morality for Christ. He cannot accept your blood. He is looking for a peculiar kind of blood.

The instant you put your faith in the blood of Jesus Christ, the glory drops into your soul. Right here we see the burnt offering and there you see your Lord again. He was consumed for us and we are to be burnt offerings for him.

The day that God's fire fell upon the church, the devil sought to baptize it with his fire. And you who are familiar with church history know that in the great persecutions he sought to destroy the men of God with his fire. Scarcely a disciple died a natural death. But the more the devil raged, the more the church grew. Thus came the old saying that "the blood of the martyrs is the seed of the church."

We can stand the devil's fire. The devil sees he is defeated by his own tactics, but he can't keep his hands off of fire-baptized men. The three Hebrew children gained in two senses by the ordeal. First, their bands were burned off, and second, the company was increased by the addition of the Lord. The Lord loves us so he can't see us in the fire and not come to us.

The world will begin to scratch matches when you get this blessing. You can't live a life out and out for God, without having a hard time as men count it.

Not only does the devil and the world burn us, but we burn ourselves. Our Lord burnt up himself for you and me. They thought he was fifty when he was in the bloom of young manhood. O, this taking care of yourself! When I was in City Road, London, I saw the graves of Benson and Clarke. On the grave-stone of the latter was a candle burned down to the socket, flickering and going out, and under it ran the legend, "In giving light to others I, myself, have been consumed." I can't tell you how the water dashed to my eyes, and I said, "O! my Lord, from henceforth I will burn for thee." The world says, "Look out for number one," but Christ says, "Look out for your neighbors." I was in a man's house at one time when he was yelling like a Comanche Indian, "Bring me a towel!" You could have heard him half a mile. And his wife, his daughter and his servant all came running from different directions, each with a towel for the infuriated Comanche. He couldn't use but one towel anyway.

We are to become peace offerings. The family will not see it at first. The church won't see it. When they see how uncompromising we are against sin they will think we are out for war. We are not. We are peace offerings. God said that his church should be a house of prayer for all nations, but we have made it a kitchen! Now the holy soul can't fellowship that and there is of necessity a controversy.

They say we are splitting the church, but we are not. The truth never splits the true chnrch. God says the kingdom of heaven is like unto a mustard tree. If Colonel Buzzard and Judge Crow and Sister Woodpecker, President of the Ladies Aid Society, are the "fowls of the air" who are in the branches, no doubt the double-barreled shot-gun of a full salvation minister will disturb *them*, but it will not hurt the *tree*.

The next offering was a meat offering. We are to get to a place where we will strengthen people. If a minister in the pulpit is not feeding people, he is not in the plan of God. It is a shame for a man to rattle a shock of fodder or shake brown paper and not feed God's flock.

The tresspass offering comes in here. Supposing a man falls after he has been sanctified; God has a scheme by which he can be immediately recovered. This does not make us presumptuous, but rather intensifies our desire to not displease Jesus.

If a man is full of wine and they hit him, nothing but wine comes out. This was what made the devil sick of Job. He got tired of having wine splashed all over him. If Paul and Silas had groaned when they jailed them there would have been no revival. The soldiers were used to groans. The prison was full of groans and sighs. But the Apostles shouted and down came the fire.

The next offering is the wave offering. When you get along in divine things so that you know how to handle the blood and rightfully divide the word of truth, God will begin to wave you. He waved Paul over to Asia, across to Africa, thence to Spain. He waved J. S. Inskip all over this country and then around the globe. But God don't wave us to show us off, but to get what is in us out before the people.

The last offering is the heave offering. Heave your troubles to God. Heave your friends and relatives to God. Heave sinners to God as Finny did. Heave believers to God as Inskip did.

I saw three men moving bricks. The first man pitched the bricks to the second and the second to the third. I noticed that without the middle man moved promptly and passed his bricks along, that he would soon be covered up under a pile of them. All the cares,—we are to heave them to God. I heaved a whole church to God in Cincinnati and God took it and deluged it with a revival. If we get into the habit of heaving things, some day we will heave ourselves up to God. Hallelujah!

SATURDAY, 7.30 P. M.

The third and last Saturday night meeting of the camp has come. The congregation is large and inspiring. The singing is the best this year. The great volume of song is a great cataract set to music. At least two hundred people have come on the ground to-day. Many of them will be new "dough" for God to "make into biscuits" as Bro. Carradine says.

Rev. Phoebe L. Hall. I want to read five verses of what seems to be the most affecting of Jesus words. I do not discount any of God's word, but I never read the 17th chapter of John but my eyes fill. These are the last sayings of Jesus, and as such ought to arouse in us a special interest. The thought that naturally comes to us first is to notice the great tenderness with which Christ committed his little flock to the Father. As he saw the billows of those last tumultuous hours rolling and dashing at his feet, his heart was filled with anxiety for his disciples. And moved by this solicitude he "sanctified himself that they might be sanctified." Not that he had any sin, but he dedicated himself. He gave up his life that they might be made holy. And he was not simply praying for the men who gathered about him, but for you and for me. I am determined that no part of his prayer shall go unanswered in my case.

We are told that tho' Jesus prayed that the disciples

should be sanctified, yet they were not converted until Pentecost; but we must remember that Christ says in his prayer, "They have kept my words."

I do thank God that when Christ died on the cross he was bearing not only the sins for which we are responsible, but the very root of sin as well. Not only was provision made then for our pardoning, but for our cleansing.

Jesus saw the danger which threatened the disciples. He saw they would have difficulty with the world, the formal church and themselves. For this very reason he cries out so earnestly that they may be sanctified. There was no remedy, no safety outside of entire sanctification for the early church, and there is none for the modern except in the same experience.

Bro. Norberry conducted the altar service and before nine o'clock many souls found salvation or sanctification.

SUNDAY, 9 A. M.

The last and great day of the feast has come. The day is perfect. A cool zephyr-like wind breathes through the trembling leaves. But best of all, the Spirit himself moves through the leafy aisles of this holy grove. The divine glory of the Shekinah, which has rested upon the camp for sixteen days, is still with us on this the seventeenth.

HALLELUJAHS FROM PORTSMOUTH.

A very pretty scene was witnessed in this morning's meeting. Two little children were dedicated to the Lord. Surely children dedicated to God in a fire-filled holiness campmeeting ought to be, like John Baptist, of special separation and sanctity.

Bro. Rees: I have one or two thoughts burning in my heart this morning. One is that it is an awful curse that some people fail to stay sanctified. If you trust the Holy Ghost he will keep you. Do not neglect protracted seasons of waiting upon God. Keep yourself clean from gossip. Let no man make a cesspool of you. You cannot stay clean and let the world dump its scavanger wagons in the shape of vile newspapers on your centre table. Walk in the light. I will not designate the things you ought to give up, but I do say, "Walk in the light," and God will instruct you. Testify to what God has done for you. Be true to God in spite of backslidden pastors and people. Do not set up bars for the Holy Ghost. Don't say too much about what you are going to do. Do what God says and live a moment at a time.

Brother. I do indeed praise God that in regard to the blessing of entire sanctification he has given me a "know so."

Brother: I went home last Sunday offended. But God would not let me rest. I walked five miles to get back to this campmeeting and now God has saved me. Hallelujah!

Bro. Cole: I praise the Lord for his saving and keeping power. He has kept me all this year.

Walter Wilson: I praise the Lord for saving me and I know he will keep me.

Sister Cole: Singing, "Oh, how the world has lost its allurement."

Elder Mix (colored): I saw when I came upon the camp ground that for numbers the colored people were like a fly in a pan of milk. But I am determined not to let the white people have all the joy. I am a sharer in the blessing of holiness. Praise the Lord!

Bro. Barron: I praise God I have the hallelujah again in my soul. He can keep me on a freight train.

Sister: I want to praise God for sixteen days on this camp. They have been the best of my life.

Bro. Jewelson of Baltimore: This is my forty-first campmeeting. It is the best campmeeting I have ever attended.

Bro. Pardin Simmons of Westport. I thought when I came down here last evening that my cup was full. But now it is running over.

George Simmons. I praise God for the second blessing.

Sister Wordell of Smith's Mills: I praise the Lord that he has cleansed my heart and made me pure.

Brother: I want to praise God for what he has done for me. I was a rumseller for eight years, but five years ago he saved me.

Sister. When I think what a quiet Baptist I used to be, and how I used to quarrel with my noisy Methodist sister-in-law and how God has changed me, I praise him with all my heart.

Bro. Rees announced the services of to-day. He mentioned incidentally that Rev. H. C. Morrison of Louisville, Ky., will be with us in the mid-winter convention. Dr. Carradine speaks of this man as "the leader of the movement in the Southland."

Bro. Norberry led in prayer.

Bro. Rees took three or four minutes for a special collection. One hundred and fifty dollars was received in almost the time it takes to write it. There are no people on earth like the holiness people. They may be confidently relied upon to meet their obligations on the line of giving for the gospel.

Dr. Carradine preaches this morning.

Text, Matt. 2: 11, "He shall baptize you with the Holy Ghost and with fire." This text teaches a second work of grace. Why there should be any objection to a second blessing I cannot perceive. And yet many people, good people apparently, are prejudiced—*præ judicium* means literally, to prejudge—to pass the sentence without looking into the evidence.

Ignorance of this grace is a great cause for opposition to it. A man may be well informed on general things and be very ignorant in respect to this great work. Folks don't take time to sit down and inquire into the question and they live in constant hallucination concerning the true nature of entire sanctification.

Another reason for opposition is that some think that this blessing discounts regeneration, but it does not. Sanctification does not make a man any more the child of God, but gives him another thing altogether.

Spiritual pride is at the root of some men's opposition. You are afraid people will think it strange that you are in the straw at the altar. That bit of pride is the very thing God wants to kill.

Well, with all the ignorance, prejudice, opposition and doubt, there is a second work of grace, for the word teaches it. I believe God, don't you? How do I know that these men received a second blessing? Because they had been converted. Zacharias said that men were to receive remission of sins through John, and here is the very John saying to the converts, "He shall baptize you with the Holy Ghost and with fire."

A birth and a baptism are two different events. It is a physical impossibility for a child to be born and baptised in the same instant. God thought we would have sense and see that.

The figure of fire shows it to be a second blessing. Fire is scarcely a proper swaddling cloth for a new born babe. Jesus comes to us with both hands full of blessing. There are two arms to the cross. I lived for years under one arm, and one day I strolled around under the other and have lived there ever since. I found pardon under one end of the cross-beam and purity under the other.

"God so loved the world that he gave his son," and "Christ so loved the church that he gave himself." I marvel that you can read the two texts and not see the second work.

The experiences of the saints show a second work. Asbury, Fiske, Cookman, Hamline, Sheridan Baker, all experienced and preached a second blessing.

Bishop Asbury says, "I live in patience, purity and in the perfect love of God. God is my portion. He fills me with pure, spiritual life. My heart is melted into holy love and altogether devoted to my Lord. I think we ought modestly to tell what we feel to the fullest.

Rev. Dr. Holdich says, "On the 10th day of Aug., 1819, at a campmeeting at Wellfleet on Cape Cod, Dr. Fisk became deeply sensible of his want of full conformity to the Christian standard. He sought earnestly unto God through the atoning sacrifice and in the course of the meeting he obtained the perfect love that casteth out fear. He lay with two other ministers three hours in a tent prostrated under the power of God."

Rev. Alfred Cookman says, "The evidence in my case was as clear and indubitable as the witness of sonship received at the time of my adoption into the the family of heaven. Oh! it was glorious, divinely glorious. I could not doubt it. Need I say that the experience of sanctification inaugurated a new epoch in my religious life? O what blessed rest in Jesus. What an abiding experience of purity through the blood of the Lamb."

Bishop Hamline says, "All at once I felt as though a hand, not feeble but omnipotent, not of wrath but of love, was laid on my brow. I felt it not only outwardly, but inwardly. It seemed to press upon my whole body, and to diffuse all through and through it a holy sin-consuming energy, under the influence of which I fell to the floor, and in the joyful surprises of the moment, cried out in a loud voice. For a few minutes the deep of God's love swallowed me up; all its waves and billows rolled over me!"

Rev. Sheridan Baker says, "Now the way of faith opened to my spiritual vision with such clearness that I definitely made the reckoning, and unquivocally disclosed the fact. This was followed immediately by a flooding of love and heavenly sweetness which I have no language to discribe. I was now fully persuaded of my entire sanctification. The attitude of my soul is now that of complete, unreserved and eternal surrender to God, self, property and everything. I find my highest delight in talking, preaching, writing and contributing of the means in my hands to spread this wonderful doctrine and experience. Just now I feel with almost unendurable sweetness the bliss of the purified. Hallelujah!"

The Acts of the Apostles, which ought to be called the Acts of the Holy Ghost, is one grand argument to show how the early church received the Holy Ghost. In the second chapter the disciples got the second blessing. If they ask you, "Who ever got the second blessing anyhow?" You answer, "One hundred and twenty praying disciples in an upper room in Jerusalem." In the eighth chapter we find a man who has steam up, chock full to the cylinder-head, can't stay in the round house, racing down the track, brakes gone and sparks a-flying! Great joy in Samaria. Now see what happened. The Jerusalem preachers heard of the revival and Peter came down and prayed for them that *they might receive the Holy Ghost.*"

We have seen how the Jews got the blessing, how the Samaritans got it, now let us see how the Romans got it. Acts, chapter ten. Cornelius was devout (religious) and he gave much alms and prayed alway. Wasn't he a beautiful sinner? If that man was a sinner, may the good Lord sprinkle the land with sinners. An angel came to him. Do angels come to sinners?

More than this, his gifts were accepted and God don't accept gifts from sinners.

Let us be true to men and tell them that their first duty is to repent; for as sure as you live God takes no money as a gift from sinners. This man was of good report among all the nations. Sinners arn't that. "Well," you say, "what on earth did God send Peter down there for?" I answer, that he might receive the Holy Ghost. That he might experience the second blessing. And the apples were so ripe that while Peter was a preaching they fell. Hallelujah!

How did the Greeks get the blessing? They had not heard whether the Holy Ghost was yet poured out. But Paul wasted no time, but opened the altar at once and they received the Holy Ghost.

"Why should a second blessing be necessary? Why can't it be done all at once?" Because pardon is what a sinner comes for. God holds the penitent to this prayer: "Lord forgive me!" "God be merciful to me a sinner!" And then it is proper that there should be a double treatment for two kinds of sin. A man can't be forgiven for a thing he isn't to blame for. A man isn't to blame for being born into the world with a depraved nature. God can't pardon inbred sin. It isn't pardonable. So the second remedy is for inherited sin. And then again it is a mercy of God that we are not to receive the two blessings at once. If we had to feel the guilt of sins committed and see the blackness of indwelling depravity at the same time, we would be so discouraged that salvation would be impossible. Another reason for two works is the slowness of the soul to grasp spiritual truth and appreciate its privilege. How many sermons did it take to convince you that you should be saved or sanctified. Scores and scores. And here you are demanding that a soul shall apprehend the whole thing at once.

If you want this blessing you can have it. You must be in one accord—no fusses—no church quarrels—you must seperate yourself—insulate your soul from men and things for a time and pray. Don't discuss it, but pray for it believingly and it will come. Hallelujah!

No sooner was the call given than the altar filled and soon the air was full of the sounds of prayer, the sobs and cries of hungry hearts. It was a gracious season and many souls date their entire sanctification to that hour.

SUNDAY, 3 P. M.

By far the largest congregation ever seen upon Portsmouth camp ground assembled this afternoon in the tabernacle. The huge audience extends far out beyond the building. Bro. John Norberry preached a most blessed and powerful sermon. We are indebted to the wife of Bro. S. G. Otis, the publisher of this book, for kindly taking the notes of this sermon.

Text: Luke 19: 5. "Make haste." These are words of Jesus. His fame had spread abroad because he was a wonderful man, a being from another world. Men and women made their way to him, and at one time they thronged him so he had to get into a ship and from there he preached a marvelous sermon, that has been repeated from that day to this. Words that no other man spake. They were so taken up with him they forgot their homes and everything. At one time they were so eager to hear him that they were with him three days, and he had to give them bread. His face shone as no other. I would that people were now concerned to see Jesus. They cried out "We would see Jesus." When officers were after him and a crowd about him, Jesus stood and cried, "If any man thirst, let him come unto me and drink." They said, "Before we can arrest him, we must get something against him." They never heard a man saying such things before. They were charmed with his words and went back without him and said, "Never man spake like this man."

Jesus wasn't afraid to touch the lepers. People came and brought divers that were sick, blind, dumb, etc., and he healed them all. This crowd wouldn't be here to-day if Christ had not been preached. Men were always anxious to hear Jesus speak, and they spread the news, "Jesus is coming this way." You remember the woman that had spent all her living on doctors and had grown worse instead of better. One of the neighbors told her one day about Jesus and that he was coming that way, and charged nothing for curing diseases; but a shade came over the face of the poor woman as she said, "But my case is incurable." The other assured her that he could cure incurable cases and this would perhaps be her last chance, so she hurried through the crowd and pressed her way till she got near enough to reach out and touch the border of his garment. She was well immediately. Jesus turned right about and asked, "Who touched me?" "That's a great question to ask," said one of his disciples, "don't you see the crowd pressing you on every side, and then you ask, "Who touched me!" But Jesus said, "Some one touched me, for I see that virtue has gone out of me." There is a way to touch Jesus that brings virtue out of him. Jesus wanted her to make an open confession of her healing before the multitude.

His fame kept spreading till one day a man named Zaccheus heard of him. He was a tax collector and a great sinner; but he got under conviction and closed his office and determined not to do anything more till he had seen Jesus. There were obstacles in the way, but he must see him, so he looks ahead and sees a tree which he reached and climbed. O! that people were as determined to see Jesus now! Satan will try to hinder, but we must jump over the difficulties. From his position in the tree, Zaccheus could see the people passing; now doubting Thomas goes by, and there is John, the beloved. Here comes one with the face of an angel, with a radiance about his countenance, and such a pure look, he is charmed. Jesus gets to the tree and looks up and says, "Zaccheus, make haste and come down." Zaccheus might have said, "Why! Lord, I didn't know you were going to make me so conspicuous. Go on up the street and I'll follow by and by." But no, he didn't argue like you do. He made his way down, the people whispering, "He's going to join that crowd." Jesus told him he was going to abide at his house that day, and Zacheus said, "Lord I'll give half my goods to feed the poor, and restore fourfold where I've wronged any one." Jesus said, "This day is salvation come to your house." Don't you suppose they watched him next day when he went to his place of business? They found he had the genuine article. There are some here to-day that will never get saved unless they make restitution.

Let these words ring in your ears, "Make haste." Time is short, life is uncertain, death is on the track, pursuing us. Jesus is coming some day when we least expect it. Jesus tells us of a rich man who had a large farm and his crops were so numerous that he had no place to store them. He was a man, perhaps, of fine physique, good health and liable to live many years. He looks about wondering what he will do, he hears the supper bell and goes to the table, giving no thanks or prayer to the God who has been so kind to him and given him everything he could desire year after year. The wife sees her husband eats nothing, and asks, "What is come over you?" "I am thinking, where shall I put my goods, and I can't eat till I get the question settled." Bed time comes and he says, "I'll not retire now." So the family leave him alone and he takes out paper, and pencil, and rule, and thinks nothing of God or heaven. Some of you farmers are more concerned about cabbage than you are about your soul. You think more about the triflings things of earth than of the life to come. This man thought he would build some larger barns and lay up stores for his children. He begins to plan, mark and figure, Some of you are planning how much you can lay up another year. He sits up all night, gets it all arranged, sits back and says, "Soul thou hast much goods laid up for many years. Take thine ease, eat, drink and be merry." Death won't come for twenty or thirty years; The doctor says I have a fine constitution, my children are well. Three o'clock and some one knocks. No time for visitors, but the death angel never tells us when he is coming. Hark! I hear the voice of God. "Thou fool! this night thy soul shall be required of thee." The man drops dead, his wife hears the thud and rushes to see what is the matter.

Some of you are saying, "As soon as I get my house paid for, as soon as I get the last thing done, I'll seek salvation." "Make haste!" Don't procrastinate! "He that being often reproved, hardeneth his neck, shall suddenly be destroyed and that without remedy."

Backslider, make haste! He'll kill the fatted calf for you. Believer, make haste! get sanctified! If we don't walk in the light we shall lose what light we have. Get saved to-day. Everything about us tells us to "make haste." That boy, that girl you laid away and promised to meet again, they cry to you, "make haste!" Every grave yard to-day cries "make haste!" Every tombstone is saying "make haste!" Every person ought to make haste. The Holy Ghost cries to us to "make haste." The angels cry down to us, "make haste!" Jesus, who died to save sinful souls cries to us, "make haste!" God help us to make haste this afternoon.

God permitted his children to witness a most glorious altar service as a result of this Spirit ordered sermon. There were many clean-cut conversions and reclamations as well as sanctifications.

SUNDAY, 7.30 P. M.

We deeply regret that we cannot remain through the service. It is the last night of this great camp. There is a great crush of people, but "the power of the Lord is over all," to use George Fox's expression. As we hasten away Dr. Carradine is announcing his text. For the notes of this grand sermon we are under obligation to Miss Nellie Wilson of Providence and Mrs. S. G. Otis of Springfield. We cannot leave the holy place with its throngs of holy people without a feeling of sadness. Nowhere but in holiness convocation is there such unity of spirit and genuine fellowship. But the day is coming, thank God, when the pure-hearted shall "gather to part no more." Our part of this little task is completed. May the God of holiness in some way bless the little book to everyone who reads it. Amen.

Dr. Carradine. Text Matt. 27:22, "What shall I do then with Jesus that is called Christ?"

These are the words of Pilate. Christ was on his hands for disposal and he is on our hands; and we must dispose of him in one way or the other, we must either accept him or reject him. Rich or poor he comes to us all, for he knows that there is no way to save us but by himself. Jesus Christ alone can rectify the soul. He alone can regenerate us and sanctify us and make life fit to live. The heart is absolutely incorrigible to all but the power of Christ. What will you do when he withdraws his hand and you are left with your own reckless miserable self forever? "My spirit shall not always strive with man." Nothing ever frightened me so much as the thought of my soul going out there in the dark unsanctified and unregenerated.

It is for each man to say where he will go. You and I, by our choices, decide our own destinies. Look at Dives and Lazarus. Rich man clothed in purple and fine linen, faring sumptuously every day. Nothing especially mean about him except his unbelief in the things of God, though he did let a beggar, a good man, die of starvation. The beggar went to the bosom of Abraham while the rich man lifted up his eyes in torment, and all because of choice.

Christ always comes pleading. He never compels, never forces the will, because God gave us free wills in the first place. The idea of heaven being crowded with people who did not want to go there! Why, it would be a hell instead of heaven. Christ presents his truth to you and you decide the matter. He treats us as free beings. We must choose Christ or hell from a God-given power which is in us. You have got to rise on the feet that God gave you and use those lips which he made and plead and pray for salvation. All heaven and hell can't make you a Christian against your will. I have been telling you in the last few days what Christ can do for you and you have sat and judged for or against him.

What will you do with Jesus? We may wash our hands of him as did Pilate. Some of you are doing that, though you do not call for water. God sees your heart. He can see your intention as plainly as a cloud in the sky, and when he sees you don't want Christ, he leaves you.

We often fail to recognize Christ. "There standeth one among you to-night whom ye know not." The Holy Ghost has been here taking pictures all through this camp, and now the Lord is going to take you into a dark room of sickness or trouble and develop the negative, and then you will see that Christ was here. The God of the Universe has been here seventeen days and you have failed to recognize him, but the time is coming when you will think of it again and when you will say, "O, I see it all now! O, that I had never left that camp ground until God had had mercy on me!" Christ is knocking. How long would you knock at an unopened door? He has knocked for years.

How may we know that it is Christ who is there? By the tender feeling in our hearts. That tenderness was not put there by the devil. It is from the Holy Spirit. People come out of theatres and the stars talk to them and they mutter, "Oh, that I was a better man!" and instead of yielding to God they laugh it off or read it off or dissipate the feeling with some worldly amusement. The feeling was nothing on earth but Christ coming to the soul.

Another reason we know it is Christ who comes is that of ourselves we are incapable of grieving over our sin. You are no more able to grieve over your sins than a dead man to rise up and walk. It is the Holy Ghost that makes us feel bad over our misdeeds.

You can deny Christ as Peter did. The denial of him goes on to-day. You deny him when you are ashamed of his people. You deny him when you are ashamed of his words, such as, "Sanctify," "holiness" etc. You are afraid of the word "Sanctification," and yet its in Christ's book!

You may sell him as Judas did. The air is just quivering with the rattling of the money that has gone in exchange for Christ. People are selling him all over the land—some for so little! He is sold for pleasure, for place, for a thousand things.

You may give him up as Pilate did. You can't seek Christ but someone cries, "Give him up." When I turned to God as a young man, the boys jeered and laughed at me. You try being a Christian and see what they will do to you. You'll hear from your family and friends if you try to be sanctified. I see lots of people give up because somebody wants them to. They have no backbone. The martyrs refused life, when it was offered them on condition that they should give up Christ. When in Rome I visited the Coliseum and stood where one hundred thousand Christians were slaughtered. Wesley was often stoned and mobbed. I was out in Texas a year ago and a girl who was saved in the meetings was turned out of the house at ten o'clock at night by her own father; she met a girl friend who took her home and in two weeks God gave her a place where she found her life work. Oh, give up everybody but Christ! If you had everything and did not have him you would be miserable. People who live on pound cake without Christ are fretting all the time because they want more; but if we have a piece of corn bread and Jesus we feel like saying, "All this and Jesus too!" He can make corn bread taste like pound cake. Don't surrender him.

Do not reject Christ as the Jews did. Jerusalem is the most desolate country of to-day. I have seen Christians reject and lose him by opposing sanctification. Christ will leave us if we are regenerated and refuse to accept him as our sanctifier.

Take Christ as your pardoner, as did the dying thief. The thief saw how patient Jesus was on the cross and he began to take his part. Suddenly the Spirit came to him and he said, "Lord, remember me when thou comest into thy kingdom." Take him as your sanctifier, as the apostles did. They had served him for years, but he had something better for them.

You can take him for your keeper, as the disciples did. Don't be afraid you can't keep it. It will keep you. Sanctification keeps us. The bank of heaven never breaks.

What would you do without Christ in the dying hour? How sweet to feel in death that Christ is near you and hear him saying, "I am with you." It is not hard to die when Christ is around. But it is an awful thing to put out your hand and feel for Christ when you are dying and not find him.

There is a time when we get where God talks to us no more. You can sin God's Spirit away so that he will never come back. It is an awful thing to put off an impression made by God. When Christ leaves there is no hope. Come to him now!

Extract of the Bill of 1897.

PORTSMOUTH CAMP GROUND is situated on Quaker Hill, on Rhode Island, about two miles from Portsmouth station, on the N. Y., N. H. & H. R. R., and is seven miles from Newport and ten from Fall River. Portsmouth Camp is a beautiful hard-wood grove, supplied with the best of cold spring water. The Island is a delightful summer resort, the sea air is very bracing, and the picturesque scenery is unsurpassed in New England.

Heaven has chosen this spot for the display of Pentecostal electricity from the upper skies, for the operation of the Holy Ghost in the salvation of sinners and the sanctification of believers. He will be there in great power. No mistake. He swept through the Camp with resistless force last year, until, while the servant of God was yet speaking, men began to fall on their faces in the straw; forty-two people lay about the altar without an invitation. At another time when there had been no hint or call to an altar service, people began to come; strong men fell prostrate before they reached the altar; sixty-five souls lay in the straw crying to God. No trace of fanaticism.

Rev. B. Carradine of St. Louis, Mo., Rev. John Thompson, Philadelphia, Rev. Wm. H. Hoople, Rev. John Norberry and Rev. Chas. BeVier of Brooklyn, N. Y., Rev. Miss Phœbe Hall, Washington, D. C., also many New England ministers and workers are expected to be with us.

LODGING.

There are society tents where lodging on single beds may be had at 25 cts. per night. Family wall tents, 10 x 12, with flies and board floors, each containing one double bedstead, straw mattress, straw pillows, pail, cup and wash basin, chair and broom for $4 for the first ten days or $6 for the entire time. In all cases bring your own bedding, towels, etc., not mentioned in the tent furnishings. Do not neglect this. Furnished rooms may be had by those who prefer not to live in tents. The tents are owned by us. They are all made of 8-oz. duck, and each tent has a fly of the same material. Free lodging for all ministers (and their wives) who are in regular connection with any Evangelical Church.

BOARD.

Good table board, $4.50 per week, 75 cts per day; breakfast and supper, 25 cts each; dinner, 35 cts. Provisions may be had on the grounds for those who wish to board themselves. All persons must procure their provisions and meal tickets for the Sabbath on Saturday, as nothing will be sold on the Lord's Day.

RAILROAD ACCOMMODATION.

Round-trip tickets from Boston to Portsmouth station, $2.40; from Fall River, 40 cts.; from Newport, 35 cts. Stage will leave Portsmouth on arrival of trains. All persons coming by way of Providence will leave the city 2.30 p. m. (on Saturdays only at 3.30) on boat "Queen City." Round-trip ticket, 40 cts. The "Awashonks," leaving Providence at 9 a. m., will carry passengers to and from the Camp Saturdays only. The boat landing is about one mile from the Camp. Passengers taken to and from the Camp for 15 cts each, trunks 15 cts. each. From Portsmouth station, 20 cts. each, and trunks 20 cts. each. Those coming by train without baggage, who wish to walk from station, can get off at Corry Lane, one mile from Camp. No Sunday trains. Let everybody come up to this feast of the Lord. Applications for tents and rooms should be sent in as early as possible.

SETH C. REES,
F. M. MESSENGER,
G. W. KIES, } Executive
W. H. WEST, } Committee.
E. G. MACOMBER,
BYRON J. REES

All communications should be addressed to Seth C. Rees, Portsmouth, R. I.

EVANGELIST SETH C. REES

HULDA A. REES (Died June 3, 1898)

BOOK 3

HALLELUJAHS

FROM

PORTSMOUTH CAMPMEETING

Number Three

A Report of the Campmeeting held at Portsmouth, Rhode Island, July 29th to August 8th, 1898

BYRON J. REES

SPRINGFIELD, MASS.
CHRISTIAN UNITY PUBLISHING CO.
1898

PREFACE.

ANOTHER session of Portsmouth Campmeeting has come and gone. The eighth annual meeting on the Island of Rhode has passed into history, and the company is dispersed abroad from Maine to Colorado and from North Dakota to Kentucky.

By the concession of all it has been the best encampment of the eight. The weather was good, the attendance was excellent, the singing was spiritual, and the preaching was dynamitical. Morrison was at his best. He is a glorious, princely preacher, a man of God, a sterling exponent of New Testament piety. Godbey, who was new to all New Englanders, delighted us all with his red-hot religion, his humble Christ-like spirit, and his crystal-clear exegesis from the basis of his Tischendorf Greek Text. All the ministers and workers, Norberry, BeVier, Messenger, Remsen, Pennington and many others seemed to have received an extraordinary douche of fresh ointment.

For the first time in the history of Portsmouth we publish an illustrated report. The faces of these people of God will look good to many a reader whose hearts these ministers cheered, whose lives they brightened and whose souls they encouraged to push on through fog and gloom and darkness to full salvation!

The sermons are of course inadequately reported. Anyone can see that, but it is the best that we could do; and while it is manifestly unfair to men of the calibre of our Kentucky preachers to let meagre scraps stand for finished discourses, yet we believe (else we would not write) that the gain beats the deficit and the blessing which readers obtain outweighs the maltreating of sermons.

May God's blessing rest upon every reader of this unassuming little book. May we all see to it this coming year that we keep humble and meek and dead to the world and deaf to the Siren calls to compromise, and buckle our belts one hole tighter and grip our swords a little more firmly and face the enemy a little more courageously, so that, should our Lord come, he might find us red as sunset glow from crest to sandaltip in the blood of the enemy, with the piles of slain all about us! Everybody say "Amen."

BYRON J. REES.

Westport, Mass., August 10, 1898.

INTRODUCTION.

THE Portsmouth Camp-ground is located on the island from which the State of Rhode Island takes its name. This island is about fifteen miles long, and something over four miles broad at the widest part. A line of electric cars run the entire length of the island making the camp-ground easy of access to the residents of all parts of the island, as well as of the adjoining cities.

The camp-ground is beautiful for situation, and there is something in the very trees, rocks and atmosphere, that seems to be an inspiration to devotion.

While this camp nestles in the very heart of civilization, and within a few miles of its sacred precincts, there are great cities full of commerce, and factories, whose tall smoke stacks can be seen from the hilltop near the grounds, with thousands of busy operatives, and fashionable world-loving Newport, with its giddy thousands seeking after the pleasures of the world, yet this is a remarkably quiet spot, where one can rest and worship God free from the world's distraction and care.

The congregations were large from the first service, and the Lord was with us all the time.

This camp is noted for the spiritual power which attends the annual gatherings here. "Where the Spirit of the Lord is, there is liberty." Here the people have great liberty in the Lord.

Rev. Seth C. Rees, the president of the association, who had charge of the services, is a mighty man of God. Large physically, larger mentally, but largest spiritually, he makes an unexcelled leader of the hosts at a great holiness camp-meeting. He is a man of much prayer, and strong faith. He puts God to the test, and things come to pass.

We must have Brother Rees in some of our Southern camp-meetings. There is no man in all the holiness movement who preaches with more fervent power, and direct effect on the masses, than Seth C. Rees.

We were delighted to have the privilege of sitting again at the feet of Rev. W. B. Godbey. He gave Bible readings from eight to ten each morning, and frequently preached to the people. One morning he read two hours, and then preached two hours, and quit apparently as fresh after the hour's labor as when he first begun.

I have never seen him in better working trim, and was constantly amazed at his simplicity, learning and wisdom.

As I looked up at the dear old man, with a great company gathered at his feet, listening to the word of God, I remembered something of the conflicts through which he had passed, enough of persecution, scorn, and misrepresentation to fill a large volume, and yet, with unswerving step he has gone forward, while those who maligned him have fallen into their graves and been forgotten, but his bow abides in strength. Few men have the undivided love of as many warm hearts helped by his ministry, as W. B. Godbey. May God's blessing continue to abide with him, and his evening be serene, and his sunset without a cloud.

At this camp I met with Evangelist Clarence Strouse. This was my first meeting with this remarkable man. Of a fine old Virginia family, educated in Paris, France, with excellent natural endowments, most attractive personal appearance, fervid eloquence, and tender, loving heart, Brother Strouse is one of the most intensely interesting men I have ever met. It will be remembered that he is editor of the *Religious Review of Reviews*, a charming monthly magazine, splendidly illustrated, which our readers ought to subscribe for by the thousands. I wish to suggest to our Kentucky pastors to secure Brother Strouse' services for revival work. Address him at Salem, Virginia. Write early, there is a great demand for his services.

Byron Rees, a worthy son of Seth C. Rees, was with us, with blessed promise of great usefulness.

John Norberry, of whom I have written often, and who is a perfect torrent of spiritual life and joy, helped forward the good work.

Prof. Mitchell, educated in music in Germany, and

filled with the Holy Ghost in Rhode Island, presided at the piano, and the same old colored brother of whom Dr. Carradine wrote last year, rattled a tamborine in a most marvelous way.

The camp-meeting was a great success financially as well as spiritually, something like $1500 dollars being raised over and above the running expenses of the meeting, with which to pay off indebtedness for improvements on the grounds.

First and last, there were many noted people on the grounds, among them Dr. Levy of Philadelphia, and Mr. Dennett, the celebrated restaurant man of America, who feeds the multitudes in many of the large cities of the nation. Here he was bowing down in the straw at the feet of Jesus, placing his all upon the altar for full salvation.

There were some scenes during these meetings which this pen cannot describe. The Holy Ghost fell in power, and there were demonstrations of His presence which beggar description.

I do not know the number of salvations, but I know the number was very large. I think the brethren claimed this to be the greatest meeting ever held on the grounds.

During the year Sister Hulda Rees, the wife of Bro. Seth C. Rees, had died in most glorious triumph. She was a preacher of rare gifts, and wonderful power. The people missed her presence, but rejoiced in her victorious ascension.

INTRODUCTION ix

Our visit to Portsmouth Camp greatly enriched us. The kindness of the people, to wife and myself, and the blessing of God make that beautiful forest on the island, between the river and the sea, one of the most sacred spots on earth to us. To God be everlasting praise. Amen.—Rev. H. C. Morrison in the *Pentecostal Herald*.

CONTENTS.

PHOTO-ENGRAVINGS.

REV. SETH C. REES,	*Frontispiece*
HULDA A. REES,	*Frontispiece*
REV. WM. B. GODBEY,	Facing page 17
REV. H. C. MORRISON,	Facing page 48
REV. JOHN NORBERRY,	Facing page 56

THURSDAY, JULY 28.

Portsmouth Campground,	13
In the Evening,	17

FRIDAY, JULY 29.

Morning,	18
Opening Meeting,	19
Sermon by Rev. John Pennington,	20
Sermon by Rev. W. B. Godbey,	25

SATURDAY, JULY 30.

Bible Reading by Rev. W. B. Godbey,	28
Sermon by Rev. F. M. Messenger,	31
Sermon by Rev. W. B. Godbey,	33

SUNDAY, JULY 31.

Testimony Meeting,	36
Sermon by Rev. Chas. B. Strouse,	39
Sermon by Rev. H. C. Morrison,	42

CONTENTS

MONDAY, AUGUST 1.

Sermon by Rev. W. B. Godbey,	44
Praise and Testimony,	46
Sermon by Rev. H. C. Morrison,	48
Sermon by Rev. H. C. Morrison.	51

TUESDAY, AUGUST 2.

Bible Reading by Rev. W. B. Godbey,	54
Sermon by Rev. John Norberry,	56
Sermon by Rev. H. C. Morrison,	60

WEDNESDAY, AUGUST 3.

Sermon by Rev. Seth C. Rees,	63
Sermon by Rev. H. C. Morrison,	67
Sermon by Rev. John Pennington,	71

THURSDAY, AUGUST 4.

Sermon by Rev. W. B. Godbey,	75
Sermon by Rev. H. C. Morrison,	79

FRIDAY, AUGUST 5.

Sermon by Mrs. H. C. Morrison,	84
Service in Memory of Hulda A. Rees,	88
Sermon Recently Preached by the Late Hulda A. Rees,	97
Sermon by Rev. H. C. Morrison,	103

SATURDAY, AUGUST 6.

Sermon by Rev. W. B. Godbey,	106
Sermon by Rev. Chas. BeVier,	111

SUNDAY, AUGUST 7.

Sermon by Rev. Seth C. Rees,	116
Service Conducted by Sister Minnie Lindberg,	123
Sermon by Rev. H. C. Morrison,	125

PORTSMOUTH CAMPGROUND
THURSDAY, JULY 28, 1898.

THERE are advantages to be gained by coming to the campground a day or two before the meeting opens. Just as there is nothing more delightful than a half hour in a quiet church before the people come, so a day or so in the grove, "God's first temple," before the bell taps for service, is refreshing and inspiring.

Today is Thursday, tomorrow "the firing begins." The campers are coming all the time, some by train, some by the "Queen City," the steamer from Providence, most by the electric cars which pass within a few minute's walk of the camp. It is a strange and novel experience to come to Campmeeting by car. The old way was to ride two miles and a half from Portsmouth station in a boiling hot sun over a dusty road. Now we pay our nickle and hum along the country roads and step out at the back-door of the Campmeeting.

This is not a sunshiny day by a good deal. The sky is gray and leaden, and stray drops of rain patter on the leaves now and then. But the birds sing in spite of the dreariness of the day. I think that that is a thrush balancing himself on a twig in front of the tent and singing with "good liberty." Perhaps he thinks of the good days coming, or, perhaps he has something in his breast which manufactures melody and he has to sing or die. And God puts into the heart of every sanctified man or woman a self-acting Aeolian which makes them make music and exult and rejoice in the fiercest tempests! Glory!

There are many changes this year. New buildings have been built and a new tent or so pitched on "Fifth Avenue," so that, as a campmeeting, we are on the upgrade. Praise the Lord! Brother Nelson R. Reed has a new cottage. It is a neat, tasty, substantial-looking building, built of hard pine and painted white. Thomas L. Lewis and Andrew R. Trafford have each had new kitchens erected.

It is now eleven o'clock in the morning and the rain has gotten down to business. "Drip, drip," the drops strike the canvass "fly" of the tent with a pleasant rhythm. Nearly everyone has gone indoors. Little Howard Roberts has taken his umbrella down and trotted into the cottage under the big beech tree. We are in for a rainy day if appearances are not deceptive. But there are compensations for cloudy weather. When we are forced to stay in, we look about for something to do, and the first thing we know the Bible falls open and God's word feeds the soul. There is more chance to pray when it rains, for even a hardened and experienced tenter, a veteran campaigner, will not brave a soaking to come to you for "a broom" or "a hammer" or "a few nails if you please." But what are we good for anyway if not to supply campmeeting folks with anything we have? We will see the time, everyone of us, when we will be glad of every little kindness we ever did to one of God's saints. Some of the oldest and queerest and most trying of people will shine in the ages to come with a lustre that Orion and the Pleiades never had, and some whom we "endure" now we will admire and honor in that City.

There is singing in the tent next to us. The sound of hymns in a tent at campmeeting! How spirit-touched songs do cheer the soul! These battle hymns which the saints have sung as they have gone into battle, which they have chanted as they crossed the dark River, how they lift the discouraged and broken spirit! As one hears the martial words and music, courage comes and one feels like standing in the hard, dark places of the earth and, like the figure on Liberty Island, holding aloft the blazing torch. O may God give his servants grace to fight on and shout on and battle on until the dusky-faced hosts of hell turn and flee to their native regions! The soldiers are being promoted from our army; let us close in the ranks and with shoulder to shoulder stand steadfastly. Like the cliffs of Marblehead breasting the surges, let us face the Euroclydon of the deep, fearless and dauntless. Amen and Amen!

There is one face we do not see at Portsmouth. There is one quiet, saintly woman-soul who has

"Passed to where beyond these voices there is peace."

What ragged, cruel chasms are made in life! One whose dear presence was to us like the incense from the censers in the sanctuary has ascended, and we are left to go on amid blinding, scalding tears and do our duty as if nothing was the matter, for the days must not be spent idly, neither must we tarry too long secluded from the world in the chamber of bereavement.

It is doubtful if any woman connected with Portsmouth Campmeeting has so large a place in the hearts of those who attend the meetings as had Hulda A. Rees. But she is with her Lord today and though her accustomed places see her no more, though "Rest Cottage" has passed into the hands of others, though she will never preach again from the platform under the Tabernacle, we are comforted with the thought that her pain and weariness are over and that she now, with all the church triumphant, sits in the galleries of the skies watching the battle on the earth! Praise the Lord!

Some of the workers came onto the grounds to day. This morning there walked through the gateway a man of medium height but of very slender figure, wearing a duster, a brown straw hat, and carrying an umbrella. His beard and hair was closely trimmed, and his alert step made him seem younger than he really was. He ap-

REV. Wm. B. GODBEY

proached very quietly, and there was an atmosphere of Christliness about the man that struck us at once. He had the air and mien of a pilgrim, a citizen of another country who was merely "passing through" this one.

"May God's richest blessing rest upon you, my brother!" And as he spoke, the benediction seemed to come upon us and we felt that unmistakable presence of the Spirit which all friends of Jesus know so well. We sat in a tent and talked for half an hour and we rapidly grew to love the man of God. The man was Dr. William B. Godbey, of Perryville, Ky.

IN THE EVENING.

A goodly number of people came this evening, over fifty in all, certainly. Tonight there are lanterns scattered throughout the grounds revealing great banks of gray fog and making the wet oak and maple leaves glisten like mica. It is a late hour and the lights in the tents and cottages are all out. Away up on the hill one can hear the hum of a late car, and the big fog-drops splash upon the tight canvas of our tent.

It is a sweet thought to us, as we sit alone in the night, that of all who are upon the campground, there is not one with whose case God is not intimately acquainted. If there is a tired, sleepless head, God knows it. If there is a discouraged heart, one into which has entered the iron and from the lacerated side of which drips the life-blood, God knows it all and like the great Father that he is, bends o'er and whispers words of consolation and peace to all who hearken. Is there in some obscure tent some child of God who is suffering under the shock and cruelty of a recent bereavement? Thank God, He yet lives and the balm of Gilead yet heals and soothes. God is here and there is not a tent under the thick canopy of leaves but He visits it.

ℒℛ

FRIDAY, JULY 29.

MORNING.

The weather is yet foggy and cloudy, but there are signs of a clear sky later. People who have tents engaged are constantly arriving, opening their "canvas houses" and settling down for ten days of life in the woods. The dining hall is open, and cooks and waiters are busy getting ready to feed the tenters. Superintendent Chase and his assistants are engaged in various parts of the grounds directing new arrivals to their temporary homes. Everyone on the grounds knows Brother Chase. It is said that no man can do more than one thing at once and do it well, but Brother Chase is a standing refutation of the saying, for he does any number of things at once and does them all satisfactorily.

Rev. John Pennington, the new pastor of the Church of Emmanuel at Providence, is here. Brother Pennington has been with us two seasons before this one, and

God has wonderfully blessed the people under his ministry. He is a tall, strong-looking man with resolute yet kindly face. There is about him a manly air which makes one involuntarily look to him as a leader of men.

OPENING MEETING. 2 P. M.

This is the opening service of the Eighth Annual Session of Portsmouth Campmeeting. By far the largest campany we have ever seen at the first meeting is gathered. It is a solemn moment, for as our eyes turn toward the platform, there is one form which we are accustomed to see there which we will never see again in this life. After a few moments of profound stillness the people with one accord joined in the singing of

"All hail the power of Jesus' name."

and

"O for a thousand tongues to sing
My great Redeemer's praise."

Bro. Pennington, after the singing of the hymns, led in prayer. There was great unity in supplication and the responses were frequent and full of zeal. Bro. Godbey followed Bro. Pennington in petition. Thus, one after another, the people of God approached the throne and the Spirit fell upon us and sealed this first service to himself.

After another hymn, Seth C. Rees, who is as usual in charge, spoke a few appropriate words. expressing great faith for the camp and exhorting all to be in a place spiritually where they could get the full benefits of "the times of refreshing."

Louis F. Mitchel is at his old place at the piano. There are pianists and pianists. There are few Holy Ghost ones. But Bro. Mitchel is not only a splendid musician, but as his fingers touch the keys God touches hearts, and many a soul is saved through this instrumentality.

Rev. John Pennington arose and preached from the text: "Nevertheless the foundation of God standeth sure, having this seal, The Lord knoweth them that are his, and let him that nameth the name of the Lord depart from iniquity."

The foundations of this world are not steady. History verifies this. Men who thought they were building steadfastly have seen that which they erected totter and fall. Perhaps some of us here have thought that some things would stand which have not. God has to teach us by repeated changes that there is but ONE foundation which "standeth sure."

Brother, build not your hopes upon earthly foundations! Thank God, there is a foundation that is as strong as Heaven! Thank God, there is a foundation grounded upon the Rock of Ages! These are shifting, changing times. Men are going down on every side. The devil is pitted against us. He is doing his utmost to undermine us. I hear the crash of falling empires, the surge of breaking seas; I hear the cries and groans of the bereaved but, thanks be unto God, "the foundation standeth sure." It does not move! It holds and will hold forever!

There is no time when the grace of God appears in so favorable a light as when it upholds us in times of awful tension. Business man, there is no secure place for you except upon "the Foundation."

This "foundation" is for us all; for the mother beside the cradle, for the young people, for the children, for the preacher in the pulpit! Hallelujah!

There are according to this text, two inscriptions. The first is: "The Lord knoweth them that are his." What a comforting thought is this! God knows us all by name. It is good for us to be known by our friends, but just think of it, God knows us and will take care of us. The second inscription is, "Let him that nameth the name of the Lord depart from iniquity." Brother, do not deflect from the rigid line of righteousness. Men do not go down all at once. The great crash comes only after a series of seemingly small deflections. You who are on this campground, if you feel that you are under conviction concerning anything at all, be frank and confess and get right.

As this campmeeting opens let us look to our foundation. It will stand "sure" for us only as "we depart from iniquity." We must be clean if we are to stand.

O may God increase the number who feel the foundation solid beneath their feet.

Beloved, if you are upon the foundation, stay! If you are not on it, get upon it immediately. Do not try to explain your action if you come to this altar. Let people say what they will, you go straight and be right. Is there a consciousness of need in your heart? Then recognize it, come out like a man, and get your lack supplied. Amen!

Seth C. Rees: "As I look into your faces after twelve months' separation, I want to testify that in all my trial God has held me and the foundation has stood without a quiver."

Rev. Frank M. Messenger: "There is a passage in the Scriptures which says that 'yet once more will the Lord shake the earth.' I feel that the shaking times are upon us. May God so save us and establish us that we will not be moved whatever may come to us."

Brother James Estes: "I have been building upon this foundation for years."

Rev. Mr. Bryant: "I feel that I ought to confess that I have in the past year ' regarded iniquity in my heart.' There was a time when I was sure that I was saved and sanctified, but I have gotten away and I feel concerned about myself. I ask an interest in your prayers."

Brother Rees: "I felt a moment ago that you ought to come to this altar. Do not delay."

As this confession was given, a sympathetic wave of feeling swept over the meeting and there seemed to be a unanimous though silent prayer that God might restore his straying child.

One brother testified that after using tobacco sixty-three years God instantaneously delivered him and he has never desired it again.

Brother Maryatt of No. Grosvenordale, Ct.: "I am standing on the sure foundation."

Sister Steere of Wickford, R. I.: "I know that God is on this ground. My soul is athirst for souls. I would give anything, suffer anything, sacrifice anything, if God would only use me in the salvation of precious souls. I do not want honor from the people. I want the smile of God upon me that I may be used in saving souls."

Sister Messenger: "I never was so thankful in all my life that I was on 'the foundation' as I am this afternoon."

There were a number of testimonies from young people yet in their teens. Bro. Rees said: "How glad I am to hear these testimonies from our young people. I remember that many of them were saved and sanctified on this campground last year. Before the services closed here last season the power of God was so present that nearly all the sinners and backsliders on the grounds were at the altar. Praise the Lord!"

The altar service which closed the service was very good and at least one soul wrestled for the blessing of full salvation.

6:30 P. M.

It is just growing dusk in the grove. The meeting tonight does not begin until 7:30, and the campers are using the interim in various ways. Some, who arrived today, are getting settled; others, who have completed the task, are talking in groups about the good meeting we had this afternoon. The bright, beautiful day is about to close in a fog. A fine, dust-like mist, so common on the coast, is drifting through the boughs and leaves of the trees. Men are carrying dozens of lighted lanterns along the paths and hanging them on nails on the trees. The tabernacle is all ablaze and looks as it did last year, a bright attractive building where the saints can gather together and worship God "in the beauty of holiness."

As we sit here in the growing darkness and think of the meeting which is to be held here for the next ten days, we thank God that in these days of ecclesiastical bondage and pastoral despotism, there are campmeetings just like this one, where the children of God can seek, find, and bear witness to, the Scriptural experience of entire sanctification, without having their shoulders lashed by self-constituted bosses. The holiness movement is moving and it is bound to succeed. Like Ezekiel's holy waters it is to grow and widen and deepen until it covers the earth. Small-sized preachers and corpulent, over-fed church dignitaries may threaten and "speak great swelling words," but Hallelujah! people are going to continue to get the blessing and, with shining faces and fire-touched lips, testify to God's great gift. Brethren, we are victors; let us act like victors. All the advantage is on our side. Let each man go up straight before him and conquer everywhere and at all times. Amen!

7 : 30 P. M.

It doesn't take much time for the meeting at Portsmouth to "get going." Tonight there is a good-sized audience gathered in the tabernacle and the singing is enthusiastic and vigorous.

Brother Rees: "Would you like to sing the last hymn my wife ever sang? It would not cause me pain. I would like for you to sing that blessed hymn." And so the people all joined in the singing of

> "How firm a foundation, ye saints of the Lord,
> Is laid for your faith in his excellent word."

After a very unctuous prayer offered by Brother Rees, Rev. W. B. Godbey preached on The Vision of the Holy Waters. (Ezek xl: 1-12.)

The caption of the chapter which you have heard is "The vision of the holy waters." This is a holiness campmeeting and so I will, as the Spirit may help, talk to you from this holiness passage.

I was much struck with one part of our brother's prayer, and that was that in which he spoke of continued progression. A Christian is like a bicycle; if he stops going he falls. Material analogies teach us the same truth. The acorn goes on to become an oak or else it rots. The little boy astride his hobby-horse must either go on and become a man or be a dwarf.

Beloved, this campmeeting ought to give everyone a grand boom. If we are sanctified we ought to acquire more in a short time than an unsanctified man in the same time. A man with a million dollars ought to be able to make more money in the Klondike gold-fields than a man with only a dollar. The more we have the easier it is to get more.

There are various symbols in the Bible. Fire stands for the Holy Ghost in his negative work. Fire burns sin. There is no fire in heaven because there is nothing there to burn. But there is "much water there," because water stands for the Holy Ghost in his positive aspect. The positive blessings of the Spirit are to increase forever.

"The waters came to the ankles." What does that mean? Well, the ankle is the walking joint, and this text means that when we get this experience we go to no place where Jesus cannot and does not go. If you walk in ankle deep, that means we are going with Jesus. As many as are going in this way raise the hand and say "Amen" as loud as you please. (Apparently the whole audience responded.)

The next thing I notice is that the second depth is to

the knee. This is the worshipping joint. O my Lord, help us to get in knee deep! If I had a thousand sons I would not send one of them to a school of theology, but I would want them all to graduate at the college of kneeology. Greatheart won his victory over Giant Despair on his knees.

Brother, professions don't amount to anything. We may profess everything and possess nothing. Do we go in knee-deep? We must get in if we want a meeting that will make heaven shout and hell groan.

Now we will go on again. We pass over a thousand paces and come to waters which reach to the loins. The loins stand for strength. When we get here we vote the whole precinct for the Lord Jesus Christ. This is where time, money, ability, everything are all for Jesus. You have heard the maxim, "Once for all!" It ought to be current in all our lives. Put in all you have! Let God have you soul and body, out and out, all in all.

Another "thousand cubits" and we are over our heads! Lord, give us floating grace! O the delectable experience of floating in mid-ocean! You wade in over your head and God will attend to the floating.

These waters of which Ezekiel speaks bring life and verdancy even to the Desert. Everywhere they go they bring plenty and richness. The glory of the holiness movement is to freshen this salty, desert world. O what opportunitites you New England people have to be a blessing to the crowds about you! You are living in a thickly-settled country, only a short distance from the metropolis of the New World—what a chance you have to sweeten the lives of poor human beings!

Now, brethren, there is no virtue in this altar, but if I were you I would show the devil that I was not afraid of it. Let everyone gather about the altar and seek for enlargement and deepening in spiritual things.

Nearly the entire audience responded to Brother Godbey's call, and a very blessed altar service was held. A little before ten the people dispersed to their tents and the first day of the meeting was ended.

SATURDAY, JULY 30.

8 : 30 A. M.

The meeting opened this morning with the hymn,

"Leaning on the everlasting arms."

Bro. Godbey is to give a Bible Reading in this service:

In the Acts of the Apostles we have the history of the founding of Christ's church. The world is full of counterfeit churches. By going back to the Acts we find the insignia of the true church.

The Acts of the Apostles was written probably by Luke at the dictation of Paul. While Luke held the pen he was only the modest amanuensis of the great Apostle.

I hold in my hand the critical Greek text from which I have read my Testament exclusively for twenty-five years. It will be well for you to follow me in your English Bibles. You will in these Bible Readings have the benefit of the very words which sprung from the mind of the Holy Ghost.

Paul appealed to Caesar that he might have an opportunity to preach the gospel to him and to his court. By appealing he forced his enemies to defray his traveling expenses to his next appointment!

In the storm on the Mediterranean, the ship could not go down because Paul was on board. John Wesley could not go down in that tempest on the Atlantic because he had not finished his work. You are immortal until your work is done. A very desperate character once drew a revolver on me, but the thing only snapped; it would not go off.

Toward the close of Paul's life he was in great suffering and close confinement. Meanwhile the epistle to the Philippians was written, and of all the epistles it is the fullest of joy and rejoicing. New Testament religion enables us to exult in times of awful trial.

After the first nine or ten chapters of Acts, Paul is the hero of the history. Luke got his material directly from Paul, for he traveled with him constantly.

We are to study God's word this morning. We are not simply to answer the question, "What shall I do to be saved?" but we are studying God's word for our edification and help. What a privilege to delve into the precious treasures of the Lord's truth! I tell you when people get sanctified, if they do not become students of the word of God they will not amount to much. Nothing is so important in these holiness camp meetings as the school of Christ, the studying of the Book.

Acts 1:1. Theophilus, "a lover of God." This book is dedicated to all lovers of God.

v 2. "The kingdom of God" was predicted by the prophet, proclaimed by Jesus and the Apostles, and is being extended to day.

v 4. "The promise of the Father is the gift of the Holy Ghost." The Holy Ghost is present here. He has been poured out and is even now in our midst. In this text the Lord commanded the disciples to tarry until the Spirit came. O, what a mistake that the church has ever gotten away from this truth! Why, no man has a right to preach until he is anointed with the Holy Ghost! In Bible phraseology, conversion makes us disciples and the baptism with the Holy Ghost makes us Christians, for the word "Christ" means anointed. When "anointed" with the Holy Ghost we are Christians according to the lexicography of the Bible.

While we have been taking these notes the people have been coming to the Tabernacle for the preaching service. It is a very close, warm morning. There is not a cloud in the sky and the air is perfectly motionless. The tents in the circle are open and the little children are swinging in the hammocks.

Brother Godbey is one of those rare men who never "run dry." When the bell for preaching tapped, the reading was not nearly completed, so it was continued through the 10:30 service until the dinner hour. Brother Godbey's quaint and characteristic style make all that he says of greatest interest.

During the prayer hour at 1:15 p. m. today there was a special out-pouring of the Spirit. This hour is always a season of great blessing to the meeting. The individual cannot afford to neglect secret prayer, and a campmeeting cannot fail to still itself before God without losing ground spiritually. There is an infallible philosophy in the successful holding of campmeetings. If the people humble themselves before God He will exalt them. If they take time for protracted seasons of prayer and abstain from everything but the practice of piety, the fire will fall upon the preaching of Christ crucified.

3:00 P. M.

The meeting opened with the singing of "I will rejoice in the Lord." Although the heat is excessive the people have made special effort to come out so that there is a good audience to hear Rev. F. M. Messenger. We always expect rich things when Brother Messenger preaches. He is a man who "walks humbly with his God," and God wonderfully uses him as a result. After the offering was lifted Brother Messenger preached the word from Isaiah xxviii: 9:

"Whom shall he teach knowledge? and whom shall he make to understand doctrine? them that are weaned from the milk and drawn from the breasts."

There are those who do not believe that God has made any revelation of himself to man. There are various classes of these disbelievers and they vary from the blatant infidel to the polished Unitarian.

Among those who claim to believe in revelation there are several classes. There are those who claim to accept parts of the Bible who reject other parts. But if one man has a right to use his shears on the written page every man has a right to do the same, and by the time a few men have cut out all objectionable things, nothing would be left but the covers of the Bible.

Opposition to revelation is due to heart aversion to righteousness. It is because men do not want to be right that they deny the Book.

God has always had at least one man he could talk to. Before the flood, God talked with Noah. When Israel was in Egypt, God picked out Moses and talked with him. He selected Samuel and held conversations with him.

The text says, "Whom shall he teach knowledge?" This knowledge is not that of colleges and schools, not that which we find in the newspapers, but the knowledge which God alone can give. If we want to possess this knowledge we must come out and be separate from the

HALLELUJAHS FROM PORTSMOUTH

world. God will not reveal himself to an unclean people.

But there is a deeper teaching in this text. God's knowledge is imparted to those "who are weaned from milk." Milk is good. It is wholesome and refreshing, but the system needs something more substantial. Too many of us are depending on sermons and public meetings and papers for our food. We neglect the meat of the Bible. If we do not feed on it we will not be recipients of God's great revelations.

Brother Messenger was *God's* messenger to the people today and many were greatly blessed.

7:30 P. M.

The people have been gathering to the Mount Zion at Portsmouth very rapidly today. Nearly every "electric" has brought three or four to swell our number. We are therefore quite a large company in the Tabernacle tonight and the volume of song is swelling louder and louder as the meeting gains in power and unction. The early part of the service was devoted to prayer and there were perhaps twenty-five short, faithful prayers. The people are getting down in humility and dependence upon God until we are expecting a spiritual deluge soon. God's order is first down, then up!

By far the most characteristic figure in the Tabernacle is our dear Brother Godbey. As we write he is kneeling at the altar in silent prayer. Goggles are on his eyes; a traveling cap with vizor is on his head. His thin saintly face, which is turned upward like the face of Hoffman's "Praying Christ," is full of earnestness and feeling. As we look at this aged, diminutive figure we remember that before us is a man who has preached as many as nine hundred and three sermons in a year and who has preached for forty-five years the gospel of our Lord. It is possible that the holiness movement west of the Alleghanies owes more to Brother Godbey under God than to any other man. He travels everywhere in America. Last month he sailed on the Pacific, this week upon the Atlantic ocean. A flame of living fire and full of unction, although sixty-five years of age, he is one of the most mighty and active of men. He preaches tonight from Numbers vi: verses 1-7. The subject is "The Nazarite."

The word Nazarite means separated. The Nazarite of the Old Dispensation was the holiness man of his time. And we who possess holiness are the Nazarites of our time. By the way, I would that we could all get into the Book of Lamentations for a time. In every work of God there is a Gethsemane and a crucifixion before there is an ascension and a glorification. Let us get down, down, down! Before we get much in this meeting we will have to get down to business with God Almighty.

In Lamentations we have a description of a counterfeit sanctification. A counterfeit sanctification is the meanest thing in the world, and their name is Legion. These spurious sanctifications are wrecking the holiness movement.

To become a Nazarite one must first be a true Israelite. So this symbolizes a second work of grace. We must be true believers if we are to be sanctified.

The Nazarite was never allowed to touch a dead body. If his father or mother or sister or brother died he could not touch their dead bodies. However near a thing may be to him he could not touch it if it was wrong. Holiness brother, do not compromise for anything!

If you want to get your friends saved you can't do it on the line of compromise. They will not even respect you. Go straight and be true and God will convict your friends.

Sampson's strength was due to his Nazaritic vow. I have seen pictures of Samson which represented him as a giant, but that is all nonsense. Samson's power was in his vow. The power of a holiness man lies in his keeping separate from uncleanness.

The Nazarite could not drink any intoxicant. The sanctified man is to "Be not drunk with wine wherein is excess, but be filled with the Spirit." The Spirit is to be his stimulant.

The altar service which followed this remarkable sermon was very precious and blessed. Thank God for His presence in this camp today.

SUNDAY, JULY 31.

8 : 30 A. M.

The people are on hand this morning for a glorious day of blessing and power. It is a still, holy morning; there is a quiet brooding sense of the presence of Almighty God.

Among the new arrivals are Rev. I. T. Johnson of Douglas, Mass., Rev. Edward M. Mix of Rockland, R. I., Rev. Arthur Greene of Auburn, R. I., Sister Abbie Lawrence of Douglas, Mass., and many other workers and evangelists.

While we have been writing Rev. Clarence B. Strouse of Salem, Virginia, has entered the Tabernacle. Brother Strouse is an evangelist whom Brother Carradine has spoken of as "the star of the South." Last winter he held a revival in Charlestown, S. C., in which seven hundred and fifty people bowed at the altar. In appearance Brother Strouse is a mere boy. Sitting upon the platform he looks like a very ordinary, tame young fellow, but when he preaches he is God's holy prophet and strikes terrific blows for God and souls and heaven. He is not only an active evangelist, but he is the editor of "The Religious Review of Reviews," a magazine which is to the field of religious literature what "The Review of Reviews" is to the secular world.

We are delighted to see in the audience this morning Brother and Sister Dennett of New York City and Brother Tatnal of Wilmington, Del.

The stream of testimony is beginning to flow and the contagious fire of witnessing is spreading.

Sister Phetteplace: "The Psalmist says, 'Let every thing that hath breath praise the Lord.' I am sure that takes me in. Glory to God for his mercy and grace."

Brother Silas Davol: "The power of God is here. I felt it the moment I stepped upon these grounds. I do thank God for the cleansing blood. Hallelujah!"

Singing:

"Blessed Quietness."

Rev. F. M. Messenger: "My debt of gratitude was never so great as it is this morning. How I do praise God for what the Holy Ghost has been to me and my family during the past year! My prayer is that I may be kept so humble and low in the dust that whenever trials and afflictions do come I may take them with the spirit that I should."

The audience took up the chorus, "Blessed Quietness," for the second time, and with great feeling and tear-besprinkled faces and uplifted hands sang it again and again. The waves of God's power seemed to roll over the congregation like combers over a beach after a storm.

Brother John Trevor: "I want to praise God for a

clean heart and a joyous salvation. I remember that under Sister Rees' ministry I was sanctified and I have had an unbroken walk with Jesus ever since."

Sister Estes of Newport: "I praise the Lord for the privilege of attending this meeting. I thank God that he gives us power to go ahead and capture other souls for him."

Elder Mix: "I want to do good and get good at this meeting. Oh, I have prayed for this camp. I have prayed that the Lord may station his angels about this camp and that souls may be mightily convicted, even as they enter the camp. 'If ye ask anything in his name he will do it.' Praise the Lord for his wonderful, full and free salvation."

Rev. I. T. Johnson: "None of us know what sorrow and bereavement are until they come to us. When my little child went to Heaven I then knew what affliction was, but God kept me. Praise the Lord!"

Sister Jennie Stromberg: "I feel that Jesus walks by my side and he is very precious to my soul."

Brother Joseph Wood of Fall River: "I cannot frame words to tell you how much I have to thank God for."

Brother Edward Doane of Westport Factory: "I am saved this morning from this wicked world. I thank the Lord for all that he does for me."

Sister Steere: "I thank God that even through our tears we can praise the Lord."

Brother Rees asked if there were not a number who desired to say a word of praise. Fully sixty immediately arose. Praise the Lord for these tokens of a deep spiritual tide!

10:30 A. M.

Rev. H. C. Morrison was the preacher of the hour. We were so rejoiced to see Brother Morrison and so eager to hear him preach that taking notes was out of the question. So we laid down the pencil and enjoyed the sermon from introduction to peroration. It was a marvelous sermon from the text, "What would you that I should do unto you?"

3:00 P. M.

After much entreaty and persuasion Rev. Clarence B. Strouse consented to preach this afternoon. He took for his text the latter part of the last verse of the 87th Psalm: "All my Springs are in thee."

I thank God that this text is not only the testimony of the great David, but it is *my* testimony as well.

This word "spring" is a very peculiar word. When I was in school in Paris a man who was learning English told me of the difficulties which he had with this word.

"Why," said he, "you talk of the spring of the year and a spring in a watch, spring when you leap and a spring of water." Well, thank God, he is all this. He puts an experience in the soul that is like the "Spring" of the year; he puts a motive power in us that keeps us running like the works in a watch; he places a "springing" experience in us that makes us leap spiritually and sometimes physically, and he himself is our "spring" of pure refreshing water.

But David referred more especially in this text to God as a "spring" of refreshing water. Beloved, are all our "springs" in God? Do our desires all seek satisfaction in God? Is he the source of all our help and recuperation?

God as a "spring" is our source of purity. Water cleanses and makes holy. All our holiness comes from God.

We find in this "Spring" constancy and perpetuity. You have all seen the wet weather "spring." It dries up at the very time when you need it most. But, if you get this experience, you will *never* dry up.

Oh, these preachers who work all the week trying to pump a pail of water to splash on the congregation on Sunday morning! But when a preacher gets this "Spring" he will have floods with which to fairly drench the audience.

This "Spring" will cool your hot tempers. Instead of being hot and irritable in your family, you will be cool and calm.

Prayer is a wonderful result of this "Spring." O it makes prayer precious, delightful, easy. I am amazed when I see some holiness preachers who spend little time in prayer. May God convict us for our lack of prayer. "O," you say, "I keep prayed up." Well, I believe in praying *down*. We do not pray enough.

This "Spring" means blessing. It means that we will be a blessing to all we come in contact with. Oh, brother, don't you want to be a blessing? Get this "Spring!"

Brother Strouse gave his experience in connection with his sermon. As this precious man of God related his wonderful experience, the people were greatly blessed. Turned from a life of worldliness and society, he is now a blessedly saved preacher of full salvation. Praise the Lord!

7:00 P. M.

Since the close of the afternoon service the Lord has sent us a refreshing rain, cooling the air and allaying the dust. Rev. H. C. Morrison is to preach again this evening. We do devoutly thank God for the presence of Brother Morrison at Portsmouth. It is the plan of God that the holiness movement should be principally promulgated by men of ordinary and mediocre talents endued with celestial fire, but now and then he sanctifies a man of real genius and natural ability and sends him forth to push the battle. And so once in a while we hear the joyful message from a silver-tongued orator, such as Henry Clay Morrison. In appearance Brother

Morrison is a man of medium height, with dark, curling hair, large lustrous eyes, fine forehead, smooth, placid Christ-like face. In the pulpit he is always perfectly at home, easy in manner, graceful in gesture. He is one of the most versatile preachers we have ever heard. The thunder-toned declaration of the law is often followed in an instant by the music of God's grace.

There is a large, interesting audience here tonight. The electric cars which have been running now for some weeks between Fall River and Newport make a large local attendance possible. We see many in the audience from Tiverton, Middletown, Newport, Fall River and Swansea.

The early part of this meeting was especially marked by a deep, intense spirit of prayer; we are expecting therefore great things in this service.

THE SERMON. REV. H. C. MORRISON.

Text: "For this is the will of God, even your sanctification." 1 Thes. 4: 3.

There is in human nature a principle which would lead us to excuse ourselves from the trouble of finding out and doing God's will on the ground that God is too mysterious for finite minds. That is a very devilish principle, for it implies that God is a tyrant and asks things impossible for us to perform.

When a man, by the grace of God, has his nature changed by regeneration it becomes perfectly natural for him to keep God's laws. Why, brother, we can get so in harmony with God's will that we will not wish anything in God's plan of salvation changed. In this sense we can say "Amen" to even the damnation of the wicked!

A good time of sobbing at the mourner's bench will settle a man about the Divinity of Christ, the reality of Hell, the falsity of Evolution. I was never in Hell, but I have had the essence of it in this breast. I haven't been to heaven but, thank God, I have a foretaste of it in my heart now.

If it is true that we are saved and sanctified there ought to be scripture for it. Well, thank God, there is Scripture for it. These texts are not to tantalize us. They are not to tease us. No, sir! God rings the bell and calls us to dinner where there is a fatted calf on every plate! There are Moses and Daniel and Paul and Peter and John, blessed characters, but we can have the same grace.

If you get this grace you will be happy if they fight you in your presence. It doesn't matter what they say, you will rejoice. We can get to a place where enemies can't move us and angels can't move us and devils can't move us! Hallelujah!

There is Scripture for sanctification and you will all agree that it will not do for a Christian to come face to face with God's will and turn his back and refuse him obedience. "God hath not called us to uncleanness, but unto holiness."

We know or we *ought* to know that sin, that which ruined Paradise, must go from our soul or we shall never enter Heaven. In the day of Judgment, I would as lief be a Jew who rejected Christ as a modern Gentile who rejects the Holy Ghost.

Oh, brother, we have got to line up with God. We must get where we love what God loves and hate what God hates. To reject holiness is to reject Jesus Christ. Oh, Christ is looking at us!

Did you ever see a sober man who wished his boy to be a drunkard? Did you ever see a pure man who wanted his boy profligate? No! No! No! And you cannot imagine a holy God being satisfied with anything less than holiness in his children.

Brother Morrison seemed simply inspired as he preached this wonderful sermon. The vast audience listened almost breathlessly to his burning words. The appeal was terrific, and men bowed like reeds before the wind. When the altar was thrown open, immediately the people pushed forward to prostrate themselves before God. Hallelujah for this sermon!

MONDAY, AUGUST 1.

10:30 A. M.

The meeting opened with the hymn,

"White raiment I'm wearing.
Purified from sin through the blood of the Lamb!"

After a number of short, importunate prayers, Bro. Godbey preached the gospel from the text, "Thou art Peter, and upon this Rock will I build my church, and the gates of Hell shall not prevail against it."

This scripture is the pillar of popery. Popery has girdled the world with ignorance and darkness and sin. It gets its scriptural support from a misinterpretation of this text.

Jesus went up to Simon and said to him "Thou art a rock." Naturally timid and vacillating, he became at Pentecost a rock able to face a whole regiment of devils. And when you get the fiery baptism you will be able to do the same.

Jesus says, "Thou art a rock," and the word means a broken off stone; but says Christ, "upon this Rock, *this* ledge, the unbroken stratum, Myself, I will build my church, and the gates of hell shall not prevail against it."

Unless we get our feet on the Rock we can never be members of the church of Jesus Christ. It doesn't matter where your name is written, you are not a member of Jesus' church unless you are sure your feet are on the Rock.

The word in Greek for church is "ecclesia," and means "called out." The Holy Ghost calls to all the world to come out, to separate from uncleanness. The word for sanctify in the Greek means to "take out the world." Conversion takes us out of the world; Sanctification takes the world out of us!

I can remember my wilderness life. O I have a big graveyard back there. I buried a college president there with a plug hat on, I interred a Free Mason there, an Odd Fellow there, and I made a bee-line at race horse gait for Canaan, fording Jordan and shouting down the walls of Jericho.

A modern form of idolatry is the worship of church edifices and preachers and creeds. Why, brother, your creed will be of no more use to you in the Day of Judgment than the Farmer's Almanac. This Book is what you will be judged by. God's word is your creed and God's word alone. Well, somebody says, "Ought I to come out of the church?" Let God answer. In Revelation: "Babylon is fallen. Come out from her ye people." When is this? *During the tribulation.* It is your mission to stay and preach to Babylon until the tribulation comes.

The important thing is for you to belong to God's church, the register of which is kept beyond the stars. Are you a member? Let the people stand and let the seekers come. Amen.

1:30 P. M.

Brother C. B. Strouse in charge.

The praise service opened with that beautiful hymn, "We are walking in the light." Full salvation will make a man with the larnyx of a frog into a sweet singer in Israel. The most unmusical people in the world learn how to make at least a joyful noise. Hallelujah! we are all getting in tune, and some day around God's throne will sing a chorus of eternal harmony. Glory! Glory!

Sister Switzer: "I am very thankful that God is able to deliver, and I am glad that this is not only in the hymn book and in the Bible but it is in my experience as well."

Brother Pardon Simmons: "I thank the Lord for the light. For over one year I have walked in all the light which God has given me. I am fully sanctified through and through. I am determined to go on in the way until I die!"

Sister Laity: "The desire of my heart is to be at my best for God."

Brother Bache of Bound Brook, N. J.: "I wandered for several years in the wilderness, but I heard of Canaan and desired to enter in and thank God I did."

Brother Kennedy: "The 'prone to wander' has all been taken out and the 'prone to love the Lord' has been put into my heart."

Sister Myra Soule: "I praise the Lord that he has set me free and I have victory all the time."

Sister Lilly Lewis: "I praise the Lord that his blood saves and sanctifies me, and although I have not been through all the testings that some have, yet I know that his grace will be sufficient for me in all places."

Brother Strouse: "Now you let me speak a word. Let me say something about testimony. I do not know what you do here, but in some places I have visited some people testify like a man that I knew of marked sheep. His own name was Israel and he was in partnership with a man named Jones. He marked the sheep with a little J and a great big I. So in testimony it is often a little Jesus and a tremendous I. O, let's magnify Christ! Let's *exalt* the blood and minify self."

2:30 P. M.

What days of privilege these are! Why, Praise the Lord, it seems to us that we are the most favored of the favored. Here we are at a holiness campmeeting among the blood-washed, with our hearts made clean, all packed up and ready for either earth or heaven. As we sit at the table we can see Rev. John Norberry coming through the grove. We are delighted to see this blessed brother again and so are the people; for as he steps upon the platform the audience breaks into a prolonged shout and clapping of hands. There is no man who comes to Portsmouth who is more generally loved then Brother John Norberry. He is singing now with a vim and an earnestness which are never seen except as they spring from the heart of a sanctified man.

Rev. H. C. Morrison preaches this afternoon. Isaiah 58:11.

"And the Lord shall guide thee continually, and satisfy thy soul in drought, and make fat thy bones: and thou

REV. H. C. MORRISON

shalt be like a watered garden, and like a spring of water, whose waters fail not."

Yesterday afternoon we heard about the spring—a most blessed discourse, and my soul was greatly blessed and refreshed. Do you know I am kind of like the miser who spent all his time counting his money. I have times under sermons just like that one yesterday when I have to go down into my bank-vaults and count my treasures, and I get awfully happy when I see how much I have!

You have heard about the wet-weather springs; the land is full of them. But I often go into a church and look over on the left and there is a *dry*-weather spring that never dries up, and there in the middle block of seats is another, and in the corner on the right is a third. Springs of water whose waters fail not.

"And the Lord shall guide thee continually." It doesn't say "the Lord shall *drive* thee," nor "the Lord shall *drag* thee," but the Lord shall *guide* thee." If you go to heaven you will not go because you have to, you will go because you choose to.

Why, there is nothing forced about salvation. There is no heaven for an unholy heart. Until we desire to be holy we will never see heaven.

God treats the race as a mother treats her child. See the patience of a mother as she teaches her baby-boy his letters. How glad it makes her when he progresses in learning! It makes the heart of God glad when we learn his lessons.

God "shall guide thee continually." We walk hand in hand with the Almighty, just follow along beside him. And don't you be fool enough to get in the way of the Almighty! I tell you I got to a place when I didn't *dare* to say anything against sanctified people. You had better stand on the track with an express engine coming down grade sixty miles an hour than to get in the way of the Almighty.

People have so many false ideas of religion that it is difficult to get correct ones into them. Why, God's idea is that we shall be guided *"continually."* Not just "on Sunday," not simply in "protracted meetings," not merely "part of the time." C o n t i n u a l l y spells "All the time."

If we want God to guide us continually we must consecrate entirely. People pray, "Lord, bring me into the blessed experience." And he takes their hand and starts off, but they balk up and say, "Why, I can't go this way," and God goes off and leaves them to shift for themselves.

God is going to test us. He wants us to learn to drill under fire. When we get so we can do that God will send us into the battle. There are lots of folks that say, "Lord, give me a gun," and they go to work and shoot their guns and fill the back of the captain with bullets! Why some of the worst wounds I have ever had were from my friends.

Commit your way to the Lord and let him bring things to pass. Just hand yourself and vour affairs over to him and hold him responsible.

If the Lord guides you you will be guided into battle. With sword and battle-ax and shield he will lead you into the campaign.

"A watered garden." When other people are thirsty and dry and arid, why, you have an unchanging spring that never fails. These trials and testings are only the plows to break up the ground so God can grow the flowers and fruits of the Spirit.

The altar service was very blessed and there were many seekers and finders. Praise the Lord!

7:30 P. M.

Rev. John Norberry is leading the singing with almost divine energy and zeal. There is a holy ground-swell in the music and singing tonight such as we have not seen in this session of campmeeting. Oh what a deluge of holy song! We will never know the magnificent and eternal results of the billows and surges of holy enthusiasm aroused by such choruses as

"I have the glory in my soul,"

or

" 'Tis a glorious church, without spot or wrinkle."

Thank God for sanctified songs, voicing the holy aspirations, desires and exultations of the congregation!

On the platform we see Rev. John Pennington, who has been away at his church in Providence over the Sabbath; John Shober Kimber of the Friend's Church, Newport, R. I.; James Estes of the same city, and Rev. Mr. Hartwig, also of Newport.

Rev. H. C. Morrison preaches again to us tonight.

"And God which knoweth the hearts bare them witness, giving them the Holy Ghost even as he did unto us and put no difference between us and them, purifying their hearts by faith." Acts 15: 8, 9.

You remember some of the difficulties of the early church. You remember how difficult it was for the Jew to think that the Gentile was as good as he was. God had wonderfully favored and blessed the Jews. He had chosen them to be his instruments in the world. But they abused their privileges and became proud and arrogant and selfish and conceited and prejudiced. It was so difficult for them to believe that God had salvation for all the world. But after the Jewish disciples were sanctified it was much easier for them to learn the stupendous truth. God gave Peter a lesson and Peter learned it; and he taught the Jerusalem conference the same invaluable lesson. And the sermon with which he addressed his hearers was so convincing that the whole conference was satisfied. "Why," said Peter, "God put no difference; he is at the helm, he will manage the whole business."

And so it is because I am sure that God "puts no difference" between us, that I preach as I do. This is the reason that I feel sure that God will sanctify a man whether he be Quaker, Presbyterian, Congregationalist, Methodist or Catholic.

What a curse prejudice has been to the church of God! When God puts the seal of the Holy Ghost upon a work it is time for us to shut up and keep still. God does not put his endorsement on falsehood. The holiness movement must be *truth* therefore, for God is putting his constant blessing upon it.

How are we to know that our consecration and faith are genuine? that they measure up to the divine standard? Now the human mind is fallible and liable to mistakes and we must have some *infallible* proof that our consecration and faith are absolutely all right. And the one infallible proof is the witness of the Holy Ghost. I sometimes meet people who say when asked if they are sanctified, "Yes, I've taken it by faith." Well, where is the witness? Brother, you have no right to stop crying to God until the baptism consciously falls.

I do not believe in fatalism, but I do not believe that John Bunyan could have died in those five years in which he was groaning and struggling and agonizing for the blessing of full salvation. I believe that if you go to work and seek with all your heart and act up to all the light you receive, God will keep you alive until you get to a place where the blessing will come.

But look here, brethren, don't you claim too early. Don't you say 'I believe' too soon. If there is any unconfessed theft in your life, any uncleanness, any sin at all, you have no right to think of believing until they are all put rigidly away.

It takes the power of the Holy Ghost to put men under *real* conviction. O, sir, if we want a really divine revival, it will take all the nerve and brain and soul you have got. You will have to lay yourself out in a sense of utter dependence upon God. We must have the supernatural if we are to have conversions and sanctification and testimonies that really count. Why, you can get up human conviction and human prayer, and men may come to the altar and remain as cold as wedges, but when the real power of the Holy Ghost is present and a holy God is on hand and a man feels that the heart is unclean, then he wilts.

This sermon, of which we have given only a mere sample, was of glorious power. The great audience was mightily moved, and the altar service was wonderful. Hallelujah!

TUESDAY, AUGUST 2.
8:30 A. M.

Brother Godbey's Bible Reading this morning was well attended, the people coming in crowds with their Bibles.

Among other interesting things which he said was this: "In the early church they had none of the kind of preaching such as we have today—that is, taking a text and preaching from it. In those days preaching was purely expository. They read the scriptures and explained them, and that was preaching."

Beloved, pray through. I am glad I got religion in the woods where there was no one to manipulate me. In repentance we give all the bad things to the devil where they belong, and in consecration we give all our good things to God. If we keep any of our sins we are thieves, for sin belongs to the devil.

Hydrotatry (the worship of water) and ecclesiolatry (the worship of a church) are very common forms of idolatry.

When man repents, God always converts.

All we have to do to be popular with the worldly churches is to die. As soon as we are dead the folks that fight us the hardest will write eulogies about us. They fought Wesley and they will fight us. But they stopped fighting and went to eulogizing Wesley as soon as he was dead.

One may be truly sanctified and enjoy the abiding Comforter and yet not possess the gifts of the Spirit to any great extent. After you have received *"the* gift of the Holy Ghost" you may, if you will, possess the gifts of the Spirit.

We have hydrolaters (water-worshippers) in Kentucky and Missouri and California who are wearing out their lives in the indefatigable preaching of their god. You see, their god is so weak they have to work themselves to death to maintain his cause.

A heretic is a man who separates himself from God and his truth.

Wesley called himself, "Homo unius libri," a man of one book. We all ought to be the same. I tell you frankly that I do not believe in ecclesiastical law at all. Why, think of a law which makes it possible for an unconverted little preacher to warn off and keep out one of God's holy evangelists. That law is diabolical and came from the pit.

10:00 A. M.

The morning audiences this year are far larger than they have been any previous year. Campers are getting blest so abundantly that they gladly eat cold dinners for the sake of attending the morning preaching service.

Rev. John Norberry: There is a conviction in my soul that the holiness movement needs a revival. Our campmeetings are getting quite barren. I know of nothing we need more than love.

I want you to open your Bibles to the 13th chapter of First Corinthians. Love is the principal thing. The first verse says, "Though I speak with the tongues

REV. JOHN NORBERRY

of men." It is a great thing to preach with the tongues of men. It is said, I think it was Dr. Hanlon of Pennington Seminary who said it, that when Bp. Simpson preached men so forgot themselves that they climbed upon the backs of the benches, they were so eager to hear the tongue of eloquence. But Paul says that though you have a tongue like that if you have not "love" you are no good.

Yes, and this chapter says something else. "Though I speak with the tongues of angels." There are people in our churches who are spending fortunes cultivating their voices so they can sing and draw crowds. But Paul says it is only "sounding brass." Did you ever hear of a man being saved or sanctified by a brass band? You never did. I like brass bands, but they do not save souls. If they did we ought to have one here. We need one badly.

"Though I have the gift of prophecy." If I have a knowledge of the future and explain the "mystery" of the "Maine" and tell how the war is coming out and do not know what it is to have holy, humble love, I am nothing, says Paul.

It is a wonderful thing to have "faith." But though we might have sufficient faith to remove whole mountain ranges, if we did not have love with it, lowly, sincere, humble love, we would be nothing.

We may be very benevolent and bestow all our goods to feed the poor and yet not have this one thing of love. There are folks in the Ladies' Aid society and the Relief Committee who need to join one more relief committee, and that is the relief committee to get relieved of inbred sin. The Holy Ghost is on that committee and he will relieve you.

Why, you may give your "body to be burned" in your zeal for a doctrine or a creed, and go to Hell for lack of pure, holy love. You may be zealous and earnest for a theory, and yet burn in perdition.

This "love suffereth long." It is like a good piece of elastic: you can stretch it and stretch it and it holds all right. Some of you suffer a little while, but you say "there are some things I can't stand!" But this love suffers long and "is kind." You suffer a while and then you are unkind! Lord pity you!

"Love envieth not." (Brother Godbey: "Brother Norberry, the word means jealousy, prejudice, revenge—these meanings are all in the word.") Thank you, beloved. What a wonderful thing it is to be free from these things! Are you free from them, brethren and sisters?

"Love vaunteth not itself." You will not want to make yourself prominent. You will seek the lowest place if you get real love. "Love doth not behave itself unseemly." There are lots of two-faced people in a meeting like this. They act good sometimes, but they change faces and act like the very devil himself at other times.

"Seeketh not her own." Love takes the smallest place. It counts self out and counts others in. It makes any sacrifice, it will go any distance, it will perform any labor for others. Some of you are professing holiness, and when seekers are at the altar you won't pray or sing or do anything for fear of tonsilitis! Lord bless you, you have got devil-itis now.

"Thinketh no evil." There are people here who are always surmising and suspicioning and back-biting. I tell you love never slanders. No, it does not *think* evil. If you have got anything in your heart that tends toward this sort of thing and are professing holiness you are a rank hypocrite!

I tell you this is an awful sin in the land. It is a stench in the nostrils of Almighty God. Love "rejoiceth not in iniquity." It is not glad when anyone falls. It does not ache to tell bad news. It doesn't itch to spread evil reports.

"Love beareth all things." You may put a thousand pounds on it and then a thousand more and it will stand it all right. O, it can endure and endure and endure! Have you got it, brother? Have you got it, sister?

O friends, come and seek this holy love! Never mind your past profession! Never mind what you have said! Be straight now, anyway. Come!

In the altar service there were some glorious cases. Hallelujah!

3:00 P. M.

After prayer by H. C. Morrison, Byron J. Rees preached from the first verse of the 91st Psalm: "He that dwelleth in the secret place of the Most High shall abide under the shadow of the Almighty."

7:00 P. M.

The praise service was a cyclone of glory. The songs were simply glorious, and there was plenty of demonstration in the Holy Ghost. One good sister was so blest that she could not keep her seat, but walked back and forth upon the platform. Truly this was a Pentecostal service.

7:30 P. M.

Among the new arrivals are Rev. H. J. Ballentine of North Attleboro, Deacon G. W. Kies of Norwich, Ct., and Dr. Edgar M. Levy of Philadelphia, Pa.

Brother H. C. Morrison preached tonight.

Text: "All the house of Israel lamented after the Lord." 1 Samuel 7: 2.

Israel had sinned and God had forsaken Israel. God cannot be true to his own nature and not forsake those who sin. I do not want you to get a false conception of God. I should hate for an indulgent father to send me to his prodigal son and I so misrepresent him as to give the son the impression that the father would not be glad of his return and would not make merry if he should go back.

When I was converted God did not change, but he looked different to me. I used to think that God Almighty desired to damn me in hell forever. And the devil helped me all he could in my false idea of God. It is the devil that wants to put us into hell. God doesn't want to put us there. He wants to save us from it and love us and take care of us.

But it is impossible for God to feel toward the sinner as he feels toward the saint. In the very nature of things when we sin against God we cut ourselves off from God. And a man may keep that thing up until everything in God's universe is arrayed against him. Every thunder-bolt seems like God striking at him. Jonah had an experience when the very winds and waves fought against him.

There is a time when God calls Mercy home and says, "Vengeance, leap for that man!" and Vengeance sticks its nose to his track and follows him. It is an awful time in the history of a man when Mercy lifts its sad wing and flies away and Vengeance takes after him.

There are some deep places in hell, and one of the deepest will be filled with people to whom we are preaching at these campmeetings and conventions. There are people who will go down to hell from a holiness campmeeting with Bible in hand. I'd rather be lost from the jungles of Africa with the bone of a missionary in my hand.

So long as we keep firing back at the Almighty from our Fort Sumpter he cannot treat us with kindness; but when we cease firing and raise the white flag then he says, "Don't let a hair of those men be hurt!"

There will come a time when the prayer of Noah, Daniel and Job, or any saint, will not avail for a sinner. I care not what progress we may have made, if we sin it doesn't count at all. And many a holy man has known what it was to come to a place where he could not pray for certain sinners.

Brother, don't play pranks on the Almighty. When you undertake that you are shoveling brimstone into your own pit. Do not, for your soul's sake, trifle with the great God.

Be careful with what hands you handle holy things. The fallen Israel carried the ark into battle, but what is an ark worth with a broken covenant? If you break the covenant you break it at both ends. Touch the ark with unholy hands and it will be chained lightning. What is a holy emblem if we have unholy hearts?

There's nothing so hateful to God as an unholy church. I do not abuse the church, but I tell you the world is made sceptical by an unholy church. C. G. Finney was led to doubt because he saw that the professed Christian did not live according to the Book. I am contending that God's church should be a holy church. Fellow Christian, the question which we are agitating is an all important question. Holiness is not something which you may take or leave as you please, it is a supreme necessity.

The trenchant Word did its work, and many souls were cut by its shining blade. "Behold, the slain of the Lord are very many." Amen and Amen.

WEDNESDAY, AUGUST 3.

10:30 A. M.

The altar service last night was marked for the number of new cases of salvation and sanctification. There are faces this morning newly bright. Conviction is deepening and widening, and men and women are constantly being brought under the searching power of the truth.

Seth C. Rees, President of the Association preaches this morning. It has been with considerable hesitancy that he has at last decided to preach at this meeting. Every hour he is reminded of an unspeakable loss, at every turn he makes he sees some object or hears some word which reminds him that she who preached so seraphically from this pulpit, and who lived so angelically in "Rest Cottage," is here no more.

Text: "And they chose Stephen, a man full of faith and of the Holy Ghost. Acts 6: 5.

This is our first introduction to Stephen. He appears in history like the flash of a meteor. We know nothing of his parentage. We do not know anything concerning his childhood. We are not told whether he came off of Fifth Avenue or the Bowery or Back Bay or Boston North End. We are at once introduced to his Christian character, and I conclude that is the most important thing.

God has his standard. Men also have their standard, but men would often find that if they came to measure themselves—not by themselves, for that is not wise, but by God's standard—they would find that they are fearfully deficient.

Stephen was doubly full. He was full of faith and of the Holy Ghost. Faith springs up spontaneously on thoroughly submitted soil. Do you know we talk too much doubt? If we would talk more faith we would have more faith.

Stephen was right in his faith. His doctrines were straight. He was orthodox in God's orthodoxy. He was right in his head and in his heart. You might think if you heard some of us only once that we depreciated doctrine. You would suppose that we do not believe in doctrine, but we *do*. Doctrine is necessary. A young lady was doing missionary work in a Catholic community and one day met the priest. Apologizing for her presence she said:

"Sir, I am not teaching my doctrine."

"And pray, what might be your doctrine?" On reflection she discovered that she had no doctrine, consequently the priest taught her *his* doctrines and soon received her into the Catholic church. "The floating ship turns out for the embedded rock," and there are positive characters in the world who are filled with error, and we must be full of truth to withstand their influence.

Stephen was correct in his outward life. He had the confidence of good people.

In my church there was a time when the word of a Quaker was as good as his bond. Now people want not only a note, but they desire security. Are we worthy of the confidence of the people about us? I would rather have the confidence of those who know me best than to preach great sermons in stone churches.

But Stephen had power to work miracles. He was familiar with the miraculous. He would not feel at home at some of our holiness campmeetings, I trow. O, how my soul longs for the supernatural in our meetings! And yet I am told that what we need is not more demonstration, but more intelligence! they told me when I came to New England that New England people were not like other people; that they were calm and deliberate and never got excited. But I find that when they get blest and saved and sanctified they act like they do when they get blest beyond the Mississippi.

Yes, sir, Stephen had the miraculous. And my soul is made weary when I see men trying to keep the very things out of God's work which God put in.

Stephen had wisdom which they were not able to resist. This wisdom comes by devotion rather than study, by prayer rather than metaphysical research. Without this wisdom we shall always fail. It is one thing to preach hell and damnation and shake men over the pit, and another thing to make a man really feel that it is only a short distance to perdition.

In those days Stephen's fullness did not debar him from church office. He was a deacon. Nowadays if a man gets full of fire and power they put him out of office.

I wish you to notice that Stephen was courageous. Do not talk about your sanctification in the same breath with your timidity, for they do not go together. They are inconsistent. If you are really sanctified you are out of any body's control but the Lord God's. You have but one Bishop. My soul longs for more of Gideon's band! There are more lion's dens now than there are Daniels to put in them. There are more furnaces than Hebrew children.

They saw Stephen as if he had been an angel. And there is something about real sanctification that puts the shine upon people, and in Stephen's case it made the Sanhedrin gnash upon him with their teeth and pick up stones and stone him to death.

Stephen had a type of holiness that made him pray for his enemies amid showers of stones. He could not rejoice in the down-fall of any man. He had such love for people that he could not secretly exult over any man's misfortunes. O for a love that will enable us to forget ourselves, deny ourselves, and neglect ourselves!

Brother, you can have the same kind of piety that Stephen had. Do you want it this morning? If you want the favor of the presiding elder more than you want this blessing, do not come to the altar. But if you want this more than anything else in the world you can have it!

Come on! They're coming. That's right!

The altar filled rapidly, and many earnest cries were offered up to God. There were many who "got through" gloriously, as we say. Praise the Lord!

3 : 00 P. M.

The meeting opened with the singing of No. 96 (Voice of Triumph), Dr. Carradine's hymn. Dr. Morrison is on hand to preach again. A little book which Brother Morrison has recently written, "The Two Lawyers," is attracting considerable attention. The first copies which have come to New England arrived today. It is a holiness book in the form of narrative. It is brimful of wit, sense, soundness and salvation. There are several excellently drawn characters in the book. Dr. Gall, Mr. Youngduck and Sister Dishrattler are people whom the reader can see with the greatest vividness. The style is easy, graceful, delightful; the words are well chosen and specific, and frequently have the force of shot bullets. The descriptions are excellent and seem real. The whole book of 240 pages glows with piety and holy power.

Text, 2 Peter 3: 1-8.

Peter is here writing of the coming of the Lord Jesus Christ. "And first of all," says Peter, "remember that in the last days scoffers will come, saying, Where is the promise of his coming?"

It was one of the most precious of the doctrines of the early church that Christ was to come back again. The hearts of the disciples were filled with sadness when Christ said, "Where I go ye cannot go." But their hopes were raised by the promise that he would come back again. "I go to prepare a place for you; and if I go and prepare a place for you, I will come again and receive you unto myself."

What a comfort it was to the disciples to feel that Christ was coming again! And what a hope it is to us, what a hope it is to *me* to buoy me up and sustain me, to feel that I am going to see Jesus. I believe with all my heart that Jesus is doing just what he said he was going to do—prepare a place for us.

If we believe the Lord is coming it will have a tendency to make us loosen our grip upon the world. And that is an awfully hard thing for us to do ordinarily.

"O," we say, "I'm on the altar," but we go and eat our three meals a day and let our neighbors starve.

Mrs. Wakeman told me that she was glad she got sanctified and heard about the Lord's coming before she built her new house, because instead of putting a great deal of money into it she built a substantial building and gave the money she would have spent thus into the Lord's work. This doctrine has a wonderfully practical effect.

When this doctrine gets thoroughly into your nature, you will be after souls. Not after Christmas trees or ice-cream suppers or oyster suppers. I had a sort of day dream the other day, and you were in the dream, Brother Godbey. I thought I could see a long line of people and you was at the head; and I saw that those people were souls who have been won to Jesus, and they were your "crown," Brother Godbey, and I woke up. All through my soul I wanted souls; I wanted a crown.

We say about the contemporaries of Noah, "How foolish not to believe Noah's faithful preaching?" And yet we are on the same track, and in our turn mock at the thought of the coming Christ.

Brother, God has given us this Book and we have no right to cut it up and take what we please of it. We must take a whole Bible.

Do you know what makes men hate the preaching of the Second Coming? Now see here, if you want to be Bishop, if you have your heart set on being a Bishop, you wouldn't care to hear that Christ was coming. The trouble is men are thinking about something they want and they do not wish their plans interfered with. To men who have elaborate plans for the world the thought of Jesus' coming is revolting.

I do not want my Lord to come and catch me making fun of the fond hopes of pious hearts who are looking for Jesus in the clouds. I do not want to be caught idle. How embarassing it is for an employee in the field to be caught idle by his employer!

Yesterday I was standing talking to a minister, and suddenly he cried out, "Why, there's Dr. Levy!" and my heart leaped, and I said, "That is the way it will be in the Millenium. We will cry out, "There's Bro. Godbey, and there's Brother Norberry! Hallelujah! And there are all the saints. Glory!"

Just as John the Baptist ran before the Lord in his first advent, the holiness movement runs before the Lord in his Second Coming.

You may just as well try to keep an apple tree growing with bark and leaves all pulled off as to try and run a holiness meeting and keep out the scriptural view of Divine Healing and the Coming of the Lord.

Why, brother, when a man gets sanctified it makes him love Jesus with all his heart, and it makes him want to believe and cherish everything that has to do with him. While all the world is indifferent to what concerns him, he is all engrossed in anything that has to do with him.

Brother, let me say this to you; we are not going

to save the world. We are not put here to save the world. We are put here to preach and pray and sing and shout and labor and try and get all we can out of the burning world.

This sermon was filled with unction throughout, and the blessing of God rested upon us all. Hallelujah, our hearts are white and Jesus is coming. *Glory!*

7:30 P. M.

In the early service this evening Brother Godbey encouraged the offering of many short earnest prayers. After perhaps twenty had prayed he asked that the entire audience pray vocally at one time. The effect was inspiring and reminded us of the text, "And Israel lamented after God." With one voice the congregation cried to God.

Rev. John Pennington of Providence preached tonight.

"He shall baptize you with the Holy Ghost and with fire."

This has been a wonderful day; the power of the Lord has been upon us. We heard this morning that we ought to be filled and this afternoon that Jesus was coming, and our souls are brought to a place where we long to be ready.

John was a preacher of righteousness. He preached

repentance, and it was prophesied that he should turn many to righteousness. Men heard his message, heeded it, and came flocking to his baptism. Some came to him in whom he detected hypocrisy. To such he did not administer his baptism, but only to those who gave evidence of having really repented.

But even as he baptized, John Baptist pointed to another Baptizer and another Baptism. There is a Baptism which Christ alone can administer. Men cannot administer it. I repudiate any statement that men can baptize with the Holy Ghost. They may help us to get ready for it, but there comes an hour when men must halt and Christ himself must step in and do his office work.

This Baptism is for believers only. It is not for sinners, nor for backsliders. The apostolic church which gathered in the upper room were God's dear children. The reason there are so few candidates for this Baptism is because there are few who walk close enough to the Lord to know their need.

Men who disobey God in any particular are candidates, not for this Baptism but for repentance. The lowest standard held up in this Book is a life free from disobedience. People sometimes talk flippantly about disobedience, but it is an awful thing. If you have been neglecting family prayer and ignoring your duties, come to the altar and get pardon for your sins! I fear sometimes that some of our people overestimate their progress in the things of God and, thinking that they are justified, seek holiness and find reclamation first because they need it first; but in misapprehension of its real nature they term it sanctification. Only those who are living justified lives are ready for sanctification.

There are comparatively few people who really want "fire." A brother minister came to Chicago with his heart hungry for the fulness of God, and in desperation he prayed, "O Lord, put me in the crucible and put the cover on!" The ordeal was terrific, but he came out pure gold.

This Baptism is for purification. There is much talk about receiving the Holy Ghost which does not take into consideration the question of purity. You say, "I had a little touch of fire last year and I want another touch now." What you need is a grand conflagration which will destroy everything chaffy.

"But," says someone, "I do not know what is combustible." You do not need to. Fire will itself find anything that can be burned. Do not stop short of a fire that will burn up the old man and kill the self-life.

The basis on which God gives this Baptism is that the life be a justified life and that the individual be walking up to all the light he has. It takes a close walk with God to reveal carnality. It is so deep-seated, so involved in the very meshes of the soul, that the white light is absolutely necessary for its revealment.

Consecration is necessary for us to receive this Baptism. Make no trial trip with God. Go over unreservedly into God's hands.

You will be startled at things you will find in your heart. The light of God will reveal awful things. God is more concerned with our *being* straight than with our *doing* so much. We want our children pure and true. We can get along without their service, but we must have their integrity. So with God.

Consecration always means more than we suspicion when we make it Settle the question, however, once for all, and let God take care of the rest. And if you keep your consecration the chances are that you will have to go for God. I cannot believe that God is having his way with us all the way when we are piled up so deep in communities that are already well worked when the millions are sinking into hell!

May the blessed Holy Ghost put in us a vigor and grit and go and stalwartness that will make us glad to go anywhere for God.

Another characteristic of genuine consecration is that the one consecrating is willing to go without what God withholds. Are you willing to go without the approval of your friends? Are you willing to go without the ornaments of the world? Are you willing to cut off everything that is in the way of your spiritual life.

There is always a last question to which we must say "yes" before the blessing comes. With different cases the last things are different, but they must all be treated by utter submission to God.

God will test us. He will have a tried people. He will put us to real trial. I can remember when God put the test to me. "Go out from your business and preach the gospel." There was nothing in sight, but, thank God, I gave up and have never gone hungry! God has seen after me!

The fire will cleanse the temple, and into a cleansed temple will come the Holy Ghost. He will bring power. If we do not have power we have not got the blessing. This must be so. The reason there are some mistaken people who think they have found a third blessing is because they have never really experienced the second. Brother, do you want this Baptism of which we have talked tonight? If so, come to the altar.

And they did come, and the altar was soon full of earnest seekers. This was a powerful message, and God honored his truth wondrously. Praise the Lord! Amen.

THURSDAY, AUGUST 4.

10:30 A. M.

Rev. W. B. Godbey preached on the "Gifts of the Spirit."

The grace of the Spirit is to convert and sanctify us and the gifts of the Spirit are to convert and sanctify others. The most important thing in the world is the establishing of the saints. Paul made long missionary tours in which he did nothing but preach to saints. My work now is to talk to the sanctified people. There are no people who need preaching to worse than they. So this morning I will talk to you about the nine gifts of the Spirit.

The first gift is wisdom. This is not the wisdom which you get in the schools and colleges. An old colored man down south said, "You white folks are getting sanctification, but what we colored people need is sanctifigumption"—*i. e.*, sanctified commonsense. And what we need now is wisdom.

Away down south a baby in a Roman Catholic family died and the family was in great distress because there was no priest to pray it out of Purgatory. They were told of a man, a circuit rider, he was not a priest, but he was something of the kind. He was a red-hot Methodist preacher, one of Asbury's men. When he came in answer to their call they asked him: "Are you a priest?" "Not exactly, but I can do anything that a priest can do." "We want you to pray the little baby out of Purgatory." "Why, I've already talked to the Lord about that baby, and it is in heaven, and hasn't cried since it got there." And how they rejoiced; and they invited the preacher to come and hold services in the house and he did, and all the family were converted, and their descendents nearly all were red-hot gospellers, and one of them is before you, for they were my ancestors. Now if that man had not had wisdom he would have missed his opportunity.

The next gift is the gift of knowledge. This is the gift that makes us to read the Scriptures understandingly. When I gave up my library I supposed that I could never know even the Scriptures, but I found that the Holy Ghost gave me the gift of knowledge until these old Greek words just blaze and flame. You can all have this gift of knowledge, but you must give up your creed and not twist and turn the Scriptures to suit your narrow creed.

The third gift is the gift of faith. He is not talking about the *grace* of faith by which we are saved ourselves, but the *gift* of faith by which we save others. O, it is a wonderful gift. It is the gift by which we pray for a meeting and get the assurance of victory before the service opens at all! This is the reason I am so glad to rush in here and lead the prayers, for I want you to get the gift of faith and take victory for the service.

The next gift is divine healing. Of course when the time comes for you to die and your work is done, why, you will die. But the Holy Ghost often bestows the gift of healing on sanctified people. I have seen many wonderful cases of healing myself. Frequently I have been taken with sciatic rheumatism so that I could not walk and I just stop and pray and it never lasts more than two minutes, and usually not more than half a minute.

In your text, the next gift is called the working of

miracles. In the Greek text it is "the workings of dynamites." God has one dynamite to knock down sinners, and another to bring them into a skyblue pardon, and another to blow up believers and set them going wholly sanctified and baptized with the Holy Ghost. Why, brother, if you will put on this panoply you can move heaven, earth and hell. This gift has predominated in many of God's preachers. In C. G. Finney this "workings of dynamites" was wonderful, and in the cotton-mill hundreds of operatives were thunder-struck with conviction.

The fifth gift is prophecy. Prophecy is to boil over like a boiling spring. If you get this gift you will be prepared to preach without a collegiate education. Of course if you have it, it will be a help to you, but it is not necessary at all.

The discernment of spirits is the sixth gift. If you do not have it you will waste your ammunition; you will cast pearls before swine and waste your gun-powder. When you go to a dead church you ought to preach Sinai before you tackle Pentecost. You can't do it without this gift. You have got to have it to make your work count.

The gift of tongues. You say, "I do not want any more languages." Well, all right, but you need to know your own language so as to talk salvation fluently.

With the gift of interpretation you can understand Holy Ghost preaching and Holy Ghost books and Holy Ghost testimonies.

3:00 P. M.

We were not able to be present to hear the glorious sermon by Dr. Edgar Levy on "The Virgin Mary and Sanctification," and through pressure to get this report through the press there was no time to correct the notes taken by those who attended the meeting. The sermon was greatly blessed and many were fed by this holy man, Dr. Levy.

There are several new faces among the ministers on the platform. Rev. D. L. Dean, Rev. Mr. Crandall of Wickford, Rev. Olin W. Rose of Iowa, Rev. Mr. Perry of West Mansfield, and several other ministers are present.

Among our advertized workers who have arrived today are Isaac B. Remsen of Jamaica, L. I., New York, and Rev. Chas. BeVier of Spring Valley, N. Y. Bro. Remsen is well known as the pioneer of the holiness work on Long Island. He has been marvellously used of God in spreading full salvation. He is an elderly looking man with gray whiskers, bent shoulders, kindly, piercing eyes, benign countenance, devout manner. Rev. H. C. Morrison preaches tonight.

I remember very well when I criticised holiness people. I never associated with them. I used to say that they neglected sinners and went for saints only. But I remember this: after I was sanctified and went to Stamford, Kentucky, where Bro. W. E. Arnold, now associated with me in the "Pentecostal Herald," was pastor, and forty persons were sanctified, that I was led to pray, "O, Lord, as result of this meeting let 500 sinners be converted." Bro. Arnold wrote me before the year was out that more than that number were converted as a result of that series of services.

I believe in holiness meetings. Do not, my brother, find fault with us because we hold just what Jesus held, viz., holiness meetings. You have chased us out of the churches and off the Brussels carpet out under the trees into the straw pile, now call off your dogs.

I knew of a horse-racer who was converted and within four days sanctified gloriously, and in four years I do not doubt but he has had thousands of conversions.

My text is Galatians 2, verse 20: "I am crucified with Christ; nevertheless I live, yet not I, but Christ liveth in me, and the life which I now live in the flesh I live by the faith of the Son of God who loved me and gave himself for me."

Tomorrow in the Bible reading you ask Brother Godbey about the two Greek words which are translated "flesh." One word refers to the meat on the bone, the other to the carnal mind. In the former there is no sin. In the latter we cannot please God. Since my heart is right my mouth has never wanted tobacco.

I was down in Meridien, Miss., and a man whose head was as white as cotton, and whose mustache would have been but for the fact that it was dyed red by amber-juice, and who had been sticking that dirty mustache in the communion cup of Jesus Christ for twenty-five years, said in desperation that he had tried many times to get rid of the appetite and could not. But he went to the locust grove and got to crying out to God and was gloriously delivered from the desire for nicotine.

A man may be delivered from the appetite for tobacco and not be sanctified, but no man can be sanctified and not be delivered from it.

The unconverted man is not conscious of trouble with the carnal mind. It is the truly justified man, striving day and night to do God's will, that feels that the old man is a source of trouble.

I tell you a really converted man has an awfully hard fight inside. It takes a Christian man to stand in the fight. Some of the blackest crimes ever committed against humanity have been committed by men who neglected to preach the doctrine that we could be delivered from civil war inside.

I would as lief go to Rome and have the pope beat me over the head with a hand-spike as to allow any preacher stand up and insist that we shall not declare that God can stop the internal war.

O wretched man that I was; I used to write out rules and put them in my coat pocket and—forgot them. I used to put them in my vest pocket, and after a long time I went to give my vest to a colored boy and was looking in it for a chance nickel and found the rules! I wrote them out on foolscap and put them on my pillow and my head on top of them so that every time I stirred I would hear them rattle! But rules were not as big as the carnal mind.

If you are not having a fight, a battle with the old man, you are either unconverted, backslidden or sanctified. If you are really converted and not yet sanctified you are fighting inside. Why, I fought and fought and fought. I prayed in every fence corner on the farm and at the foot of every tree and everywhere, I was so anxious to please God and serve him and love him.

As long as we are in the world there is going to be a fight. O, may God grant that our fight may be on the *outside*. May God grant that none of us shall continue to have to fight on the inside. There is enough on the outside to engage all our attention and strength.

Paul once had the carnal mind, but when he penned this text it had been crucified, destroyed. There is something in corrupt human nature that does not die easily. There is grief and violence and pain in crucifixion. Understand that I am not casting up any breastworks to keep folks out of the blessing, but God forbid that we should break your bones and take you off the cross before you are dead.

We want to be willing to go through to death, give up entirely, die out absolutely! Do not let anything deter you from Canaan-land. You will find high grass on Jordan's banks, but do not stop there. You will find many refreshments as you approach the blessing. You will get many an insight into the Bible; but do not stop there. Go through to entire crucifixion; die out and get sanctified.

I can remember that Brother Henck preached in my church and just run me through and through with the sword, and by his very faithfulness was made a great blessing to me and I died the quicker for it.

If the carnal mind dies today you will die tomorrow. If you get sanctified you will "die daily" as various things come up. The folks that keep in the power are people who go right ahead and die out to presiding elders and preachers and people and everything as they come to them.

Do you know what it is to be crucified? I told a lady who was seeking holiness at Beulah Heights in a half-hearted way, "Sister, you do not want me to tell you how you can get the blessing. You want a cross done up in a comforter and a board nailed to the beam for you to rest your feet on and then the cross tilted back like a divan and your hands tied up with ribbons." O, friend, in God's way die out. Even though on a rough cross, with vinegar to your lips and the nails in the palm and feet and the sword in the side and the thorns on the brow we must be crucified!

After Jesus was dead, the Roman soldiers tested him with the sword. He thrust the cruel iron into his side and jerked it out and said, "O, he's dead!" and they never troubled him after that. And while we will always be tempted and while we will always be tested they will have to admit that we are men of God. Even the centurian said: "Truly this was the Christ!" And our enemies will admit that we live the life! We have got to be willing, first, to go out of sight and be buried. Who is it that says tonight, "I am willing to go all the way with Jesus?" "I am willing to have my church bury me and my family bury me and my pastor bury me and every body bury me?" Is this the language of your heart?

While Brother Morrison was yet speaking the seekers began to drop upon their knees at the altar. From all around they came, some from the platform, many from the audience. The movement was very general, for God was most graciously in our midst. This vivid, pungent, powerful, searching, tender, holy sermon was a marvel of effective preaching. Glory be to God! Hallelujah!

FRIDAY, AUGUST 5.

10:30 A. M.

There was a tempest last night. A cannonading of thunder, an illumination of lightning, a down-pour of water. But wet weather does not deter the people of Portsmouth from coming to the Tabernacle. So there is an excellent audience, one of our largest, to hear Mrs. H. C. Morrison, the wife of Dr. Morrison.

It was a great surprise to me last night when Mr. Morrison came home and said that I was to speak this morning. I do not have the trouble that some of these ministers have in selecting a sermon, for I have but one sermon. I can tell you of nothing this morning but of Jesus and his love.

I want to call your attention to Romans, the twelfth chapter and first and second verses. I can remember the first time I heard of entire sanctification. It was through a testimony, and I thank God for testimonies! A schoolmate of mine had an experience which I saw was far better than my own. She gave herself day and night to the salvation of souls, and she seemed as happy a creature as I ever saw. I began to seek a like experience, but as I bowed before God He revealed to me that I was not even a child of God. I was not even on speaking terms with God. But, Glory be to God, He did save me and taught me that I must be separate from the world and must keep myself from the fashions and follies and pleasures of the world.

It was so delightful to love Christ that I wanted to know more about him; and when He revealed to me my inbred sin it was easy for me to give up every thing to him—all except one thing, and that was my mind. I lacked faith in my Savior. But when I finally presented myself a living sacrifice, God honored the sacrifice and cleansed me from all sin. Glory to his Name!

I beseech you to give yourselves fully to God, for he

is not a hard taskmaster. God is love. He does not ask you to see the end. He simply asks you to put your hand confidingly in his and trust him to lead you safely. "He leadeth me beside the still waters."

Ye are not your own, "Ye are the temple of the Holy Ghost." And, that he may dwell in you, He desires to cleanse the temple and make it clean.

Saint Paul goes a little farther and exhorts us not to be conformed to the world. Many of us are conformed I fear, but let us not be. We cannot afford to lower our testimony for anybody. We cannot afford to attend a church entertainment to please our friends even. We are of a heavenly kingdom. We are of another clime, There are young women who spend more of their time over the fashion plates than over this beautiful book; they spend more time in thinking about what they shall wear to church than they do about the food which they shall find when they get to church!

But we must not only not be conformed to the world, we must be *"transformed* by the renewing of our minds." God will give us new minds. He will change our habits of thought and conform us fully to the pattern of Christ.

Thus we will prove that good and acceptable and perfect will of God, not thinking more highly of ourselves than we ought to think. O, friends, let us think soberly, esteeming others better than ourselves. Instead of seeking to have our own way let us get together and pray over the matter and get the will of *God.*

If there is an unconverted person in the audience I want to assure them that if they will come to Jesus he will save them, for he has saved me and "God is no respecter of persons."

Christian brother, this is God's will concerning you, "even your sanctification." He says, "Be ye holy, for I am holy." That trouble in your heart called "inbred sin," which has given you so many times of sorrow, ought to be removed today. If you will present yourself a living sacrifice God will today take away all sin. Let us stand and sing!

The altar service was very blessed and many souls "got through" to victory. Glory to God! As the audience sang,

> "Just as I am without one plea
> But that thy blood was shed for me,
> And that thou bidst me come to thee,
> O, Lamb of God, I come, I come."

the seekers kept coming until the kneeling space was well nigh full.

1:30 P. M.

The praise service was in charge of Sisters Reed and Williams, two very prominent holiness Evangelists in the New England field. Sister Williams has a remarkably clear, strong voice which she uses in singing full salvation. Sister Reed is an excellent example of the fulfilment under the Pentecostal outpouring of the text,

"Your sons and *daughters* shall prophesy," for she is a thoroughly equipped minister of God's holy truth. The power of the Spirit was very evidently present and many souls were helped toward God.

3:00 P. M.

In Memory of Hulda A. Rees.

Singing,
> "How firm a foundation, ye saints of the Lord,
> Is laid for your faith in his excellent word."

Mrs Mary Kimber of Newport, R. I., a minister in the Society of Friends and a personal friend of Hulda Rees, led in prayer. After the prayer, in which all seemed to join, Sister Rose Williams sang that beautiful hymn, "Saved by Grace," in a most beautiful way. The throng of people was very great, and as the voice of this holy evangelist floated out over the congregation there was not one untouched heart beneath the roof of the Tabernacle.

Rev. John Pennington: "If I should say at the opening of this service that Hulda Rees is sorely missed I should but feebly express what everyone who ever attended this campmeeting feels to be true. We shall not trespass at this hour upon her dying request, for she asked that no eulogies be passed upon her after she was gone."

Brother Pennington then read from "Hulda, The Pentecostal Prophetess," as follows:

We have now come to the last period in the life of this noble woman of God. Everyone who saw her felt that there was no human hope. Relatives came from Iowa, and the two sons hurried to her bedside from New England. With what a beatic holy smile she greeted us! There are scenes that strike themselves upon the brain and heart to remain forever, and there were many such during the last three weeks of her life. She was a great sufferer. And yet with what patience she bore it all! Never a murmur passed her lips, never a complaint was heard by any of us. Her one care seemed to be that she might honor her Lord in everything.

We saw from a distance the end approaching, but we could not fully realize the truth. It did not seem like "the valley of the shadow." We had read of the triumph of the saints when approaching the River, but surely this excelled anything of which we had ever heard. Such sweet resignation to all God's will, such divine unction in prayer, such holy tenderness in exhortation and admonition, such victory and gladness in the furnace of pain and agony!—these luminous beacons did much to dispel the gloom and lighten the shades of the nearing evening.

Many visitors came to see her—some from considerable distance,—and whenever her strength permitted it she always had them admitted to her room. Her words were ever full of cheer and eternal hope. On one occasion, when a minister called whom she had known for years, she said to him with the greatest exultation, "The glory holds!" Yes, thank God, it did hold. The gospel she had preached to so many thousands with emphasis and assurance was found true and unshakable in this time of earnest testing. One day her husband said to her:

"My dear, is it all true that we have preached?"

"Yes, yes; we have not put it strong enough! It is all true, and more!"

At another time she said: "If the Lord takes me, it will be from the evil to come. Perhaps He sees something coming to me from which He wishes to protect me by taking me to Himself."

In one of her prayers she said: "Thou hast put, O Lord, a great laugh in my heart. Glory! Glory be to Thy Name forever! No evil can come to me! All is turned to blessing!"

She said one day: "You need not mourn over me when I am gone because I died young. If I go, it will be because my work is done. If I go now, God will round out my life-work."

Examining the diary of her husband, we find this recorded for one day: "In the afternoon we fell into conversation and then into prayer, and finally into shouting and laughing. When we looked at the clock we found that two hours had passed."

From the same source we quote the following: "May 23d—At 3.15 this afternoon Hulda had an awful spell of suffering, which lasted an hour and fifteen minutes, except for a brief intermission in which she sang the hymns: ' I Shall Be Like Him,' and

> ' The cross is not greater than His grace,
> The cloud cannot hide His blessed face;
> I am satisfied to know
> That with Jesus here below
> I shall conquer every foe.'

The glory of the Lord filled the room."

"May 24th—Hulda suffered awful pain for four hours, but in the midst of it all she sang: ' Glory to His Name, ' and quoted Scriptures and praised the Lord."

One evening, just at dusk—how well we remember it!—she prayed the following prayer: "O my precious Saviour, how much I have to thank Thee for! For all Thy many, many blessings I do devoutly thank Thee. I praise Thee that in all this suffering Thou hast kept me from charging Thee foolishly, or complaining in any way. O, Thou 'Man of sorrows, acquainted with grief,' who didst 'give Thy back to the smiters, and Thy cheek to them which plucked off the hair,' how much more Thou didst suffer for us than any of us ever did or could suffer! With thy servant Paul, I would gladly 'Fill up that which is behind of the suffering of Christ.' Lord Jesus, my precious Savior, Thou hast said we should be Thy 'joint heirs if so be we suffer with Thee,' and that we should sit together with Thee and reign with Thee. Lord, *I* would sit with Thee, and if I were to go to heaven tonight, where there are loved ones gone before, and I were told that thou wast not there, that Thou wast yet on earth bearing the cross, it seems to me that I would much rather come back to earth and suffer with Thee, than to remain in heaven separated from Thee. I thank Thee that Thou hast conquered death. I shall never die! I shall not taste of death! I thank Thee death does not flap its dark wing in my face and oppress my soul and spirit. The grave has no terror for me. Thou hast conquered all. O, my very soul is in rapture! O, my Saviour, if they who give a cup of cold water in the name of a disciple shall receive a disciple's reward, how great will be the reward of these loving hearts who have such patience with me! I pray, and I know that Thou dost hear me when I pray, for these loved ones, and I know that the reward of these whose hands are scarcely ever off my body will be *wonderful!* Thou knowest whether or not this is to be a night of the cough. If it is, Thou wilt give Thy grace. Sometimes it has seemed to me, as I have looked forward, as if more was coming than I could endure, but it was not so. When the time came Thy marvelous grace was with me. Praise the Lord!"

When the prayer was ended she sang with clear, strong voice:

"I must tell Jesus all my trials,
I cannot bear my burden alone."

Three nights before her translation she sang:

"Through grace I soon shall conquer,
And reach my home on high,

> And through eternal ages
> I'll shout beyond the sky."

Her voice failed her at the end of the verse, and her two sons sang the hymn through for her, while she nodded her head and smiled and said: "That is it! Amen! Amen!"

One afternoon, the family were all gathered about her, when her face suddenly lighted up as if a candle was burning beneath the transparent skin. With the brightest, sweetest smile and a far-away look as if she was gazing off in the distance, she said in a soft, reflective tone: "I didn't know it was so beautiful." After a moment or so she exclaimed, rapturously: "Can it be that the glory of the Lord is risen upon me?"

Thus this daughter of the Most High drew near to her exit from this world. It was indeed to her, as she said, "all bright and glorious ahead."

The night before she ascended she attempted to sing:

> "Fear not, I am with thee;
> Oh, be not dismayed,
> For I am thy God,
> I will still give thee aid."

But she could only whisper the words. Her husband read the entire hymn to her.

In the evening of Friday, June 3d, as the darkness was deepening about us, we watched her slip quietly away. There was no struggle. She passed from us as calmly as a child falling asleep. We knew that she was with the Lord, both hers and ours.

The funeral was very large. Seldom indeed, has Cherry Grove Meeting House been the gathering-place of so great a throng. John Pennington, who, assisted by Esther Tuttle Pritchard, conducted the services, preached a gracious gospel sermon. There were no eulogies, and little mention was made of the life-work of the departed one. A few days before her translation she had especially requested that the services be extremely simple and that her work should not be eulogized. "If I have done anything," she said, "it is through the grace of God." And as we followed the sacred dust to its quiet resting-place beneath the pines we felt that all was as she would have desired it.

Hulda A. Rees.

BY MRS. E. E. WILLIAMS.

We remember the beautiful star-like face,
  So quietly calm and serene;
We remember the regal womanly grace
  That would well have become a queen;
We remember her voice, so tenderly soft,
  And her hand clasp, so true and fond.
And the faith that ever *would* look aloft,
  Through the clouds, to the Light beyond.

We remember her zeal for the cause she loved,
  Her labors for perishing souls;
And the courage grand that remained unmoved
  Through breakers, and storms, and shoals.
And as we remember our eyes o'erflow,

Though our hearts feel so strangely glad,
For she rests from her labors—and well we know
   That she would not have us be sad.

We have seen her stand in the battle shock,
   'Midst the enemies of our Lord,
With her feet placed firmly upon the Rock,
   As she wielded the Spirit's sword;
We have seen her prostrate upon the ground,
   Regardless of sneer or of stare
From the wondering throngs who gathered round
   While she won the fight through prayer.

And though always womanly, modest, sweet,
   Yet her soul was so brave and strong,
That she knew not how to accept defeat
   From the allied hosts of wrong.
So she marched, a conqueror, through this world,
   Till at last, with the sword laid down,
And her unstained banner in victory furled,
   She has gone to obtain her crown.

"Is she dead?" Ah, no! We deny Death's claim!
   Such women can never die!
She is living and loving just the same
   As she did in the days gone by.
She has just gone Home—and more slowly we
   Are traveling on in the way
That she trod so buoyantly, soon to be
   With her in the realms of Day.

    *   *   *   *   *   *   *

Oh! brother mine, though thy heart may ache
   And thine eyes may be wet to-day,
In her name I bid thee fresh courage take,
   For thy wife is not far away.
In that beautiful Home beyond the Sea,
   Where so lately she's gone to dwell,
She is watching and waiting, my friend, for thee,
   And the boys that she loved so well.

And over and over, when thou shalt be
  In the work, by the Master's will,
Her spirit, unseen, shall stand by thee,
  As she shares in thy labors still;
For though God has called her away to rest,
  And she walks by thy side no more,
Yet second to Jesus, she loves thee best,
  As she did in the days of yore.

And, by and by, when thy work is done,
  And the battle for thee is o'er,
And thy face shall turn toward the setting sun,
  And the foe thou shalt meet no more;
When death shall be swallowed up in life,
  As the Master for thee shall come,
Thou shall spend eternity with thy wife,
  Forever with Christ at Home.

Seth C. Rees (husband of the departed one):

"I do not know as I can say anything to add to what has been read to you. I simply want to say that God's grace holds me. In the sleepless hours of the night God has held me. I want to give glory to God. I want to magnify his wonderful salvation."

Singing:

    "Jesus, lover of my soul,
      Let me to thy bosom fly
    While the nearer waters roll,
      While the tempest still is high.
    Hide me, O my Saviour, hide
      Till the storm of life is past,
    Safe into the haven guide;
      O receive my soul at last.

Plenteous grace with thee is found—
  Grace to cover all my sin;
Let the healing stream abound,
  Make and keep me pure within.
Thou of life the fountain art,
  Freely let me take of thee,
Spring thou up within my heart,
  Rise to all eternity.

Thou, O Christ art all I want;
  More than all in thee I find.
Raise the fallen, cheer the faint,
  Heal the sick and lead the blind.
Just and holy is thy Name,
  I am all unrighteousness;
Vile and full of sin I am,
  Thou art full of truth and grace."

This service was of especial blessing to a great many souls. There was a tenderness and unction and power about the meeting that are seldom seen on such an occasion.

The following is a sermon recently preached by the late Hulda A. Rees:

THE THESSALONIAN CHURCH.

"And the very God of peace sanctify you wholly, and I pray God your whole spirit and soul and body be preserved blameless unto the coming of our Lord Jesus Christ.... Faithful is he that calleth you, who also will do it."—1 Thess. 5: 23, 24.

The holiness preachers are sometimes accused of twisting and perverting Scripture in order to get a holiness text. But certainly this one needs no twisting to make it a holiness text.

We are told by Greek scholars that the Greek of this passage is much stronger than the English translation, but the latter is certainly far beyond our highest conceptions of truth.

In order to comprehend fully the meaning and import of this passage, we should consider the characteristics of those to whom it is addressed. Many handle the Word of God indiscriminately. It is a crime to break the seal and appropriate to yourself that which belongs to another.

By turning to the first chapter of this epistle we will find that this Church was gloriously justified. Soon after Paul and Silas sang themselves out of prison at Philippi they went down to Thessalonica and preached the Word in power and in the Holy Ghost. Thus we notice that when he addresses them the apostle speaks of them as "in God and in the Lord Jesus Christ."

They were a converted Church. To be "in God" means more than to be "in the Church." They had been transplanted from the kingdom of Satan to the kingdom of God. It is a very common and easy thing to add men to the Church, but Pentecost adds them to the Lord.

This Church had conscious salvation. They were "born of much assurance." They knew they were saved. They were not of those who "hope so," or "guess so" about religion. If asked about their salvation they could give a ready, positive answer in the affirmative.

"Our gospel came not unto you in word only, but also in power and in the Holy Ghost, and in much assurance." Paul's preaching was not merely in letter, but he was an unctuous preacher. He did not preach science or philosophy or *mere theology*. He did not preach rocks or stars or bugs. He preached Christ crucified and resurrected. He says: "We were allowed of God to be put in trust of the gospel." He did not have trust money or trust property, but he had trust gospel, and he felt the responsibility. It is an awful thing for a man to squander the money or property of the widow or orphan; how much worse it is for a man to squander the gospel, or misapply, so that they to whom it really belongs get no benefits from it! Preachers who do thus will have a fearful time at the last day.

May God give us preachers and preaching which will make converts who have "much assurance!"

These Christians received the word in "much affliction." It cost much to be a Christian in those days. It does not mean so much to be a professor now. To be an identified, despised Nazarene meant reproach. It implied not only ejection from the synagogue, but suffering at the scourging-post, in the dungeon, at the stake or block. And yet, though the Word and cause of Christ was espoused through affliction, it was "in joy." How few now rejoice in affliction! The majority of modern converts succumb to a very little persecution.

Again, these Christians were exemplary Christians—"Ye were ensamples to all that believe." There was no cause of reproach to the work in their living. They had a practical type of religion. They paid their debts one hundred cents to the dollar. They could be trusted to meet their obligations. Their word was as good as their bond. Thousands of professed Christians today are lax in these matters. But it does not take sanctification to make a man straight in his outward life.

This was a working Church. They were neither lazy nor indifferent. They were not the kind who fold their arms and sit down. Every real convert hears the injunction: "Enter thou into my vineyard and labor."

It was a labor of love and faith. He tells them that he is informed of their "work of faith and labor of love." Why, there is much so-called "church work" now that is not a "work of faith." A work of faith is something that no one can do but a spiritual person. Unsaved church members may carpet the parsonage or beg a cake, but that is not a work of faith.

There is but little "love-labor." Oh, that we might engage in a "labor of love," every one of us! When a woman fries oysters until eleven oclock, or washes dishes until one for a church festival, she may tell herself that she is doing "love-labor;" but it is not true, for we hear her say the next day that she had to work nearly all night, and Sister B. never did anything.

And then these things, said to be done in the interests of the church, are not real labors of love, for they give trouble afterwards. Often it cannot be pacifically agreed as to what society shall have most of the proceeds. If it was a labor of love, it would never result in hard feelings between church members. In evangelistic work we are all the time having to help fix up some church trouble resulting from these things.

When you perform a labor of love you are willing to do all the work and some one else take all the glory.

Again, they "waited for His Son (Jesus) from heaven." They were not only a converted Church, a working Church, an exemplary Church, a joyful Church, but also looked for their Lord from heaven.

"Well," many a preacher would say, "if I had a church as good as that I would never bother them about sanctification!"

Perhaps you would not, but Paul would, and did. But, then, Paul was not like many preachers anyway. He shunned not to declare the whole counsel of God.

Here is a gloriously justified Church. Paul prays for their sanctification. He wants them sanctified "wholly," entirely, completely, and with great confidence assures them that "Faithful is he that calleth you who also will do it." "Will do what?" Sanctify you wholly, and preserve you, body, soul and spirit, unto the coming of our Lord Jesus Christ. Praise be to God!

BETWEEN SERVICES.

The storm has entirely cleared away and the sunlight falls in bright, beautiful figures upon the ground under the trees of the grove. The children are at their play again, merry as if there had been no storm. The cars are bringing new arrivals constantly. The cottagers are sitting on the verandas. The fact that God is charging and surcharging the camp with his gracious power makes us humbly thankful, and our hearts are full of praise. Hallelujah!

6:30 P. M.

The testimonies this evening are "red-hot." Brother Norberry is leading the meeting and the flow of witnessing is steady, full, and strong. There is no mistake, these people certainly enjoy what they believe. There is nothing in the spirit of this meeting which resembles the long-faced, solemn sour-pickleism of so many of our so-called churches. As we sit on this platform we look into scores of faces which are the mirrors of souls transparent as crystals and white as arc lights. While the singing was going with the greatest enthusiasm tonight, Brother Norberry headed a triumphant march around the large tabernacle. None of us have forgotten the wonderful night last year when the joy of the Lord so flooded the people that the congregation, headed by Brother Carradine and the President, marched around the auditorium with glad faces and singing voices. We have none too much joy and gladness and cheer in our holiness meetings. May our God give us truly Pentecostal demonstration, fit concomitant for the blessing of heart purity.

7 : 30 P. M.

Just before preaching, Rev. Charles BeVier and Jennie A., Stromberg sang that solemn and effective hymn, "A Dream of the Judgment."

Rev. H. C. Morrison preaches tonight. Hebrews 6: 1 to 8, inclusive.

"Therefore leaving the principles of the doctrine of Christ let us go on unto perfection; not laying again the foundation of repentance," etc.

I have preached the last ten years to many audiences in many places and I find large numbers of people who believe the Bible to be an inspired book and are what we call orthodox people. There are people here who say, "Come in, Truth, at any cost, and cast out what you will. I must have you at all hazards." Do you know, friend, that we ought to be able to look any Bible truth full in the face without "batting" our eyes. One of the most dangerous things a man can do is to turn his back on revealed light. And if you turn your back on light and go on in sin you will go to hell as sure as God is holy and good!

I believe in restitution, and I was preaching about it

down in Kentucky and a man said, "Why, if that doctrine is true, it would ruin this community." Well, that showed that he was hit. I do not mean to say that a man cannot have peace with God and yet be in debt. But I do mean to say that if he can *possibly* pay he has got to pay or go to hell!

Of course there are cases where a man is not able to pay his debts. With all his effort and striving, he is not able to meet his indebtedness. I want to say this man can be saved *now* and shout in the face of debt and the devil!

There is nothing of no importance with God. He tests big folks with little things, and little folks with big things. He tested Frances Willard and asked her to shed her jewelry, and he asked me (and I am "little folks") if I would sell out for a cotton factory sometime and run for Congress!

As holiness preachers we do not want to carry any whitewash with us. We must be frank and honest and sincere and faithful and longsuffering with our fellow beings. And, by the grace of God, here is one preacher who is going to try to be this as long as he is on the earth.

Here is a question which men are asking and they have a right to an answer: "Can a man who is justified but not sanctified go to hell?" Well, let's try to answer the question. No justified man can enter hell and no unsanctified man can enter Heaven. Well, suppose a man is justified but dies unsanctified? Halt right there; no man ever did or will. He will either get sanctified before death or backslide. Unholy people *could* not live in peace with a holy God and holy angels throughout a holy eternity.

If a man claims to have religion and yet does not want more of it, we begin to doubt if he has really got religion. It is bad enough for a sinner to refuse Jesus, but it is far more awful for one who has been moved by Christ and taught by Christ to reject the Lord! It is most shameful and terrible, and Christ must turn away with a sad heart.

O, brother, do not reject your Lord. Let him sanctify you tonight.

SATURDAY, AUGUST 6.

10: 30 A. M.

Rev. H. C. Morrison preached from 1 Peter 2: 3. We were compelled to be away on important business. The sermon was wonderful, according to all accounts, of great conviction to the un-right and of great help to the sanctified.

3: 00 P. M.

The people have been coming in large numbers all day, for tomorrow is the last day of the camp. The attendance this year exceeds that of any previous year. There have been more tents occupied, more diners at the dining-hall, more seekers at the altar, more outpourings of the Spirit than even Portsmouth has ever witnessed before.

At the noon-hour when the morning service was spoken of almost *everyone* seemed to have been greatly blessed by Brother Morrison's glorious sermon. God has not left us, but is still with us. Conviction is deepening all the time and new comers are being struck by the power of God. It is very gratifying to watch the work of the Holy Ghost among sinners and backsliders. Often as a group of sinners stand and talk and laugh, the power of God strikes them and jests die on the lip and laughs turn into a hollow cackle. Many a sinner comes onto the campground unconcerned and disinterested, but is speedily smitten with the power of God and brought to a place of deep and sincere penitence and sky-blue conversion.

Rev. W. B. Godbey preaches at this hour. His subject is "The Symbolism of David and Solomon."

While we live in the New Testament dispensation and while the New Testament is of the greatest use to us, yet the Old Testament symbolism is of great interest and blessing to the soul.

David symbolizes Christ in his first coming. He was hounded by enemies and always in war. Solomon symbolizes Christ in his second coming—not an enemy in the country, wearing a crown gleaming with celestial lustre.

David also symbolizes a soul in the justified state; Solomon, the soul in the sanctified state. "Yes," you say, "but Solomon fell." Well, we do not claim that we cannot fall. The Bible teaches that we are on probation and *may* fall. But I believe Solomon after writing Ecclesiastes in the blackness of conviction was gloriously reclaimed. The burden of Ecclesiastes is, "All is vanity and vexation of spirit." O, take warning, sanctified friend, if you backslide and go back to the world you will never enjoy it. After reclamation Solomon wrote that beautiful poem about the love of Christ and his church, called the "Song of Songs."

All that Solomon had to do when he came to the throne was to look his enemies in the face and they fled. And all the sanctified soul has to do is to face the dusky cohorts of hell and they will vanish before him.

Solomon has left everywhere in Palestine monuments of his power and magnificence, which will stand forever. The quarries of Solomon, the sealed fountain of Solomon, these monuments will stand until the end of time. And if we are sanctified we are making history; we are erecting monuments that will last forever. Who can tell me the names of the spies who brought back an evil report? Nobody. Why, what were the names of the men who fought John Wesley and George Fox and John Bunyan? None can answer. They have all rotted. You are publishing your "Hallelujahs" and the next generation will read them. We are erecting monuments.

Solomon had wisdom. The Queen of Sheba came to see his great wisdom. And the sanctified man ought to be taught in the things of God. Not in the things of the world, but in the things that concern the Kingdom of heaven. When we get sanctified they will come to see us. When we get on Solomon's throne, folks will want us to come and see them. If I had not got on the throne, I would not be here. There were more D.D's in my conference than any other in the convention, but you will never hear of them. But the grace of God takes a little, shabby fellow like me and brings me out here to preach to you.

The throne is white, made of ivory. And when we get under the blood we are made white. You have got to have a clean snow-white religion or make your bed in hell.

There are six steps in the devil's ladder to hell.
1. Doubt,
2. Discouragement,
3. Despondency,
4. Despair,
5. Death,
6. Damnation.

If you never doubt, you will never be damned. I would fight a platoon of devils and fall in my tracks before I would doubt. Don't you, dear folks, ever doubt.

As many as promise me they will die rather than doubt, raise your hands. (Hundreds of hands went up.) Now I will tell you a secret: If you never doubt you will never die. "He that believeth on me shall never die," says Jesus. This body is immortal. It will sleep while the soul is with Christ, but it will never die.

The first step toward sanctification is faith—i. e., an intellectual faith, a belief that there are things spiritual to be sought. You cannot be sanctified without you believe there is such a thing as sanctification.

The second step is conviction—deep, pungent conviction.

The third step is resolution. What is that? "I will have it or die." Grit your teeth and say, "I am bound to obtain." If you want sanctification; make up your mind that you will get the blessing or perish in the attempt.

The fourth step is consecration. This means we turn all, all, all, *all* over to God. I suppose more people have had to go to Africa at this point than any other place. That is the test! Maybe God doesn't want you in Africa, but he does want you willing to go.

The next step is faith of the heart. The reason so many people "take it by faith" and do not get it is that they take it with a *head* faith and not a heart faith. O, may the Lord help us to take this fifth step!

There are lions spoken of in the text. Twenty-four lions, twelve on each side. The twelve patriarchs of the Old Testament and the twelve apostles of the New.

These are all to help us up the heavenly road. They are in the Bible; they, under the Holy Spirit, wrote the Bible and they will bite the heads of the devils right off.

Who wants to ascend to the throne? While we sing, come forward!

6:30 P. M.

In the service this evening Evangelist Rose Williams sang that beautiful hymn, "Get Somewhere in Jesus To-day." As the audience took up the chorus and filled the woods with a volume of song, every heart was impressed with the importance of steadfastness in the Christian Life. There is a large and intensely interested audience tonight. Providence is well represented and so are Bristol, Warren, Fall River, Newport, New London, New Bedford and other cities. Some are here from Iowa, Colorado and the Dacotas.

We are nearing the close of this glorious encampment. We are landing our boat on the crest of a high wave. White linen waves in the air, joyous shouts burst from the lips, bright faces abound, and salvation is plenteous. Glory!

Bro. Rees: "Everybody that is dead enough to wave a handkerchief for the Lord, get out your bandana!" The effect was tremendous. It was as if a great white lily had burst into full bloom in an instant.

Before Rev. Chas. BeVier of Brooklyn, N. Y., preached the word, Rev. John Pennington led in prayer.

Brother BeVier is at Portsmouth and our hearts are glad in consequence. He is an example of what God desires to do for many a business man. God has girded him with spiritual strength, and like a holy Jehu, his energy is almost irresistible. In his ministry he is at times a John Baptist, laying the axe at the root of the tree; at others, a Jeremiah weeping over the church's lack of holiness; at others, a seraphic John filled with ardent love for Christ and the brethren. In person, he is a man of rugged figure with strong masculine face and keen, penetrating glance. His style as a preacher is that of a man who has deepseated, unshaken, unshakable convictions, a man in whom one naturally and instinctively has confidence.

Text: John 11 : 38 to 44, inclusive.

One of the gifts which Brother Godbey spoke of the other day was the gift of wisdom. I thank God that He has at times bestowed this gift upon me. Not having had much sermonic education I have had to depend the more upon God. And frequently as I have waited upon him he has given me whole sermons, outline and filling, in less than five minutes. And I want to speak a little while this evening on a subject which God gave me one day in prayer.

When Adam came from the hand of his Creator he had no sin. But by eating the forbidden fruit he died—i. e., his connection with his God was broken. Just as truly as

Lazarus was dead, just so truly a sinner is dead in trespasses and sins.

The sister of Lazarus remonstrates when the opening of the tomb was suggested, for, she said, by this time he stinketh. And a sinner is totally corrupt and depraved. It does not matter what clothes the sinner wears or what manners he has or what food he eats or of what colleges he is a graduate, if he does not repent and come to Jesus he will as truly sink in hell as a harlot who runs the streets or a gambler who rakes in his winnings.

Lazarus was unconscious, and so is the sinner. He rushes on in pleasure and frolic and fun and is not alarmed and yet hell is certain and damnation is sure. The sinner is asleep on the edge of a precipice, and the slightest movement would dash him over the awful cliff! How is it he can lie in a snow bank unconcerned? It is because he is unconscious, so benumbed are the sensibilities by sin. If one does not heed an alarm clock and obey its summons it will cease to arouse and awaken. The thing that alarmed me was that I was not under conviction. O, I can see how a man may cross the dead line and yet be breathing and living. Sinner, it is an awful thing to reject the Spirit. Beloved, it is an awful thing to grieve the Spirit by refusing to seek holiness. You cannot with impunity treat this matter lightly. Added light gives added responsibility. If you keep rejecting light you will come to a place where you *cannot* choose right. This is what makes the devil the devil, and damned souls damned souls.

It is a wonderful thing to me that Lazarus could hear the voice of Christ. It is a marvelous thing that a sinner dead in trespasses and sins, can hear the voice of the Son of God.

You can be convicted if you want to be. If you gaze upon Jesus, if you will stop long enough to think of your condition, if you will take time, you will find conviction settling upon you. A man who shot a picket on guard in the Civil War, in a moment of curiosity stopped to examine the dead man, and as he drew near and looked into the fine face and read the letter which protruded from the pocket, his heart broke and he was convicted for what he had done. Look at Jesus, sinners, and be convicted!

We must roll the stone away. We must remove hindrances and obstructions. We must make a clean, clear path for the Lord to come to us on.

I want to go back to the thought that sin makes men unconscious of their condition. I want to say in all love that many of our churches are dead and unconscious of their deadness. With these barn-dances and festivals and suppers and teas they are going on in deadness and worldliness and sin.

When a soul is really converted there comes genuine life into the soul. There is a *bona fide* impartation of the Christ nature to the soul. It is a wonderful thing for a soul to be quickened into life.

Well, Lazarus was alive but he was still bound hand

and foot. He needed liberty. He needed to be freed from the bandages and grave-clothes and cerements of the tomb. And you, young converts, need more liberty than you have now. The difficulty with backsliders is that after they were converted they did not go on to perfect deliverance.

Who wants perfect deliverance tonight?

This was a grand, plain, Anglo-Saxon, fire-filled sermon and many hearts were cut to the quick with the sharp edge of the truth. Praise the Lord! Great God, send us floods of power and conviction on the morrow in Jesus' name. Amen.

SUNDAY, AUGUST 7.

8:30 A. M.

The last day of the great campmeeting has came, a bright clear day in the morning at least. Although the crush of people last night was very great, sleeping places of some sort were found for all. "The Holiness people are the easiest people to suit in the world," says Superintendent Chase.

Brother W. B. Godbey is giving one of his wonderful Bible-readings. The audience is very large already. The people have taken their Bibles and have crowded close up to the platform, intent on hearing every word that Brother Godbey utters.

HALLELUJAHS FROM PORTSMOUTH

"Brother, if you are right with God you are not trying to twist the Bible. I am satisfied with the Word of God, every bit of it." This utterance of Brother Godbey is a key-sentence to the spirit of Portsmouth Campmeeting. We are in for all the truth of God whatever it costs. We cannot afford to close our eyes to any of God's holy truth.

W. B. Godbey has become wonderfully popular with the Portsmouth saints. His evident godliness, his deadness and indifference to the world, his meekness and humility, his scholarship, his love of truth and his unction in preaching have won the affection of the Lord's children.

Can it be true that this campmeeting will end today? Holiness is the one grand unifer. In ten days God's people have become so truly a unit that they feel perfectly at home and dread the thought of separation. What delightful, holy seasons of blessing we have had about this great platform! What blessed shouts have smitten the sky from the straw of the altar! Is there anything more glorious than to be in the midst of a Portsmouth altar service while the saints sing,

> "The fountain lies open,
> The fountain lies open,
> You had better come to Jesus and be saved."

and hard hearts melt and obdurate wills relent and our glorious Lord is glorified? But in a few days the lights will all be out, the straw will be raked up and thrown into a pile, the tabernacle will be closed and locked, the tent bottoms will be deserted, and dawn and twilight will come and go through desolate trees. But, glory be to God, the fire that has burned so brightly here for ten days will not have vanished. It will be simply disseminated throughout many states and many churches. Tongues have been set going on this campground which will never stop glorifying God by witnessing to full salvation; lives have been brightened which will light foreign countries and home kitchens; hearts have been cheered and comforted which will cheer and comfort other stricken hearts. Glory, glory be to God!

10:00 A. M.

Singing, "It is Good to be Here," and "There is Sunshine in My Soul."

The audience does not seem at all wearied by the services of the past week, but is as fresh and bright as if today was the opening instead of the closing day of the encampment.

Seth C. Rees, President of the Association, preaches this morning. Just before preaching an offering was taken in two minutes of ninety-one dollars for the support of the gospel. At Portsmouth the gospel department is supported solely by the free-will offerings of the congregation. Subject of sermon, "The Service of Difficulties."*

"Thou hast caused men to ride over our heads; we

---

*This sermon was reported by Mrs. S. G. Otis, and is published in tract form by the Christian Unity Publishing Co.

went through fire and water, but thou broughtest us out into a wealthy place." Psa. 66: 12.

The margin says a moist place, which means a fertile place. The subject treated in this text is the use of difficulty. Opposition and oppression have always been favorable to national success. It was this that drove the fathers of the revolution to independence. Men come to the front in times of great struggle who would otherwise have spent their days in obscurity: the civil war brought out Grant and Lee and Sherman and Lincoln. The Spanish war has made Dewey and Hobson and Schley household words. Many a man stands out today as a flaming torch in consequence of trials and opposition. These bring out the strongest qualities of the soul; they prove our real value.

Israel gained more by the bondage under Pharaoh than she lost. Difficulty awakened courage and self-reliance in the breast of the Hebrew. The Lord never tests a worthless soul, and the devil never tempts a soul which is already his. If a man has trials it is because God sees there is something in him; he sees something worth putting in a crucible. If you see others living in prosperity and luxury and ease, it is because they are not worth testing. Brother, if you and I are severely tested we ought to be comforted in the thought that God has conferred upon us the honor. He knows we are able to stand, and he lets just the things come to us that we can endure to the glory of his name.

Satan has sense enough to know where the valuables are and he goes for them. A pirate goes for a loaded ship. When a man is promoted through grace the devil holds a caucus and sends a committee to wait on him.

When God sees there is hard wood which can be polished he lets the testing come. Our trials, whether they be at the campmeeting, in the kitchen, in the counting-room or in the field, are to wake up the latent power in the soul. You can never wear the same clothes after you have been through a lion's den or an Egyptian prison. You are never the same after passing through the furnace. You outstrip everything you ever had. There was Joseph; his pathway to the throne lay through the prison cell. Daniel was never promoted till he slept with lions. The Apostle Paul preached in Caesar's household with irons on his wrists. John Bunyan did his best work in Bedford jail. Thousands have come to their best through overwhelming difficulties. We have got a God who is able to take these very things and glorify his name through us.

I would rather associate with people who will rub up against me and cuff and kick me and jostle me, for that will bring out the dormant strength which God has built into the soul. It was the weights on my old grandfather's clock that made it go. It is the adverse wind that propels the tacking ship. And God puts us in straight jackets and in stocks in inner cells, in order that we may shout and sing and hold meetings at midnight.

We go from this camp to meet the stern realities of life, each heart knowing its own bitterness, its own trials, each to go through God only knows what, to develop us, to make us giants instead of pigmies, men instead of babies. Just as the wind carries the ship to its destination in the face of the tempest, God will waft us to our haven. "All things work together for good to those who love God."

Isaiah prophesies that Israel will return to Palestine on the shoulders of the Philistines. God's people need to learn that through difficulties we climb to higher heights and sublimer altitudes. Two men are traveling together and they come to a mountain. One man says, "I cannot go farther," the other says, "This is here that I may climb nearer to the skies."

Trial makes us appreciate our resources as nothing else will. You have been handing in drafts for five dollars and ten dollars and getting along with small amounts, till a great trial or bereavement or sorrow comes into the life and you walk up to the paying teller's window and present a check for a million dollars, and it is honored as quickly as if it was fifty cents. Many a man wouldn't know God had much if he wasn't put to the test. The greater the difficulty, the greater the triumph. The greater the trial, the greater the opportunity to show God's power. Heaven is exhaustless. Don't complain if severe things come into your life; only thank God and take courage. Beloved, I want to say you can choose between being a delicate, weak, ordinary Christian, and taking God to make you extraordinary. There are ordinary preachers enough; there are ordinary churches enough. It is the extraordinary that comes from the upper skies I'm looking for.

Opposition and difficulties are my servants to serve me, my helpers to help me. It is God's will and purpose that sanctified people shall ride over all difficulties. It is God's will that we should understand that our enemies are our helpers. When the mother eagle wants her young to fly, she takes out of the nest the feathers and the cotton and leaves the thorns. Is she unkind? No; she knows they will be dwarfs if they stay there. God treats us in some such way if we are bound to be true. He stirs up the nest in order that we may learn to mount into the azure of the sky. It was persecution that scattered the disciples and sent them everywhere, preaching the word.

You cannot tell what a man is made of by the way he preaches. Look at him in his every-day life. Look at him in great grief and loneliness, watch him when he is nagged and persecuted. Does he keep sweet? Is he still sanctified? That is the time. God knows I don't depreciate demonstration, but you will be safer to make your estimates of the genuineness of piety at home than at campmeeting. Brother, the way you act at home with your wife and children proves what you are. That's the place to measure yourself. It is more important that my own children believe in me than that I should have the confidence of a godless world and an almost Christless church.

It is God's thought for us that we shall triumph with a great reservoir back of us. It is one thing to go through the furnace and another thing to go through triumphantly. If you've got what God wants you to have, trials may come, friends may leave you, the very thing may come that you said never could occur, but you will walk right through in victory.

Fire and water are the two destructive elements in the world. If God can keep a man in fire and in water, where can't he keep him. God can make us fireproof and watertight. It matters not how difficult the situation, God can keep us safely and securely. "When thou passest through the waters, I will be with thee, and through the rivers; they shall not overflow thee; when thou walkest through the fire thou shalt not be burned, neither shall the flame kindle upon thee." Glory to God for a salvation that protects against fire, that fixes us up so we can stand fire anywhere. Beloved, when you get this experience you won't grumble or complain, but you'll take everything as from God. If God is putting you through a hard place, you ought to feel honored that he can trust you in a hard place. I'd rather do heavy work in the trenches and be a real soldier with marks on me showing that I've seen real service, than to have all the ease and luxury this world can give.

It is time we began to loosen our grasp on temporal

things, as Moses did, and tighten them on things eternal. We can afford to wait. We are the only people who can. Our hearts must be set on things that will last. A soldier who fought in the Battle Above the Clouds was wounded and carried to the rear. "Where were you wounded, my dear sir?" said the surgeon. "I was almost at the top." "But where were you wounded?" "Almost at the top." He had forgotten his wounds and was thinking of how near he had come to reaching the summit of the mountain. O may the Lord help us as Christian workers to forget our grievances and trials and injuries, and think of the success of Christ's war. We may press on to the heights, we may walk over everything in victory. God lets us do it.

Let me call your attention to the place spoken of in our text. It is a wealthy place, a moist place, a place of high clover, a place of plenty, a place where drought never strikes, a place where there are springs whose waters fail not, a place of entire sanctification, a place of second blessing. A man who is sanctified wholly always lives in a moist place. Glory to God!

"Thou hast brought us through fire and water, but into a wealthy place." Are you rich this morning, beloved? Have you reached the fertile place? Are you rejoicing evermore? Are you where you can go out to battle conquering and to conquer? God help us to secure the riches that will never fade. O, this blessing will do wonders for you. It will make you peculiar, I know, but it will put joy in your soul and will be a propelling power to make you go through difficulties. Beloved, shall we go through?

A great company arose for prayers and came quickly forward.

1:30 P. M.

As was announced this morning, this service was given over to Sister Minnie Lindberg, returned missionary from East Africa. Many of our readers will remember that three years ago Miss Lindberg received a call to Africa from the Lord at Portsmouth Campmeeting, and inside of a week was on the way to the field. And now, after these years which have been years of hardship and peril and affliction for her, this brave woman of God has returned to America on a brief furlough.

Singing, "I'm over in Canaan now," and "The Half has never yet been told."

Prayer by Rev. John Pennington.

Seth C. Rees: "Many of you remember very well when Sister Minnie Lindberg left us three years ago for her field in Africa. We are devoutly thankful that God has preserved her life and brought her back to us. She will talk to you a few minutes."

Miss Minnie Lindberg: " It was nothing else but the love of God that led me away from this campground to Africa. I saw in God's word that 'God so loved the world that he gave his only begotten Son.' And I read that the heathen, those dear ones in Africa, 'cannot believe except they have a preacher.' And my heart was so full of the love of God that I gladly went with Jesus.

"We settled among a very large tribe, and while there were many hardships, we were contented because Jesus was with us. My Redeemer has been with me in all things. Glory to our God!

"The tribe with which we worked were devil worshipers. When they need rain they have a rain-dance. Sometimes they have war dances in order that they may have victory in battle."

Sister Lindberg talked for some little time concerning the religious ceremonies and social customs of the East Africans. She made the subject very interesting and instructive.

Toward the close of her address she described the poverty of the missionaries and the death of Peter Cameron Scott, and then made a very effective appeal for aid for the missionary cause.

Miss Jennie A. Stromberg sang, at the request of Sister Lindberg, a missionary hymn. Sister Stromberg followed up her hymn with a very earnest, powerful testimony and exhortation.

Miss Frida M. Stromberg also sang, and delivered a short, earnest address.

Seth C. Rees: "I never was more deeply impressed

than today that we have got to do more. We have got to sacrifice more and deny ourselves more than we have in the past. I believe in shouting but shouting is of no earthly use without it is backed up by a life of Christ-like self-denial. Let us all pray!"

Brother Rees led in prayer.

This missionary service was one of the most spiritual we have ever attended. The Holy Ghost was wonderfully present and sealed the words of his hand-maidens to the conviction of many hearts. We devoutly believe that many a soul received a definite, distinct call to the foreign field. God help everyone to obey the call.

3:00 P. M.

The largest audience we have ever seen upon Portsmouth Campmeeting Grounds is gathered at the Tabernacle this afternoon. There are rows and rows and rows of faces.

Rev. H. C. Morrison preached.

"Good Master, what shall I do to inherit eternal life?" also "Lord, remember me when thou comest into thy kingdom."

I have read you these two passages because I desire under the grace of God to bring a message to every soul.

You notice that there is a wide difference between these two prayers, and they are answered differently. I have no hesitancy in saying that the man who prayed the first prayer was a young Jew and a man who was what we would call justified in our day and dispensation.

The fact that this man was a young man and a rich one made it difficult for him to be a man of great devotion. Now, mark you, I am not trying to rob the rich man either of his wealth or his peace; for Job was a rich man and yet he was "perfect and upright." But I am simply stating as a truth that few rich men are holy men. The whole Bible teaches us that there is great danger in wealth. O, "when riches increase set not your heart upon them!"

It is no matter how great a man's devotion if he does not watch and pray; when prosperity comes he will find the gold eagles are perching on his soul. He will get in the habit of kneeling with one foot firmly planted to facilitate rapid movement toward the store and the office.

That man is greater than Alexander who can say to business, "Thus far shalt thou come and no farther." It is a very pleasant thing to be regarded as a great success as a business man, and there is a snare right here. You have got to die out to all men's approval.

This young man who prayed the prayer of the first text was a ruler. I have been about a good deal, but I do not remember to have ever met a really devout man who was an earnest politician. I am not here to say that you cannot be sheriff or assessor and be sanctified, but I will say that there is an awful danger to the soul in the making of political friends and in the struggle for office.

The man was an humble man, for he came kneeling and he came running. And he prays direct, and I like that in a man. And now he puts the question, "Good Master, what must I do to inherit eternal life?" He recognized the Messiahship of Jesus. He was more consistent and devout than our modern Unitarian. Jesus answers, "One thing thou lackest." Brother Godbey will tell you that a sinner needs a great many things. But this man needs but *one* things. As Jesus looked into his face "He loved him." This man is a truly converted child of God, but he lacked one thing, namely, total, entire, whole-souled devotement and consecration to God. The young man has come to a crisis in his Christian life and so must you and so did I. There comes a time when we must go clear over to God or go away from Christ forever. There comes a time when we must either do the will of God forever or do the diabolic will of devils throughout eternity.

O, woe to the man who, feeling his need and counting the cost, turns straight away from God! I have seen a man whose left side was a graveyard in which he had buried laughter and tears and fear of hell and desire for heaven. He was still alive, but he had passed beyond the "dead line."

The time comes when we must give to Jesus Christ the place we have given to dogs and horses and stocks and farms and books. I do not mean that we can't pat a dog on the head or enjoy a horse, but I do mean that Jesus must fill our hearts and lives.

There is a place in the spiritual life where the absence of Jesus is agony. There is an analogy in human relationships and attachments. You go into an art gallery and you long for a certain one to enjoy the pictures with you. You see Niagara and you feel that there is one person who would make it beautiful to you; you look at the sunset and yet feel hungry and lonely. And the sanctified soul cannot and could not be happy except Jesus is the constant companion.

We have got to be just as truly under the complete command of Jesus as were the troops under Shafter. We must give our all to Christ. We must be willing to spill our blood and spend our strength for Jesus Christ.

Now let us for a few minutes turn our attention to the other man, the thief on the cross. Fortunately for him he had been apprehended and was crucified with Jesus. But Jesus did not look like a Messiah. It would have been easier to believe in Him when he was performing miracles; but now He is alone and disgraced and about to die almost without a friend. But this thief saw Jesus and even then, O, wondrous faith, he believed in his divinity. He was dying and he had just breath enough for one prayer. So in spite of the black-winged bats of doubt he said between the gasps, "Lord, remember me when thou comest into thy kingdom!" And the next moment he was sailing over forest and dale and city and lake, safe in the arms of Jesus with his head upon his quiet breast.

O, brother, you can start for heaven from that post, from that chair, from that curtain of canvas. Come to Jesus! Come to Jesus! My heart says to you—I cry to you right out of my heart, Come to Jesus! O, Lord, *save* this afternoon!

The peroration of Brother Morrison's sermon was the most wonderful piece of Holy Ghost eloquence we have ever heard. He described a visit to heaven and to hell and probable conversations with the blessed and the damned—a trite conception, but originally treated and, best of all, surcharged with the omnipotent force of the Holy Ghost.

There were many, many seekers. Praise the Lord!

6:30 P. M.

As this is the last testimony meeting of the camp-meeting there are hundreds eager to get a chance to speak. Rev. John Pennington is leading the meeting.

Rusha W. Swift: "My all is on the altar. I'm waiting for the fire!"

Sister Chapman: "I praise the Lord that I am in the land of Canaan and enjoying the fruits."

Rev. Mr. Dorey: "I praise the Lord for a salvation that saves."

Mrs. H. E. King: "What a wonderful Saviour is Jesus my Lord; he keeps me day by day."

Sister Kennedy: "How I praise the Lord for the privilege of being at this meeting! There are loved ones who have passed on but, praise the Lord, we are going to meet over the river."

Singing,

> "There's a land that is fairer than day."

7 : 30 P. M.

Singing,

> "When the roll is called up yonder."

After the collection the congregation sang,

> " 'Tis a glorious church,
> Without spot or wrinkle."

Rev. H. C. Morrison preaches the closing sermon of this meeting.

"And thou, Solomon my son, know thou the God of thy father and serve him with a perfect heart and a willing mind, for the Lord searcheth all hearts and understandeth all the imaginations of the thoughts; if thou seek him he will be found of thee, but if thou forsake him he will cast thee off forever." 1 Chron. 28: 9.

David, step by step, came from the most humble circumstances to the head of a great nation. But suddenly the wheel of Fortune seemed to fly backward as swiftly as it had spun forward. Saul became jealous and David was driven from a palace to a hole in a hill, and from the board of a prince to the fare of a beggar. This trouble was all caused by the injudicious praise of David by the singing women.

I want you to notice that the action of these singers was in all probability thoughtless and unintentional. The people who are bringing wreck and ruin into lives frequently, little realize what they are doing. Why, there isn't a bar-tender so low that he really designs the downfall of a man; he simply says, "He has money and for the chinks I'll pass the drinks." I knew of a case where a man was taught to gamble by thoughtless girls in a euchre party, and he went on and wrecked his fortune, and one Sunday morning he put a self-acting revolver to his temple and his brains spattered on the wall, and that very instant the girls who taught him to play were teaching Sunday School in a high-toned, abominable church up-town!

I want to enforce that text of the apostle's, "No man liveth to himself and no man dieth to himself." And what wilt thou do, O man, when thou standest before the great tribunal of the great God with the blood of souls clotting your skirts?

I have heard that "boys have to sow their wild oats," but a backslidden Methodist sister told me that "girls have to sow *their* wild oats." Well, I have seen a few girls with blistered hands in the burning sun reaping a harvest which stretched away till the horizon came down and touched the earth. This "wild oats" maxim is a blatant lie of the black devil.

There are a giddy set of people who are so conceited and self-centered that they are not content to have people hunt them up to worship them, but they go to a church appointed for the worship of God and attract attention to themselves. I want to say that these are the worst people out of hell. And they will sink deeper in the pit than any other class under Heaven.

When I was a young preacher and rode up mud-lanes and had saddle bags for my trunk and got five dollars a month, the devil used to point out prospering young sinners and try to make me envious of them; but I have seen those whom I was tempted to envy make ship-wreck and failure and I have been ashamed to remember that I ever listened to the voice of the devil.

"Son, know thou the God of thy fathers." Brethren, we can't leave our children a better heritage. I'd rather be born in a hut, rocked in a sugar trough, wear a tow frock and crawl over a puncheon floor and have a prayerful mother than to have millions of money. Friend, it would be an awful thing to leave your children no inheritance of devout memories.

I notice that the text says, "Know God." Not know *about* God merely, but know him personally. And, mark, he does not say, "serve God and know him," but "know him and serve him;" for the knowledge must come before the service.

Not only are we to serve him but we are to serve God with a *perfect* heart. Say, my friend, are we to cut this out of the Book? Are we? (Cries of No, No!) Well, then if we are to leave it in the Book let me tell you that when the throne is set the books will be opened and this passage will be opened and this passage will face you. Somewhere, somehow, we must reach a place where we serve God with a perfect heart.

I want you to notice that the text does not say "perfect service." He looks at the heart. Just as you appreciate the service of your little boy even if it is imperfect, because he *is* your little boy and loves you, so God looks at our motives and smiles at us even in our blunders. O, the considerateness of our God! What a heavenly Father, what a compassionate God we have! God wants the heart! If he can get the heart he knows he has got your service and your all. Bring your broken heart to him and he will fix it and he will set it by the clock of heaven which is the heart of God, and it will go on ticking with the big clock.

But "if thou forsake him he will cast thee off forever;" but "if thou seek him he will be found of thee." Come, brother, seek him tonight! God bless you, what will you do? The Lord help you! Amen.

As Brother Morrison preached this sermon he seemed inspired with the Spirit of the great God. The vast audience was thrilled with the power of God. Away out in the darkness beyond the burning lights men were seized with conviction. From the bright light about the platform away back to the dark, forbidding faces in the back of the Tabernacle, all souls were stilled by the breath of God. The altar service was glorious and the meeting was hard to close, for the saints part relunctantly.

We have spent ten days with God. We have had the grandest and most blessed meeting this year of all the eight. And now may the blessing of God rest upon us all and may we honor our Christ by faithful living and definite testifying in the twelve months between the present and the next encampment! Amen and Amen! Hallelujah!

THE END.

EXTRACT OF THE BILL OF 1898.

PORTSMOUTH CAMP GROUND is situated on Quaker Hill, on Rhode Island, about two miles from Portsmouth station, on the N. Y., N. H. & H. R. R. and is seven miles from Newport and ten from Fall River. Portsmouth Camp is a beautiful, hard-wood grove supplied with the best of cold spring water. The island is a delightful summer resort, since the sea air is very bracing and the picturesque scenery is unsurpassed in New England.

Heaven has chosen this spot for the display of Pentecostal electricity from the upper skies, for the operation of the Holy Ghost in the conversion of sinners, the sanctification of believers and the healing of the sick. God will be there in great power. No mistake.

Rev. H. C. Morrison of Louisville, Ky.; Rev. W. B. Godbey, Perryville, Ky.; Rev. John Norberry, Brooklyn, N. Y.; Chas. BeVier, Brooklyn, N. Y.; Mrs. Margaret Bottome, N. Y., President of "King's Daughters;" Rev. John Pennington, Mt. Pleasant, Ohio; Isaac B. Remsen, Jamaica, L. I., N. Y., and also many New England ministers and workers we expect to be with us.

LODGINGS.

There, are society tents where lodging on single beds may be had at 25 cents a night. Family wall tents, 10 x 12, with flies and board floors, each containing one double bed-stead, straw mattress, straw pillows, pail, cup, wash basin, chair and broom for $6.00 for entire time. In all cases bring your own bedding, etc., not mentioned in the furnishings. Do not neglect this. Furnished rooms may be had by those who prefer not to live in tents. The tents are owned by us. They are all made of

8-oz. duck and each tent has a fly of the same material. Free lodging for all ministers (and their wives) who are in regular connection with any evangelical church.

BOARD.

Good Table board, $4.50 per week, 75 cents per day; breakfast and supper, 25 cents each; dinner, 35 cents. Provisions may be had on the grounds by those who wish to board themselves. All persons must obtain their provisions and meal tickets for the Sabbath on Saturday, as nothing will be sold on the Lord's Day.

RAILROAD ACCOMMODATIONS.

Round-trip tickets from Boston to Portsmouth station, $2.40; from Fall River, 40 cents; from Newport, 35 cents. The stage makes four trips a day to Portsmouth. All persons coming via Providence will leave the city at 2:30 p. m. (at 3:30 on Saturdays) on boat "Queen City," round-trip tickets, 40 cents. The "Awashonks," leaving Providence at 9 a. m., will carry passengers to and from the Camp Saturdays only. The boat-landing is about one mile from the Camp. Passengers taken to or from the Camp for 15 cents each; trunks, 15 cents each. From Portsmouth station, 20 cents for each passenger; trunks, 20 cents each. Those coming by train, without baggage, who wish to walk from the station should leave the train at Cory's Lane, one mile from the Camp. (No Sunday Trains.) An electric car line passing within a short distance of the Camp runs between Fall River and Newport. Let everyone come up to this feast of the Lord. Application for tents and rooms should be sent in as early as possible.

SETH C. REES,
F. M. MESSENGER,
G. W. KIES,   *Executive*
W. H. WEST,   *Committee.*
E. G. MACOMBER,
B. J. REES.

All communications should be addressed to SETH C. REES, Providence, R. I.

WORDS OF LIFE.

A series of Gospel Tracts, issued monthly by the
CHRISTIAN UNITY PUBLISHING COMP'Y

These Tracts are just the thing to enclose in every letter you write, or for general distribution.

SUBSCRIPTION PRICE,   10 CTS. PER YEAR, POSTPAID.
4-page Numbers, 5 cts. per dozen; 25 cts. per hundred.
8-page   "   10   "   50   "
16-page   "   15   "   75   "

No. 1. The Word of Life. 4 pages.
No. 2. Poem—The Months of the Year as Applied to Human Life. By Mrs. Jane Pardon.
No. 3. How There Came to Be Eight. 4 pages. By Abbie C. Morrow.
No. 4. Poem—On the Ocean of Life. 4 pages. By Mrs. Jane Pardon.
No. 5. Water Lily Money. 4 pages. By Abbie C. Morrow.
No. 6. "Whatsoever." 4 pages. By Abbie C. Morrow.
No. 7. Thoughts on the Divinity of Christ. 8 pages. By A. A. Pease.
No. 8. The Days We Live In. 16 pages. By Rev. T. J. Campbell.
No. 9. How to Love the Bible. 4 pages. By Abbie C. Morrow.
No. 10. Position We Should Occupy if We Wish to Fulfil His Highest Will 4 pages. By Hezekiah Davis.
No. 11. Receive Ye the Holy Ghost. 4 pages. By E. K. Sellew.
No. 12. God's Call to Separation. 8 pages. By Eld. Wm. A. Burch.
No. 13. Choice Thoughts. 4 pages. From the pen of H. L. Hastings.
No. 14. Not Commonplace. 4 pages. By Edgar K. Sellew.
No. 15. Lost Power. 4 pages. By Seth C. Rees.
No. 16. Apostolic Christianity Needed To-Day. 4 pages. By W. J. Gladwin.
No. 17. Take Heed to Thyself. 4 pages. By Abbie C. Morrow.
No. 18. Stillness. 4 pages. By E. K. Sellew.
No. 19. Saved and Healed, or the Touch of Faith. 16 pgs. Mrs. J. C. St. John.
No. 20. The Sin of Unbelief. 4 pages. By E. K. Sellew.
No. 21. The Service of Difficulties. 8 pages. By Seth C. Rees.
No. 22. The Blessings of Abraham. 12 p. By Arthur A. Pease.
No. 23. The Wine Blessing. 4 p. By Louis F. Mitchel.
No. 24. Hallelujah. 4 p. By Louis F. Mitchel.
No. 25. Given to Prayer. 8 p. By Abbie C. Morrow.
No. 26. Man's Wants Supplied. 4 p. By Louis F. Mitchel.
No. 27. God's Rushing, Mighty Wind. 4 p. By Louis F. Mitchel.
No. 27. Extra. The New Song. 4 p. By Louis F. Mitchel.
No. 28. The Thessalonian Church. 4 p. By Hulda A. Rees.

Address all Orders to
S. G. OTIS, Evangelist Building, Springfield, Mass.

The Ideal Pentecostal Church,

BY SETH C. REES,
Quaker Minister and Evangelist.

CONTENTS: Chapter I—Opening Words. II—The Ideal Pentecostal Church is Composed of Regenerated Souls. III—A Clean Church. IV—A Powerful Church. V—A Powerful Church—Continued. VI—A Witnessing Church. VII—Without Distinction as to Sex. VIII—A Liberal Church. IX—A Demonstrative Church. X—An Attractive Church—Draws the People Together. XI—Puts People Under Conviction. XII—Will Have Healthy Converts. XIII—A Joyful Church. XIV—A Unit. XV—The Power of the Lord is Present to Heal the Sick. XVI—A Missionary Church. XVII—Out of Bondage. XVIII—Entering into Canaan. XIX—The Land and Its Resources. XX—Samson. XXI—Power Above the Power of the Enemy. XXII—Compromise and Its Evil Effects. XXIII—Sermon. XXIV—The Author's Experience.

The following are a few sample drops from the
CURRENT OF COMMENDATIONS :

Dr. Carradine—"As for Brother Rees, I know of no man in the Holiness ranks today who preaches more convincingly and unctiously than himself. I do most heartily commend him and his wife to my friends and brethren, North and South, who desire a man filled with the Holy Ghost, and one who is as good a leader as he is a preacher."

W. B. Godbey—"The Pentecostal Church, by Rev. Seth C. Rees, the fire-baptised Quaker, is a Niagara from beginning to end. It is orthodox and full of experimental truth and Holy Ghost fire. You can not afford to do without it. I guarantee you will be delighted and electrified from Heaven's batteries."

Christian Standard—"It is safe, sound and evangelical, uncontroversial and admirably adapted to circulation among all believes."

Michigan Christian Advocate—"He writes in a sweet and attractive spirit. We could wish it a wide circulation."

Religious Telescope—"It is written in clear, nervous English and glows throughout with the evangelical fervor of its author."

Rev. George Hughes, Editor of the Guide to Holiness—"I like it, it is square out, and that suits me. It ought to have a good sale."

Rev. John M. Pike, Editor of Way and Faith—"The book glows and burns with Holy Ghost fire, and has stirred our spiritual being to its very depths."

It is well printed on good paper, and is neatly bound. It contains 134 pages, making a beautiful and very cheap book.

Price 50 cents. Address

BYRON J. REES,
Office of Revivalist, - - Cincinnati, Ohio.

BOOK 4

HALLELUJAHS

FROM

PORTSMOUTH CAMPMEETING

Number Four

A Report of the Campmeeting held at Portsmouth, Rhode Island, July 28th to August 7th, 1899,

BYRON J. REES.

SPRINGFIELD, MASS.
CHRISTIAN WORKERS UNION.
1899.

PREFACE.

THE little volume, "Hallelujahs from Portsmouth," has well nigh become an annual affair. The people ask for it year after year, and the testimonials to the good it does are numerous. We therefore praise God for the privilege of sending these pages forth, believing that the fiery words of God's dear children written therein will not fail to do much for Jesus' cause.

This ninth camp-meeting has been the best of the nine. God favored us with good weather, a large attendance and plenty of faithful preachers of the Word. The tide rose higher and higher on up to that wonderful last night when Dr. Walker preached on "The Blasphemy against the Holy Ghost." No one who was present will ever forget that meeting.

We take this opportunity of expressing our indebtedness to Mrs. S. G. Otis for her kind assistance in taking notes when it was impossible for us to be at the writing-stand.

The report of some of these sermons and meetings will doubtless sound very flat to those who remember how wonderful was the display of God's power at times. There was an unction and potency and feeling of God's presence that no pen can describe. We can only give a faint outline of the wondrous work of the Spirit in our midst.

May the Lord use these pages to the blessing, consolation and edification of His children.

BYRON J. REES.

Westport, Mass., August 9, 1899.

INTRODUCTION.

BEAUTIFUL for situation, the joy of many saints in New England and elsewhere, even to distant mission fields, is Portsmouth Campground. On the island of Rhode Island, between Narragansett Bay and Sakonnet River, on the old historic battle-ground of Quaker Hill; roofed by a leafy grove of ample proportions, the foliage of which is thick enough for shade yet open enough to let in the bright New England sun; well watered by "upper and nether" cold-spring wells and gently fanned with refreshing breezes from the broad Atlantic; conducive to both physical and spiritual appetites and abundantly provided with supplies for both; an ideal place for a genuine holiness camp-meeting—such is the campground of Portsmouth Camp-meeting.

From its incipiency the human leader of the meeting has been Seth C. Rees. Brother Rees has frequently been spoken of as "the Earth-Quaker evangelist," yet he believes in the still, small voice as thoroughly as in the earthquake demonstration of the Spirit, and is as still much of the time as the traditional Quaker, and is always as reliant upon the leadings of the blessed Spirit as a genuine "George Fox Friend." He does not "drive" nor "boss" the meeting; but his firm hand is pliant to Him who wittingly guides His own work, and the people are impressed that the Camp is in "the hands of the mighty God of Jacob" and that the Executive of the Godhead is in supreme command. Praise the Lord.

The ninth annual meeting (1899) has been much larger in attendance than any previous one, and has been, both in its spirit and results, most blessed.

A full gospel for spirit, soul and body has full right of way here. The truths and experiences of regeneration and sanctification are kept most prominently and emphatically in the forefront; yet the kindred truths and experiences of divine healing and the personal and imminent return of the Lord are not relegated to the outside, but given their *proper and proportionate* emphasis. They occupy their rightful place in their relation to "the scheme of redemption."

Although but one service (and that was not announced for the public) was held in the interest of bodily healing and not much was said publicly about it, yet it was an alive subject and many were anointed with oil in the name of the Lord, and took and realized Him as their Healer.

The spiritual tide rose higher and higher. Nothing hurt or destroyed in all these holy meetings. Everything seemed to contribute to the treasury of spiritual power up to the glorious climax of the final service. Many of God's ministers, evangelists, pastors and teachers were in the holy convocation, and all were given opportunity for the exercise of their gifts in the Holy Ghost. While several were regarded as "leading workers," yet no one was exalted as the "star attraction." The glorious Sun of Righteousness Himself eclipsed all "stars." He increased while each worker felt "I must decrease." Praise the Lord!

Four years ago it was my first privilege to be in this Camp, and now have I had "a second benefit." As the meeting was then a great blessing to my whole spirit, soul and body, increasingly, gloriously was my whole being blest and enriched in the Lord at this year's meeting. Forever will it be most precious in the casket of my memory. "Hallelujahs from Portsmouth" shall re-echo through me while I have any being.

EDWARD F. WALKER.

Portsmouth, R. I., Aug. 7, 1899.

CONTENTS.

PHOTO-ENGRAVINGS.

A View of the Tabernacle—A View of Some of the Tents—Seth C. Rees' Tent—A Group of Preachers and Workers—N. R. Reed's Cottage.

FRIDAY, JULY 28.

Portsmouth Campground,	11
Opening Services,	15
Between Services,	22
Sermon by Dr. Walker,	24

SATURDAY, JULY 29.

Breakfast Hour,	32
Mrs. Morrow's Bible Reading,	34
Sermon by Rev. John Pennington,	37
Dr. Walker's Sermon on "The Church,"	42

SUNDAY, JULY 30.

Sermon by Seth C. Rees,	54
Mrs. Morrow's Reading on "Love,"	59
Dr. Walker's Sermon on "Sanctification,"	60
Sermon by Rev. William H. Hoople,	67

MONDAY, JULY 31.

Bible Reading by Mrs. Morrow,	72
Dr. Walker's Sermon on "Fruit Bearing,"	74
Sermon by Rev. John Norberry,	83

TUESDAY, AUGUST 1.

Brother Hoople on "Perfect Love,"	89
Bible Reading by Mrs. Morrow,	92
Sermon by Dr. Walker,	94
Sermon by Rev. J. H. Norris,	99

WEDNESDAY, AUGUST 2.

Mrs. Morrow's Reading on "The Vine Chapter,	103
Sermon by Dr. Levy,	111
Miss Curry's Sermon on "Naaman,"	116

THURSDAY, AUGUST 3.

Bible Reading by Mrs. Morrow,	120
Dr. Walker's Sermon on "Nazarites,"	123
Minnie Lindberg's Missionary Address,	127
Sermon by Rev. W. H. Hoople,	128
Sermon by Rev. John Norberry,	132

FRIDAY, AUGUST 4.

Mrs. Morrow's Last Bible Reading,	134
Sister Cassie L. Smith's Bible Reading,	137
Sermon by Rev. John Pennington,	139
Sermon by Sister Mattie Curry,	142

SATURDAY, AUGUST 5.

Sermon by Rev. F. M. Messenger,	144
Sermon by Dr. Walker,	147
Sermon by Rev. Wm. H. Hoople,	152

SUNDAY, AUGUST 6.

Sermon by Sister Mattie Curry,	155
Rev. Byron J. Rees on "Knowing Christ,"	157
Sermon by Dr. Walker,	163

PORTSMOUTH CAMPGROUND.

FRIDAY, JULY 28, 1899.

MORNING.

TO some, at least, there is no sight more beautiful than Portsmouth Campground on a fair July morning. The clear, wholesome air, the quivering green leaves overhead, the brown carpeting of dry foliage underfoot, the white canvas tents glimmering among the dark tree-trunks, the pretty cottages, the sloping hills and the shady valleys, all combine to form a picture dear to the heart of every true Portsmouth camper.

The campground is not a large one: there are, perhaps, eight acres in our lovely grove. But while the area of the camp is not great, yet into these eight acres are crowded many things which make it a most precious spot to hundreds of souls.

Of course, "Portsmouth" is admirably situated. It is but seven miles from Newport, and ten from Fall River, and in connection with both these cities by electric cars. The Providence boat lands within a mile and a half of the gates, while the New York and New Haven R. R. brings passengers to Portsmouth Station, two miles and a half distant, and to Cory's Lane, a flag station, a mile and a half west of the camp.

The friends who come by way of New York find "Portsmouth" easy of access. The magnificent "Fall River Line" steamers leave Pier 19, foot of Murray St., every evening, landing the next morning at Fall River, from which city the trolley cars soon carry one to the campground. Providence people come by way of the Seaconnet Steamer, "Queen City," landing at Newtown Wharf. In these ways the encampment is placed in direct connection with all points near and remote.

But Portsmouth has certain characteristics that would bring people to its services if they had to walk long distances. It is peculiarly *God's* property. From first to last this camp-meeting has been God's camp-meeting. By a series of unique events He gave it birth and His hand has sustained it until now. By His marvelous wisdom it has been kept clear of a thousand threatening catastrophies and by His glorious power it has continued to be a wonderful agency in the salvation of sinners and the sanctification of believers.

The ministry at Portsmouth is of a high order. God has ever sent us men of power and fire. They have come to us from all parts of the country, from Missouri, from Kentucky, from Indiana, and from many other states. God has given us His best, seemingly, and the results have been most glorious.

Portsmouth has a *personel* of its own. It is like no

other camp and copies none. It is content to be as God would shape it and seeks not to mark out a path for the Divine feet. Consequently the steppings of Jehovah are to be heard at Portsmouth, and the work of the untrammelled God goes forward continually in our midst.

The attendance this year is most promising. Already the campground is dotted with the forms of tenters, and the open tents begin to look homelike. The big Tabernacle is filled with chairs and is all in readiness for the opening service to be held this afternoon. The dining hall is filled with busy servants, and loads of trunks appear here and there on the grounds.

Rev. John Pennington, Pastor of Emmanuel Church, Providence, is on the grounds. His hearty welcome to strangers, his inspiring faith and courage and his overcoming joy are contagious. He is filling a difficult post this year, having kindly relieved the President of a part of his arduous duties by serving as "committee on letting tents." When we remember that to many who come, tenting is an entirely novel experience, we realize the necessity of a firm hand and a kindly, courteous heart such as John Pennington possesses.

Rev. Edward F. Walker came upon the grounds this morning. In person Brother Walker is of ordinary height, rather stout, quick and nervous in manner, cheery in face and voice, a little bald, round in face and full of salvation. We have met Brother Walker many times but never with more joy than today. He is a

Presbyterian, but, as we say sometimes, has "strong Geo. Fox tendencies." His book, "Sanctify Them," is a sample of the kind of work Brother Walker does. It is clear, clean, simple, potent.

It is wonderful how God is picking men out of all churches and states, cleansing their hearts and crowning them with fire, and sending them far and wide heralding the glorious gospel of purity.

The President of Portsmouth Camp-meeting, Rev. Seth C. Rees, arrived last evening from Wichita, Kansas, where he held his last meeting. He looks worn and tired, but his health is good. His new book, "Fire from Heaven," composed of red-hot gospel sermons reported *verbatim*, is selling well throughout the land. By tongue and pen our beloved President continues to spread the news of full salvation.

Among other new arrivals we notice S. G. Otis, the full-salvation publisher, whose tracts and papers God is using so widely; Abbie C. Morrow of New York, whose name is a household word all over the United States, and whose pen the Spirit has so touched in writing for children, for God's people, and particularly for Sunday-school students; Rev. Mr. Gill, a sanctified descendent of Ponce de Leon, the famous seeker for the Spring of Perpetual Youth. Mr. Gill has had a unique and interesting history, having been saved from Catholicism and sanctified at the Peniel Mission in New York.

2.30 P. M. OPENING SERVICE.

The bell taps brought the people quickly together and in a few minutes a hundred and thirty persons were in the Tabernacle. After a few moments of quiet, the president, Rev. Seth C. Rees, in a few brief words gave us the opening keynote. It was *prayer*. "I trust," he said, "that we have come to camp-meeting prepared to pray. I hope we have on nothing which kneeling will soil. Let us sing No. 67 in Part I of 'Tears and Triumphs,' and then go to prayer." The audience arose and sang, "A Charge to Keep I Have," very solemnly, even tearfully, and then engaged in earnest, silent prayer. After a little time, Mrs. Abbie C. Morrow of New York prayed: "Father, we are here at Thy bidding and for Thy glory. We pray for ourselves. Let there be nothing in us that can possibly hinder one hungry heart from thy blessing. There are hungry ones coming to this place for food; there are suffering ones coming for comfort; there are sick ones coming for healing; there are struggling souls coming for rest. Burn out of us all just now any thing that may hinder other souls. Thou hast said 'Ask,' and we are asking, and we believe that *just now* Thou art perfecting Thy will in us."

Brother Rees also prayed and among other things said: "O God, we have met Thee in the way and like Joshua, have resigned all captainship to Thee. Thou art Captain of Thine own host. Help us to loosen our grasp upon all that is at all earthly that we may see the infinite possibilities which are within easy reach of Thy saints. We believe that Pentecost ought to be repeated more frequently than it is. If it is not repeated here it will be because of the sin of Thy people. O God, we do now pray Thee to search us, for we cannot afford to retard the battle of the Lord."

It is impossible to describe the intense nature of this blessed prayer service. There was a perfect unity, a concurrence of faith and desire, a vehemence of holy petition that betokened marvelous things ere this camp closes. God's people "stirred themselves up to take hold on Him." We felt that past victories would not suffice for the present conflicts. We were conscious that the devil is not dead; that he hates the servants of Jesus; but we were also sure that if we met all the conditions God would put a divine pressure upon the camp that no diabolical power could resist. The city is doubtless surrounded by strong enemies, but, with the prophet, our eyes see mountain sides covered with horses and chariots of fire. As Brother Walker prayed, we believe that all has been done on the divine side that *can* be done to make this a most glorious occasion.

Why should this ninth session of Portsmouth Campmeeting not be the best of all? We are all the *Lord's*. Our voices, our hands, our tongues, our all, are His. Shall we not allow Him to have His own will and way throughout? Yes, praise God, His we are and for His

A VIEW OF THE TABERNACLE.

glory only will we live and think and act and work. Amen.

Louis F. Mitchel is again our pianist. We would miss him sorely were he not. He is ever at his post, and his inspired playing is one of the important factors which go to make Portsmouth one of the most spiritual meetings in the country. His rare talent is all consecrated to Christ. He now spends his days, not in teaching worldly music, but saving souls. His tracts and leaflets go far and wide, and his service is ever precious and fragrant. God bless Brother Mitchel and touch his fingers anew to the glory of God.

After singing "All Hail the Power of Jesus' Name," Brother Rees said:

God is in the camp. He lives and reigns and gives victory, and every one may have it who wants it. We are glad that God has let us come to this hour. This is a period of great days and great hours. We might as well believe it now, for it is true. We had better abandon all our doubts. now, for they will have to go sometime, and meanwhile they will do us no good.

If you are here, tired heart, having come up from the battlefields of life scarred and weary, let me say God is here to rest and strengthen you.

I am in sympathy with the spirit of this meeting. Our God is a great God and can do great things. But only where there are people who will trust Him for tremendous things can He do the wonderful exploits which it is His will to do.

Beloved, we are on the edge of glorious things. Why not launch out into the midst of them? Shall we not get on the spring-board and leap into the middle of the pond?

Let's all get blest. Let's not be afraid to get blest. It is time we had something extraordinary in spiritual blessings. This is no formal meeting, this is just a free open service for you all. Feel at home. We gladly greet all strangers and say with all our hearts, "Welcome to Portsmouth."

Brother Walker: I was just thinking, beloved, that there is one person who is always glad to come to Portsmouth camp-meeting. He is always here. Some of us are acquainted with Him. Our blessed Lord is ever on hand at His own camp-meeting. I pray with all my heart that we may all meet Him and know Him. I have met Him and seen Him with the inner eye. The Lord has anointed my eyes with the holy eye salve, and let me see His beatific vision. The more I see Him the more beautiful He is to me, mighty to save and strong to deliver.

I would rather have Him here than anybody else. You might get a hundred of the best evangelists and preachers in the land around this platform but if Jesus was not to be found in the midst I would be disappointed. We must have Him. If we cannot have Him we ought to close the meeting. But, Glory! He *is* here. Praise the Lord!

And He will use you. You may feel that you are nobody, but God can use you. It is easier for Him to do something with nobody than with these "Somebodies." He can speak a world into being easier than He can sanctify a preacher, especially if he is a D. D. Is there a Mr. Nobody here? Is Mrs. Nobody here? If you are, Jesus will use you if you will let Him.

Mrs. Abbie C. Morrow: Brother Rees said "Let" and Brother Walker has been saying "Let," and this morning in my room the Lord said "Let." *Let God.* O how much this means! This means so very much—more than many seem to realize. But when one is in the habit of saying "Let" to God it is easy to always agree with Him. In my own experience whenever I have not "let" God love me I have ever suffered in consequence. But when we let Him love us into the place of prayer or the place of suffering we get the will of the Lord which is always the best thing for us.

John Pennington: I am glad He saves and sanctifies and keeps, even up to this very minute. This has been the best year I have ever had. Bless the Lord.

Singing: "Since I Have Been Redeemed."

F. M. Messenger: God most wonderfully blessed my soul at this camp last year. As I took the car to leave last year I had a feeling that I was to go through some new experiences, and I *have*. Some strange, fierce, hot places have been along the way, but, with Brother Pennington, I can say that this has been the best year of my life. So far as I am concerned I am determined to "let God" have His way with me.

Louis F. Mitchel: God was never so big to me as He is today. Satan is small compared with our great God.

Dr. Littell of New York: I praise the Lord for the great privilege of coming here. I little thought a short time ago that I would be here, but the blessed Lord has led me. There is no place that I am not willing to go with Jesus. He has led me to slum work and I am at His service forever.

Brother Joseph Wood of Fall River: I bless the Lord that during the past year I have been able to overcome the devil. I never loved Jesus so much as I do today. I am ready for anything as long as the Lord abides with me. I bless God for the victories I have seen in the past year.

Sister: Jesus is so good if we will only let Him be good to us! Oh, I want nothing of this world. I want Jesus and Jesus only. He is so precious to my soul. He has promised to never leave me nor forsake me.

Singing: No. 180, Part II.

Sister: I can never tell how much the Lord has done

for me. He has been inexpressibly good to me. Oh, my heart thanks Him!

Frida Stromberg: I praise the Lord for answered prayer. I have been praying that God would greatly manifest Himself in this first meeting, and He has. I want to thank Him too for all His goodness the past year.

Charles Dore (Assistant Superintendent of Camp-Grounds): I want to not only fill beds and pillows but I want to be filled myself with all the fulness of God and launch out into deeper waters than ever before.

Rev. Mr. Gill of New York: I want to thank God that although the theology of my church taught me I could not be sanctified until death, I have found out better and am sanctified today. I was raised a Roman Catholic, but God has wonderfully led me out and on until now I am free in Christ Jesus. I have not only been a Catholic but a Presbyterian and a Baptist, and I want to say that whatever your denomination, you may be filled with the Holy Ghost just now.

Brother Walker started the chorus: "Oh, Hallelujah! Hallelujah!"

Bro. Rees: I wonder if there are not some hungry souls here who would love to be filled. You can have fulness this very hour. There are those here doubtless who ought to have victory. If so, I wish you would express your need. Whether you speak or do not speak, be sure you meet God. This evening, at the 7:30 o'clock service, Brother Walker will preach. I want to request the saints to spend the early part of the service upon their knees. I believe it makes a difference how we come into God's services. Do not sing all the time. If you do the sermon will not be at its best. Mix in a large amount of prayer. At seven o'clock tonight, then, let us come together and begin our services humbly in prayer. This is a gracious opening. We have never had an opening that exceeded this. There were never so many people here at the first service as today. There is a prospect for a large attendance. Now we who are accustomed to tunnel through to victory, let's get to business! Needy hearts are coming. Shall we not make it easy for souls to "get through" by praying much? Let us close this service on our knees. Brother Pennington, I will ask you to lead us.

Brother Pennington thanked God for the auspicious opening, for His care of us, for the coming of God's messengers, for those who minister to temporal things at the dining-hall. He prayed for the waiters and the cooks, and for ourselves that we may behave ourselves before the world as becometh saints.

BETWEEN SERVICES.

About supper time there was quite an influx of new people. Part of them came by steamer, many of them by cars. The new faces greet us kindly and we rejoice in these arrivals. Among others we see dear Brother Norberry. We have come to regard Brother Norberry as a fixture at "Portsmouth." He has a warm place in all our hearts and his messages are always well received as from the Lord. From the way the people are coming we are evidently to have a large crowd over the Sabbath. Praise God for the people. Oh, that we may prevail with God for their blessing and profit!

Many are commenting upon the new improvements. There are old tent bottoms replaced by more substantial ones; the two lodging houses are resplendent in new roofs, and one pretty cottage has an addition in the way of an excellent new piazza.

7.00 P. M.

The people gathered, as Brother Rees had suggested in the afternoon, for a season of prayer and waiting upon God. It is a touching sight to see scores of people waiting expectantly for the Lord to give assurance of victory. Before we rose from our knees many of us felt that God was about to answer.

7.30 P. M.

The preaching service opened with the singing of No. 37 in Part II ("Tears and Triumphs"). The front part of the Tabernacle is well filled tonight. We cannot refrain from thinking of the ten days ahead of us. Night after night the crowds will gather under the bright light of the Rochester burners. Night after night the Word will be preached in faithfulness and power. Night after night the altar will fill, souls will meet Jesus, shouts will ascend and heaven will gain multitudes of souls. What battles will be fought! How Satan will snarl and snap as his prey is jerked from his ravenous jaws by the Rescuer, Christ! How angels will exult over sinners saved and hearts made white!

There are doubtless spots on earth dear to all the angels. If so, Portsmouth altar is one of them. Think of the anointed messengers of the Lord who have stood behind this altar and preached a holy gospel! Think of the poor loaded souls who have dropped their burdens here! Think of the broken hearts that have been bound up by the Nazarene! Truly this is a precious place and will be more precious ere the camp closes.

After a number of hymns were sung, Miss Eva Pennington, daughter of Rev. John Pennington, led in prayer.

Singing: "We'll Girdle the Globe."

DR. WALKER'S SERMON ON "CHRISTIANS."

Rev. Edward F. Walker is the preacher this evening. He took his text from Acts, eleventh chapter, twenty-sixth verse: "And the disciples were called Christians first in Antioch." There were two Antiochs, Antioch of Pisidia and Antioch of Syria. The latter was the Antioch referred to in the text.

The common name by which the followers of Jesus were called was "disciples." They were "learners." They were at times called "servants" by Jesus Himself, who also spoke of them as "friends;" because they were docile, they were called "sheep;" in their relation to each other they were termed "brethren;" in their relation to God, they were called "sons." Thus they were called by many names.

The word Christian was not a common one. It is found three times in the New Testament. Agrippa used it when he said, "Almost thou persuadest me to be a Christian." Simon Peter used it when he said, "If a man suffer as a Christian, let him not be ashamed on that behalf;" and it is used again in the text.

The disciples at Antioch so conducted themselves that they were called after Christ. They were called Christ-ians.

The word Christian is, I fear, altogether too commonly used. It has been prostituted to base uses until the term is valueless. "Christian nation," for example, means nothing. The heathen are mixed as to our Christianity, and it is no wonder. We hear an argument about the Philippines that we "should give them a better Christianity." It is said that we ought to take away the bull-fights. But will we not simply introduce the prize-fight? The first cargo that followed shot and shell and soldiers to the Philippines was *rum*. The natives call it *Christian rum*.

But there are some heathen who distinguish between nominal Christians and real Christians. The one class they term Christians; the other they call *Jesus-men*.

New England Unitarianism is no more Christianity than Mohammedism is Christianity. It denies every principle that differentiates it from infidelity. And right here in this boasted New England professedly evangelical ministers are exchanging pulpits with Unitarians!

There are professing Christians, persons who have made a *profession* of faith in Christ and have *submitted* to the administration of the Christian ordinances and have *submitted* to church membership, and they have no true, vital Christianity.

A preacher in Pittsburg some time ago went to a lawyer and said, "Now, brother, you ought to join our church."

"But I am not even a believer, I have so many doubts."

"Oh, that doesn't matter much."

"But I don't believe the Bible."

"Oh, well, join us anyway."

"All right, if it will do you any good, take my name."

No sooner was the preacher departed than the lawyer turned to a friend and said, "What hypocrisy; it confirms me in my unbelief." With such "joiners" the church is *cursed* today.

And then there is a denomination which will not let itself be called by the name of their founder but insists upon being called the "Christian Church." But frequently even they are most un-Christlike in their iron-clad dogmatism.

Thus we see the name bandied about, misused and abused.

I have here a number of answers to the question, "What is a Christian?" Dr. A. T. Pierson says: "To be a Christian is to believe heartily on the Lord Jesus Christ and accept Him as Saviour and Lord." Joseph Cook answers in an almost similar way. I might go on and give answers from Francis Willard, Lucy Rider, and Dr. Parkhurst. We would find that they all agree in essential points.

To be a Christian is to *love, serve,* and *obey* Jesus Christ, i. e., *in love, service, and obedience* take Jesus as prophet, priest and King. Take him as prophet to teach us, priest to settle for our sins, and King to lord over our lives.

We must come like Nicodemus and see him as the great Teacher. We must take His teachings as our curriculum. If we have our own notions and push them in the service of Christ we are not Christians. We must leave *our* notions, *our* ideas, *our* fancies. We must take Jesus' words, Jesus' ideas, Jesus' thoughts. A Christian stands by and accepts every statement made by the

Lord Jesus. There is no truth which our Lord uttered which he does not accept. Are *you* a Christian?

I believe in Jesus. Brother Messenger, I am not peddling "Yankee notions." I have sent all my old ideas to the junk shop as no good. I have espoused Christ as my prophet and will accept of no other.

But we must take Jesus Christ as our Priest. We are utterly bankrupt and deserve hell and damnation. "No man cometh unto the Father but by Me." We have no merits. We have nothing to recommend us to God. Our sufferings do not recommend. Our own works, our own righteousness, these will not, cannot recommend us to God. The blood of Jesus alone can make us pure. His righteousness only can help us.

Brother, look here; I do not expect to outgrow any sin. I cannot, you cannot, grow out of sin, nor grow sin out of you. *The blood of Jesus cleanseth from all sin.* No part of salvation is an attainment; it is all obtainment.

Again, I must bow at Jesus' feet as King. I must have no will, no way of my own. To be a Christian I must be a bondservant unto Jesus Christ. In proportion as a man fails of obedience to Jesus Christ he fails of a Christian character. Do not imagine that you can join a church and have a little rose-water religion thrown over you and then go ahead and nine cases out of ten do as you please without consulting Christ, and then truthfully call yourself a Christian. It would be false.

To put this matter more specifically, let me say that to be a Christian is to be Christlike. "As the Father hath sent me into the world even so send I you into the world." "As He is, so are we in this world." We ought to live and love and labor as He lived, loved and labored. O brother, do not think that to be a Christian is to be "carried to the skies on flowery beds of ease." Paul said "the love of Christ constraineth us," taketh us, driveth us forth to holy labor and Christlike service. Not love *for* Christ but the love *of* Christ, the kind of love Christ has—this constrains us to labor.

Jesus was God, was the eternal Son of God, before the Spirit came upon Him at His baptism; but not till then was He Christed. The *chrisma*, the anointing oil, made Him Christ, and then He went about doing good propelled by the anointing from on High.

Brother, are you a Christian in this distinctive sense? "I will put my Spirit within you and *cause* you to walk in my statutes," says God. After His "Christing" Jesus was *driven* of the Spirit into the wilderness. The true Christian is driven, possessed, compelled by the Holy Ghost.

"The disciples"—we are nearly all disciples here—were called *Christians*. Oh, that we may all have the Christ marks upon us! Oh, that tonight we may be not only sanctified but Christed by the blessed Holy Spirit!

This was a thoroughly searching sermon. All hearts were pierced with a sense of need and we all felt a great cry in our hearts for increase in grace. Oh, for the stature of the fulness of Christ! The meeting was dismissed and the audience dispersed quietly to the tents and cottages, finding the paths by the light of the lanterns hung on the trees. May God grant a night of rest and a morrow of great blessing and power. Amen.

SATURDAY, JULY 29.

6 A. M.

About thirty people are out for our early meeting. They have come with expectant hearts and pray as if they meant to get something. There is no kind of meeting more helpful than a deep, earnest, spiritual prayer-meeting. These six-o'clock meetings start the day well. Not infrequently the day that follows receives its keynote from the early service. The Lord did not say "Where two or three are gathered together in My name I will be in the midst," He says, "there *am* I in the midst." Yes, Christ is here this morning. These unctuous prayers, these glad shouts, these thrilling testimonies all betoken the presence of the Master.

S. G. Otis: I thank the Lord for this place, and I wish that all the hungry ones could come here. We must not attend this meeting simply for the pleasure there is in it for ourselves. We must carry the glad tidings to others.

Sister Cressy: Last night while they were singing, "Never Alone; No, Never Alone," there came to me a new sense of the presence of the Lord. I feel so sure that He will never leave me.

Sister Cunningham: I have been trying this salvation for a number of years and I find that it grows better and better all the time.

A Sister: That sermon last night just seemed to "put me nowhere," as the saying is. I feel that I have come so far short. Oh, I want to measure up and be like Christ! I am so glad I listened to the truth last evening.

Singing: "I Want to be Like Jesus in My Heart."

Brother: I rejoice that we are not redeemed by corruptible things, but with the precious blood of Christ. I am so glad that I can rejoice in a full salvation.

Brother: The Lord Jesus saves me from murmuring. These Scriptures have been running through my mind: "In every thing give thanks," and "Rejoice evermore." I am determined by the grace of God to live Christ out in my life.

Dr. Walker: "Looking unto Jesus" means "Looking away to Jesus;" this is the secret of holy victory. I am convinced that we grieve Him by looking too much to our feelings. We ought to learn to feel as good *in the Lord* when we don't feel good as when we do. Do you get my thought? I mean that we should hold steady by faith in Jesus Christ at all times, in all places.

Louis F. Mitchel: We can go down from this meeting and break bread to the multitude. I believe that hundreds of revivals will result from this camp-meeting. So let us get filled up with the plenty that God provides.

Singing: "Praise God from Whom All Blessings Flow."

BREAKFAST HOUR.

The morning is particularly beautiful. The peace of God seems to brood over the camp. The sound of voices in prayer and the hum of holy conversation in tents not far distant remind us that our purpose here is "the King's business."

Close to our tent, No. 70, are a number of huge "pudding stone" boulders, massive, immovable. Around them stand straight, lofty maples lifting their branches sixty feet in the air. Just now our hearts go out in prayer that all God's people here may have both the rugged steadfastness of rock and the towering symmetry of tall maples. Let us be rooted and grounded in God; let us also reach toward Heaven in our spiritual altitude. We must have both "depth" and "height." Amen.

The beauty of the grounds has been increased by a number of signs, beautifully painted and lettered by

A VIEW OF SOME OF THE TENTS.

Brother Wakeman of Nantucket. As one walks up the main avenue toward the Tabernacle he is greeted by the precious words, "Victory Through Our Lord Jesus Christ." Nearer the Tabernacle is the sign, "Holiness Becometh Thine House, O Lord, Forever." Not far from the Dining-hall is the precious legend, "Delivered from the Bondage of Corruption Into the Glorious Liberty of the Children of God." Over the pulpit in the Tabernacle is the inspiring reminder, "The Comforter Has Come." The holiness which is to be inscribed upon the bells of the horses has already appeared upon the trees of the forest. Praise the Lord.

8.30 A. M.

Late last evening Rev. Wm. Howard Hoople appeared upon the grounds. Brother Hoople is to have charge of the singing this year. He and Brother Mitchel, the pianist, work admirably together. The people are rapidly learning the hymns in the new song book, "Tears and Triumphs," and the song services are becoming more and more blessed. Brother Hoople plays his cornet now and then and, blended with the voices, it makes splendid music.

Mrs. Abbie C. Morrow is on the platform and will give a Bible Reading at this hour. Mrs. Morrow is visiting Portsmouth for the first time, but she has already found a warm place in the hearts of the people. It is no small treat to us to have this wonderful woman of God in our meeting. She is of small stature, dressed in simple black costume, clear spiritual countenance, modest and humble in manner and carriage.

MRS. MORROW'S BIBLE READING.

"The Humility of Jesus" is God's thought for us this morning. Andrew Murray says, "The beauty of holiness is humility." Many of us perhaps have never understood that this is true, that the true beauty of holiness is humility.

We have sung, "We will go every step of the way," not realizing perhaps that there is a Gethsemane and a Calvary. Perhaps we would not have said that we would go had we known.

There are "enemies in the land." Our Joshua, Jesus, the Holy One, can teach us how to drive out the enemies.

The humility chapter is the second chapter of Philippians. Let us read the first sixteen verses. (Let the reader turn to his or her Bible and read this passage.) Now, beloved, unity is the way to humility. We can only have unity by having the mind of Christ.

The reason there is so much confusion in the home is because there is so little humility. If we learned to trust people they would measure up to our trust.

One reason there are so many boys in the saloons and so many men in the clubs is because we wives, some of us, lack humility. We do not possess that Christliness of spirit that has the effect of impressing our loved ones with the Lord.

"Look not every man on his own things but every man also on the things of others." The things of others! To follow this may take out of your life every luxury that was ever in it. It may take out things which you have considered necessities. But the great lesson which the Lord thus teaches you is well worth the pain.

Jesus "made Himself of no reputation." It was at one time my custom in reading the Bible to skip the first chapter of Matthew. But one day the Spirit seemed to whisper, "Read it." And I read it. I saw "David" and remembered his black sin. I saw Abraham and his sins. I saw Rahab and Ruth and others. Thus I saw a commentary on the verse, "He made Himself of no reputation."

"Of no reputation." Oh, beloved, we do so love to have people think that we are all right and that we say the right thing. Oh, that we had the lowly mind of Christ!

Christ made Himself of no reputation, even in His birth. The world pointed the finger of scorn at the cradle of Jesus. They called the babe the child of Joseph, the child of shame. Oh, what humility was there in the babyhood of Jesus!

He made Himself of no reputation in His boyhood. The mother chided Him when He was found in the temple. His answer was eager, "Wist ye not that I must be about My Father's business." But the next sentence is so sad—"They understood not." And He submitted to the misunderstanding and went to Nazareth and was "subject unto them."

He made Himself of no reputation in His manhood. Together with the common sinners he was baptized of John Baptist in Jordan. The crowd said, "He also is a sinner like the rest."

He made Himself of no reputation in his ministry. He sat by a well and talked with a woman whom the world despised. Oh, how careful we are as to those with whom we talk and associate. "Of no reputation."

When His long service was ending and the last night was at hand did He rejoice because He was going? Did He say, "I am going to the Father, I am going back to the worship of the angels?" No! No! He said: "In my Father's house are many mansions....I go to prepare a place for *you*....I will come again." Jesus was thinking of His disciples, not of His own prospects.

But His humility came out most evidently in the Cross. There on the cruel Roman Cross, suffering infinite pain, His thought was not for Himself but for His enemies. "Father, forgive them for they know not what they do." Let us pray.

This was by far the deepest service of any we have had this year. Mrs. Morrow's words seemed to possess a power well nigh heavenly, and the people were bathed in tears as the wonderful Bible Reading was given.

10.30 A. M.

The meeting was opened by singing, "When I see the blood I will pass over you."

Oh, that we may realize that we are absolutely dependent upon the blood for salvation. We have nothing in our favor. Our sermons, prayers, alms, testimonies, cannot give us merit. *We must have the blood!* The people are clinging to this blessed chorus this morning and singing it again and again with great earnestness.

Singing, No. 138, Part II, "By and By, We Shall Meet Him."

SERMON BY REV. JOHN PENNINGTON.

Rev. John Pennington will preach this morning. He took for his text Ephesians 5: 25, 26 and 27.

In this meeting we are catching a glimpse of what it means to "belong to the Son." We apprehend that there is a blessedness in belonging to the Lord which we have as yet only skirted. There is in the text a blessed relationship spoken of which is even better than sonship.

Sonship is most glorious. It is more important than many of us dream. Brother Rees' prayer touched my heart this morning. He spoke of what the Lord has saved us from. Beloved, the Lord found me low down. It was a glorious start and how glad I am that I was born into God's family.

But under the familiar type of marriage an even more precious relationship with Jesus than that of sonship is taught. "They two shall be one flesh." Now in order for there to be unity there must be established first of all the relationship. Some are trying to live the united life with Christ without first of all being joined to Him in sanctification.

There are people trying to live this holy life without being killed out to all sin. They stand to all calls, profess everything and yet are not joined to Him. The Lord help us to see our heinous crime.

"New occasions teach new duties," and for us to be married to the Lord Jesus brings new responsibilities and tasks. If we walk on with Christ there will be increasing fulness and joy and beauty. But there are those who have left the Lord and there is a chasm between them. The world may not know it, but the former oneness is no more.

This spiritual marriage implies fidelity. Having been married to her husband a true woman is his only, and cannot consider other claims. And so with the heart married to Jesus. Other voices call, other interests are clamouring. There are people who say you ought not to follow Him so closely, but to these voices the heart is deaf and pursues its way with Christ.

The duties and obligations of the present are greater than ever before. Sanctified friends, we must quicken our pace and measure up to present light. Leave every thing that you feel you ought to drop. Abandon all that God does not sanction. We must not stop at any point. We must push forward and take new territory continually.

Both human and spiritual marriage imply the sharing of service. We ought to share Jesus' labor for souls. There are some, God help us, who want the joys of marriage with Jesus but do not care for the trouble which being a co-worker with the Lord implies. Oh, shall we not go with Jesus fully?

We sing, "*Gladly* will I toil and suffer," and then many of us groan when awakened at night to wait on some sick person! Shame on us!

This sacred relationship implies the possession of whispered secrets. A friend of mine in business lived near enough to God to hear Him whisper advice just before the financial panic. God told Him of the coming stringency and warned him in time. He obeyed God and when the "hard times" came he had wherewith to bless others by helping and aiding them with his means.

I believe if we are as close to God as we ought to be He will whisper to us about our families, our problems, our troubles, our griefs. He has the answer to every hard puzzle, and will whisper to us the solution if we are close to Him.

If we are living very close to God we will doubtless be much misunderstood. The more one tries to please Jesus only the more the world misunderstands us and the more our best friends will misconstrue our actions.

The "offence of the Cross" has not ceased. The fact that the holiness movement has assumed huge proportions does not free the godly life from reproach.

If I live close to God I am going to make moves and do things which people will not approve. Your own relations or your wife's relations may say "It is folly." But you have heard the whisper of the Divine Bridegroom and must walk in a way pleasing to Him.

If we follow God's will we shall find ourselves sharing a very keen reproach. Shall we not bear it gladly? We will share it in regard to dress. There will be a simplicity and modesty that will make God's own different from the worldlings.

Our dear Brother Stalker knew no better than to mind God and leave "Old Bet and the plow," and travel far and wide. Friends said, "He is crazy," but he laughed and went on. God has supported him. Sent him again and again to the Pacific coast, used him to bless his own relatives and help thousands of souls. He had heard the whisper of Jesus, and no one could deter him from the path He had marked out.

If we share the reproach of Jesus we will also share in

His coming glory. He is coming again! The true wife wants her husband to return. It is the false wife who does not think of his return with joy. If you do not want to see Jesus it is because you have drifted from Him in your heart.

I am feeling more and more that the Heaven above and the Heaven below are close together. I do not know how long it will be ere the partition breaks, but I know it will break.

Meanwhile are we ready? Are our garments white? Are your lives clean and pure and filled with Christliness? Who is there here who wants our prayers?

A number responded and a very powerful altar service was witnessed. One brother in particular was in great earnestness and prayed with great fervency. In a few minutes the fire fell and the meeting closed in victory. Praise the Lord!

2.00 P. M.

This meeting, which is in charge of Rev. John Norberry, opened by the singing of a few hymns.

Since our morning meeting Evangelist Mattie Curry has arrived. Sister Curry is well known among the holiness people in New England, having served widely as a preacher of full salvation. She will doubtless have messages from the Throne for us during the camp.

Brother Hoople is leading the singing and the people are learning a new hymn (No. 130, Part II), "We Will Not Compromise." May the Lord help us after the camp has closed and we are dispersed to our homes and churches, to plant our standards resolutely and *"Not Compromise!"*

Brother Norberry: Let me say that there are plenty of people who were at one time sanctified but are not sanctified today. When we were giving ourselves to God and making a consecration for sanctification we little knew how much was implied. Our consecration means more to us today than it ever meant before. Oh, there are so many people who take things off the altar! Now may the Lord search our hearts for a little time. Let us pray!

There was a time of earnest waiting upon God and many received light.

3 P. M.

Singing, No. 46, Part I, "It Comes O'er My Soul Like a Wave," also No. 3 in Part II, "I Now Have the Spirit."

DR. WALKER'S SERMON ON "THE CHURCH."

The preacher of the hour is Dr. Walker. After the singing of "Blessed Quietness," he rose and gave out his text: Matt. 16: 18. "My Church."

We hear this expression from the lips of men very

frequently, "My church." People of many sects and denominations use this phrase. But here we hear Jesus saying "My church."

Last evening we discussed the word "Christian." Just as the word Christian is greatly misused so the word "church" is wofully prostituted.

At the word church many think at once of a building. They think of something of brick and mortar—what old George Fox called a steeple-house and something that might properly be called a meeting-house.

But according to the Bible, Priscilla and Aquila had a church *in their house*. So a church is *not* a building. It is a gathering of two or three disciples in Jesus' name.

Sometimes we hear of "churches" in the New Testament. This refers to the different gatherings of God's people. But the word "church" is also used to denote the entire family of God in heaven and earth. It is composed of all to whom the Divine call has come effectually, who have been called out from the world. The word *ecclesia*, which is translated "church," means "the called out ones."

This is not the Presbyterian sect or the Baptist sect or the Quaker sect, it is as Christ says, "my church." There may be members of sects who are not members of Christ's church, and there may be members of Christ's church who are not members of any sect. Christ is the only one who can receive members into the church and He alone can put them out.

The Lord not only died for His church but *it is His body*. He is the Head, we are the members. Now, brethren, I want us to examine ourselves this afternoon and see whether we are in full connection with Christ's church. Are we in true church fellowship?

All of the members of Christ's church are living members. They have passed from death or "out of death into life" (John 5: 24). The only way to enter this church is by the way of the new birth. To be "in trespasses and in sins" is to be "dead." No man can be dead and belong to Christ's church. There are some who go on in sin and yet think that in some way, in spite of that, God will get them through to heaven. This is a sad mistake. God undertakes to save no man unless that man is determined to *do without all sin*.

To be carnal is death. In proportion as you are carnal in that proportion you are not a full member of Christ's *ecclesia*.

Members of Christ's church have passed "out of darkness into light" (1 Peter 2: 9). Sinners are in darkness. Christ is light. If we are in darkness then we are not in "full connection" with Christ's church. When we know Christ as we ought to know Him we not only walk in the light as He is in the light but we have fellowship with Him and are cleansed by His blood.

If we are "effectually called" and made members of Christ's *ecclesia* we are freed from the snares of the devil (2 Tim. 2: 26). The devil is the chief hypnotizer. He makes men serve him and at the same time fancy that they are free. If a man is not Christ's He is in slavery to the devil. Satan can transform himself until he appears as an angel of light that he may if possible deceive *the very elect*. But the members of Christ's *ecclesia* are free entirely from the spell of the devil.

Christ's church are called out of the world (John 17: 14. If we are worldlings we are not members of Jesus' *ecclesia*. People who serve the lust of the flesh, the lust of the eye and the pride of life are not members. I said to a lady on her way to Atlantic City: You will see more of the world, the flesh and the devil there than any place I know of. It is a worldling's resort. O beloved, if you have a love of worldly things you are yet without the pale of the true church.

If you would study the world's fashion-plates go to a modern "church." But you find no fashion-plates in my church for it is the church of Jesus Christ!

Are you a member of the true church? If you are, the world is mad at you. The world is mad at every member of Christ's church and I am glad of it, for I do not want the friendship of those who crucify my loving Lord.

If you are a true church-member you are freed from "vain conversation"—that is, "empty mode of life." You live for nothing in this world but rather for the eternity beyond.

We have people in Indiana who are "in business" they

say. What are they doing? They are raising hogs. What for? To make more money. What for? To buy more land. What for? To raise more corn. What for? To raise more hogs! What for? To make more money! And so this is the round. Hogs, money, land, corn, hogs, money, land, corn, etc., etc. No view for eternity! No thought for the world beyond! Vain conversation! Living to no purpose!

We have Methodists and Baptists who would rather give their sons and daughters an education than salvation. Oh, how sad! Vain conversation!

The real member of Jesus' church is in the business of "glorifying God and enjoying Him forever." This world's business is not His business. His work has respect to the heavenly world and the will of God.

Again, the members of the church of which I am speaking are freed from the habit of sinning. Jesus saves His people *from* their sins not *in* them (Matt. 1:21). It is His will that we should "serve Him in holiness and righteousness all the days of our life." If you are a servant of Jesus Christ you are out of the sinning business. You have not only quit doing business but you have taken down the sign and no longer advertise that you "sin in thought, word, and deed every day."

Of course a man may fall into sin. For such a case provision is made: "If any man sin (single act, aorist tense), we have an Advocate with the Father."

But the man who makes a business of sinning, who

expects and plans to sin, is not saved and cannot be saved until he stops sin.

Full connection with "Christ's church" redeems you from (or out of) all iniquity" (Titus 2: 14). There is an iniquity which a man does not commit. It is born in him and from it he must be saved.

The church of Christ began, as our candidates for the Presbytery correctly answer, at Pentecost. Dr. Parkhurst says that a church without Pentecost is as much a delusion as a church without Christ. A church without the Spirit is not in the apostolic succession. If you are anointed with the Holy Ghost you are in the succession.

"Out of death into life, out of darkness into light, out of Egypt into Canaan!" Not simply "Out and Out" but "Out and In"—Out of sin, in holiness. Hallelujah!

The audience listened most attentively to this pungent sermon. There was a convictive power in it that went straight to men's hearts.

7.30 P. M.

Our audience this evening is very large. For a little time after the prayer service, in which Brother Walker led us so fervently, the meeting was opened for praise. Testimony after testimony pealed out and glad tongues witnessed to God's great salvation. The power of the golden bell of testimony is beyond all comprehension. The Lord help us to ring it.

SERMON ON "CANAAN," BY MISS MATTIE CURRY.

Rev. Mattie Curry preached this evening. Her text is to be found in Deuteronomy 31: 6, 7.

This is a part of Moses' last sermon. He has rehearsed the deliverance from Egypt and the fall of the fathers with a view to inciting Israel to cross Jordan.

God, when He saves people, has an object in view: He designs to fit them up to live with God. And when men stop with the conversion of their souls they thwart God's plan.

It is an awful thought to me that great as God is and small as man is yet man has the power to thwart God's plan. And let me say to every heart in divine presence that unless you have been made holy you have not had God's complete will carried out in you.

The "fathers fell in the wilderness." They fell forever. God called them carcasses, showing that they were not His children. They died disobeying God, and for them there can be no place. Brethren, if we die outside of holiness we have no chance of salvation.

Now I want to call attention to some of the directions which God gave the Israelites concerning possessing the land. In the first place he told them that they were to be a special people unto the Lord. There has always been a people who were God's own, who walk in the fear of God. All up and down the length and breadth of the land there are those who have not bowed to the

Baals of worldliness. The prophet was discouraged and felt, as we perhaps are at times tempted to feel, that there were but few who knew Jehovah, but God told him of seven thousand faithful ones.

Let us not forget that we are to be peculiarly the Lord's. We are not to act like the Philistines around us, we are to look to Jesus for direction and order our lives according to His will.

Israel was commanded to diligently obey the commandments which God had given. Sanctification does not change the value of choice. After we are cleansed we must diligently choose God's will at every point, and carefully hearken to the word of the Lord. God cannot keep us full of love unless we keep in the love of God. We must constantly choose God: then we will be constantly preserved from falling.

Again, they were commanded to teach the commandments to their families. When God saved you He intended to use you to save your families. And yet there are people professing sanctification who have no regular family devotion! Oh, may God help us to see that if we do not diligently teach these commandments and pray with our children we are only raising them for sin and misery.

I travel a good deal and go into many different homes and I can tell pretty quickly by the way the children talk about divine things how much spirituality there is in the family.

God commanded Israel not to marry their sons and daughters to the heathen. I want to say to you that close and intimate associations with this world either in marriage or lodges or partnership will rob us of all spiritual life. I know a man professing holiness, and I noticed that he never prayed a prayer that helped a soul toward God, and I wondered at it. But I found out that he belonged to the Grand Army and the Masons and the Odd Fellows. No wonder he was weak and worthless!

Another thing which God commanded Israel to do was "profess" that God had given them the land. They were to gather the fruit of the land, put it in a basket and carry it to the priest and confess God's goodness; and when we get sanctified we ought to take our baskets of fruit and carry them about advertising the goodness of the Lord.

If people ask you how you know you are sanctified, just set your basket down and exhibit its contents! Tell them how proud you used to be and how sweetly Jesus keeps you now. Tell them how the old anger is gone. Relate the glorious work, shake your grapes and display "the fruit of the land."

The Lord also warned them that they must not get lifted up and say that their own hand had delivered them and brought them into Canaan. The Lord teach us how to walk humbly with Him and give Him all the credit all the time.

Beloved, are you in the land? Have you a basket of

fruit tonight? The Lord help us tonight to search our hearts. The Lord "brought us out" of Egypt that He might "bring us into Canaan." God grant that we may all fulfill His purpose for us this evening.

God gloriously honored this powerful message, and several seekers bowed at the altar. Thus this wonderful day is closing with prayers answered, hopes quickened, and shouts shaking the air! Praise the Lord.

SUNDAY, JULY 30.

6 A. M.

We were awakened early this morning with the quick patter of rain-drops on our tent fly. The air is cooler than yesterday and considerable rain has fallen. But the people are not discomfitted by rainy weather. Umbrellas and mackintoshes are brought out and the six-o'clock meeting is well attended. Victory is sure to those who are determined to win it at all costs. Praise the Lord.

8.30 A. M.

The meeting opened with the singing of a number of the favorite hymns, such as No. 79, Part I, and No. 6, Part II. Brother Norberry gave opportunity for people to state requests for prayer. One after another the people arose and asked that prayers be offered for sons and daughters out of Christ, for husbands unsaved, for backslidden friends. The season of prayer which followed was very unctuous and prevailing.

Brother Norberry read Paul's prayer for the Ephesians, commenting as he read. He said that we need to be strengthened because human nature is weak. Some of us may not know that there is a weakness, but frequently holiness meetings like this reveal to souls their lack of strength. You may be strong in many points and yet if unsanctified there are sore places. These sore places are all of the devil. Oh, may the Lord help us to have the sore spots all cut out and get healed with the balm of Gilead!

After Brother Norberry's talk the meeting was thrown open for testimony.

Sister: I thank the Lord that I am here and that the Lord has perfected my heart in love.

Brother: I thank God for the ceansing blood. When God sanctified my soul He put upon my heart a burden for others, and I do not feel any hesitancy in speaking to people about their getting sanctified.

Sister: I thank God that He can speak directly to us without human words. This morning as I was walking through the grove He impressed me with these words, "Who are these that are arrayed in white robes?" I am so glad to be a member of this blessed company.

Brother: I came here with an awful appetite for cigarettes, but last night the Lord delivered me from all desire for them. My wife said to me as I left home, "You'll have to fight it out;" but God has settled the fight by removing all appetite for tobacco.

Brother Messenger: Six years ago today, the 30th of July, I believed God and the blessing came into my heart. I did not feel any great ecstasy, but I felt quiet and peaceful—I was believing God. This went on for a week. At the end of that time I went to a meeting and testified to what I believed, and no sooner did I take my seat than it seemed as if heaven dropped into my soul and I was filled with unutterable joy.

Brother Norberry: Now let us have a number of short testimonies. Let all stand who want to speak.

Over one hundred rose to their feet and many burning words of witnessing were uttered. Praise the Lord for free, glad testimony; it convinces and convicts. The preaching of the Word and testimony, together with experience, go hand in hand.

10.30 A. M.

The Sunday morning audience, despite the cloudy sky, is large and attentive. Those blessed songs, "When the Pearly Gates Unfold," and "When I Get to the End of the Road," were especially blessed to the people.

> "And the toils of the road will be nothing
> When I get to the end of the way."

Oh, that we could get our eyes off present toil and

difficulties! How small they will all appear when we reach the end! When Boswell spoke to Johnson about a spiteful thing that was said to him, the great man replied, "Think how small it will appear in a hundred years. It were well for us all if we took our stand on the peaks of eternity and went through the petty things of life as seeing Him who is invisible."

Brother Walker led in prayer.

SERMON BY SETH C. REES ON "GOD'S THOUGHTS."

Rev. Seth C. Rees, President of the Association, arose and announced his text:

"For my thoughts are not your thoughts, neither are your ways my ways, saith the Lord. For as the heavens are higher than the earth, so are my ways higher than your ways, and my thoughts than your thoughts." Isaiah 55: 8, 9.

The world makes much of the thoughts of men. Our libraries and art galleries are filled with the chrystalized thoughts of great men. The thoughts of Plato, Homer, and Shakespeare are treasured up and read and studied over and over.

I have read my text from the Book which contains God's thoughts. I would not undertake to say that it contains all God's thoughts, but it contains His choicest thoughts for us while on earth.

It is a great mistake for men to get wise above that which is written. God has told us all we need to know about heaven—about its locality, its nature, its inhabitants. He has told us of hell and its tortures, what men are doing there. He has spoken concerning our destiny, whether we are saved or unsaved.

"What is truth?" Truth is what God thinks. If we can find out God's thoughts, that is enough, we are satisfied.

Most of people miss God's thought concerning themselves. Colleges so often teach that man is a glorious success, an evolved and developed paragon of perfection. But God sees man as a failure, "full of wounds and bruises and putrefying sores." God knows that we are in the mud, and that unless His strong arm saves us we are forever ruined.

I am convinced that we are too apt to think of ourselves more highly than we ought to think. We forget "the hole of the pit from whence we were digged," and ignore God's thoughts concerning things. God says to the sinner, "Repent and Believe," but man neglects God's sermon and says, "Believe, that is all." Missing God's thought we make spurious professions of religion.

How frequently men go on and profess salvation when they have never truly repented! But all such profession is vain.

It has been suggested that the days of miracles are ended. If so, it is because of the sin of God's people. The days of miracles ought never to pass, and if we obey God and walk with Him they never will.

If we want success on this campground we will have to put away all sin. We will have to make restitution if we have defrauded, and make apologies if God directs; in short, we will have to clean up altogether if God is to work mightily in our midst.

God's thought is that His people shall be mighty like "an army with banners," each banner a token of a great victory in battle. The army does not need to be large to be mighty. Gideon's crowd numbered but three hundred. God does not count on numbers.

Pharaoh doubtless thought that nothing was so great as the pyramids and the splendid court of Egypt, but God was thinking of a little babe floating among the rushes on the bosom of the Nile. Today Pharaoh is only a wizen-faced old mummy in a glass case in the British Museum, while Moses is the most illustrious character in all the history of Egypt.

Caesar undoubtedly thought that his empire was the chief thing in the world. But God was again thinking of another babe, this time lying in a manger. Jesus is conquering today while Caesar and his empire are dust and ashes.

The conquering armies marched up the Appian way to Rome, but I doubt if an angel looked on the splendid array. But a poor preacher, an arrested tramp with irons upon his limbs trudged up to Rome, and I will guarantee that there was not standing room in all the galleries of heaven, for all the inhabitants of the glory world wanted to see Paul plant the infant church in Rome.

We have missed God's thought concerning the world. We are high farming in spots when God says "Go!" He has not said that all the world would be converted. He is not so inconsistent as that. But he has undertaken to give everyone a chance. And our business is to cooperate with Him.

God's thought is that His people shall be victors—that "with a conquering tread they should push ahead and He will roll the sea away." Brother, God's thought for you is that you should overcome. He put Jericho in Joshua's way that he might knock it down with ram's horns. He put Danel to bed with the lions that he might wake him up with the voice of the penitent king. He put the apostles in prison that He might bring prisoners out with them.

Oh, that we might learn God's lessons! How slow we are to get God's thoughts. Oh, I feel ashamed that I ever complained, that I ever spoke of my own difficulties. That Rough Rider who, wounded and faint, lying upon a blanket in the hot son, insisted that his comrades carry him to the front, had the kind of spirit that we ought to have in spiritual war. That man at the battle of Lookout Mountain in the Civil War, who, fatally wounded, could not think of anything but capturing the guns of the enemy, ought to have brothers in this holy war.

I stood on the battlefield of Franklyn, Tenn., and witnessed in my mind the great battle fought on that bloody plain. General Hood sent word to an under officer to take a certain dangerous Yankee battery. Word came back, "the officer is dead." He sent a messenger to another. He also was dead. He sent to the youngest officer. The young man knew that it meant almost certain death to attempt the task. He knew that most of his men would be left on the field. But with true bravery he charged forward and captured the deadly battery.

Pentecost will give us moral courage; it will fit us for all the spiritual conflicts that we get into. Have you received it? Do you enjoy the presence of the Holy Ghost? If you want to come to the altar, come on!

A large number came, and the most glorious altar service since the camp opened was held. This has been a most marvelous meeting! Glory be to our God for "His wonderful goodness to the children of men."

The meeting is beginning to take on great depth. If God's people will now stay on their faces in deep humility and faith, Pentecostal dynamite will blow up some tremendous boulders and icebergs of prejudice and indifference ere long.

1.30 P. M.

At this hour Mrs. Abbie C. Morrow gives one of her blessed Bible Readings. Her ministry is especially a *heart ministry.* It has in it those spiritual elements which *help* people. Though she speaks in a very quiet, even tone, there are times when her words cut clear to the heart core or bring the tears to the eyes with their pathos. The reader will doubtless remember that Mrs. Morrow is the editor of *The Illustrator*, also the *Word and Work* (Springfield), agencies which God is mightily using to bless thousands of souls. There is a large company here who are eager to listen to the message of the Lord through His prophetess. Some few months ago Rev. M. W. Knapp issued from his Cincinnati publishing house a little volume entitled "Sweet Smelling Myrrh," which is an account of the life of Madame Guyon. It has seemed to us sometimes that Mrs. Morrow with her clear spiritual intuition and delicate refinement was not unlike the devout French lady. May the blessing of the Lord continue upon Mrs. Morrow.

MRS. MORROW'S READING ON "LOVE."

The law said, "Thou shalt love thy neighbor as thyself," but the gospel said, "Love one another, even as I have loved you." Let us turn to 1 Cor. 13, "Now abideth these three; faith, hope, love, but the greatest of these is love." Faith brings us to God. Hope anchors us in God. Love makes us like God, for God is love."

"Though I speak with the tongues of men and of angels and have not love I am as sounding brass or a tinkling cymbal." If I spoke to you this afternoon without love it would do you no profit—no more than the beating of a tin pan. Love makes words worth something.

"Though I have all knowledge" and yet have no love it is of no avail. Though one died for one's belief, if there is no love in him it would not count toward a reward.

Mrs. Morrow went through the 13th chapter of 1 Corinthians giving each verse a little attention. The people were held well-nigh spell-bound so potent was her entire address.

3 P. M. DR. WALKER'S SERMON ON "SANCTIFICATION."

Three hundred and fifty people have gathered to hear Dr. Walker. After the singing of "It Reaches Me," Dr. Walker arose to preach:

1 Thess. 4:3: "This is the will of God, your sanctification." You notice that in reading the text I leave out the word "even." This is because the word is not to be found in the Bible. It was put in by the translators. Just as they put in "easily" with the verse "Love is not provoked." They did this, perhaps, because some of them had just been provoked. They doubtless felt that sanctification was extraordinary and so inserted "even." But sanctification is not an extraordinary experience. It is the normal experience and should be common.

If we are God's children we must desire God's will

carried out at whatever cost. We cannot scout God's will. We must welcome it and experience it.

What is sanctification? Now of course the idea of separation is always connected with sanctification. Separation and more is frequently meant, but separation is *always* meant.

There are plenty of people who seem to desire to limit sanctification to the idea of separation. Some go as far as to say "separated unto God." But no one can be separated *unto God* unless he is separated *from sin*, for sin is the great separator from God.

The text translated most literally is: "This is the will of God, the sanctifying of you." It is a personal sanctification, a personal cleansing. The Bible idea of sanctification is not to suppress sin or repress it but *express* it, i. e., cast it out. So long as there is sin in the heart there is not purity.

There was never a vessel separated unto the tabernacle service except it was first subjected to a thorough cleansing. The animals offered must always be clean animals. The priests had to be made pure and clean ere they could take up the service.

If you have any pride in you, you will have to get rid of it when you get sanctified. We must also be freed from envy, and from doubt. If you doubt God in any particular you are condemned. Selfishness is not of God. If you are selfishly hoarding anything for yourself you have got to have that old selfish man crucified or you cannot have the will of God carried out in your heart.

It does not matter what kind or degree of sin you may have, you must get rid of it if you are to be sanctified.

On the negative side of sanctification is purity; on the positive side is holiness. That lamp (pointing to the pulpit lamp) has no sin in it, yet it is not holy. Holiness is wholeness and includes likeness unto our blessed Lord so that all His lineaments are stamped upon the heart.

Both the negative and positive elements of sanctification are wrought by the Spirit of holiness. This is the Pentecostal blessing. The baptism with the Holy Ghost means the purgation with the Holy Ghost. When the apostles were baptized with the Hloy Ghost they were made pure. Jesus was not baptized with the Holy Ghost for He had no sin to baptize away; He was anointed with the Holy Ghost. We are to be baptized with the Holy Ghost under the symbol of fire because we have sin in us.

After the conflagration there is room for the Spirit to dwell, shedding abroad in our hearts love, the very essence and nature of God. The Holy Ghost then dwells in you filling your whole being.

Now I believe that these two sides, negative and positive, make up the full complement of Biblical sanctification.

If Paul desired these disciples of Thessalonica to be

sanctified then they were not yet sanctified in the sense in which he here uses the word.

It is true that they were already "saints," i. e., they had been born of holy seed. But it does not follow that because of that, they were pure and free from all sin and filled with the Holy Ghost.

So sanctification is for "the brethren," for "the saints," for those who are members of Christ's church; and a man who is not a member of Christ's church is not a divine nominee for sanctification. You must be clearly regenerated before you are a candidate for sanctification.

This Thessalonian church was an active church. They had the three distinguishing marks, faith, hope and love. They had a "work of faith, a patience of hope, and a labor of love." The "word came unto them" not in word only but in much assurance." If any body asked them if they were saved they had "much assurance" and could doubtless say "Yes, bless the Lord. I am!"

"But," says some one, "they were in need of a little brushing up. They were a little backslidden." Paul himself had had some solicitude about them and had sent Timotheus to inquire, and on his return had rejoiced greatly. So these men were not backslidden.

And yet Paul prays for them that he may come to them to perfect "that which is lacking in their faith." They were not wholly sanctified. He did not want to simply indoctrinate them. He wanted to lead them into entire sanctification.

If it was the will of God that these Thessalonian brethren be sanctified it is no less the will of God that these Rhode Island and Massachusetts and Connecticut brethren should be sanctified. Beloved, this is the will of God, *your* sanctification.

One reason why the apostles wanted these disciples sanctified was to keep them from falling into sin. They were exposed to sin and needed something to keep them from sin. Let me make an assertion. It is my judgment that there are but few who are keeping their justification who are not at the same time sanctified. Mere justification is not a *normal* Christian experience. God designs sanctification for us in order that we may keep justified; you are not a Christian as you ought to be unless you are sanctified.

"Well," you say, "it is not my will." Look out. You are arraying yourself against God. A little farther on the text reads, "He that despiseth (or rejecteth) *despiseth not man but God.*" Do you imagine that you can be a child of God and despise God's will?

Some of you say, "O well, this is the annual meeting and we will hear these folk's doctrine." It is not man's doctrine; it is *God's* doctrine. They say to me, "Walker, what are you preaching Methodist doctrine for?" I answer, "It is not Methodist doctrine, it is God's Word." This doctrine of holiness belongs to no sect, no man; it belongs to God.

It is God's will. Are you allowing some man to

SETH C. REES' COTTAGE.

come in between you and God? Is a husband big enough in your eyes to balk God's will for you? Are you going to permit relatives or preachers to stick their puny wills up against God's and defraud you of God's will for you? Read the first commandment—"Thou shalt have no other gods before me."

This *is* the will of God." In this text in the Greek the verb "is" is emphatic. God is willing *now*. It is God's desire for you at this moment. After you have been in heaven 10,000 years it will be no more God's will to sanctify you than it is *today*. *Now* is God's time.

Are you a subject of God? Well, here is God's will for you, God's law for you. "Be ye holy." And the Greek means, *"Be ye completely and instantaneously and continually holy!"*

If this is God's will it matters not who is opposed to it. If I place my will in sweet submission to God it will come to pass. I will be sanctified in spite of men and devils. Let us pray.

Brother Walker followed his prayer with an earnest exhortation. A number of people came forward and nearly or quite every one came into the light.

Interim.

The sky has cleared and the sun is shining brightly. The grove is greener than before the storm, and the smile of God seems to rest upon every leaf! Oh, that sunlight may break on many souls during these days! We believe it will.

7.30 P. M.

We notice that Rev. M. D. Jewelson of Baltimore, Md., is with us, also Rev. Mr. Hartwig and James Estes, of Newport. Rev. Delia Rees, formerly associate editor of *The King's Messenger*, is attending the meeting.

The spiritual tide is rising. There is no doubt about it. The marshes are already covered and many old barges are beginning to float. Some schooners are getting out to sea which have not seen old ocean in quite a while. Thank God for full moon high tides! When the tide is in, a camp-meeting moves for God. Sin is washed away. Fences are covered if not destroyed and Baptists and Quakers shout together. Hard old cobble-stones which have bleached in the sun for a long time are pulled down under water while the pure white surf exults in the fulness of the flood. There are tides and there are tides. There are ordinary high tides; these are every—yes, twice a day—affairs, but once a month along the coast we witness extraordinary tides. We believe that before long we are going to see one of these in this camp-meeting. Praise God!

After a number of hymns were sung by the congregation, Miss Nickerson sang a beautiful solo, "Beyond."

We feel that this is to be a blessed night, an occasion of blessing. The saints are filled with expectancy, there is a scent of victory in the atmosphere. Brother Walker says he feels like the locomotive Brother Rees spoke of this morning. It ran across New Jersey drawing a heavy train at the rate of fifty-six miles an hour, but no sooner had it halted at the Jersey City depot than it began to blow off steam! Brother Walker is blowing off "Hallelujahs" and "Bless the Lords" at a prodigious rate. The Lord give us more high-power engines.

REV. WILLIAM H. HOOPLE'S SERMON ON I THESS. V. 23.

Rev William H. Hoople of New York, preached this evening. Text, 1 Thess. v. 23: "And the very God of peace sanctify you wholly, and I pray God that your whole spirit, and soul, and body be preserved blameless unto the coming of our Lord Jesus Christ."

How hopelessly we are in debt to God! If we were to engage all our faculties in repaying God for the temporal blessings merely, we would find after a life time of effort toward repayment that there would remain a large amount of debt.

How much greater than this is our indebtedness to God for His goodness to us in grace. And yet I fear that the majority of this audience do not appreciate God's grace and mercy! Oh, for a renewal of the old-time revivals and the old-time power! Oh, that in these closing days of the century there might come a mighty awakening! Oh, I am looking for it! I have turned my back on failure. I have turned my back on all past defeats! I am looking for God to step in and put His great red seal of salvation on these pages of nineteenth century history.

Let us look into this text tonight and see the great privileges which are indicated in it for us. "Sanctify you wholly." This is our theme. Many are talking about this glorious subject who know nothing of its true character. This is the cause of the third-blessing theory—lack of genuine sanctification.

People who are sanctified are unusual in power and blessing. Moreover they are free from all evil tempers. No sinful appetite or desire is left in the sanctified heart.

There will come into our lives, if we are sanctified, an automatic adjustment to the will of God. We will learn to discriminate between excess and temperance. We will be free from breaking God's plan and God's will.

"Tell me," says D. F. Brooks, of Jonesville, N. Y., "what a man's theory of sin is, and I will tell you what his theory of holiness is." We must get to a place where we see the loathsomeness and the grewsomeness and the awfulness of sin if we are to understand what holiness means. If your idea of sin is misty, undefined, illusive, your idea of holiness will be misty, undefined, illusive.

Man was born pure, but through a wicked choice fell. After the fall trace the race down. Here are two brothers, sons of the first parents. Abel had a right idea of sin and his mind leaped over the centuries and fell on the cross and he realized that blood was necessary to atone for sin. Cain looked at sin more lightly, avoided God's commanded way of worship, lost his temper through envy and slew his own brother. How far the race fell in a short time. It doesn't take sin long to drag us down to awful depths.

But however black a sinful life may be, God can cleanse it. The poor harlot, and the brutal murderer, dyed in sin, without hope, can bow at God's knee and receive a perfect pardon and have all their sins washed away.

Oh, I see such possibilities for us in justification! I see how every habit may be broken. I can see how every appetite may be corrected, I see men rising up out of the ashes of a misspent life and blooming for God and His glory.

Oh, a sight of Jesus' face does it! A poor old drunkard staggered into my church a week ago tonight. He was so drunk he could not get to the altar alone. But he began to pray. Soon he saw Jesus and that look sobered him, that look saved him, and he jumped up as sober as any one. He knew he was saved and the witness was clear and beautiful.

But not only is there salvation from sins and habits, but there is salvation from sin as a nature. Inbred sin is something which we inherit. We all have different varieties of inbred sin, but it is always vile and hellish in its tendency. We are not guilty because of its presence. We would not have chosen to have had it, perhaps, but it was put in the heart. It was in the heart after conversion. We grieved over it. Its presence agitated us and we were sorry for its being there.

We must get rid not only of sin as an act but of sin as a nature. Nothing that defileth can enter heaven. Sin as a nature cannot any more be cleansed by human power than sin as an act. But Christ can do it. "I will sprinkle clean water upon you." "Wherefore He is able to save to the uttermost all that come unto God by Him." "Sanctify them through thy truth: thy word is truth." Christ "loved the church and gave Himself for it that He might sanctify it." Oh, there are so many Scriptures which prove this precious doctrine.

And then there are witnesses to this grace all through the history of the church. St. Ignatious says: "O Lord, I thank thee that Thou hast honored me with a perfect love for Thee." John Fletcher: "I tell you all to the praise of God that I am free from sin." Wm. Bramwell: "I have walked in this freedom 26 years." Hester Ann Roges: "Inbred sin no longer hinders close communion, and God is all my own."

We do not deny that there are many faults in all professors of holiness. "We have this treasure in earthen vessels." But we have the treasure if we are earthern! Glory to God! In some way, I don't know how, but some way God patches up the vessels and makes them so they will hold God's glory. Awkward, homely, clumsy as we may be, we can all be clean. We used to berate ourselves, but when we got clean we found a luxury in being ourselves for Jesus' glory.

Jesus is here tonight. Oh, that you may gaze on Him! The stream is flowing. Will you not look to it tonight? There is both pardon and cleansing in it for us. Who will come tonight? O come, come to the foot of the Cross and look into Jesus' face!

What a wonderful night this is! God was wonderfully with His servant. Sinners and opposers were cowed, and tarried while saints shouted aloud with joy. At times the joy was so demonstrative that the preacher was forced to stop for a moment to let the exuberant glory burst forth. There were a number who bowed at the altar and to them Jesus spoke pardon, purity and peace. Praise the Lord for this glorious day.

MONDAY, JULY 31.

6 A. M.

The six o'clock meeting was led by Brother Sherman of Newton, and was a profitable season. Many of the saints prevailed with God for victory in the battle throughout the day. The current is flowing with greater and yet greater swiftness, and people are getting to God all the time in meeting and out of it.

8.30 A. M.

The meeting for a time was opened for praise.

Little Boy: I am glad that I am saved.

Sister: I want to praise the Lord this morning that He has cleansed my heart.

Brother White: Four years ago I was converted and three months after I received the blessing of a clean heart.

Singing, "Speak to Me, Jesus." (No. 171, Part II.)

Sister Morrow: Now let those who really want Jesus to speak to them come and kneel at this altar.

Nearly all came, and a precious season followed. One after another we asked the Lord to speak to us, and of course He did! Praise His matchless name!

MRS. MORROW'S READING ON "THE WILL OF THE LORD."

Ephesians, the fifth chapter, 1st verse. I will read the entire chapter. In this chapter we have many things which are the will of God for us. In verse 17 it says, in the Revised, "Understand the will of the Lord."

One thing which is the will of the Lord for us is that we "be filled with the Spirit."

How often people come to me not knowing what to do! The reason you cannot find out the will now is because you have not obeyed before, where God told you what to do. Go back to where you disobeyed and begin right there.

"Understand what the will of the Lord is." Remember that God is never in a hurry. He often wants us to walk quickly but He never hurries us. There are three voices, the voice of the evil spirit, the voice of the Holy Spirit, and the voice of our own desires. Hannah Whitall Smith taught her children to listen and hear what Jesus says. One day she asked one of them how she knew the voice of Jesus. "Why, He always speaks so smooth and sweet." "Does not the devil ever speak to you." "Yes mamma, but he always talks so whiny!"

[Mrs. Morrow told us at some length about her call into public work. It was intensely interesting and thrilled many hearts.]

Another thing that is the will of the Lord for you is to give "thanks for everything." Even things that are unpleasant and painful—we can thank God for these things for they are stepping stones to lift us up to God.

"Wives, submit yourselves unto your own husbands." If wives would but speak gently and submit in the Lord, their husbands would be convicted. Look at the submission of Jesus. Three times in the garden He prayed that "this cup," the cup of dying in the garden rather than on the Cross, might pass from Him. He came to earth on purpose to die on the Cross. This was the cherished desire of His heart. And yet so true and deep was His submission that He prayed, "Not My will but Thine be done." And when a little later the soldiers came for Him He spoke two words, "I am," and they fell to the ground. He had the power to destroy them all but He withdrew the power and let them take Him. Before Pilate He answered nothing. One word and the people would have been lying about dead for miles. On the Cross He submitted. O the submission of Jesus! Do you want to be like Him? Shall we not follow Him all the way?

10.30 A. M.

The audience is of good size for Monday morning. The clear, bright weather has encouraged many in the neighborhood to come in. The new song book, "Tears and Triumphs Combined," is gaining in favor. The audience is singing that unique piece, No. 112, Part II, "I've Found the Secret Out."

After announcements were made, Dr. Walker preached from John 15: 8: "Herein is my Father glorified that ye bear much fruit; so shall ye be my disciples."

DR. WALKER'S SERMON ON "FRUIT BEARING."

The chief question with the true Christian is, "How may I glorify God?" A Christian will find joy in positive pain if so be it glorify God. Paul said that he rejoiced that he was counted worthy to suffer.

"The chief end of man," it is said, and so we believe, "is first to glorify God, and second to enjoy Him forever." The glory of God is the first consideration.

"Bearing fruit" and being true "disciples" are the two thoughts of the text. Now what is the fruit that we are to bear? Much is counted as fruit which really is not. There is much "creaturely activity" which is called fruit. Persons who make themselves numerous in church offices and positions are considered as the most "fruitful Christians."

I had a dear relative on the Pacific coast who was more active in the social and financial work of the church than any other person in the church. She was the best to the real, legitimate work of the church, to soul winning and spiritual labor, she was of no use. She could decorate churches, make the strawberries go farther and find the poor oyster which had got lost in the soup more frequently than anyone else, but she was utterly devoid of spirituality.

The fruit of the Spirit, love, joy, peace, etc., is the fruit referred to. This is the kind of fruit we must have.

One species of the fruit is love, not human love, not natural love but divine love (*agape*), such love as is described in the Psalm of Love, the 13th of 1 Corinthians. This is something very different from being naturally affectionate. My dog Duke is the most affectionate animal I know of, but Duke doesn't even profess to be a Christian.

Again we must distinguish between a bright, sunny character and divine joy. People often mistake happiness for joy. Happiness is "happenness," something that depends upon what happens. But joy is something that does not depend upon natural temperament or circumstances at all. This is a supernatural grace of which I am speaking this morning. When you have it no matter what surrounds you, you can "joy in God your Saviour." Then there is peace in the fruit of the Spirit. We must distinguish here also between naturally tranquil natures and true, divine peace. There are people naturally peaceful. They would be willing to lie in a hammock forever and forever and not have energy enough to fight the flies.

The most sensitive natures in the world may be kept in peace. Jesus was the most sensitive being in the universe, and yet He said, "My peace give I unto you."

"Longsuffering." Now there are people who are supposed to be patient who are naturally indifferent. But the work of grace is to take out of a naturally resentful and impatient disposition all that is unkind and un-Christlike. It is truly a supernatural work.

And there is gentleness and goodness and fidelity and meekness and faith and temperance in the fruit of the Spirit. Notice that "fruit" is singular number. "The *fruit* of the Spirit *is*." Here is the cluster of Spiritual graces. Jesus wants us to be characterized by every species of the fruit. We are not to take it all out in temperance or love or faith. We are to possess all the grapes in the bunch.

"Herein is My Father glorified that ye bear *much* fruit;" not only love, but perfect love; not simply faith, but perfect faith, etc.

How may we bear much fruit? In the first place it is necessary that we have a real vital, not artificial, connection with the vine. "Without Me ye can do nothing."

Now a branch may be in the vine and yet be fruitless. "Every branch in me that beareth not fruit." What happens to this branch? "He taketh it away." So you cannot remain long without you bear fruit. I believe in the perseverance of the *saints*. If you remain a saint you will persevere. If you do not continue a saint the doctrine does not deal with you at all. I want to speak a word of warning. There is danger of your *falling* if you are in a fruitless condition. *God says so.*

"He purgeth it." I came home one day from a long trip and my wife said, "The bugs are taking the potatoes." I said, "I'll fix the bugs;" so I went to the drug store and bought some London purple and Paris green and I sprinkled the vines and the bugs became discouraged and turned their toes up to the stars, and you ought to have seen the potatoes take on new life! We had a fine crop, but we would not have had any potatoes at all if I had not sanctified the vines!

The purged vines are the fruitful people, the prayer-meeting people, the soul-saving people. If you want to be a success spiritually apply to the Husbandman for purgation.

Did you know that it is always the most spiritual people that seek purging. Backsliders do not come. Worldly people do not come. They are not in a position to want added grace. The "best members in the church" are the first ones to seek the blessing.

If we *abide* we will bear *much* fruit. There are people who get cleansed who do not abide. Sanctification is the establishing grace but there is such a thing as a man being cleansed and yet not being *established in the establishing grace*. Oh, beloved, get established.

But the first thing to do is to seek cleansing. Establishment will be the fruit of continual abiding after sanctification. Who will seek purging now?

Some responded to the call and the Lord was soon at His same old business, blessing and cleansing hearts. Praise the Name of the Lord!

2.30 P. M.

After a season of song, Brother Hoople threw the meeting open for witnessing.

Deacon Kies (who has just come on the grounds): Jesus Christ has cleansed me from all sin, and the Holy Ghost fills the temple.

Singing: "Running Over."

Sister: We have just sung my experience. Praise the Lord! The Lord enlarges the cup and then fills it up till it runs over!

Brother Doane: The Lord has sanctified me and is preserving me unto His coming.

Singing:

> "If you would be happy
> I'll tell you what to do;
> Just give your heart to Jesus,
> And be saved through and through."

"That's it!" shouted Brother Hoople. "Now let's take a trip through the week! Come on!"

> " On Sunday I am happy.
> On Monday full of joy;
> Tuesday I have peace within,
> The devil can't destroy;
> On Wednesday and Thursday
> I'm walking in the light;
> Friday is a heaven below,
> And so is Saturday night!"

Sister: I am so glad I found Jesus, the chiefest of ten thousand to my soul.

Sister Lewis: Saved from sin; cleansed by the blood.

Brother: I can say it is good to be here. My heart says "Amen" to all the will of God.

Singing: "Softly and Tenderly Jesus is Calling."

Brother Chapman (whose saintly wife has recently departed for heaven): I thank God that in these days of tears and afflictions I find that God is my comfort and portion.

Sister: I have victory over the world, the flesh and the devil.

Brother: Praise God this afternoon for an indwelling Victor.

Sister Mamie Macomber: I am trusting in Jesus for all. He is my satisfying portion. Oh, I do praise His Name for His wonderful goodness to me!

Brother Frank Messenger, Jr.: I thank God that I am saved and sanctified. Sanctification just suits me and I enjoy living for Jesus.

Brother Rees: Let us have a few short prayers. Let all pray who feel led to do so. After we pray Rev. Mattie Curry will again speak to us.

A number offered fervent prayers for the meeting, for God's messenger, for the message, for those who hear.

MISS CURRY'S SERMON ON "WAITING ON THE LORD."

"They that do wait on the Lord shall renew their strength; they shall mount up with wings as eagles; they shall run and not be weary, they shall walk and not faint."

People are waiting upon almost everyone but God. They listen to almost everyone else. They who wait upon the Lord are few.

But they who wait upon the Lord get something from God that makes them strong in Him. It is so much more satisfactory than anything else.

The sinner gets to a point in seeking God where he has to just wait on Him. He has to quit depending on men's prayers and people's counsels. It is when he lets go of men that God catches hold of him and saves him.

After people are saved they are strong in proportion as they pray. We ought to so live in prayer that we would not come to meeting to get fired up; we ought to come already fired up. We ought to be so in God's hands that He can couple us into connection with the spirit of the meeting in an instant.

People seeking sanctification have to wait on God. A person may come to the altar time after time. People may try to help, but God only can help after all. No one can show us our own hearts but God Himself. Wait on Him in earnest prayer until He shows you what is hindering you from the blessing.

I remember that when I was seeking sanctification I got clear to the end of my strength. After the family had retired I went into a room alone and prayed and agonized and tried to believe. Then I got to my rope's end. And in the stillness of the night the Lord showed me the true cause of my failure to enter into the blessing. I had to "wait on the Lord" to know my own heart.

Beloved, if you will wait on the Lord He will give you strength. Are you weak? Then wait on the Lord; He has all the strength you need. They that wait will change their weakness for strength. Praise the Lord.

We need to wait on God for wisdom. If we do not we will get into trouble. I tell you there is a great deal of this getting down and telling God a great many things from our own standpoint instead of waiting on Him and getting His view of things. A quiet, unhurried waiting on God will do more for us than anything else in the world.

In ten years' experience I have never seen a defeat that was not due to failure to wait on the Lord. Beloved, do you wait on the Lord? David said, "My soul, wait thou only upon God." Are you doing it?

Are we waiting on God in this camp-meeting? In our hearts, in our tents, in our walks about the grounds, are we waiting upon the Lord? Oh, may the Lord put this spirit of waiting upon God upon us this afternoon.

At the close of her address Sister Curry invited all God's saints to come forward for a time of waiting upon the Lord. They accepted the invitation and God answered by "renewing strength."

7:30 P. M.

What a sweep we are having! Glory to God! The God of fire is answering the petitions of His people. The melody of song is surging out all over the great audience this evening and victory is in the air.

Among our new arrivals are Rev. J. H. Norris and wife of Pittsburg, Pa.; Dr. and Mrs. Levy, Lidie Kenney and Mrs. Stewart of Philadelphia; Brother Horton of Denver, Colorado; Charles Potter of Norwich, Conn;

Evangelists Rose Williams and Mrs. M. J. Reed of Willimantic, Conn.; Evangelist Switzer of Boston; Rev. Frank E. Talbee of Bristol, R. I., and Rev. Bro. Merrell of Pawtucket.

Just before prayer the Misses Stromberg sang a duet, "Eternity."

Sister Stewart led in a very unctuous prayer. Mrs. Stewart knows how to pray. We remember some prevailing petitions at Pitman Grove and Douglass. O Lord, increase the number who know how to pray the "fervent, effectual prayer" which "availeth much."

Rev. John Norberry will speak tonight.

REV. JOHN NORBERRY'S SERMON ON "GOD'S CALL."

I ask your prayerful attention to these words: "For God has not called us unto uncleanness, but unto holiness." Also, "Follow peace with all men and holiness, without which no man shall see the Lord." Our theme tonight is that wonderful one of holiness. Holiness is the only thing that wins. A camp-meeting which does not press a second work of grace is a failure. There was a time, say thirty years ago, when it was possible to have revivalistic camps without the distinctive preaching of a second work of grace, but that time is past forever. Light has increased since then, and unless holiness is put to the front a camp will not have success.

Rev. George Hughes said in an article in *The Standard* years ago, that the reason so many sinners were converted at Ocean Grove was because they put holiness to the front.

I love holiness. The holiness movement is bound to move. It does not depend on any one man or two. The movement began six thousand years ago. There were two charter members and they both backslid, but the *movement* went on. Abel got the blessing and Cain, full of inbred sin, killed him. The movement, however, went on. You can kill the holiness people but you cannot stop the movement.

The text says that *God* calls us unto holiness. It is a serious thing when God calls a man to anything. It is not like the call of a parent who doesn't more than half mean what he says, it is a call of the great God who means business.

One way in which God calls men is by His Spirit. Oh, fathers, mothers, brothers, sisters, friends, God has been calling to you ever since you came on the encampment! Oh, I pray you do not harden your heart as in the day of provocation!

Another way in which God calls us is by the Word. If you had never heard a holiness sermon or never attended a holiness camp-meeting, there is enough in the Bible to tell you plainly about sanctification. You will be judged by the truth as revealed in the Word of God. It is our guide, our chart and our compass.

We are also called of God to holiness through His messengers. "He that despiseth, despiseth not man, but God." My dear brother, you cannot afford to reject any of God's messengers. When God speaks through a man you cannot afford to reject the message.

The contemporaries of Noah perished because they failed to obey the word of the Lord through Noah. Ninevah was saved because the inhabitants hearkened to the preaching of Jonah.

Oh, have you had a leakage of love and power? I went to a camp-meeting the other day and took a couple of pails to get some water. But when I pumped the water into the pails it all ran out again. They were dry, they needed soaking. And so there are lots of people who come up to camp-meeting who are of no immediate use because they are dry! They have to soak awhile before they are of any use to God. Oh, beloved, get soaked clear through and keep soaked all the time ready for the Master's use at a moment's notice.

Are you sure you have this blessing tonight? How many of you by rising will say, "I want you to pray for me?"

A glorious break followed the earnest exhortations and before long the altar was filled with seekers, many of whom were children. The fire is striking among the young people. Some of us remember what glorious conversions and sanctifications there were among the children last year. The Divine Lord is ever standing with outstretched arms toward the little ones. They are the hope of the church. If early in life they begin to follow Jesus, they will have unbroken lives to count for Jesus, and are not pained as are some others by feeling that they are offering the fag end of a life to God, having spent all that was valuable in their beings in the service of Satan.

TUESDAY, AUGUST 1.

8.30 A. M.

After a period of song and testimony, Brother Rees said: "You must all know how I feel about woman's ministry. It gives me great pleasure to say unto you that Sister Lidie Kenney of Philadelphia has a message for you this morning."

Mrs. Lidie Kenney:

I praise God that He has put my heart in tune to enjoy a place like this. As I came upon the ground last evening I said within myself, God is in this place and I know it. This meeting reminds me of the National camp-meeting that Brother Inskip used to lead.

The first time I ever met Brother Inskip was at Oakington Camp-meeting. I was in the blessing when I went there, but, oh, I received such an uplift, such a re-girding for the battle! Oh, the camp was so pervaded with the spirit of holiness!

One lesson which God taught me there was that it is not presumption to claim God's promises, neither is it humility to refuse to claim them.

As I went home from that camp-meeting I felt so rich I felt that God was all my own, and that I was a child of a King. When I reached home I told my experience at the bedside of my sick father and to my father's friend, Mr. Taskell, and my pastor, and everybody. Said my pastor: "I do not approve of the National brethren at Oakington, they allow no one to preach at the camp-meetings who are not in the experience of holiness." "Oh, brother," I answered, "it is such a nice place to die to self!"

And I have an intense hunger this morning—not a hunger of destitution, but a hunger of relish. I am so glad I am here. This is a heavenly place to my soul.

This blessed experience is for all: the illiterate and the learned, the poor and the rich—it is for all of them! The young—it is for them! I was so rejoiced to see the children getting saved last evening. Oh, that they may go on to sanctification! Sanctification is so suited to the young.

I thank God for a radical conversion. My regeneration was so deep and true that I was hungry for full salvation. A little while after my conversion I was invited to go to a holiness meeting, and when I got there the first word I heard was "sanctification." I sought it that night. The Holy Ghost talked to me and led me along, and He said to me, "Say: I do believe, I do believe;" and my faith took hold and I realized that the blood cleansed from all sin. My whole being is so filled with glory this morning. Praise the Lord.

Singing: "It Reaches Me."

Mrs. Stewart was asked to speak. She is a remarkable woman, mentally and spiritually. She not only manages a large and successful business in Philadelphia, but travels widely, proclaiming a full salvation.

Sister Stewart:

Brother Rees says I can talk as long as I want to. I shall never get through in this world and I am sure I will never cease in eternity. Our salvation is so great that we cannot say too much about it.

Oh, how I love to commune with God! My cup is so full this morning among these blessed, sanctified people, I feel that God is here.

When I was first sanctified the devil cheated me out of my experience by telling me that I was "too young to be sanctified." Oh, young people, do not let Satan cheat you out of the blessing. But God showed me the wiles of Satan. Oh, how blessedly, how gloriously, how tremendously He sanctified me. Oh, praise the Lord!

God wonderfully blessed His servants, Sisters Kenney and Stewart, this morning. Their faces were radiant with holy joy and their words were freighted with divine power. Praise the Lord for these prophetesses of Jesus Christ!

HALLELUJAHS FROM PORTSMOUTH

10.30 A. M.

Brother Walker is leading the singing. He is a splendid leader, and throws his soul into the matter in hand. There is no one in the entire audience who sings more enthusiastically than he. He is a much older man than the Brother Walker who was at Portsmouth a few years ago. Two hard trips in the Southern camps have aged him far more than the years warrant. Oh, these dear men who are working themselves old and gray for the Master! Oh, these self-denying battlers who are willing to spend their lives away from home, away from comfort, away from the studies they love and dear ones about whom their affections twine. All for Jesus' sake! God is not unmindful, and will repay in that day when camps like Portsmouth are all history, and the holiness conventions and meetings are all past forever. Fight on, brethren! Let nothing deter you from pushing on to the end! Amen.

Brother Rees called attention to the book-stand. The importance of holiness literature is not understood as it should be. People who are sanctified ought to "give attention to reading," that they may know the truth and help not only themselves but others.

BROTHER HOOPLE ON "PERFECT LOVE."

Rev. W. H. Hoople preached the morning sermon. Text: 1 John 4: 17, 18—"Herein is our love made perfect, that we may have boldness in the day of judgment: because as He is, so are we in this world. There is no fear in love; but perfect love casteth out all fear . . . He that feareth is not made perfect in love."

I remember some time ago seeing a drunken man on a trolly car in Brooklyn. He talked about his family and he told us that he was just home from Europe and was looking forward to the welcome which his wife and daughter would give him. Doubtless they were glad to see him, but, oh, what a pang must have pierced their hearts when they saw his intoxication.

God is glad the church is trying to get to heaven but when He sees how she is intoxicated with worldliness how pained His heart must be!

If that man meant to give his family unmixed pleasure he would have had to leave his cups and dissipation. And the Church of Jesus Christ, if she is going to please her Lord, must leave things about which the tendrils of her heart have encircled. We will have to get untangled. God wants to loosen up on the straps that bind us; He wants to set us at perfect liberty.

Oh, thank God that there is such a thing as freedom—freedom from the bondage of sin, freedom from the dungeon of evil desire, freedom from the load of reputation! Praise the Lord!

Now God wants us to have this perfect love spoken of in the text. Jesus was perfect in love and the Word says that "As He is so are we in this world." Again, we are "in this world," a place where we need a perfect love.

"There is to be an absolute resemblance to Jesus in that," says Dean Alford, "we are to be righteous." God so changes character that the generous man becomes liberal and the dark heart is filled with love and joy.

Perfect in love. God is not speaking here of His love for us but our love for Him—the principle of love in our hearts. "God is love," and when we are made perfect in love God Himself comes into our hearts and abides there.

One result of receiving this love will be that we will be free from fear of what is coming—rid of apprehension as to the future. We can see the Divine side to all questions. We will lose sight of doubts and questions and fears and see the bright side. We will see the silver lining to every cloud.

When we have perfect love there is not a craving in the soul that pulls one downward. All our desires are upward toward heaven. Praise the Lord!

Love is a loving, tender principle that keeps us from fanaticism. It guides the heart away from harshness and censoriousness, and keeps us in the wisdom and unction of the Holy Ghost.

There were five seekers at the close of Brother Hoople's sermon, and God quickly heard their earnest prayers for perfect love. Let us all say, Praise the Lord!

1.30 P. M.

The hour of Mrs. Morrow's Reading has been changed from 8:30 a. m. to this hour.

MRS. MORROW'S READING ON "SEEING THE KING."

"Thine eyes shall see the King in His beauty." Isaiah 33: 17. Let us see who it is that see the King in His beauty. (v. 14). "The sinners in Zion are afraid; fearfulness hath surprised the hypocrites: who among us shall dwell with the devouring fire? Who among us shall dwell with everlasting burnings?"

For a long time I read this verse carelessly, supposing that it meant hell, everlasting burnings, and I said, "I am not going to hell." But one day I read, "Our God is a consuming fire." When I read that I shrank back a little.

I had known God as a mother comforting me. I had known Him as sanctifier. I had known Him as my healer, but I had not known Him as fire.

Again I read, "When thou walkest through the fire it shall not kindle upon thee." The three Hebrew children went into the fire. What was burned? Only the bands upon them.

Now who is it that sees the King in His beauty? (v. 15). "He that walketh righteously, and speaketh uprightly." "Walketh righteously." Tells the truth in all things—is right in his life. He that "despiseth the gain of oppressions, that shaketh his hands from holding of bribes, that stoppeth his ears from hearing of blood and shutteth his eyes from evil." You must close your eyes to earthly things if you are to see the beauty of the King.

Oh, beloved, we must be right if we are to see the King. We can do right in the great things, but in the *little things* are we correct and conscientious? Only thus will we see the King in His beauty.

In the forty-fifth Psalm we see more about beauty: "Leave thy people; leave thy father's house." Why? That thou mayst come unto Me. "So shall the King desire thy beauty." If you wish the most tender and intimate relationship to Christ you must go out from the world and sometimes even from your loved ones.

We feel sometimes as we take notes that it is well nigh absurd to attempt to report these beautiful talks of Mrs. Morrow. One cause for this is that Mrs. Morrow's personality, manner and intonation are even more impressive than her words. Her language is exquisitely beautiful, and yet there is a delicacy of style and attitude and expression of countenance of which no pen can give even a meagre representation. One thing is sure: those who are so fortunate as to be in attendance at these marvelous readings will never forget them. When Mrs. Morrow was a babe in her mother's arms the mother was frequently heard to say by those of the family who passed through the room, "O God, make my baby daughter a blessing to the people." How God has answered the prayer of that mother heart! To how many thousands have the words of this His chosen handmaiden been the words of the Master!

3 P. M.

Rev. E. F. Walker preaches: Text "If ye love Me keep My commandments," also verses 16 and 17 of John 14.

There are tests of the sincerity of love. Mere profession of love does not avail.

Jesus presents a test here: "If ye love Me keep My commandments." Here were disciples who professed to love Jesus, and He Himself put a test to them. No one else would have had a right to make so absolute a test as this. No one else would be free from the mistake of asking too much or too little.

It is a libel on God's goodness to say, "I am trying to serve the Lord." God never asks anything of us that we cannot by His grace perform. When He tells us to do anything at all it is a pledge that He will help us through. It we fail it will be through a failure of *our love*.

So here is the test, beloved, if we are true lovers of Jesus we *are*—not trying to—we *are keeping His commandments*.

Now if we love Him and keep His commandments then He will pray the Father and He will send the Comforter unto us. Notice the Trinity here in this passage. We are living in the dispensation of the Trinity. Not simply the dispensation of the Holy Ghost, but of Father, Son and Holy Ghost. We are to baptize into the name of the Three.

We want to call attention especially to the Paraclete. We have two Advocates, Christ at the throne of the Father and the Spirit in our hearts. Both are making intercession. He who is in our hearts is the Omnipotent Spirit. "Greater is He that is in us than he that is in the world." "When the enemy comes in like a flood, then the Spirit of the Lord will lift up a standard against him."

These are times when it seems as if the devil casts sort of hellish spells over congregations so that it seems impossible to overcome them. Sometimes the people of God give it up. But I believe that if we would but rely on Him who is in us we would always conquer, always drive the enemy off the field.

We have a Comforter. Oh, we have trials, we have sorrows, we have wounds, but the balm is close by to heal the wound! When our first-born was struck by a locomotive and killed before my eyes I had an awful wound in my heart, but, O beloved, I did have the consolation of the Spirit.

You remember that when the disciples were toiling in rowing all the night and Jesus came, *immediately* they were at the land.

When Lazarus was dying doubtless the sisters said, "Oh, if Jesus was only here!" They felt that all would have been well if He had been present. But He stayed "beyond Jordan." O friend, a Christian does not get along very well unless God is continually with him. Therefore said Jesus, "It is expedient for you that I go away," that the Comforter might come. The temple of the Holy Ghost is the human bodies of sanctified people, so He can be everywhere at all times, comforting, blessing, sustaining, keeping.

Now we are not to think of the Persons of the Trinity as *essentially separated*. Jesus comes in the Spirit. He has promised to be with us unto the end. The Father is here this afternoon. The Son is here this afternoon. The Spirit is also here. Praise the Lord!

"Whom the world cannot receive." We have here the plain statement that no one can receive the Holy Ghost who has not previously received Christ. We must be converted before we can be baptized with the Holy Ghost. We are told that the natural man cannot receive the things of God because they are spiritually discerned. He is as a blind man. No blind man (who has been blind from birth) has any *idea of sight*. The natural man has no idea of the spiritual world. He is blind.

We may not know how to define the Holy Ghost and yet we may know the Holy Ghost. A child may know a posy and yet not know what you mean when you say

A GROUP OF PREACHERS AND WORKERS.

"Botany." There are lots of theological professors who are not experimental possessors.

None of us can define light, but we all enjoy it. Diogenes, the Cynic, sat in his tub in the sunlight and the shadow of the great Alexander fell upon him. "Get out of my sunlight," cried Diogenes. He was enjoying it. And we enjoy the light of the Holy Ghost. When some big theological professor undertakes to obscure our light by his ambiguous definitions we can say, "Get out of my sunlight."

A lady down South got the blessing of entire sanctification. Her pastor believed that we "got it all at conversion," or we "grew into it," or we "got it at death," or else a mixture of all three. She supposed that he would rejoice to hear of her new-found joy. On the contrary he said critically, "How do you define it?" "Oh," she said, "I do not define it; I enjoy it."

Dr. Godet says in commenting on the text, "He is *with you* and shall be *in you*." "The distinction between the external operation of the Spirit and His indwelling are well-nigh effaced from Christian consciousness." This ought not to be so. His baptism, His girdings, His anointings are His gifts. But He Himself is the Abider, the Dweller. We must not forget this.

There are, it is true, some who say "Come in, Come in" to the Holy Ghost but forget that He will not come unless He can perform certain operations. He will not come into old dirty shanties. He is not only the Inhabiter but the Builder. He wants to come in as Renovator. He will enlarge some rooms and make others smaller. He will do away with some closets and put in new stairways. Oh, take Him, beloved, with all He is and all He does!

Some of you are saying, "I want to be sanctified, but I am afraid I coudn't live it." When will we learn that we are to be passive to the Holy Ghost. God is the Operator. Look at that piano, it is not trying to play, it is silent in itself. It is the soul of the musician who makes it make music. It is a heresy to say "I am trying to serve the Lord in my poor, weak way." You ought to serve the Lord *in His power*, not *"try to serve Him,"* not do something in *"your poor, weak way."*

"I will walk in you." Not use you for a garden or a promenade. Not walk about in you as a pleasure ground, but "I will walk in you," I will walk as you walk.

"I will *cause* you to walk in my statutes." When you are sanctified God causes you to go right. His power bolsters your poor, weak will and enables you to keep the Lord's commandments. Not automatic working and walking, but *vital*. Glory!

Oh, come on, beloved, let's lay our deadly doings down and forget about "trying to serve the Lord in our poor, weak way" and serve Him *in the Holy Ghost*!

7.30 P. M.

One of the thrilling events in this evening's praise service was the singing by Evangelist Rose Williams of "When I Get to the End of the Way." Yea, brethren, "the toils" may seem very large to us now. It may seem to us that our difficulties are very huge and awful, but at the end, when we sit like "the fathers of Troy" upon the walls of the city and look back over the battlefield they will seem very small, oh, so infinitely small! And our labors, too, will seem nothing. We may think that we are of some importance. The Lord have mercy! It is so easy to get an exaggerated idea of the importance of our own work. But the end—that will shrink our puffed ideas. O Lord, help us to remember the end of the way.

Brother Walker devoted a little time to speaking about a few of the books on sale at the book-stand. He spoke of "Holiness Text-Book," "Sweet Smelling Myrrh," "Fire from Heaven," "The Heart Cry of Jesus," and others.

Rev. J. H. Norris, from Pittsburg, Pa., preaches this evening.

REV. J. H. NORRIS' SERMON ON CHRISTIAN PURITY.

1 John 3: 3: "Every man that hath this hope in him purifieth himself even as He is pure."

God's word reveals to us the great fact that the holy life is the only life that pleases God. "Without holiness no man shall see the Lord." "He that saith he abideth in Him, ought himself also to walk even as He walked."

There are two classes of men in the world, saved and unsaved. Those who are not saved are already lost. It is a wonderful advance to make toward salvation when a man realizes that he is now lost—not that he will be lost by and by, but that he is lost *now* if he is without Jesus. Men seem to treat this matter as if to be saved was to get into heaven and to be lost was to fail to enter into it. But there are those here who are already lost. God help us tonight to see this truth.

The saved class may be subdivided into two classes: (1) those who are on the stretch after holiness, (2) those who have holiness. If you do not have holiness and are not on the stretch for it you are a lost man.

No one will deny that there are unsaved people. There are men here tonight who know that in their present condition they are lost men. Jesus died to save men from that which damns men's souls—sin. If you were to go to heaven with sin in your heart you could not be happy. So God has heaven begin here in this life by destroying sin in the heart.

When a man refuses to walk in all the light God gives him he becomes a backslider in the sight of God. You have tremendous responsibility resting upon you. You have had great light. Christ died for all His disciples that he might sanctify them, and you have heard this.

When the apostle came down to Ephesus and talked

to the Ephesian church about the Holy Ghost he did not find a lot of holiness fighters, He found men who were glad to hear about a second work. No wonder that they were soon sanctified.

After I was converted I had a good, healthy, normal appetite for holiness. I went to Hollow Rock campmeeting and gave myself fully up to God, "paid the price and took the goods." I knew that I was sanctified, and if you will meet the conditions God will do the same for you.

All churches agree with the Bible in saying that we must all be made holy before entering heaven; but most believers do not believe it is possible to live a holy life in this world.

But God's word teaches that purity is possible here. "Blessed *are* the pure in heart for they shall see God." Jesus prayed: "Sanctify them through thy truth: Thy word is truth." Jesus never prayed for an impossibility.

Again, this blessing is practical in its results. It unifies the church of Jesus Christ. The purpose of sanctification: "That they all may be one." Oh, the strife and backbiting and quarrelling among Jesus' professed followers! It makes the world stand aloof. Oh, we need samples! We need examples of the work of the grace of God!

If Jesus came to baptize with the Holy Ghost, what mean we to refuse the baptism? God help us to come to Jesus tonight and seek for this blessed baptism. Oh, let us not delay!

Every one that is a child of God is seeking after this purity. If you turn away from this altar tonight it is evidence that you are not fully justified.

The latter part of Brother Norris' sermon was a powerful exhortation. His words were well-nigh irresistable. Conviction was deep and powerful. Consciences were appealed to and men felt themselves to be caught by the steel fingers of truth. The preacher insisted that we were offered a present, perpetual sanctification and if we refused it we would be bringing guilt and damnation upon our own souls.

This was "the night of the break." Over thirty came to the altar and all but one or two were either converted, reclaimed, or sanctified. The meeting continued until a late hour. Our God has come down in power. Praise the Lord!

WEDNESDAY, AUGUST 2.

6 A. M.

After Rev. Frank E. Talbee, who was in charge of this early meeting, had expounded the Scriptures, the meeting was opened for testimony.

Deacon Kies: I rejoice that my "strength is renewed like the eagle's." The goodness of my God increaseth every day. Oh, I can never praise Him enough for what He has done and is doing for me.

Brother: Jesus took me just as I was and cleansed me from my unrighteousness. Glory to God!

9 A. M.

We are indebted to Mrs. S. G. Otis of Springfield, Mass., for the notes of this and the 10:30 service this morning. Mrs. Otis' notes are much fuller than we are accustomed to take, but on reflection we have decided to leave them substantially as she wrote them out.

MRS. ABBIE C. MORROW'S READING ON "THE VINE CHAPTER." JOHN 15.

Jesus wants to call our attention especially to the 14th verse: "Ye are my friends if you do whatsoever I command you." Some one says, "Whosoever is the door of God's house and whatsoever is the door of God's treasury." If you and I will hear Him say, "Whatsoever ye would that men should do unto you, do ye even so to them," then we may hear him saying, "Whatsoever ye shall ask of the Father in my name that will I do."

"Whatsoever I command you." It's the *I* in there that ought to make us willing. He said it that awful night when He took your place and my place. He bore your sins and mine, your sorrow and mine, your sickness and mine, and He wants to bear them still; so when we grieve over things which Christ has borne we are robbing God.

You and I know what it is to be lied about. They never can say a word about us that they did not say about Him. They said he was guilty of blasphemy, that he was a glutton, that He cast out devils through Beelzebub, the prince of devils. What He suffered *from* man we know something of, but of what He suffered *for* man we can have no conception. Can you think what it must have been to have the Father put the sins of the whole world on Him? Has your heart ever ached on account of the sins of the few you have loved? Then think of it, "The Lord hath laid on Him the iniquity of us all."

"Do whatsoever I command you." There is no circumstance in our life where we cannot have the clearest leading. Take, for instance, the matter of money. We read, "Give to him that asketh of thee." If they ask money and you haven't it, do as Peter did: give something that will enable them to earn their own living. I used to think that passage meant that we must give just the thing they asked for. If you can't give anything else, give time, sympathy, love.

In 1 Cor. 10: 31, we read, "Whether we eat or drink or whatsoever ye do, do all to the glory of God." How few of God's sanctified ones have ever seen this text as *written for them*.

10:30 A. M.

Byron J. Rees preached on "Crucifixion." Text: Gal. 2: 20. "I am crucified with Christ; nevertheless I live, yet not I, but Christ liveth in me; and the life which I now live in the flesh I live by the faith of the Son of God, Who loved me and gave Himself for me."

There are some deep places in the Bible and this is one of them. There are places too deep for us to fully comprehend, and while this text goes down, down to depths we cannot fathom, yet we may receive great blessing from it if we take heed to it.

A little reflection will show you that the apostle had a very deep experience. No ordinary man would ask to be crucified. Lots of us want to be "blessed," but here's a man who wants to die with Christ. A man must have a deep spiritual life to want to be crucified.

A sinner cannot be crucified, for he is "dead in trespasses and sins." A man must first be alive in order to be crucified. A sinner sees no loveliness in crucifixion. He can see how Christ's dying for him is beautiful, but he sees no beauty in being spiked to the cross with Christ. It takes a man who knows God and desires to walk all the way with Him, to desire crucifixion. Crucifixion must come after the new birth.

God is bound to have a crucified people, a people dead to the world; and when a man is born again He begins to plan to bring him to a place of complete crucifixion. That's why he wrings your heart with pain and grief. That's why the afflictions come. God is seeking to untwine the tendrils of your love for earthly things and place them on heavenly things.

Crucifixion implies separation, estrangement. Right here men fail. To walk out with Christ alone, to go out with the thorn-crowned Man alone, an object of scorn and ridicule, Oh, how hard it is! But as sure as God is God and Christ is Christ we must be separated from every thing to go out with "Jesus only." There must be a separation between you and old associations. You must be content to walk out solitary and conspicuous. Don't for your soul's sake try to bridge the chasm.

Crucifixion means pain, suffering. You can't dance a jig on the way to the cross. You can't laugh and shout through crucifixion. You've got to die, and when a man dies with Christ, there may be accessories, but the one thing is to die. It is so hard to quit having your own way, you've had it so long. It's so hard to say, "I'll take God's plan, whatever it may mean to me." I think of the sneers and taunts, I think of Him dying there on Calvary, I hear Him say, "My God, my God, why hast thou forsaken me?" And yet I'm sure every true child of God says, "I want to die with Him." Paul understood it, he knew about the Roman spear and the nails, but he said, "I'll go forth unto Him bearing His reproach."

The attitude you take toward crucifixion is the index to what you have in your heart's volume. The way you look at this, determines your standing in grace. As you look at the crowd on a steamer at the pier and see the people chatting with each other, you cannot determine just who are passengers and who are not. You don't know who hold tickets and who do not; but by and by you notice a man who calls out, "All ashore that are going ashore," and then there is "no small stir." It is evident then who the passengers are. All who do not hold tickets leave the boat.

So we can't tell just who hold tickets for glory. We have our songs, our prayers, our sermons, but we don't just know who has paid the price and is going through till one comes along with the gold braid of divine authority on his cap and epaulets of divine approval on his shoulders. "All ashore that are going ashore." A good many leave, but those who stay are real passengers, and you can't make the real passenger get off the boat! They are eager to leave the pier and proceed on their journey toward sanctification.

Crucifixion means to be misunderstood. They took that man who said He was the Son of God and crucified him like a common thief. You've seen pictures of three crosses and the middle one was higher than the others, but in truth Christ's cross was no higher than the thieves' who were beside Him. They said He was "a bandit," "a thief," "a breaker of the law." *He was con-*

tent to die misunderstood. He did not jerk the spikes out and come down and say "I'll explain it to you." If we come to the altar we think we must explain why we came. We are afraid some one will think we are sinners! Don't explain, beloved.

"But," says some one, "there's a man who goes to the altar and talks with seekers and I know he's a hypocrite. I won't go and have him talk to me." Well, I'd die if I were you. You and I must be content to die anywhere, misunderstood like Christ.

This experience implies deadness to sin. Some say if we are dead we feel nothing. You'll know when you are hurt, of course; your feelings may be lacerated, and if you are alive you'll be up in arms, but dead men don't move. A sanctified man is conscious of insult but does not retaliate. You may go to the cemetery, and call a dead man names, but the grass over him won't stir; he is dead. When they call us names we feel it, but if sanctified do not answer back. We do not explain if crucified with Christ. If you explain you lose the blessing out of your heart. Many times Christ could have set folks right, but He didn't. He simply did His work and went back to glory.

These times demand crucified people. Sinners go to extreme worldliness, building as if to stay here for centuries. We need to counteract this by extreme piety. We must be filled with the life of Christ if we are to cope with the world.

Men who die must expect to be tested. The Roman soldier shoved the spear into Christ's side. But Christ did not move. Oh, these iron spears! They may come from your brethren, from your loved ones. Some one may come along and say some devilish thing about you, but if you are dead you will not move. So many fail here. There is the test of poverty; many fail here. There is the test of plenty; how many go down here! There is the test of the sharp word from the friend. It is possible, beloved, to get into a place where we will remain calm and quiet, with a halo of holiness about us, unmoved and unshakable because "founded on the Rock."

One result of this experience is that we will have power. There is a divine sense in which you will be feared. You will carry a mysterious power with you that will make sinners tremble. When we are dead indeed to sin and filled with the life of Christ, God will put this fear on people and cause them to know that God is dealing with them.

Another result is that we will have Christ dwelling in us. Oh, how we would love to sit at His feet, to have Him speak to us! We can be indwelt by Christ *now*. We must wait for His visible coming but we have His spiritual presence *now*.

To have Christ live in us is to be able to endure things. There are some places you can't jump over nor crawl under nor go through, you must just endure them; and

God undergirding and sustaining you will take you through tribulation and you will rejoice in it all.

If we are crucified with Christ, God will use us. I want my life and your life to help somebody. Oh, how many poor souls need help! May the Lord help us to so get Christ in us as to live helpful lives. We may be small instruments, but God can use us in His great orchestra if we are crucified with Christ. Let every one who wants to die come forward!

2:30 P. M.

Brother Hoople is in charge of this meeting; under his enthusiastic leadership the songs are very full of fire and unction. Praise the Lord for Holy Ghost songs!

Young Sister: I am saved and cleansed and filled with the Holy Ghost.

Brother Gill of New York: I came here with a burden on my heart, but Jesus has lifted it.

Mrs. Abbie Ann Simmons: I praise the Lord I have victory in my soul. My heart has been cleansed and purified from all sin.

Sister: I used to be troubled with my patience giving out; now, since I have been sanctified, the Lord keeps me in perfect peace.

Sister Levy: I love to read that motto there (pointing to the motto over the platform, "The Comforter Has Come") for the Comforter *has* come into my heart. In these days I am testing the gracious promises. Praise the Lord.

Sister Gifford of Vineyard Haven: I am drinking at the fountain this afternoon.

Sister Rose Williams sang that solo which she always sings so effectively, "Get Somewhere in Jesus Today." The people love to hear her sing, and she always does us good because she sings in the Holy Ghost.

Sister Otis: By the grace of God I will not compromise to the world, the flesh or the devil. I mean to stand true to Him at all costs.

Singing, "When I see the Blood."

DR. LEVY'S SERMON ON "GOD'S WILL IN EARTH."

After prayer by Brother Pennington, Rev Edgar M. Levy of Philadelphia, preached to us from Matt. 6: 10: "Thy will be done in earth as it is in heaven."

The corruption of human nature may be seen in its opposition to the will of God. The carnal mind, we are told is enmity against God.

Civilization and refinement have doubtless had certain influences upon the carnal mind but not to change its nature. It is the same in its opposition to God.

When a bolt is broken in a piece of machinery the parts may all be present but they clash and are not harmonious. The will is the bolt of the soul, and when that falls from God the soul is brought into confusion and commotion.

The groans and tumults and murmurings in the world are only indications of the warfare of the will with God. We see man uplifting his puny hand and will against the Lord's holy will.

After conversion we find there is that in the heart which opposes God. Say what you will, brethren, the seventh chapter of Romans is a picture of many a justified man, "The law of sin in my members." What is that but the carnal mind?

Look at this prayer, beloved! What a wonderful prayer this is! How much it means! It is on the lip of millions, and yet I aver that no one can pray it truly and naturally but those whose hearts have been cleansed.

To whom is this prayer offered? "Our Father which art in heaven." It is the prayer of a child of God. When we enter into an experience of sonship it becomes an exquisite privilege to say "Father." It has been truly said that the man who serves God as His Creator merely, is a very different man from the man who serves Him as Father.

"In earth as in heaven." When we read this there comes to mind the innumerable company of angels. His government pleases them. They stand about the throne in readiness for service with unselfish hearts. They do not serve from fear of punishment or desire of gain. Their desire is that He should be glorified rather than that they should be happy.

They do His will with profound humility. Isaiah

saw the celestial being covering his face in humility and his feet in utter self-abasement. It is the very life and triumph of heaven to ascribe everything to God and nothing to self.

How busy are the inhabitants of heaven! One is seen at a night's work in Egypt slaying the first-born. Another kills the army of Sennacherib. A great company of them ascend and descend the golden stairs before the astonished eyes of Jacob; and others bear the soul of the beggar Lazarus to Abraham's bosom. They are God's constant workers and servants.

Thus we are to fulfil the will of God in earth. Many voices are heard contrary to this but let us remember that Christ has come that we may be saved and that we may "serve Him without fear in holiness and righteousness all the days of our life."

Why, I ask, should Jesus put this prayer in our hearts and mouths if there can be no answer? Praise God, His will can be done. God asks no more. The child of God desires no less.

We may do His will in holy love. Paul was an example of this. From his sanctification until his head dropped into Nero's basket he was a flame of love, "living and loving for God."

[Dr. Levy quoted at some length some beautiful words of Madame Guyon in speaking of pure love for God.]

A handmaiden of the Lord of the early church was seen running with a pitcher of water and a firebrand.

When questioned as to her purpose, she said, "I would quench the fires of hell and burn heaven that men may serve God from pure love."

The will of God can be done by us with delight. St. Francis Xavier was not full of regrets when he left his beloved mother. He wept, but raising his hand into the air said to his comrades, "On to the heathen, I will have all eternity to see my mother." Thus we can gladly deny natural affections and do all for Jesus that He asks of us.

Angels can serve with unwearied constancy. And while the physical powers of man are less, yet up to our strength we can serve God with equal constancy. The endowments of God's children are various. Some are strong in body like Luther, some are weak in body like Baxter and Watt. Some are strong in mind, men of gigantic intellect like Milton and Edwards. But up to our ability we can serve him with equal constancy and fidelity. Are you doing it today, beloved?

The altar service was victorious and fruitful.

7.30 P. M.

After the prayer service, Brother Hoople announced No. 17 in Part II,

> At the cross, at the cross
> Where I first saw the light,

and after this was sung the congregation all joined in

Brother Pickett's hymn, "Wonderful Story of Love."

How well we remember hearing Brother Pickett sing this precious hymn in Cincinnati this last winter. As this man of God sang our hearts swelled in eagerness and we vowed that as best we could we would

> Preach it, and pray it, and sing it, and shout it,
> Wonderful story of love.

This is our business. Oh, may God help us to devote ourselves entirely to this wonderful Evangel, the "wonderful story of love."

Miss Hutchinson of No. Attleboro sang a solo:

> "I have given up all for Jesus,
> This vain world is naught to me;
> All its pleasures are forgotten
> In remembering Calvary."

Among the new arrivals this evening are Evangelists Fanny Simpson and May Frost. Just now we notice that Sister Cassie Smith has entered the Tabernacle. Praise God for the "elect ladies" whose number God is increasing in the land and on whose devoted ministry He is putting the golden seal of His approval.

While the congregation was singing,

> Glory, glory to God
> My heart is now cleansed from sin;
> I've abandoned myself to the Holy Ghost
> And His fullness abides within,

the tide kept rising higher and higher. Brother Hoople first asked the people to wave their handkerchiefs, and when they had bloomed out like Century plants, he then asked them to clap their hands in unison with the music. The result was inspiring. No one could fail to perceive the presence of the Holy Ghost in the manifest liberty and freedom of spirit of the children of God.

Sister Amelia Stewart led in prayer.

After the offering was taken Evangelist Mattie Curry spoke to us, 2 Kings 5, and verses following, giving the account of Naaman and his healing.

MISS CURRY'S SERMON ON "NAAMAN."

Leprosy in the Bible is a type of sin and there are many respects in which this disease of the body resembles the disease of the soul.

Naaman was a successful man. A man of wealth and position. He had led the army forth to battle, and conquered. He was second to the king only in Syria. He was probably regarded as a man to be envied.

But with all this Naaman had a disease which doubtless tortured him day and night. All his wealth and friends could not improve his condition. Leprosy is the worst disease that afflicts the body.

Leprosy is like sin in that it is inherited. The children of leprous parents look as pure and beautiful as children of other parents. But the years go by and at fourteen or fifteen the disease appears in the palm of the hand, then spreads all over the body. The fairest children have sin in them and it will show itself in time.

Leprosy is like sin also because there is no human cure for it. When once it makes its appearance the person is doomed, the beginning of the end is at hand. There is not even any alleviation of the trouble.

So long as sin is in the soul we are in fearful danger and peril. Full salvation is the only perfect cure. It is a necessity. Oh, people ought to be told that there is a complete remedy! That is why I am in the work of the ministry.

The horrible things from which we shrink are only the manifestations of sin in the soul. Of course, they are, as a rule, the things over which we grieve. But that which lies back of the manifestation is just as loathsome and vile and devilish as the outward symptoms.

If sin is not gotten rid of the disease will grow on us. The eyebrows will whiten, the flesh will rot, the bones will decay and finally the putrid carcass will drop into Hell!

We are not perfectly saved, unless we have full salvation. You are only half saved if you have only had your sins forgiven. You cannot be fully saved until God has washed all disease out of your soul.

Sin-leprosy will manifest itself in the heart as pride, haughtiness, an unsubmissive spirit. It shows itself in jealousy. I remember how God first showed me that I had inbred sin in my heart. For two months after I was converted I had a glorious time. But one day I was talking with two or three girls in the place where I was working and something was said that made me very angry. I choked it down, but I saw myself as never before. God revealed me to myself. I never felt so sure after that. I was not so confident that I was thoroughly saved. I knew that inbred sin must go if I was to be kept continually.

Here was a man that knew he had the disease. Our friends may make excuses for us, the old man may plead hard, but we know that we are diseased, are conscious that we need cleansing. The longer leprosy stays in the body the deader it gets, and the longer sin stays in the soul the deader it becomes. Oh, may God help us to see that if sin is not removed from our souls it will destroy us forever!

Naaman wanted healing and God sent him a little messenger. And if one wants to be healed let us be sure God will send some one to tell one about it.

That little maid may have been tempted to withhold her experience, but she gave it and God wonderfully used it. Oh, friends, never withhold your testimony!

Naaman thought to buy healing with gold. Oh, you can't buy grace! Grace is grace and is therefore a gift.

He also supposed that he would be healed in the way that he had marked out. He was accustomed to elaborate heathen ceremonies and supposed that the prophet would go through some impressive routine that would make everyone feel the importance of the occasion.

You have to put your own thoughts away. The prophet had sense enough not to show his face. He taught the haughty prince a lesson. God never comes in the grooves we mark out for Him. If we plan for Him to come in a cloudburst of glory He will come as a still, small voice. If we plan to get the blessing in a dignified way He will smash us all to pieces!

When a man is sent of God men ought to heed his words. There is altogether too little reverence for God's messengers in these days. Naaman had to come to a place where be obeyed.

The leper dipped himself in Jordan seven times according to the commandment. Seven typifies perfection. I do not suppose that his faith was perfect until he dipped the seventh time.

Naaman had the proof of the power of God in his healed body. If men doubted his cure he could show them his hands. "See them," says he, "they are like the flesh of a child!"

Oh, friend, "wash and be clean!" You can't grow sin out of you. The blood only can cleanse you. Will you not accept the cleansing?

Brother Hoople followed the sermon with an earnest, fiery exhortation. Many responded and the day closed with a blessed altar service in which many souls were saved and sanctified.

THURSDAY, AUGUST 3.

8.30 A. M.

One brother's testimony was "Glory to God! I am in love with holiness. It doesn't do to take people's advice unless God is in the advice. Some time ago a certain person came to me and sought to direct my attention from this distinctive work of holiness and turn to milder work; but I could not accept such counsel because God said differently."

Sister Cassie Smith: I am here to "celebrate the Lord." I have learned to try the spirits and learn the precious will of God by waiting upon him.

After a song was sung Sister Abbie C. Morrow spoke on "The Joy of the Lord."

MRS. MORROW ON "THE JOY OF THE LORD."

"He, for the joy that was set before Him." And He had almost no other joy. In order that we may see the connection, let us turn back a little.

So we will read some in the faith chapter (Heb. 11).

"Faith is the *substance*," not the shadow. "Through faith we understand," not "through commentaries we understand," but through faith. I believe in commentaries, but I believe in faith more.

"Heir of the righteousness which is by faith," not by strength. Oh, how hard I tried to be righteous, but one day the Lord whispered, "It is *by faith*."

"By faith Abraham went out not knowing whither he went." Beloved, if we get anywhere we will have to go out by faith, ignorant of our journey's course and terminus.

"God is not ashamed to be called their God." Beloved, do you believe God so little that He is ashamed to be called your God?

"By faith Joseph gave commandment concerning his bones." He knew that they were going up out of Egypt, and he said: "When you go up out of Egypt, two or three hundred years hence, take my bones with you and bury me in Canaan."

"By faith Moses was hid of his parents, and they were not afraid of the king's commandment."

Faith and fear do not go together. If you have fear, you are not faith-full."

"Lay aside every weight." I shall never forget how God expounded this passage to me. I was writing one day at a camp-meeting and God said, "Go to the testimony meeting." I sat on the platform, and a woman arose and looking straight at me said, "Laying aside every weight." I said, "Father, what is it?" He said, "You say that your bonnet is heavy." "I will take off the heavy jet when I get home!" But no one testified. They had been popping up all around before that. I said, "Father, if you want me to take it off now, don't let a soul speak;" and He didn't. And I arose and told the people, and a brother loaned me a jackknife and off came the heavy jet. "Laying aside every weight."

"The sin which doth so easily beset us." What sin is this? Well, remember the connection. Faith has been the theme for many verses. Unbelief is the sin. "The sin of unbelief." When we doubt God then the trouble comes. Oh, may the Lord show us the truth!

"Run with patience." Patience with others. Patience with ourselves. We so love to get to places with a hop, skip, and jump. We must learn to have patience even with ourselves.

The only reason God lets any sorrow come to you is that He may turn it to joy. The only reason He lets stones come into your way is that He may roll them away and show you the angels.

Sister Morrow related some of her marvellous experiences in trusting the Lord. She spoke of her desire to give for missions, and how the Lord permitted her to give. She referred to the school of teaching through which the Lord has been leading her. Her message was especially helpful this morning, and the tearful eyes and joyous countenances testified to the presence of the Holy Spirit.

10.30 A. M.

Rev. E. F. Walker speaks to us again this morning: Lamentations 4: 7. The book of Lamentations is written in the minor key and yet there are strains of joy in it.

DR. WALKER'S SERMON ON "NAZARITES."

Our subject this morning is the "Nazarites." The word means "separated." They were a typical people and were intended by God as a type of God's holy people. In the sixth chapter of Numbers we have a description of these separated people. We find that any Israelite could become a Nazarite by taking the vow. The Nazaritic vow was not restricted to any tribe or sex. Any one can become a member of the Independent Order of Nazarites by taking the vow and assuming the obligations.

If we decide to become Nazarites we must abstain from "dead bodies" (which means sin), and from "wine" (which means worldly pleasure), and we must show our badge of separation, corresponding to the long locks of the Nazarites.

You will notice that the description of the Nazarites in the text is in the past tense; the verses following state the condition of the Nazarites at the time of the writing of Lamentations. "Their faces," says the weeping Jeremiah, bewailing the low state of the holiness people, "are as a coal." The light has gone out of their countenences. "Their skin is dry like a stick." No symmetry, no beauty, no grace.

Now let us notice some of the characteristics of the normal, genuine, thorough-bred Nazarite. First, they are pure. They are 24 carets fine. There are no unclean passions, no selfish desires, no unholy ambitions.

"Purer than snow." This is an extraordinary purity. We regard the snow-flake as very pure but in its journey to earth through the atmosphere it becomes contaminated. And so our hearts must be even "purer than snow." Not simply pure "as far as I can see," but pure *as far as God can see*. The Lord God Himself puts the certificate to our purity upon us. No other alchemist is equal to the responsibility of pronouncing us clean.

In the Old Testament it was commanded, in regard to the cleansing of leprous garments, that after a piece of cloth was washed if the leprosy departed from it then it should be washed again. That is, if it was clean as far as man could see then God said "Cleanse it again. Give it a second work." It may look to you, Christian friend, as if you are all clean. Frequently the young convert feels that he is all right. But the Word says you need another cleansing, "a second cleansing," as Wesley sometimes called it.

Now, next, we have a superlative expression in regard to whiteness. The garments of the saints are "clean and *white*." Cleanness and whiteness are not the same thing. A thing may be clean and not be white.

Purity is a negative trait. It means absence of all extraneous matter. But whiteness emblematizes moral excellence. It is a positive characteristic. In Roman history a man who was chosen to serve his country because of his excellence of character was clothed in a white robe. The word "candidate" means "a white-robed one."

It is not enough for us that we should be clean, we must also be white. We must not only be pure, but we must be filled with love, joy, peace, etc., etc. This is *holiness*. Cleanness is emptiness; *holiness is fulness*. We are all the time neglecting the positive side. We are saying, "Be clean, be clean," but let us not forget the other side.

The Nararites were "ruddy." "Ruddiness" means a splendid, robust, spiritual condition. Now a man may be clean and filled with graces and yet not strong in the Lord, not able to do exploits. Ruddiness indicates iron in the blood. There is such a thing as being *filled with power*.

Little Sammy the prophet was a true Nazarite, and all the days of his life he persevered in the way of the Lord. Oh, what strength of character! John Baptist was filled with the Holy Ghost from his birth. He had a camp-meeting by himself in the wilderness, and was equal to all the crowds that came out to see him.

There was Samson. He was not strong because of muscle but because of God and his vow. He did not even have much hair, for he did not miss it when it was cut off for he went out and shook himself as aforetime, not knowing that the Lord was *departed from him*. Oh, the secret of his power was *the Lord with him* because of a kept vow.

"Like rubies." The ruby stands for zeal. My boy got home from a trip round the world. And then, though I have tried to make a man of peace out of him, he joined the heavy artillery. But finding that the heavy artillery was going to stay in Fort Slocum instead of pushing to the front he asked for release and joined the Sixth Regiment and went to the Phillipines. It was his regiment that defeated the four hundred and fifty Filipinos the other day. Oh, I would to God that we as Christians would get away from the idea of "Hold the fort" and go to the vanguard!

Here are a lot of you who instead of fighting are staying around the commissary's wagon and eating all the time. Eat, eat, eat. Stuff, stuff, stuff—do nothing but feed all the time! Oh, shame on us! Shame on us for our indolence!

We need the "polish" of "sapphire." Sapphire is the color of the sky and the color of the sea at times. It is broadly disseminated. Oh, how we need *broadness*! The Lord put the polish of sapphire upon us!

When the Kohinoor diamond was purchased for Victoria, although it had been in the hands of royalty for years, it was subjected to polishing for twenty-three days. A steam engine was necessary to furnish the power. Oh, let us pray that God may polish us! Let us submit to all the wheels God lets come our way!

Where are you this morning? Are you clean and filled with holiness? Are you ruddy as rubies? Are you polished like sapphire? While we stand and sing a simple hymn, I want all who want to join the Nazarites and all who have not yet put on the regalia—I want all these to come to the altar.

A number, ten or twelve, perhaps, came quickly forward and engaged in prayer. Vows were made and the band of Nazarites was increased. Glory!

2 P. M. MINNIE LINDBERG'S MISSIONARY ADDRESS.

A large company gathered to hear Miss Lindberg's talk. She went to the African Inland Mission in 1895 and returned last year. Many of our readers are already acquainted with the account of God's dealings with her during her sojourn in the Dark Continent. That the climate is deadly we have all doubtless heard. Miss Lindberg's party lost three members by death in three years. A party of twenty-four on the West Coast was depleted by death of eleven in four years.

In spite of all the hardships Sister Minnie said: "I do thank God that He counted me worthy to go to Africa to suffer. It is sweet to suffer with Him.

She said that frequently the funds sent by friends were intercepted and they received no benefit from it. The journey to the coast required three months time. Their destitution was great. For four months they were without salt. In answer to prayer God sent them a cupful by the hand of a native. Another time an ungodly man gave them ten boxes of provisions.

In her appeal to the Christian people in the audience Miss Lindberg said: "Oh, the ignorance and the awful filth of those people! And what suffering I saw among little children and women and old people just ready to step into the grave, only they do not put the bodies in graves out there but throw them into the bushes for the wild beasts to devour. I wish I could tell you of the suffering but I cannot.

"There are three hundred millions in Africa who don't know God. Oh, beloved will you not pray that God will call some one from here to go to that dark, heathen land? Will you not ask God to supply the money? He has it. Christ died not only for us but for the heathen, and He's not blessing you here that you may sit down and fold your hands, but that you may be ready for His work.

"Since my return to this country, thousands have died of starvation. I received a letter recently from one who said she saw 50 bodies lying dead on the ground at one time. All these Jesus died for and yet they died without Him. We know what God has done for us, beloved, and yet we are often so selfish."

3 P. M. W. H. HOOPLE'S SERMON. I JOHN 1: 7.

"If we walk in the light as He is in the light we have fellowship one with another and the blood of Jesus Christ His Son cleanseth us from all sin."

N. R. REED'S COTTAGE.

This is a text God wants every one to hear. I am glad holiness is something bigger than the soul and overflows into the life. A holiness that does not make us feel in our pockets and leave less there when we take the hand out than when we put it in is not the kind spoken of in this verse. Some people try to see how much they can reserve for themselves, but may the Lord help us to see how much we can give.

You are in a dangerous position if you are not hating sin and trying to get rid of it. God help us to cut a swathe in the ranks of sin that will make the devil howl. If we go in on this line we will have all Heaven back of us. Oh, brother, sister, we must get on the war path! We hardly protest against sin! Is it any wonder that infidelity has captured the church when most Christians have escaped the fire of the Upper Room?

It is sin that mars the home and eats into the character; and it is the old-fashioned truth that is going to rouse men. We need more hell-fire preaching. We've been telling people they are "pretty good," when they needed Sinai.

Jesus can reconstruct and rebuild the soul that everyone else has cast off. He can make a success of what seems a hopeless failure. I have been in the slums of New York and seen Jesus illuminate those dungeons of night. He can cleanse the abominable; He can save those who are lost to all decency and respectability; He can reach the sore spot in any case and start such a song of praise out of the lips as will cause other lost souls to see Christ. Oh, beloved, its time we put on white; its time we got something that would startle all hell.

My text says "the blood of Jesus Christ cleanseth us from all sin."

> "There is a fountain filled with blood
> Drawn from Immanuel's veins."

Thank God for an open fountain! There used to be one troubled at certain seasons but here is one open day and night and in it you may wash and be clean.

Oh, how this fountain has attraction for my heart today! I love to stay around its borders and see the disgraced, unsightly crowd as they plunge into it, and how different they look when they come out! We hear their glad cries and see their shining faces! I would not give much for a salvation that did not find expression some way. The real thing will bring a shining face and some response of gratitude.

As we watch the crowd we see them walk on for a time but soon we hear the clank of chains that bind them still. We look about, pitying their condition and say, Is there nothing more?

I am not here to minimize justification; it's a mighty work of grace. The devil points to works and to various other resources, but God points right back to the blood. The apostle don't refer to justification in my text; this verse was spoken to the converted soul.

There is power in the blood. The application of the blood is not given as a reason for walking in the light but as a result of it. Dean Alford says the conjunction "and" connects the sentences as an additional result of walking in the light. He also says it is not a thing but a state of faith and holiness in which the blood is always applied. We must be divinely empowered and in continual communication with the blood.

To say all sin cannot be cleansed away now is a flat denial of the text. All means *all*. If some one comes along and throws mud at my character while I am walking in the light the blood will wash it off and it will not stick. It is an affront to God not to seek the second work of the blood.

If the sinner who has a litle light is on the way to hell how much greater the condemnation of those who have much light and refuse to be cleansed from all sin!

The cure of sin is not found in yourself nor in death nor in works, but in the Blood.

7.30 P. M.

The song service this evening is full of the tones of victory. People who have recently "got through" are singing with a freedom and enjoyment they never dreamed of before. Oh, the joy of being dead to people and prejudices and formality and false propriety! Sanctification destroys the affected and the conventional in one and makes one natural and simple, free to serve the Lord in any way the Holy Ghost dictates.

Sisters Simpson and Guild sang Brother Nasbaum's hymn, "His Way With Thee," with great power. As the song floated out over the congregation every heart was touched with the beauty of the words, of the music, and of the thought, and God used the hymn to convict many souls. Praise the Lord for consecrated voices!

Sister Simpson also sang a solo full of joy and victory, and her companion in the ministry, Miss Frost, led in prayer.

Rev. John Norberry preached the evening sermon.

We invite your attention this evening to Isaiah 4: 1. The persons spoken of in this text are types of many we see today. There are a host of people who have no desire for Jesus to save them; they refuse Jesus; they do not want their characters changed; *but they would like to be called Christians.* In some quarters it is quite *fashionable* to be a member of a church.

In many of our watering places it is socially necessary for visitors to identify themselves with some church. Some of the newcomers inquire, "What is the most popular church here?" And many preachers call on summer boarders and put forward the plea that their church "will give better social standing to its members than any other in town."

And these people join churches to have "the reproach removed" but they "eat their own bread and wear their own apparel." They are nominally Christians but feast on worldliness and frivolity and dress to suit their own carnal minds.

We are living in the days of religious laxity. We have in these days "Union Meetings" which take in Methodists, Baptists, Unitarians, and Universalists. Oh, may God give us a revival of justification! If we had such a revival we would subsequently have a revival of holiness.

In some quarters it is becoming popular to belong to the holiness movement. At a camp-meeting like this for instance it is unpopular to fight holiness. A preacher who does not believe in sanctification wouldn't preach here. And so there are preachers who come to our camp-meetings who, *at the camp-meeting*, pass as believers in holiness, but at home say nothing clear and definite about it. They escape the reproach but they get no "bread" from God and no "apparel" from Him.

Are we willing to quit "eating our own bread" and wearing our own filthy rags of self-righteousness?

Beloved, it pays to go straight! How out of place it is for sanctified people to complain. Why, if it had not been for holiness they would never have heard of us. We have gained more than we have lost. Let us quit telling "what we might have been." Our names would never have been heard had it not been for sanctification. Nearly all these holiness preachers whom God has anointed and lifted into prominence would have died in obscurity if it had not been for the holiness movement.

Oh, get a principle in your heart and life! Quit being a jelly-fish and get a back bone. When you stand straight for God He will give you success and souls.

Brother Norberry conducted his own altar service, and a glorious one it was. Seekers came at once and the fire soon fell. Brother Hoople also exhorted powerfully and many were the wills which yielded under the fiery admonitions of God's servants. Praise the Lord.

FRIDAY, AUGUST 4.

8.30 A. M.

MRS. MORROW'S LAST BIBLE READING.

After prayer Mrs. Morrow said:
In the seventeenth chapter of Revelation, fourteenth verse, we find "These shall make war with the Lamb, and the Lamb shall overcome them, for He is Lord of lords and King of kings. And they that are with Him are called and chosen and faithful." It takes the strength of a lion to live the life of a lamb.

Our calling. (1.) Called out of darkness into His marmellous light.

[As an illustration of this text Mrs. Morrow related the story of "Delia, the Bluebird of Mulberry Bend," who was so wondrously saved through Mrs. E. M. Whittemore's "Door of Hope" work.]

(2.) "Called to be holy." "I have not called you to uncleanness but to holiness." "Be ye holy for I am holy." The life of Jesus was filled with doing and teaching. A certain disciple was said to be mighty in word and deed, but Jesus "began to do and to teach."

I want to read a little from the Sermon on the Mount (Matt. 5: 23, 24). The meaning is, "If thy brother hath ought against thee, leave thy gift at the altar and go and make that thing right, if possible." We think that we have done well if we have no anger in our hearts; but this text says that if our brother have ought *against us*, we must go and do our best to make it right.

"Not rendering evil for evil or railing for railing, but contrariwise blessing." Send presents to those who hate you most, who will have nothing to do with you.

(3.) We are called to patient suffering that we may inherit a blessing. Oh, if we would only believe away down in our hearts that all that comes to us is a blessing for us it would change our whole lives.

The only reason there is anything in our hearts that is not right is because we do not trust the blood. Reckon yourselves dead and *God will make the reckoning good.*

"Called, chosen, faithful." He that is faithful in that which is least is faithful in that which is much. O Lord, teach us how to be faithful in that which is least today that we may discharge our higher duties when we come to them.

10.30 A. M.

After singing, Brother Rees said: "I feel that this ought to be a time of general expression concerning the dealings of the Lord with us. Through the sermons and Bible Readings such light has come to me that I desire more thoroughly than ever to measure up to all the will of God as revealed in His Word. Let us pray for each other that we may not disappoint Jesus in any way.

"I have a burden, a deep concern, for my brethren in the ministry. If ever there was a time when there was danger of the plough running out of the ground, it is today. I feel that one reason that we do not have a greater sweep is due to the lack in the ministry.

"What is the use of going to Pitman, to National Park, to Denver, if we cannot have victory right here. I believe there is victory for us in this meeting. Shall we not have it? Let all who feel convicted to come to this altar, come."

We spent the preaching hour upon our faces before God. Satan did all in his power to break up the spirit of supplication, and defeat God's people, but victory came and the atmosphere cleared beautifully.

1.30 P. M.

SISTER CASSIE L. SMITH'S BIBLE READING.

Sister Smith opened her Bible to 1 Cor. 13.

Jesus said: "This is my commandment, that ye love one another as I have loved you." Theologians tell us the emphasis is on the *as*. That's the standard, and don't, beloved, lower the standard because you don't measure up to it.

If we have Christ's love, our love for one another will be continuous. You think you have a friend, and by and by he ignores you and finally becomes your enemy. Christ's love loves to the end. It will stand any strain brought against it. My one desire for Holiness Israel is that they may be examples of the pure love of God. Oh, may we get a baptism that will make us love our neighbor precisely as we do ourselves!

We regret that we cannot give a full report of this deep address. None of the saints who profit by Sister Smith's messages forget her ministry to them. Her long experience in the Lord's dealings helps God's people wonderfully wherever she goes.

Sister: Jesus is the one altogether lovely to me.

Sister: I want to praise God for the blessing I have received here.

Singing: "Oh, 'Twas Love, 'Twas Wondrous Love."

Sister: I have been wonderfully blessed since coming here.

Sister: "My all is on the altar."

Brother Mitchel: I praise God for the blood that washes whiter than snow; I never get disappointed when I go to Jesus.

Singing: "Hallelujah! I'm so Glad to Tell."

Sister: My greatest desire is to grow more like Him each day.

Sister: He saves, sanctifies and keeps me.

Brother Bacon: If I know my heart, there is nothing there but love.

Singing: No. 31 of Part I. "My Heart is Enraptured with Love."

Sister: I not only believe He saves but I know it, and I know he heals the body too.

Brother: He keeps me sweet when sour things are all about.

Brother: I'm glad I have the sweet consciousness that I belong to God. He saves and I enjoy His presence. There's nothing can satisfy but God, and He satisfies *my* soul.

Sister Porter sang, "Love Brings the Glorious Fulness In."

Sister: I thank God that I ever cried to Him and that He heard me.

Sister: I love Him with all my heart and with all my soul, and my neighbor as myself.

Singing: "The Comforter has Come."

Brother: I'm glad I live where the air is pure and the

view unobstructed. Some people are glad they belong to the Methodist Church, but I'm glad I belong to God. Bless His name!

Sister: I praise God so much for what He has done for me in these meetings. He has filled me, and I want to do a work for Him.

Sister: I bless God for the Comforter. He has come to my heart. The thought of loving as Christ loved never meant so much to me as it does today.

Brother: I found yesterday my temper was not all taken out, but it is now.

Brother: When God heals you lots of folks will shun you and say you're a little off, but you'll love them better than ever if you are sanctified.

3 P. M.

A large number have assembled at the preaching service this afternoon.

Rev. John Pennington preaches to us:

"And I said: I will never break my covenant with you." This was spoken to backslidden Israel by the angel of the Lord, and God is speaking to us today. He is a Sovereign and has a right to declare upon what terms we shall receive His favor and blessing. Puny man may lift his arm against God's will, but he will ultimately perish.

God is a covenant-keeping God and never breaks His

covenants. We may break our part of the covenant, but God does not forget His part, but performs that which He said He would do. If you have broken your vow, do not be surprised if there is an awful punishment in store for you. If you have kept your covenant look out for God's blessing; it will come!

Opposite to this truth is the awful one that we are a covenant-breaking people. Witness the laxity in financial contracts. Look at the looseness in respect to the marriage vow. See the lightness with which vows made in joining the church or at the sacrament are disregarded.

All that we get in grace comes under covenant. We came to God as rebels against Him, and He took us in under covenant. Are we keeping the covenant? Are we doing as we said we would do when we were sanctified.

There are people who have made vows and have broken them. Such people are here today. If things go hard and you are having a difficult time do not excuse yourself on the line of "a hard field." Get down on your knees and see if you can find the break in the vow. If your family is going astray do not take the matter too lightly—humble yourself in the sight of God and have Him reveal to you the crack in your covenant.

If you have less power, less zeal, less love for lost souls than you once had, you are in awful danger. I *fear* anything like a lapse from the deepest spiritual life. Oh, this line of peril!

We break vows and then wonder why God doesn't use us. We made vows at the open grave in times of affliction, in close places financially. We vowed, for example, in a time of temporal stringency that we would give a tithe, but when God heard and prospered us we forgot our promise. Oh, that is the road to financial and spiritual bankruptcy!

"Yes," you say, "that's all right, but I can't do it." *Yes, you can!* Circumstances do not bear the blame. People are not at fault. The fault is *in yourself*.

I would to God that we would all have done with trifling and renew our covenants and then keep them. Vows grow upon us. They mean much more now than they meant when they were made. But it is an awful peril to break vows. Keep your covenants! *Keep your covenants*, for so very much depends on it! If you are a covenant-breaker today, promise God you will never break vows again. I want all who *really want* to come to the altar to come.

A large number, fifty at least, came quickly forward and covenants were made and renewed on every side. The opposition was badly crippled by this landslide for fidelity and covenant-keeping, and the outlook is even better than ever. The ministry went down deeper this morning and the congregation is breaking up in tears and sobs this afternoon. Praised be the name of the Lord!

7.30 P. M.

As the days pass by and we approach the end of the meeting, the audiences grow larger and larger. This evening's audience is very large and attentive. The glorious hymns are rolling out like choruses from the upper world. The songs can be heard away down in the village, and the land is filled with the praise of God.

Sister Rose Williams sang, "When I Get to the End of the Way."

The people are receiving the prospect of "Hallelujahs from Portsmouth, No. 4," with jubilation. They are subscribing eagerly for the books in advance this evening.

Sister Mattie Curry preaches.

Rom. 8: 1-9: "There is therefore now no condemnation to them which are in Christ Jesus," etc.

There is a law of sin and death in the world. It is strong, fearfully strong; so strong that God's law is broken by its power. Had God not brought in grace, we would have been left helpless in the power of the law of sin and death. This law of sin does not always manifest itself in the same way, but it is always of the same nature.

Men know God's law, but there is something in the

human heart, so much stronger than their fear of God's law that they go on and break His statutes right in His sight. Everybody admits that we ought to do right, but in the face of conscience, that which was left us from the fall, mankind, for the great part, continues in wilful sin.

What the law could not do because of the weakness of the flesh, Jesus Christ came to accomplish. The law was weak; Christ is Almighty.

Men love darkness because their deeds are evil. The burglar who is robbing a house flees if the electric lights are all turned on. Light has been turned on at this camp-meeting, and people who are staying away from the altar and shrinking back from the truth are simply showing that their deeds are evil. Some have had little light. There are some in this world who never had much opportunity. There are others, such as have attended this camp-meeting, who have had floods of light thrown upon their pathway. The latter will receive far greater condemnation at the Day of Judgment than the other class.

Oh, I would to God we would accept light! If light comes and shows us that restitution is necessary, we must make restitution or lose our souls. We must obey God at all costs. *We must make things right!*

You can't substitute any kind of service for real obedience. You say, "I don't know what I ought to do." What is that thing that has been running through your mind the last few days? Do *that* thing. *Obey God, and daybreak will come into your heart.*

When you are converted you are set free from the *power* of the law of sin and death. It still remains, but the power is broken. But there is a better salvation than this. There is a salvation which saves us from the *inbeing* of the law of sin and death.

The altar was quickly filled with earnest seekers. Many of them were gloriously delivered, both from the power and inbeing of the law of sin. It has been a glorious day and this is a glorious night.

SATURDAY, AUGUST 5.

10.30 A. M.

The meeting preceding this was in charge of Evangelists Reed and Williams. There was a time of prayer, and then the meeting was opened for testimony. Many spoke for the first time since they were sanctified. Each successful altar service brings on a new family of witnesses.

Brother Pennington spoke of a few of the books on sale at the bookstand. He referred to M. W. Knapp's "Impressions" as a most valuable help for God's children. He also made mention of "Fire from Heaven," and "Christlikeness."

Rev. F. M. Messenger preaches. Text: John 16: 8, 9, 10, 11. (Read these verses.)

God has always had a people to whom He revealed Himself and made plain His will.

In the old dispensation God revealed Himself as the Father. He and Enoch walked together. He met Jacob and changed him from a "supplanter" to a Prince of God. He showed Himself to Isaiah, Daniel, Ezekiel, and many others.

God also revealed Himself as Saviour in Jesus Christ. The life and death of Jesus were for the purpose of our salvation. Jesus said, "My Father worketh hitherto, and I work," showing that He was having a dispensation in which He was pre-eminently active. Jesus also spoke of the Holy Ghost, the Comforter, who was to come to the disciples at Pentecost.

Christ found but few men who were "Israelites indeed." Nathanael was commended as "a man in whom there was no guile," but there were few of whom He could say this.

"When He is come," says Christ, "He will reprove the world of sin, of righteousness, and of judgment." I remember the sins I committed when I was a boy. Do you remember how, when as a child you did what was wrong, the Spirit showed you your guilt? Later we became hardened with oft-repeated sin. But it is the office of the Holy Spirit to break up the hardness of heart and make us feel afresh the awfulness of sin.

The revised version says that "He will convict the world of sin." Dr. Fowler says that the word "convict" here means the act of a man who goes out to arrest an evil doer and bring him before the judge and jury, and face to face with the statutes. The Spirit has been doing this very thing for the last few days on this campground. People have come here thinking that they are all right, and God has arrested them and shown them differently.

Do not read the text as if it said, "convict the world of judgment *to come?*" The last two words are not there. The meaning is that *judgment is pronounced against sin now*; and the Spirit shows us this fact and makes us wofully conscious of it.

When light comes we have to walk in the light or go into condemnation. I know of a deacon who got under conviction and went to the altar and God spoke to him of a desk which he had bought with somebody else's money. He got no further after he saw the desk. He came to the altar the next night, but the desk was there before him and he could not get by it, and he had to make that thing right before he could find peace. Brother, if you want to be right you will have to obey God *at every point*.

Are you willing God should have your pocketbook? Are you willing for Him to take care of your reputation? It takes lots of strength and time to chase down lies. "Oh, but there are people in my own community who ought to be set right about me." Well, God can attend to that. If these people need to know anything God will tell them or explicitly reveal to you that you ought to go and explain.

Let God have all there is of you! Let Him own you altogether.

2.30 P. M.

Brother Norberry suggested that, as the testimonies were given, the people tell where they were from. Some of the testimonies were thrilling in their earnestness. We note a few of the places from which our people have come to Portsmouth: "No. Scituate, R. I.; Providence, R. I.; St. Kitts, West Indies.; North Attleboro, Mass.; Wilmington, Del.; Vineyard Haven, Mass.; Clinton, Mass.; Bristol, R. I.; New Bedford, Mass.; Bluff, North Carolina; Plainville, Mass.; Hopkinton, R. I.; Anthony, R. I.; New York, N. Y.; Keene, N. H.; Newport, R. I.; Norwich, Ct.; Springfield, Mass.; Boston, Mass.; Pawtucket, R. I.; Dartmouth, Mass.; Westport, Mass.; Fall River, Mass.; Centredale, R. I.; Sag Harbor, L. I.; Chatham, Mass.; Lafayette, R. I.; Sterling, Ct.; Wickford, R. I.; Denver, Col.; and North Grosvenordale, Ct.

After the testimonies a little time was devoted to the sale of camp-meeting stock. About five hundred dollars worth was sold in a few minutes.

Brother Walker preaches:

Whether or no I preach this afternoon I feel led of the Lord to speak just a little while along the line where my brother left off this morning—that of "Spiritual Discernment."

It is so easy for us to undervalue a man's testimony because he followeth not us, *i. e.*, he got the experience in a little different way than we got it. It is such a frequent thing for people to sit in judgment on certain of God's dear children because they do not train in the same religious company as the criticisers.

Brethren, these things ought not so to be. We ought to have spiritual discernment enough to see Jesus wherever He is.

On the day of Pentecost there was tremendous noise, and God was in it. In Elijah's time He was "not in the fire" nor "in the rushing, mighty wind," but in the still, small voice. Now, there are some who see God only in "the still, small voice." There are others who see Him only in great demonstration. Now we ought to be so fitted up that we can recognize the Holy Ghost wherever He appears.

Our text is one word, found in 1 Thess. 5: 23—"Wholly." Now there are some who suppose that Paul was praying for the sanctification of the entire church rather than of the individual. But the mention of the body, soul and spirit is conclusive proof that the entire sanctification of the individual is meant.

This word "wholly" is not only not found anywhere else in the Bible, but it is found nowhere else in Greek literature. August Meyer says that it means "to the entire extent." The German text has this translated as "through and through." Wesley says "it means perfectly and thoroughly." The Latin Vulgate has *per omnia*, "through everything."

So this word refers to every part of our spirit, soul, and body. First, the *pneuma*, the spirit, is to be sanctified. It is my view that no one but a child of God has the *pneuma*. He has no spiritual discernment and no spirit life. After receiving this it is proper for it to be sanctified and made fit for the indwelling of the Holy Spirit.

The next part of our being is the soul. It lies between the spirit and the body. It is the sphere of the conscience, the affections and the desires.

The third part of man is the *soma*, the body, that which has ponderosity, our flesh and bones, the physical part of our being.

The place where sanctification is *chiefly* wrought is the soul. When this is sanctified, high imaginations are cast down. Your ambitions become clean and holy. God will be in all your thoughts. You will not forget God. You will be more conscious of God than of yourself. You will be a Godly soul. You will say:

> "I worship thee, sweet will of God,
> And all thy ways adore,
> And every day I live I seem
> To love it more and more."

Every faculty of your being will be saturated with perfect love for God. You will live by faith and rejoice in hope.

You will not let anyone be a rival of God in your heart. You will be garlanded with victory every day. I am talking about *entire* sanctification.

When you are wholly sanctified you can say with the Psalmist. "Bless the Lord, O my soul, and all that is *within me* bless His holy Name."

Entire sanctification also has to do with the body. *Sin is not in the body, but the body may be the instrument of sin.* Your body should be "the temple of the Holy Ghost." "The body for the Lord and the Lord for the body." We are to glorify God in our body, which is His. If you are wholly sanctified you have no unclean physical habits. If you were to get a dear dirty tramp converted and sanctified this afternoon the first thing he would do would be to ask for a bath tub. The work of entire sanctification affects your whole spiritual life. It will make you temperate in all things. If coffee does you any injury you will *stop drinking* it if you are sanctified.

Sanctification will alter your dress. One cannot be sanctified and governed by the laws of Paris at the same time. Simplicity is true beauty.

Now you can work this out for yourself, but sanctification makes us obey the Bible in everything. If we are sanctified we must measure up to God's revealed will.

The God of peace Himself sanctify you wholly. The *Lord* must sanctify you. You can sanctify no part of you. He must do it all. Neither death, nor growth, nor affliction can do it, the God of peace alone can make you clean throughout.

No one has a God of peace but the justified man. A man must be converted before he is at peace with God.

If the spirit, soul and body are to be wholly sanctified and then preserved unto His coming, then this must be a sanctification for *this life*.

Again, this must be an experience for this world because the apostle prays for the *preservation* of the disciples. We cannot pray for the preservation of those who are in heaven, for we know they are secure. Therefore this blessing is for this life.

This work of entire sanctification is wrought instantaneously. A man cannot be sanctified completely, wholly, gradually. There must be a time when the work is completed, perfect. That time must be an *instant*. The tense (Aorist) admits of nothing else than instantaneous sanctification.

How can we get this blessing? In the first place, we must want it. And this is usually the trouble. People "would like the blessing, provided, etc., etc." There are preachers who would like a complete sanctification at 90 per cent., the usual discount to preachers.

There are people loafing around altars and saying they "don't know what is the matter." I'll guarantee that you could guess at it and strike the trouble the first time and not try very hard either.

There was a man seeking at the altar for days. He

was a Methodist, but he was breaking the Discipline which says that we are not to have many words at a bargain! At last he got at the little end of nothing and fell off and cried out, "Yes, Lord, take the pony too." He had a fine colt and had set his heart on seeing him trot around the race track *just once*.

Oh, give up everything, put yourself entirely on God's altar and say:

> "Here I give myself to thee—
>   Friends and time and earthly store,
> Soul and body thine to be,
>   Wholly thine for ever more."

Put yourself forever in His hands. Leave yourself there. Cry out with John S. Inskip, "Lord, I am wholly and forever thine." You will not wait long. Come, give yourself fully up to Jesus!

Without singing and without the audience standing a number came quickly forward. Brother Walker's earnest soul is stirred within him in exhortation, and the Spirit is speaking to the hearts of the people. Several of the seekers had clear, indubitable evidence of Jordan-crossings, and praised God for their new-found purity and joy.

7.30 P. M.

After the usual preliminary singing, Sister Rose Williams sang, "It is Well with Me," as a preface to the preaching of the Word.

Rev. Wm. H. Hoople preached from Acts 1:5: "For

John truly baptised with water, but ye shall be baptised with the Holy Ghost not many days hence."

Our space forbids our giving more than a few thoughts from Brother Hoople's sermon.

Victory brings honor to the soldier; failure covers him with approbrium. If the church is to be respected and honored, whether in heaven or among sensible people on earth, she must be victorious.

If you have not had the baptism with the Holy Ghost, you have not had the crowning blessing God intends you should have.

If you get hungry while I am preaching, don't wait for me to get through—come to the altar at once.

The baptism with the Holy Ghost is always a *sudden experience*; the man who has it *knows* it.

What is in us will come out. If we are filled with worldliness, that will appear; if it is salvation, that will show itself in speech and life.

When a man is filled with the Holy Ghost he is as ready to go to work at 12 o'clock midnight as at 10 a. m. The baptism with the Holy Ghost is always a *sudden* experience.

SUNDAY, AUGUST 6.

8.30 A. M.

We have come to the last day of this glorious feast. How quickly the days have passed! The people seem to feel that the time is short and have come out to this meeting *en masse*. The testimonies are ringing out with a clear, sweet assurance that cannot fail to carry conviction to the hearts of all those here who are not right with God.

Chas. Gifford: Years ago God wonderfully saved me at this place, and this year He wonderfully sanctified me. Business is all in His hands.

Sister Harris: I praise the Lord for the help and comfort these meetings have been to me. I have had great blessing since I came here.

Sister: Four years ago God saved me, and two years ago He blessedly sanctified me, and this morning He keeps me safely.

Sister Frida Stromberg: I know that this moment the blood cleanses me from all sin.

Brother: I praise God that sometime ago the Lord cleansed me and gave me the blessing of sanctification, and I am sanctified this morning.

Bro. Rees: Now, let all who have been saved or sanctified during this meeting and have not testified, stand up. A large number arose and gave definite testimony to pardon and cleansing.

Brother: I was sanctified last night and I am determined by the grace of God to go every step of the way.

Another Brother: I want to go to the front and stay there. I do not want to be a coward and fall back to the rear.

Sister: I saw last night that I did not have the power

I used to have, and I came to Jesus and was sanctified.

Singing: " 'Tis a Glorious Church," and "When I see the Blood."

Brother Rees: I want Brother Young to sing a piece which always blesses me. Brother Young, come to the platform.

Brother Young sang a beautiful hymn, "God Leads His Dear Children Along," which God used to the blessing of us all.

Brother Rees: The spirit of holiness is supernatural and divine. We were never so crowded for lodging room as we are now, and yet there has been no murmuring, no complaining; everything has gone so smoothly and blessedly! As I watched the brethren last night making up their beds in the straw of this Tabernacle, I said: "What hath the Lord wrought!" Only the blessed Holy Ghost is able to take all the grumbling and fault-finding out of our hearts.

A special offering was taken this morning for the needs of the gospel department of this meeting. One hundred and thirty-five dollars were quickly and quietly pledged.

Singing: "Rock of Ages."

Sister Mattie Curry preached the morning sermon from Titus 2: 14: "Who gave Himself for us that He might redeem us from all iniquity and purify unto himself a peculiar people, zealous of good works."

Who was it that gave Himself for us? It was no mere man that died. God committed the work of atonement to the Son of God Himself.

Christ is God. Wherever the word LORD, spelled with capital letters, appears in the Old Testament, Christ is referred to. Isaiah saw Him in the temple. We read in the New Testament that Moses esteemed the reproach of Christ greater riches than the treasures of Egypt. It was Christ who parted the Red Sea. It was the Rock, Christ, who furnished the water for Israel in the wilderness. Jesus was called "Emmanuel," which means "God with us." He is spoken of as "the great God," and "God over all."

Christ created the world. All things were made by Him. "In the beginning was the Word, and the Word was with God and the Word was God." This was the Word who made all things and by whom all things consist."

"No man hath seen the Father at any time save the Son and He to whom the Son hath revealed Him." We hear people talk about the All-Father, but *there is no Father save He whom Christ reveals.*

Christ is living today. We worship, not a dead Christ, but a living Christ. He is risen and is alive today at the right hand of the Father. When you see things going wrong, just remember that Christ still lives and will work out His eternal purpose.

O Lord, get people's eyes on Thee so thoroughly that

they will trust Thee through everything that seems to threaten God's work. Christ lives; He will vindicate His truth. What is truth will abide. What is God's will will last forever.

Jesus Christ gave Himself for *you*, my dear brother, my precious sister, that you might be redeemed from all iniquity. He gave Himself for you, dear church-member, that He might purify you unto Himself for a peculiar possession.

* "KNOWING CHRIST," SERMON BY BYRON J. REES.

"Yea, doubtless, and I count all things but loss for the excellency of the knowledge of Christ Jesus my Lord; for whom I have suffered the loss of all things, and do count them but dung that I may win Christ. That I may know Him and the power of His resurrection and the fellowship of His sufferings." Phil. 3: 8, 10.

I want to call especial attention to this part of the text: "Yea, doubtless, and I count all things but loss for the excellency of the knowledge of Christ Jesus my Lord." "That I may win Christ." "That I may know Him." Jesus Christ is God. As the preacher of the morning said, if Christ is not God Himself, our hopes are entirely vain. We are lost in a trackless forest in a starless night without a ray of hope. The text implies we can know God. Mr. Spencer says God is the Unknowable, but "to

---
*Reported by Mrs. S. G. Otis.

the law and to the testimony." God's word declares explicity that we may know Him—yea, more truly than we know each other.

The Apostle said, "I count all things but loss." His heart was so set on knowing Christ, and he had received such visions of Christ that nothing was so dear but he counted it loss, in order to know Him. Everything goes to show that Paul was a man of learning, of position, of power, yet in this verse there is an undertone of hunger. He had seen Jesus in such a peculiar sense that earthly things could never satisfy, and his heart turns toward Christ and he seeks to know Him. There comes a time in every Christian life when earthly things lose their attraction, when books, music, paintings and everything of earth fail to attract and the soul thirsts and pants for something else.

Now, of course, sinners are not in a position to desire to know Christ for His own sake. When a sinner comes sobbing to the altar, he prays not for the lovliness of Christ; he "wants pardon," or he wants to "escape hell," and get a safe passage to Heaven; but the child of God who has learned of Him, desires Christ in a new and profound sense.

Men cannot know Him except as they become like Him. There must be some plain on which we can meet Him. There must be some common plateau of thought and feeling. Men cannot be in league with worldly institutions if they are going to know God. Christ said,

"Repent; drop your sins, come unto me and I will give you rest. *Learn of Me,* for I am *meek* and *lowly* in heart." It's to the man who has given up earthly ambitions, who has lost all desires for position that Christ shows Himself most inwardly.

To be like Christ is to be pure. He not only did not commit sin, but He had none in His own heart. He did not have what we call depravity. If we are to know Him we must be pure. But you say, "I don't see how I can be cleansed from all feelings and motions of sin." The point is not that we *understand* how, but that *we accept God's word.*

The man who says, "I'm a pretty good sort of a fellow," has never seen his own heart. The more we see our own depravity, the more we see that no human power can help us.

We can't conceive of Christ having an impure thought, and God's word says we must be "pure even *as* He is pure." "How can two walk together except they be agreed?" How can my heart understand the heart of the Nazarene if I am mean or filthy or proud or haughty?

If we are to know God we must be willing to suffer the loss of all things, part with everything. If a man really dies out he consecrates everything, and from that time calls nothing that he possesses his own; he is simply a steward of God's property.

Christ is a pure Christ. The Holy Spirit is a Holy Spirit and cannot abide where there is sin of any kind.

He may come to see you, He may witness to your conversion, but cannot abide with sin; He must reign in your heart without a rival. But you say, "I can't cleanse myself." No, but you can take sides against sin, you can *put* it away and the blood will *cleanse* it away.

If we know Christ we shall understand His plans. Oh, how few understand Him! I imagine Christ feeling lonely as He walks up and down in our great churches. I can conceive of His looking on the great crowds and going away sorrowful because they do not fellowship Him. We sing our hymns and have a great time, but I wonder how many Christ sees that understand Him. Eighteen hundred years ago Jesus said, "Go ye into all the world and disciple all nations." What has been done? Men tell us that there are more heathen today than ever before. We seem to have made no progress. We boast of our scientific age, and we have great light, but have we great piety? We have great light and in consequence great damnation if we do not live up to it.

Oh, how Christ shrank from sin! How it filled His heart with horror! Would to God it were as loathsome to us. Some of us have gotten so accustomed to sin that it no longer seems an awful thing to us. We even find holiness people advising others to soil their white garments by reading the daily papers. If you are living with God as you ought to live you'll hate sin so that you won't even want to hear of its doings; you'll have no part in it, except to oppose and denounce it.

Oh, what peace Jesus had! There were the trials, the scourgings, yet He had peace undisturbed. Look at Him on the sea when the disciples asked Him, "Carest thou not that we perish?" Christ put out His white hand and said, "Peace, be still!" and there was a great calm. We may know Him in the storm. When the surf dashes about us, when the storms of sorrow wring the heart, there is something within that says, "Peace, be still!" In time of discussion and debating, we can have peace in our vicinity. Then the patience of Jesus. We must know Him in His patience.

This knowing Christ implies knowing Him in his loyalty. See Him in the garden when all the powers of darkness were seeking to kill Him there, and hear Him say, "Not My will, but Thine." Our griefs look so big, our hardships so hard! Oh, that we may learn to say, "Not my will!"

How can we know Christ? In the first place we must make a complete consecration. Shut out every thing but Christ. Shut ought all earthly things. If we are to see Christ, we must shut out the advice of people, the creeds of the churches. There must be no light but that which streams from the face of Jesus. We cannot have the other suns if we are to have the Sun of Righteousness. Look at Him with the look of faith. There is not enough looking at the Christ who died for us. It is Christ that saves, not man. He who knows Christ knows Him in His joy. A joy not of earth, but the kind He had.

When you are put aside for Jesus' sake, don't complain, but rejoice in the light of His face. You may be cast out, but Christ will find you and take you in. Oh, brother, you may know Christ so thoroughly that no earthly cloud can make His face shine less brightly! Praise the Lord.

6.30 P. M.

This is the last service of the last day of the encampment. The Tabernacle is filled with people and many are standing up outside. The platform is loaded with full-salvation preachers and workers. The air is full of holy jubilation and the sound of victory. Brother Norberry reminds us that the Judgment is coming, and asks the congregation to sing repeatedly:

> "Judgment is coming,
> All will be there.
> Who have rejected,
> Who have refused?
> Oh, sinner, hasten,
> Let Jesus in,
> Then God will pass,
> Will pass over you!"

It is a solemn time as well as a joyous time. God grant that many who are not right with God may see the solemnity of this hour and find peace and safety in Jesus.

A young colored evangelist from Boston sang, "The Great Judgment Morning" with great power. The vast audience was stilled with a stillness like that of death by the power of her song. Oh, that hundreds may be stricken with conviction tonight!

Dr. E. H. Walker preaches: "The blasphemy against the Holy Spirit shall not be forgiven unto men."

"Jesus Christ is preached unto us that we may receive forgiveness of sins and inheritance among them that are sanctified." We rejoice in being heralds of this good news and are glad that we can declare the mercy of God.

In the midst of our joy we find a text like the one I have read to you. There is a sin that has no forgiveness, either in this world or in the world hereafter. There is such a thing as being doomed before we are damned. A man may get to a place in this world where he is just as hopelessly doomed as if we had been shut up in hell a million of years.

Let us not suppose that the text implies that one may sin against the Holy Ghost without at the same time sinning against the Father and the Son. The Holy Ghost is no more holy than are the other Two. Neither let us suppose that there is any special, particular *kind* of sin referred to in the text. *Any kind* of sin can be forgiven. There was never a sin blacker than the crucifying of Jesus, and yet He prayed that His crucifiers might be forgiven. He would not pray for an absurdity. There is no one act which is always the sin against the Holy Ghost.

Any sin persisted in will become the sin against the Holy Ghost. The sin against the Holy Ghost is more an *attitude* than a single act.

Notice the circumstances under which Jesus spoke the words of this text. Nothing that Jesus could do convinced the Pharisees that Christ was God. They kept saying (imperfect tense), "He hath a devil." In the face of His mighty deeds, and in spite of their own consciousness, they blasphemed against the spirit, by whom Christ performed all His works, by calling Him a devil.

Why was this sin unpardonable? *Because unrepentable.* No one can repent except the Holy Ghost demonstrate the truth to him. These men rejected His demonstration and therefore shut themselves out of all help and hope! And when you quench the holy light He brings to you, you are rejecting the only thing that can give you aid in escaping the hell to come.

What is there left for the spirit of truth to operate upon when a man persistently rejects the convictions already given? When a man becomes untrue to himself and wittingly believes a lie and makes himself rotten at heart and turns himself upside down in his moral make-up, there is absolutely nothing to which the Holy Ghost can appeal.

We are gladly reaching up and ringing the gospel bell tonight, but oh, brother, sad, sad thought, if you were to reject the truth you would be converting the gospel bell into the funeral bell of the death and damnation of your own soul. Every act of rejecting light is a step in the transformation.

The devil is the greatest hypnotist in the universe. He blinds men and leads them down to Hell with his strong delusions.

He who fools with truth is being doomed. He who blasphemes God will be damned. In the days of Noah men fooled with truth and suddenly the bolt leaped from the sky and shut Noah within the ark, and the scoffers outside the ark.

I believe in the total depravity of the human heart. I do not mean that it is always as bad as it can be, but that the devil is boss and depravity is ruler. It does not naturally want any part of truth. Stephen preached the truth and the depraved doctors of divinity put their fingers in their ears, rushed upon him, gnashing with their teeth, cast him out of the city and stoned him. *They stoned the truth.* They wielded a boomerang which not only struck the truth but struck their own souls.

To whom did Christ utter the words of this text? To the immoral? The profane? The harlot? The drunkards? The vile? No, *the church bosses, the ecclesiastical rulers.* The people who had heard the truth times without number. They had become *confirmed sinners.* They had rejected the light for years and their fate was fixed.

The most fearful condition for a man to be in is to have no fear. If you have fears there is hope for you.

If the fear is dying out, take alarm! Haste to God! Flee to the cross!

The devil does not make his dupes afraid. They have no apprehension of danger. They are perfectly easy and comfortable. They are duped by the devil.

Justification is in order to sanctification. It gives a man a title to get sanctified. If you do not go on after justification and get sanctified you will soon lose your justification.

One of the bishops in the Methodist church said before a conference of preachers: "It is my conviction that not more than one person in ten in the Methodist Church is living in a justified relation with God." Why not? Because the mass of so-called Christians are rejecting the light of the gospel of holiness.

We will not attempt to reproduce more of Brother Walker's wonderful sermon. Suffice it to say that it was the sermon of the camp, and that between sixty and seventy persons crowded around the altar. *It was an awful night!* Hardened sinners and wilful backsliders rushed to the penitent form. The great crowd was held by the power of God in almost unearthly stillness. At one thrilling and convicting point the entire body of preachers and workers turned like one man and fell upon their knees.

One beautiful characteristic of the service was the quickness and clearness with which the seekers found that for which they sought. The rejoicing was great, and in celebration of the release of bound hearts and burdened spirits the saints encircled the Tabernacle in a victorious march. They looked to us like troops of angels, and reminded us of the celestial band in heaven who praise the King.

At a late hour the camp is still and silent. The lanterns twinkle on the trees and the light wind rustles the shadowy leaves. The calm stars look down upon us through the open spaces between the trees and seem to beam God's approval and love. On the morrow the camp will break up, the dear children of God will scatter throughout the land, the tents will disappear from their floors and the ground will look strangely bare and worn.

But doubtless the angels will not utterly forsake the hallowed place. Again and again they have rejoiced as sinners repented and turned to God. Again and again they have shouted His praise as souls became white through the blood of the Lamb. Their wings will fan the empty altars and their forms will glide swifty through the leafy corridors of the grove. They will protect this holy place from the foul touch of hell, and keep it inviolate until July 27th, 1900, the date of the next encampment.

Let us all come up next year with expectancy and faith in God. Meanwhile let us live unto the Lord, walk in the light, trust the Spirit for unction, sweetness, and power. Amen.

EXTRACT OF THE BILL OF 1899.

PORTSMOUTH CAMP MEETING will hold its Ninth Annual Session beginning at 2 p. m., Friday, July 28th, 1899, and continuing until August Seventh, Seth C. Rees in charge.

Portsmouth Camp Ground is situated on Quaker Hill on Rhode Island, about two miles from Portsmouth station, on the N. Y., N. H. & H. R. R., and is seven miles from Newport and ten from Fall River. Portsmouth Camp is a beautiful hard-wood grove supplied with the best of cold spring water. The island is a delightful summer resort, since the sea air is very bracing, and the picturesque scenery is unsurpassed in New England.

Rev. Edward F. Walker, Greencastle, Ind.; Rev. Wm. Hoople, Brooklyn, N. Y.. together with a good corps of other workers from New England, will be present.

There are society tents, where lodging on single beds may be had at 25 cents a night. Family wall tents, 10 x 12, with flies and board floors, each containing one double bedstead, straw mattress, straw pillows, pail, cup, wash-basin, chair and broom for $6.00 for the entire time. In all cases bring your own bedding, etc., not mentioned in the furnishings. Do not neglect this. Furnished rooms may be had by those who prefer not to live in tents. No rooms will be reserved for the last Sunday unless occupied for one week. The tents are owned by us. They are all made of 8 oz. duck, and each tent has a fly of the same material. Free lodging for all ministers (and their wives) who are in regular connecton with any evangelical church.

Good table board, $4.50 per week, 75 cents per day; breakfast and supper, 25 cents each; dinner, 35c. Provisions may be had on the grounds by those who wish to board themselves. All persons must obtain their provisions and meal tickets for the Sabbath on Saturday, as nothing will be sold on the Lord's Day.

Round-trip tickets from Boston to Portsmouth station, $2.40; from Fall River, 40 cents; from Newport, 35 cents. The stage makes four trips a day to Portsmouth. All persons coming via Providence will leave the city at 2.30 p. m., on boat "Queen City;" round-trip tickets, 40 cents. The "Awashonks," leaving Providence at 9 a. m., will carry passengers to and from the Camp Saturdays only. The boat landing is about one mile from the Camp. Passengers taken to or from the Camp for 15 cents each; trunks, 15 cents. From Portsmouth station, 20 cents for each passenger; trunks, 20 cents each. Those coming by train, without baggage, who wish to walk from the station should leave the train at Cory's Lane, one mile from the Camp. An electric car line passing within short distance of the Camp runs between Fall River and Newport. Let everyone come to this feast of the Lord. Application for tents and rooms should be sent in as early as possible.

SETH C. REES,
F. M. MESSENGER,
G. W. KIES,
W. H. WEST,
E. G. MACOMBER,
B. J. REES,
JOHN PENNINGTON,
} *Executive Committee.*

All communications should be addressed to John Pennington, 363 Lockwood St., Providence, R. I.

The Ideal Pentecostal Church,

BY SETH C. REES,
Quaker Minister and Evangelist.

CONTENTS: Chapter I—Opening Words. II—The Ideal Pentecostal Church is Composed of Regenerated Souls. III—A Clean Church. IV—A Powerful Church. V—A Powerful Church—Continued. VI—A Witnessing Church. VII—Without Distinction as to Sex. VIII—A Liberal Church. IX—A Demonstrative Church. X—An Attractive Church—Draws the People Together. XI—Puts People Under Conviction. XII—Will Have Healthy Converts. XIII—A Joyful Church. XIV—A Unit. XV—The Power of the Lord is Present to Heal the Sick. XVI—A Missionary Church. XVII—Out of Bondage. XVIII—Entering into Canaan. XIX—The Land and Its Resources. XX—Samson. XXI—Power Above the Power of the Enemy. XXII—Compromise and Its Evil Effects. XXIII—Sermon. XXIV—The Author's Experience.

The following are a few sample drops from the

CURRENT OF COMMENDATIONS:

Dr. Carradine—"As for Brother Rees, I know of no man in the Holiness ranks today who preaches more convincingly and unctiously than himself. I do most heartily commend him and his wife to my friends and brethern, North and South, who desire a man filled with the Holy Ghost, and one who is as good a leader as he is a preacher."

W. B. Godbey—"The Pentecostal Church, by Rev. Seth C. Rees, the fire-baptised Quaker, is a Niagara from beginning to end. It is orthodox and full of experimental truth and Holy Ghost fire. You cannot afford to do without it. I guarantee you will be delighted and electrified from Heaven's batteries."

Christian Standard—"It is safe, sound and evangelical, uncontroversial and admirably adapted to circulation among all believers."

Michigan Christian Advocate—"He writes in a sweet and attractive spirit. We could wish it a wide circulation."

Religious Telescope—"It is written in clear, nervous English and glows throughout with the evangelical fervor of its author."

Rev. George Hughes, Editor of the Guide to Holiness—"I like it, it is square out, and that suits me. It ought to have a good sale."

Rev. John M. Pike, Editor of Way and Faith—"The book glows and burns with Holy Ghost fire, and has stirred our spiritual being to its very depths."

It is well printed on good paper, and is neatly bound. It contains 134 pages, making a beautiful and very cheap book.

Price 50 cents. Address

BYRON J. REES,
Office of Revivalist, - - Cincinnati, Ohio.

WORDS OF LIFE.

A series of Gospel Tracts, issued monthly by the

CHRISTIAN WORKERS UNION

These Tracts are just the thing to enclose in every letter you write, or for general distribution.

SUBSCRIPTION PRICE, 10 CTS. PER YEAR, POSTPAID.

4-page Numbers, 5 cts. per dozen; 25 cts. per hundred.
8-page   "   10   "   50   "
16-page   "   15   "   75   "

No. 1. The Word of Life. 4 pages.
No. 2. Poem—The Months of the Year as Applied to Human Life. By Mrs. Jane Pardon.
No. 3. How There Came to Be Eight. 4 pages. By Abbie C. Morrow.
No. 4. Poem—On the Ocean of Life. 4 pages. By Mrs. Jane Pardon.
No. 5. Water Lily Money. 4 pages. By Abbie C. Morrow.
No. 6. "Whatsoever." 4 pages. By Abbie C. Morrow.
No. 7. Thoughts on the Divinity of Christ. 8 pages. By A. A. Pease.
No. 8. The Days We Live In. 16 pages. By Rev. T. J. Campbell.
No. 9. How to Love the Bible. 4 pages. By Abbie C. Morrow.
No. 10. Position We Should Occupy if We Wish to Fulfil His Highest Will. 4 pages. By Hezekiah Davis.
No. 11. Receive Ye the Holy Ghost. 4 pages. By E. K. Sellew.
No. 12. God's Call to Separation. 8 pages. By Eld. Wm. A. Burch.
No. 13. Choice Thoughts. 4 pages. From the pen of H. L. Hastings.
No. 14. Not Commonplace. 4 pages. By Edgar K. Sellew.
No 15. Lost Power. 4 pages. By Seth C. Rees.
No. 16. Apostolic Christianity Needed To-Day. 4 pages. By W. J. Gladwin.
No. 17. Take Heed to Thyself. 4 pages. By Abbie C. Morrow.
No. 18. Stillness. 4 pages. By E. K. Sellew.
No. 19. Saved and Healed, or the Touch of Faith. 16 pgs. Mrs. J. C. St. John.
No. 20. The Sin of Unbelief. 4 pages. By E. K. Sellew.
No. 21. The Service of Difficulties. 8 pages. By Seth C. Rees.
No. 22. The Blessings of Abraham. 12 p. By Arthur A. Pease.
No. 23. The Wine Blessing. 4 p. By Louis F. Mitchel.
No. 24. Hallelujah. 4 p. By Louis F. Mitchel.
No. 25. Given to Prayer. 8 p. By Abbie C. Morrow.
No. 26. Man's Wants Supplied. 4 p. By Louis F. Mitchel.
No. 27. God's Rushing, Mighty Wind. 4 p. By Louis F. Mitchel.
No. 27. Extra. The New Song. 4 p. By Louis F. Mitchel.
No. 28. The Thessalonian Church. 4 p. By Hulda A. Rees.
No. 29. Saved to the Uttermost. 4 p. By Mrs. Jennie M. Allen.
No. 30. The Will of God. 4 p. By Andrew Murray.
No. 31. What Must I Do to be Saved? 4 p. By E. K. Sellew.
No. 32. Opportunity. 4 p. By Lucy R. Phetteplace.
No. 33. Gems of Thought, 4 p. Sel. by Robert McJannet.
No. 34. Trees of Righteousness. 4 p. By L. F. Mitchel.
No. 35. The Holy Seed. 4 p. By Louis F. Mitchel.
No. 36. Be Ye Holy. 4 p. By Louis F. Mitchel.
No. 37. The Spirit-Filled Life. 4 p. By M. W. Miller.
No. 38. "If Children, then Heirs." 8 p. By B. M. Smith.
No. 39. The Corn of Wheat. 4 p. B. M. Smith.

Address all Orders to

S. G. OTIS, Evangelist Building, Springfield, Mass.

WORD AND WORK.

A MONTHLY MAGAZINE.

Edited by Abbie C. Morrow.

It has departments for The Word, God's Lessons, International Sunday-school Lessons, Work at Home and Abroad, Health, Home Circle, and Young Folks.

It is filled with good spiritual matter for old and young, and is free from sectarianism, controversy and politics.

Subscription Price, 50c per Year. 5c per Copy.

CHRISTIAN WORKERS UNION, Publishers,

S. G. OTIS, Superintendent,

EVANGELIST BUILDING,   SPRINGFIELD, MASS.

OUR GOSPEL LETTER.

A Four-Page...... Weekly Paper. £2 Free from Sectarianism and Controversy.

It is filled with good, practical, Religious and Temperance reading, and is just the paper needed for our Prisons, Jails, Almshouses and Reformatories, and among the unsaved everywhere.

Subscription Price, 25 Cents a Year. £2 For Mission Work, 25 Cts. a Hundred, Postpaid.

CHRISTIAN WORKERS UNION,
...PUBLISHERS...

S. G. OTIS, Superintendent,

EVANGELIST BUILDING,   SPRINGFIELD, MASS.

www.ingramcontent.com/pod-product-compliance
Lightning Source LLC
Chambersburg PA
CBHW021953160426
43197CB00007B/114